Retail Nation

*Department Stores and
the Making of Modern Canada*

Donica Belisle

UBCPress · Vancouver · Toronto

21 20 19 18 17 16 15 14 13 12   5 4

Printed in Canada with vegetable-based inks on paper that is processed chorine- and acid-free.

_____

Library and Archives Canada Cataloguing in Publication

Belisle, Donica
   Retail nation : department stores and the making of modern Canada / Donica Belisle.

Includes bibliographical references and index.
ISBN 978-0-7748-1947-3 (bound)
ISBN 978-0-7748-1948-0 (pbk.)

   1. Consumption (Economics) – Canada – History. 2. Department stores – Canada – History. 3. Retail trade – Canada – History. I. Title.

HC120.C6B44 2011   306.30971   C2010-905126-2

e-book ISBNs: 978-0-7748-1945-9 (pdf); 978-0-7748-1946-6 (epub)

Canadä

UBC Press gratefully acknowledges the financial support for our publishing program of the Government of Canada (through the Canada Book Fund), the Canada Council for the Arts, and the British Columbia Arts Council.

This book has been published with the help of a grant from the Canadian Federation for the Humanities and Social Sciences, through the Aid to Scholarly Publications Programme, using funds provided by the Social Sciences and Humanities Research Council of Canada.

Printed and bound in Canada by Friesens
Set in Galliard and New Baskerville by Artegraphica Design Co. Ltd.
Copy editor: Jillian Shoichet
Proofreader: Lesley Erickson
Indexer: Patricia Buchanan

UBC Press
The University of British Columbia
2029 West Mall
Vancouver, BC V6T 1Z2
www.ubcpress.ca

Millions in merchandise. Cheapness unmeasured.
They bring happiness.

— Simpson's Department Store, 1896

Contents

Figures

Acknowledgments

THIS BOOK HAS BEEN the fortunate recipient of money and encouragement, both of which have immeasurably improved its offerings. Funding from the Social Sciences and Humanities Research Council of Canada (SSHRC) kindly enabled most of its research, while grants from Trent University and Athabasca University graciously covered the rest.

Aspects of this research have appeared in the Fall 2006 issue of *Labour/ Le Travail* ("A Labour Force for the Consumer Century: Commodification in Canada's Largest Department Stores, 1890-1940") and in the Spring 2007 issue of *The Journal of Women's History* ("Negotiating Paternalism: Women and Canada's Largest Department Stores, 1890 to 1960"). Thanks to both journals for their support. For allowing reproduction of copyrighted images, I am obliged to Sears Canada, the Hudson's Bay Company Archives, the Archives of Manitoba, *The Beaver: Canada's History Magazine*, City of Victoria Archives, Wyatt Heritage Properties, and the PEI Museum and Heritage Foundation. For permission to quote from poetry, I am grateful to *The Beaver: Canada's History Magazine* and to the Hudson's Bay Company Archives. Thanks as well to Marcia Stentz, Leah Sander, Bronwen Quarry, Debra Moore, Debbie Keffer, Adriana Arredondo, Elana Sadinsky, Jean MacKay, Fred Horne, Mark Reid, Garry Shutlek, Carey Pallister, Jeannie Hounslow, Michele Pacheco, Christopher Kotecki, Kateryna Kramchenkova, and Andrew Cunningham, all of whom helped locate records, provide images, and gain permissions.

Comments from participants at the "Cultural Approaches to the Study of Canadian Nationalism" conference at Nipissing University in 2004, the Windy Pines Writing Workshop at Trent University in 2005, the Canadian Historical Association Conference at the University of Western Ontario in 2005, the "Labouring Feminism" conference at the University of Toronto in 2005, the Association for Canadian Studies' Annual Conference in Gatineau in 2007, and the North American Labor History Conference at Wayne State University in 2007 have greatly improved this book, as have insights from those who attended my talks at the University of British Columbia in 2008 and Memorial University in 2009.

For their exceptional support, encouragement, and advice, I am grateful to Bryan Palmer, Joan Sangster, and Veronica Strong-Boag. Constance Backhouse, Penny Bryden, Gary Cross, Bettina Liverant, Todd McCallum, Brian McKillop, James Struthers, and Keith Walden also offered important tips and insights, and I am indebted to Andrée Lévesque and Tom Mitchell for sharing not only their ideas but also their research. Thanks as well to my many wonderful colleagues at Athabasca University and in Alberta for making my first year in the province fruitful and enjoyable. To my editor, Melissa Pitts, I owe a special thanks, both for her support and for her expertise; Ann Macklem, Emily Rielly, and the rest of the production team at UBC Press were also extremely helpful. I am grateful to this book's anonymous reviewers for their insightful and incisive comments, and to Adrian Naylor, Lisa Pasolli, Kelly Pineault, and Carolyn Webber for their superb research assistance.

Thank you to my parents, Julia Belisle, Garry Belisle, Larraine Taylor, and Harold Taylor; to my siblings, Michael Belisle, Jennifer Simpson, David Belisle, Betty Froese, Kat Belisle, and Luke Postl; and to all my wonderful family members and friends, including Jennifer Jans, Jeremy Morrison, and Lisa Raymond. Thanks, finally, to my long suffering and much loved partner, David Taylor. His laughter, insights, and cups of tea, given freely and at all the right times, have enabled this book's existence.

Retail Nation

Figure 0.1   "Dreams That Have Come True" (cover of Eaton's 1919-20 Fall and Winter Catalogue) | Used with permission of Sears Canada Inc.

Introduction
Canadian Consumer Society

*This is emphatically an age of PROGRESS. The golden age is
before us, not behind, and those who're unwilling to keep up with
the procession will have the decency to STAND ASIDE.*

– Eaton's advertisement, 1892

THE COVER OF THE Eaton's Fall and Winter Catalogue of 1919-20 was a
sight to behold (Figure 0.1). Titled "Dreams That Have Come True," it
represented symbolically the modernization that had occurred between
1869, the year Eaton's was founded, and 1919, Eaton's fiftieth anniversary.
It proclaimed loudly that progress had been made. Yet what kind of
progress? During the first decades of the twentieth century, the types of
buildings depicted in the clouds (sites of commerce, industry, retail, and
government) were common to all of Canada's urbanizing areas, but only
in Montréal and Toronto were they present in large numbers. The cover
thus suggests that readers should be pleased with the growth of capitalism,
industry, merchandising, and the state, and that they should be happy
these institutions made their homes in southern Québec and Ontario.
Even more central to "Dreams" is the idea of the progressive nature of
retail. One of the largest stores in the British Commonwealth, Eaton's was
Canada's biggest retailer. Bringing the wares of progress to the corners
of the dominion, it brought Canadians into modernity.

Between the 1880s and the 1920s, the growth of cities, industry, the
state, and capitalism transformed Canada into a modern nation. Historians have paid substantial attention to some aspects of modernization,
especially urbanization, industrialization, and the expansion of the federal
government. Still underexplored, though, are the ways mass merchandising changed Canadian life during this time. Canada is today saturated

with advertising and commodities, but the emergence of mass consumer capitalism, and the consequences this would have, have yet to be fully examined. This book brings the history of Canadian consumer society to the centre stage by investigating Canadians' relationships with Canada's largest department stores. Between 1890 and 1940, Eaton's, Simpson's, and the Hudson's Bay Company (HBC) became Canada's biggest retailers. The pages that follow look closely at their activities. They also touch on the histories of such major regional stores as Woodward's and Spencer's in British Columbia and Morgan's and the Dupuis Frères in Québec. Department stores were not the first retailers to utilize modern merchandising methods, but they were the first to employ them to reap unprecedented profits. All the big stores experimented successfully with aggressive capitalist accumulation, bureaucratization, the employment of women, the creation of feminine consumer spaces, bulk buying, and low prices. These characteristics made them symbols of Canadian modernity, as did the stores' assertions that their goods and services would enhance democratic life, strengthen the Canadian nation, and create citizen fulfillment.

The study of department stores offers particularly insightful pathways into modern consumer society because the stores were active in all three realms of the marketplace, namely, production, distribution, and consumption. They purchased manufactured goods, they processed their own commodities, they advertised and sold merchandise and services, and they organized shopping according to modern innovations. By examining department stores' activities in production, distribution, and consumption, historians can gain new perspectives on separate developments within these realms, as well as pinpoint the effects of the commodity's movement among them. They can gain insight into the experiences of people who produced commodities, sold commodities, bought commodities, and criticized mass retail. And, as it highlights employees', consumers', and critics' thoughts and actions, department store research can illuminate how Canadians worked and lived through the rise of modern consumerism.

An enduring debate exists within consumer historiography. Is consumption evidence of manipulation? Are consumers tricked by advertisers into buying ever increasing numbers of useless commodities? Or is consumption evidence of liberation, in that individuals can choose freely from a range of different commodities, using them to enhance their well-being and express their identity? Consumer historians generally agree that the origins of this debate can be traced to mid-twentieth-century arguments about what leftists referred to as the false needs of consumer capitalism. According to some writers, commodities lulled citizens into complacency. Most famously, Theodor Adorno and Max Horkheimer (1944) argued that consumption was a tool of "mass deception," wielded by capitalists consolidating their reigns. Variations of the consumerism-as-manipulation theory dominated critical thought on capitalism throughout the 1960s, even appearing in Betty Friedan's famed *The Feminine Mystique* (1963), whose major premise was that advertisers tricked women into believing their proper role was happy consumers of domestic goods.[1]

Portrayals of consumers as dupes produced a major backlash in the 1970s. As early as 1971, as Canadian historians Cynthia Wright and Joy Parr both note, American feminist Ellen Willis argued that women's consumer activities were not unconscious manipulation, but conscious labour. "One of a woman's jobs in this society," Willis wrote, "is to be an attractive sexual object, and clothes and makeup are tools of the trade." According to Willis, women's purchasing of domestic goods was one of their household responsibilities, and most assuredly work as well.[2] By the early 1980s, some cultural theorists were arguing that consumers did not necessarily use goods in ways that advertisers intended; in their efforts to express their individuality or group identity, consumers could use commodities to make, as Parr puts it in her analysis of research on youth cultures in Margaret Thatcher's England, "fabulous and carnivalesque recuperations for their own purposes." In the 1980s and 1990s, scholarly interest in consumer motivation exploded. By the end of the twentieth century, researchers who wished to understand more about how and when Western consumerism emerged, why people consume, and how they express themselves through consumption had a wide range of works to consult, of which the most compelling remain those by American authors Susan Porter Benson, Kathy Peiss, and Nan Enstad.[3]

In their quest to understand consumers' motivations, as well as to rescue consumers from the condescension of intellectual theorists and cultural critics, none of the historians of the 1980s and 1990s depicted consumption as completely liberating. The best studies acknowledged that race, class, and gender limited the social power that any one consumer could wield. In spite of a late-twentieth-century nod to the limitations of consumerism, however, at the turn of the twenty-first century scholars started calling for a move beyond the manipulation-liberation debate. Erika Rappaport argues that views of the consumer as passive "cast the consumer as a feminized victim of masculine (economic) aggression." And yet the "celebratory view of consumption ... adopts entrepreneurial narratives about freedom in the marketplace that have been prevalent both in the nineteenth and the twentieth centuries." Rappaport illustrates an alternative approach to consumer history in *Shopping for Pleasure,* in which she shows that business and consumers together turned London's West End into a premiere shopping district at the end of the nineteenth century.[4]

Other publications also chart new paths. Using what Joy Parr terms a "third, less dichotomous" method,[5] these works suggest through their own rich examples that consumer society should be portrayed not in a one-sided manner that stresses either capitalism's hegemony or consumers' agency, but as a multifaceted phenomenon that involves a range of historical agents. Among the most sophisticated of these studies are Parr's *Domestic Goods* (1999), Lizabeth Cohen's *A Consumer's Republic* (2003), and Victoria de Grazia's *Irresistible Empire* (2005). Together, their research demonstrates that consumer society unfolded after the Second World War as a complex interplay among business, the state, and consumers, with various other groups such as lobbyists and product designers intervening. Borrowing a phrase from Foucault, de Grazia aptly describes this method as "cutting across societies on the diagonal."[6] This technique avoids simplistic depictions of consumers as either passive or liberated and allows for explorations of the historical agents involved in consumer capitalism. It further illuminates power relations among those groups.[7]

Their authors might not explicitly state that they take this third, multifaceted approach, but recent Canadian books can also be viewed in these terms. Karen Dubinsky's *The Second Greatest Disappointment* (1999), Valerie Korinek's *Roughing It in the Suburbs* (2000), Craig Heron's *Booze* (2003), Suzanne Morton's *At Odds* (2003), Jarrett Rudy's *The Freedom to Smoke* (2005), and Steve Penfold's *The Donut* (2008) all focus on the history of a particular industry or commodity – Niagara Falls, gambling, *Chatelaine* magazine, alcohol, tobacco, and donuts, respectively – and explore it over a specific time period. These publications document the beliefs and actions of past distributors and consumers, and some examine the power dynamics of distributor-consumer interactions. Parr's *Domestic Goods* (1999), which consciously applies this new, third approach, offers the most sustained exploration of government policy on consumption. Putting domestic goods consumption in broader political, economic, and cultural context, she shows that production, distribution, and consumption are mutually dependent.[8]

It is in this spirit of complexity that this book is situated. Instead of focusing on a particular commodity-centred industry, though, it explores the rise of mass retail. Between 1890 and 1940, department stores were among the most powerful agents of Canadian modernization. Companies such as Eaton's, Simpson's, and the HBC helped revolutionize the ways Canadians thought about and experienced shopping, living standards, and goods. An examination of these department stores' activities, together with consumers', workers', governments', and critics' responses, yields invaluable insights into the emergence of consumer capitalism in northern North America. This study demonstrates that corporate monopolies wielded a tremendous amount of power in the consumer marketplace, but it also reveals that governments, consumers, retail employees, and anti-retailing activists influenced the direction and character of modern Canadian consumption.

Chapter 1 documents Canada's largest stores' retailing ascendancy and situates it in an international context. Unlike department stores in Great Britain and the United States, between 1890 and 1940 Canadian department stores monopolized the Canadian retailing market. In 1930 alone, just three department stores – Eaton's, Simpson's, and the HBC – earned 14 out of every 100 dollars spent in the country. Yet Canadian department stores did not build their empires through sheer determination alone. As Monod reminds us, "innovations in marketing did not happen without the stimulus of demand."[9] To flesh out why department stores were able to construct such colossal enterprises, this chapter also tracks the changes in demand that occurred in Canada during this period.

An oft-made connection between department stores and Canadian national identity is taken up in Chapter 2, which argues that the voluminous publicity of Eaton's, Simpson's, the HBC, and other department stores forged links between mass retail and Canadian heritage. Eaton's catalogues in particular helped define what it meant to be a citizen of the modern Canadian nation. Showing that department stores' publicity portrayed the stores, their commodities, and their consumers in nationalist, gendered, racialized, and classed forms, this chapter reveals that department stores defined modern Canadian life as consumerist, middle class, and white.

Chapter 3 investigates department stores' strategies of customer and labour management and finds that retailers used paternalism to manage relations in both these realms, bringing both the best and worst of paternalism into the twentieth century. Canadian department stores' particular brand of paternalism entailed treating customers and employees benevolently when possible, but strictly when necessary. This meant that shoppers and staff at times received unprecedented attention and care from the big stores. Yet it also meant that when department stores decided to flex their authoritative muscles, customers and staff both felt the consequences. In particular, department stores' assumptions of masculine authority over female customers and staff, white superiority over non-white customers, and managerial power over employees created an oppressive retail environment for women, visible minorities, and wage earners.

Chapter 4 explores another aspect of department stores' labour strategy, demonstrating that image making and consumerism were central features of employment in the big stores. In their efforts to sell goods, department stores commodified their workers; that is, they turned their employees into advertisements. Making over such staff activities as sports tournaments and drama performances into public relations stunts, they marketed employees' bodies and activities. Department stores incorporated what they portrayed as employees' wholesome appearance and submissive behaviour into their advertising, and they turned sales floor transactions into carefully orchestrated selling pitches that extracted value from employees' bodies, gestures, and speech. In these ways and more they commodified employees' beings.

Chapter 5 inquires into female customers' perceptions of Canada's largest retailers. Since department stores would never have achieved market dominance without female consumers' support, this chapter asks why women chose to patronize the giant retailers and how they experienced shopping. By arguing that women's consumer activities must be understood in relation to their historical position as homemakers in the gendered division of labour, this chapter reveals that thousands of Canadian women became department stores' customers for reasons of both labour and leisure. Whereas some women enjoyed their shopping experiences, others viewed them as inefficient and irritating. Further, because of department stores' paternalist, bourgeois, and Eurocentric paradigms, some women experienced shopping as alienating.

Chapter 6 examines another group of women central to mass retail: female employees. Department stores were major agents of the twentieth-century feminization of retail labour, employing women much earlier than other retailers. By the interwar years, female staff made up more than half the total Canadian department store labour force. This chapter considers the age, marital status, class, race, and ethnic backgrounds of female department store employees; their reasons for seeking jobs in the big stores; their wages, hours, and working conditions; and their attempts to make their occupations fulfilling. It finds that Canadian retail employees have a complex history of oppression, resistance, conviviality, and solidarity.

Whereas the first six chapters explore the inner worlds created by Eaton's, Simpson's, the HBC, and other stores, the last chapter steps outside these bounds to examine critics' responses to mass retail. Small retailers, labour leaders, co-operators, and social reformers all took issue with the big stores. Their concerns differed, but they agreed that department stores endangered the purity and future of white Canadian women. Yet despite their ongoing actions, the critics never significantly restrained the big stores. Two factors, this chapter suggests, prevented them from doing so. The first was the critics' failure to adequately address consumer demand for convenience, selection, service, quality, and affordability. The second was their inability to convince the state to take serious action against the big stores.

For the sake of precision, a few explanations of terms are in order. The history of the words "consume" and "commodity" is rooted in the rise of capitalism, and these terms are used herein specifically within the context of capitalist economic activity. According to the *Oxford English Dictionary,* prior to the 1400s "consume" and "commodity" had no economic connotations. The former meant "devouring" and "decay" while the latter meant "that which is convenient" and "that which is useful." Only in the fifteenth century did English writers begin using "commodity" to denote "material advantages" and "wealth." In the 1500s, writers began to use "consume" to describe the acquisition, use, and destruction of commodities. Then, in the 1600s, philosophers began employing the word "consumption" to discuss the "utilization of the products of industry." Over the next two centuries, "consume" and "commodity" would take on their contemporary economic meanings. The binary opposite of "produce," "consume" now connotes the demand side of capitalism. A commodity is a good, service, or other entity that is produced, distributed, and sold in the capitalist marketplace.[10]

In this book, "consume" refers solely to activities associated with the pursuit, purchase, and use of commodities, which are themselves defined in the following pages as objects, services, and other entities that are bought and sold through capitalist means. The word "consumer" denotes an individual who is pursuing, purchasing, or using commodities. The term "consumerism" indicates a social, cultural, and economic predisposition toward consumer activity, and the phrase "consumer society" refers to a society in which much social, cultural, and economic activity is oriented around consumer activity. A consumer culture is one predisposed to consumerism, and "consumption," finally, refers to the process whereby commodities are pursued, purchased, and used.

The emergence of consumer society throughout Canada as viewed through the lens of mass retail is a large subject. This book aims to be as comprehensive as possible, but it does not cover the entire fields of Canadian retail and consumer history. Future investigators are encouraged to conduct further analyses into this area, and they are particularly urged to inquire more deeply into the history of retail and consumerism in French Canada. Canada's largest department stores – Eaton's, Simpson's, and the HBC – were owned and managed by anglophones, and though they served customers of varying ethnic and linguistic backgrounds, their primary language was English. This book investigates constructions of English Canadian forms of retail and consumerism, and in doing so it attends to Canada's largest retailers' essentialization of English Canadian culture as quintessential Canadian culture. The book also explores the oft-discriminatory treatment by department stores of French Canadians, touches on the history of Canada's largest francophone store, the Dupuis Frères, and offers insights into French Canadians' perceptions of anglophone retail. French Canadians' interactions with francophone stores and French Canadians' relationship with commodity culture, however, receive less attention. To gain a fuller understanding of mass retail and consumer history in northern North America, it is imperative that further investigations into these topics be conducted.[11]

Researchers might also explore the relation of masculinity to retail. By catering more often to women than to men, and by employing more women than men, department stores between 1890 and 1940 played a tremendous role in the creation of feminine shopping and wage-earning roles in twentieth-century Canada. Since they scaffolded their operations upon the notion that men were superior to women, department stores also perpetuated patriarchal gender hierarchies and contributed to the economic marginalization of women. For these reasons, and because Canadian women's economic history remains underexplored, this book focuses more on department stores' construction of femininity, as well as upon female shoppers and workers, than it does on masculinity and male shoppers and workers. Those curious about the latter topics would do well to conduct their own investigations. Provided that such research begins with an awareness of male privilege, it has the potential to offer further insights into Canadian retail and consumer history.

What this book does do is show how and why mass retail and consumerism emerged in Canada between 1890 and 1940. It demonstrates particularly that the rise of modern Canadian consumer society was a complex historical event involving the beliefs and actions of five major social groups: retailers, governments, consumers, wage earners, and anti-retail activists. Department stores' introduction of new merchandising methods lowered consumer prices, increased commodity availability, made available new retail services, and helped make shopping a national pastime. Federal, provincial, and municipal governments largely let department stores do as they pleased, though they did occasionally implement tax, employment, and other laws in response to various critics' concerns. Consumers, too, played a role in the rise of mass retail and Canadian consumer society, for without their purchasing support and consumer activities, mass retailers would not have survived. Workers were influential as well, for not only did they provide the labour necessary for the emergence of mass retail and consumer capitalism but their workplace actions also affected stores' and shoppers' decisions. Finally, the beliefs and actions of critics were important. Concerns about department stores' merchandising and employment policies influenced department stores' advertising and labour strategies; they also triggered governmental interventions, albeit minor ones, into certain realms of retail and consumption.

Retailers, governments, consumers, workers, and critics together shaped the character and trajectory of twentieth-century Canadian consumer society, but they did not do so equally. Most Canadian federal and provincial governments between 1890 and 1940 assumed that *laissez faire* economic policy, or the belief that the marketplace functioned best when left unregulated, was the best path toward happiness, wealth, and stability. For this reason, Eaton's, the HBC, Simpson's, Morgan's, the Dupuis Frères, Woodward's, and Spencer's enjoyed much freedom in their building of stores, employment of workers, and selling of commodities. Labour unions, small businesses, and feminist groups occasionally convinced governments to legislate reforms, but such changes were usually piecemeal and of limited consequence. Hierarchies of race, gender, and class also contributed to unequal relations among stores, customers, and employees. Between 1890 and 1940, Canada's largest retailers supported the assumption that bourgeois Anglo-Celtic men were superior to workers, non-Anglo-Celtics, and women. Consequently, working-class, non-Anglo-Celtic, and female customers, as well as non-managerial, non-Anglo-Celtic, and female employees experienced racial, ethnic, class, and gender discrimination at Canada's largest stores. This did not mean, however, that they did not engage in individual and collective actions against Canada's giant shops. As the following pages reveal, critics, shoppers, and wage earners from a range of racial, ethnic, and class backgrounds all over the country worked hard between 1890 and 1940 to make mass retail a more democractic, enjoyable, and accountable method of commodity distribution.

1

Rise of Mass Retail

In the beginning there was Timothy Eaton.

– *Cover of* Financial Post
magazine, 1978

THE DEPARTMENT STORE, Margot Finn observes, has "gained an almost totemic status as the quintessential symbol of Victorian modernity." Tired of a growing body of literature that portrays retail as "instrumental to Victorian women's liberation from the domestic circle," she welcomes approaches to modernity that investigate pre-Victorian contexts.[1] Finn is not the only scholar to criticize department stores' association with modernity. Claire Walsh states that department stores' supposedly innovative marketing techniques were evident in Britain "throughout the eighteenth century."[2] This skepticism tempers department stores' declarations of their own importance, but it also minimizes their historical significance. Department stores were the first mass retailers to appear on the world's stage. In every country they appeared, they were the most visible manifestation of retail's transition from local economies to international economies. Between 1890 and 1940, department stores were also the earth's largest stores. Their buildings were massive, their advertisements encompassing, their services extensive, their displays breathtaking, their prices low, and their assortments vast. Department stores did not invent modern retail, but their size and success did make them harbingers of modern consumerism.

International department store historians have directed most of their attention to Europe and the United States. Canada, however, was home to some of the world's biggest stores. After the T. Eaton Company of Toronto became a department store in 1890, it went on to become the world's eighth largest retailer by 1940. Unlike American stores, which rarely ventured into mail order or established branches, Canadian companies experimented widely with both. By the Great Depression, Eaton's had forty-seven retail stores and one hundred mail order offices. Its main competitors, Simpson's and the Hudson's Bay Company (HBC), also operated branches and catalogues. In 1929, these three major companies pulled in 70 percent of national department store sales. In contrast, it took seventeen American department stores that same year to realize 34 percent of their nation's department store business. Canada's three major department stores also differed from their European and American counterparts in that they sold not only to the bourgeoisie but also to the *petit bourgeois,* working-class, and agricultural populations. Canadian department stores' regional and class diversity enabled them to capture larger proportions of national retail markets than did department stores in France, the United States, and the United Kingdom.[3]

At the same time, Canada's largest stores did share important characteristics with their global counterparts. Eaton's, Simpson's, the HBC, and Canada's smaller department stores emerged as part of an international transformation of commodity distribution that had its beginnings in the middle of the nineteenth century. Prior to this period, the majority of the earth's population obtained goods by trading and bartering, in many cases at small locally managed stalls and shops. By 1920, however, in several industrializing countries, modern merchandising methods coexisted with older distribution practices. Marked prices, packaged merchandise, a precise arrangement of stock, the encouragement of browsing, and the offering of goods acquired in distant markets characterized these modern methods, as did increased retail specialization. Throughout the industrializing world, shops selling particular lines of goods, such as clothing, pharmaceuticals, and dry goods, became more common. General stores, such as those that dotted rural North America, also offered modern merchandising techniques.

Distribution's modernization was most visible in the department stores that were springing up in North America, Australasia, Japan, and Europe. Distinct from all other forms of retailing, these new retailers sold multiple merchandise lines. At all times these lines included clothing, draperies, "furniture, floor coverings and home furnishings," as Canada's 1931 census put it.[4] Department stores' size, appearance, services, and location further set them apart. Generally employing more than one hundred staff members over several floors, department stores were famous for their multistoried architectural beauty; their lavish interiors; their range of services, including refunds and restaurants; and their metropolitan downtown locations. By the Great Depression, department stores were present in Argentina, Brazil, Mexico, the United States, Canada, Great Britain, France, Switzerland, Germany, Belgium, Italy, Egypt, New Zealand, Australia, Malaya, China, Korea, and Japan. The Soviet Union, too, had department stores, though unlike those in capitalist nations, they were owned and operated by the state.[5]

Offering detailed comparisons between Canadian department stores and department stores elsewhere, this chapter situates the rise of Canadian mass retail within the international context. Paying attention to department stores' merchandising techniques, business operations, employment figures, branch store openings, and sales totals, it offers the most comprehensive account yet published on the history of Canadian mass retail between 1850 and 1940. It explores a range of data pertaining not only to Eaton's, the most famous retailer in Canadian history, but also to such less studied enterprises as Simpson's, the HBC, Woodward's, Spencer's, Morgan's, the Dupuis Frères, and many smaller department stores. It reveals that although department stores sprang up throughout the country during the late nineteenth century, two Toronto firms – Eaton's and Simpson's – dominated Canada's national retail market. Their low prices, services, merchandise selection, catalogue operations, and branch stores enabled them to remain at the top of Canadian retail well into the 1950s, when shifting consumer preferences and increasing competition brought to a close the decades-long reign not only of Canada's largest department stores but also of many in England, France, Australia, and the United States.

Beginnings: 1800s to 1870s

Mass retail did not exist in British North America (BNA) prior to Canadian Confederation. Instead, during the first half of the nineteenth century, most of the colony's three million inhabitants obtained their goods and services by trading and bartering in small, local markets. In rural areas, where the vast majority of the population lived, people brought furs, flour, dairy products, fish, livestock, poultry, garden produce, and homespun textiles to trading posts and general stores, where they traded these items for other goods. Trading posts located west of Lake Superior were owned by the Northwest Company and the Hudson's Bay Company (exclusively by the HBC after 1821); general stores were scattered throughout the colony and owned by merchants as well as by local mining, mill, lumber, and other primary and secondary resource companies. Trading posts tended to accept furs and related products in exchange for food, furniture, guns, and other items necessary for life on the frontier. Merchant-owned general stores accepted a combination of goods, credit, and cash in exchange for their products. Company stores paid their workers in truck. Instead of paying their employees wages that they could spend where they pleased, they gave them scrip that they could only spend at their employers' store, where products tended to be overpriced.

In pre-Confederation Canada's towns and cities, of which the largest was Montréal, which had a population of 57,000 in 1851, general stores and more specialized shops existed. Some of these latter enterprises were owned and managed by artisans, including tailors, dressmakers, cobblers, cabinetmakers, jewellers, and blacksmiths. Others were owned by merchants who tended to carry specific lines of merchandise, such as dry goods, haberdashery, and medications. Montréal had a large cluster of specialty shops along its waterfront, a common site of market activity during the pre-railway years. Like the country general stores, urban specialty shops were family-owned and managed. Only the largest employed outside help; such workers never numbered more than five, and they tended to hold the positions of clerks and apprentices. The position of clerk was fairly prestigious and offered some opportunity, however slim, for advancement into bookkeeping or shopkeeping. The position of apprentice was less prestigious, generally reserved for young boys whose parents wished them to become shopkeepers. Apprentices received room, board, and training, but little or no pay.[6]

Whether they were rural or urban, most of the people who lived in northern North America during the first half of the nineteenth century earned, produced, traded, and used what they could, but they did not amass significant commodities or wealth. Their predominantly rural locations and limited budgets, however, did not preclude an awareness of the variety of goods and services available both domestically and internationally. Trading posts, general stores, company stores, and urban specialty shops offered goods produced in pre-Confederation Canada as well as in the United States and western Europe. Small colonial shops placed notices in local newspapers to inform readers of "newly arrived goods" from elsewhere. Affluent colonials, as well, tended to own more goods than their poorer counterparts; the clothing, houses, and other possessions of the wealthy would have acquainted the less privileged with the vast assortment of commodities beyond the reach of the majority of pre-Confederation

Canada's population. Québec's male professionals, including lawyers and doctors, invested heavily in fashion, spending "a greater proportion of their income (some 20 percent) on attire than any other class," as Jan Noel writes.[7] Rural British North Americans, too, were aware of material trends beyond their local communities. Early-nineteenth-century immigrants from France and Britain brought with them items produced by industrial methods, including dishes, cutlery, furniture and, increasingly, ready-made clothes. Some western European immigrants also brought above-subsistence expectations of quantity and quality. Susannah Moodie's journals, written in rural Ontario during the 1830s, bemoaned the lack of amenities in the region. From a middle-class English family, Moodie was accustomed to larger homes and more commodious surroundings. British immigrant Mary Moody, who lived in rural British Columbia between 1859 and 1863, also experienced settler life as deprivation, writing to her parents to see if they could ship to her some "children's furnishings and sewing notions." She also asked her English friends who planned to immigrate to the colony to bring out ready-made dresses.[8] Such complaints and entreaties indicate an awareness among arrivals about differences between northern North American living conditions and living conditions elsewhere; they also demonstrate that as British immigration to Canada increased in the nineteenth century, middle-class English settlers became determined to replicate the levels of material comfort they left behind.

Prior to the mid-nineteenth century in western Europe, living standards were indeed changing, at least among the bourgeoisie. During the eighteenth century, credit emerged, advertising grew, imperialism enriched the bourgeoisie, and such imports as coffee, sugar, and tea became staples in the diets of the affluent. As wealthy Europeans increased their expectations for material comfort, Europe's manufacturing output also increased, as did commodity assortment. Growing materialist expectations encouraged subtle transformations in goods distribution. Before the 1830s, shops in major European cities sold specialized merchandise, practised bartering, sold exclusively on credit, and had limited stock turnover, high overheads, and high prices. After the 1830s, though, some shops began to change their practices. Advertising became more frequent, and shops began to promote browsing, one-price ticketing, and cash sales. In 1840s Paris, which reached a population of one million in 1846, merchants also began experimenting with a broader assortment of stock. *Magasins de nouveautés*, which sold both fancy goods and heavy bolts of cloth, challenged older conventions by combining two forms of goods in one store. They also began increasing their stock turnover by lowering their markups and offering frequent sales. Urban shops of this period did not specifically target working-class customers, but their new strategies indicated their response to changing shopping practices. Customers were becoming more inclined to browse and compare items and prices, to pay anonymously with cash, and to seek broad assortments of merchandise.[9]

The American retail landscape was also transformed during this period. Prior to 1850, America's country and small-town stores resembled those of BNA. They were small, had limited stock and turnover, practised bartering and trading, and operated almost exclusively on credit. As in BNA and western Europe, America's cities offered both general stores and specialty shops, the latter of which were either owned by craftspeople or by merchants who specialized in narrow merchandise lines. In New York, however, new kinds of stores were developing. With a rapidly growing population that reached 516,000 in 1850 and 814,000 in 1860, New York was the largest city in North America and had the capacity to support large shops. In 1846, merchant A.T. Stewart razed his sprawling emporium to the ground and in its place erected a massive multi-levelled shop called the Marble Palace. Like the Parisian magasins de nouveautés, Stewart's new store offered low markups, frequent stock turnover, free browsing, cash sales, and one-price ticketing. Also like its French counterparts, it was primarily a dry goods store, selling deep lines of fancy goods, drapery, and furniture. Stewart's enterprise reigned over New York City until the 1870s, when increased competition, combined with Stewart's own managerial difficulties, set the firm on a long decline that ended with its sale to retail giant John Wanamaker in 1896.[10]

During the 1860s and 1870s, retail in France and the United States underwent further changes. As the productive capacity of each nation increased, manufacturers hired jobbers to sell larger and larger orders to wholesalers and retailers, often at unprecedented low prices. Merchants with sufficient capital reserves took advantage of these bargains to increase both their sales volume and their share of the consumer market. Such merchants were most often those who had in the preceding decade experimented successfully with what was becoming known as modern merchandising methods. These included the holding of frequent sales in order to generate stock turnover and to achieve greater sales volumes, the provision of one-price ticketing to ensure predictable returns, the encouragement of cash sales to create capital internally, and the promotion of free entry browsing to stimulate customers' desires and to increase shopping traffic. Some also began pricing their merchandise at rates lower than those of their competitors. So profitable did the combination of high turnover, low and predictable prices, free browsing, and cash sales become that a few began to accumulate sums of capital hitherto unseen in retail.

It was at this time that the department store was born. Recognizing the profitability of predictable and ever-increasing sales volumes, enterprising storekeepers such as Aristide Boucicaut in Paris, R.H. Macy in New York, John Wanamaker in Philadelphia, and Marshall Field in Chicago began to consciously pursue a policy of growth and diversification. By constantly enlarging and diversifying their stock, they were able to secure favourable rates from manufacturers and wholesalers; they were also able to avoid having their livelihoods dependent on the relative success of one kind of merchandise. As their merchandise offerings and lines grew, they began separating their stock into departments that were organized according to merchandise lines. Each department was then assigned its own sales and clerical staff. Departments such as millinery, dressmaking, and furniture also frequently boasted their own craftspeople. When department store owners' existing buildings became too cramped, they purchased surrounding properties and added piecemeal expansions to their existing structures. When they accumulated sufficient capital, they then demolished their ad hoc assemblages and in their place constructed massive multistoried buildings. Using the most modern building materials, ventilation and heating systems, lighting techniques, and decor available, these buildings dominated urban landscapes by sheer virtue of their size and architectural beauty. Boucicaut was the world's first merchant to create such a store: constructed between 1862 and 1870, his Bon Marché had 52,800 square metres of floor space, glass skylights, gallery-style merchandise departments, balconies along the upper floors, and curving staircases. When he died in 1877, Boucicaut had 1,788 employees and was owner of "the largest retail enterprise in the world." America's major department stores appeared slightly later than the Bon Marché; Macy, Wanamaker, and Field built their colossal structures during the 1870s and early 1880s.[11]

Industrialization, with its drastically increased production, was one of the key historical factors that made possible the debut of the department store in France and the United States. Urbanization, an outgrowth of the Industrial Revolution in that it encouraged people to move to cities to take up industrial and, increasingly, white collar jobs, was also key. The Bon Marché, Macy's, Wanamaker's, and Marshall Field's appeared in cities that had well over one thousand residents; cities of smaller populations simply did not have enough people to sustain large multi-storied shops. Other significant factors were changes in transportation. Streetcars enabled shoppers to travel from outlying areas to urban downtown centres, and cross-country railways enabled both people and goods to move more quickly across greater and greater distances. Steamships enabled merchants, shoppers, and goods to cross oceans. Finally, changes in purchasing power and demand were important factors. Merchants could enlarge their premises, lower their prices, diversify their stock, encourage browsing, and introduce one-price policies, but they could not guarantee their sales returns. That function was performed solely by shoppers, whose consumer expectations began to increase steadily, not only in France and the United States but also in other industrializing countries around the world.[12]

In contrast to the rapid emergence of mass retailing in France and the United States during the 1860s and 1870s, Canada's merchandising environment continued to be characterized by an abundance of small shops that offered a mixture of credit, cash, trade, and in some cases truck to their customers. Changes, however, were afoot. Railway construction began in BNA at mid-century, and by 1859 the Grand Trunk Railway enabled people and goods to travel between Québec City and Sarnia. It also linked the Canadas with Chicago, a major industrial hub. Construction continued through the next three decades, and by 1885 it was possible for goods and people to travel from Canada's Atlantic coast to its Pacific coast entirely by rail. Industrialization also increased during this period, as did the populations of major industrial centres. By 1871, the population of Hamilton was 27,000, Saint John was 28,800, Halifax was 29,000, Toronto was 59,000 and Montréal was 115,000. Other major cities at this time included Québec City, with a population of 60,000, and Ottawa, with a population of 24,000.[13] In response to both the increasing availability of goods and their cities' growing populations, such enterprising merchants as Henry Morgan in Montréal, Timothy Eaton in Toronto, and Robert Simpson in Toronto began enlarging their operations. Morgan's had opened in 1843 and by the 1870s was Canada's biggest store. In 1874 its Scottish-born owner had 150 employees in several departments selling "dry-goods, apparel, and accessories."[14] Eaton's Toronto shop opened as a dry goods store in 1869; by 1875 the Irish-born Eaton had nineteen employees and was selling the same type of merchandise as his Montréal counterpart. Scottish-born merchant Robert Simpson established a dry goods store in Toronto in 1871. By 1880 he had thirteen employees. Since all three stores sold primarily dry goods merchandise, they were not yet department stores. Yet their inclination to use modern retail methods, including cash-only policies and one-price ticketing, marked them as innovative, as did their owners' determination, especially strong in Timothy Eaton, to buy direct from European manufacturers and thus to pocket for themselves Canadian wholesalers' profits. The stores' ongoing expansion further set them apart, as many of their competitors continued to operate as small shops in which only family members laboured.[15]

Years of Growth: 1880s and 1890s
In the last two decades of the nineteenth century, France and the United States remained home to the world's largest and most elaborate department stores, but at this time department stores also debuted in Britain, Germany, Switzerland, and Canada.[16] In Calgary in 1886, American investors William Charles Conrad and I.G. Baker built one of Canada's first department stores. Two storeys high, the building was 30 feet across and 100 feet long. With merchandise ranging from groceries to carpets to clothing, it offered goods purchased in "Toronto, Montréal, Chicago, and New York City" and served not only Calgary, which had a population of 3,867 in 1891, but also the surrounding agricultural area.[17] Toronto and Montréal's stores were larger than Baker's, but they did not achieve the same level of diversification until the 1890s. During the early 1880s, Robert Simpson and Timothy Eaton each moved locations, buying up properties in the emerging shopping district of Yonge Street in downtown Toronto, razing the existing structures, and in 1883 erecting massive multi-storied buildings. In 1886, Eaton's expanded further, bringing the total floor space to more than 50,000 square feet, the number of merchandise departments to thirty-five, and the number of employees to three hundred. With three-storey light wells, a basement section, electric lighting, and elevators, it was Canada's most ambitious shop. In 1884 Timothy Eaton began distributing catalogues, some of them to addresses as far away as Manitoba. He perhaps modelled his approach on that of the Bon Marché, which had been carrying on a successful mail order service since 1871. Closer to home, R.H. Macy had started a catalogue trade in 1861, as had John Wanamaker in 1876. Montgomery Ward, too, was operating a catalogue trade, but not until 1908 did he open a department store. Eaton's was therefore among the first department store catalogues in North America. No doubt also inspired by international examples, in 1883 Timothy Eaton offered in-store lavatories as well as writing rooms and restrooms for women, and in 1887 he built an in-store restaurant and a

coffee room. By 1889, Eaton's was realizing $1 million in sales annually. This figure was lower than the Fr123 million the Bon Marché earned annually during this period, lower than Macy's US$5.5 million, and lower than Harrods in London's US$2.4 million. Nonetheless, Eaton's sales were the highest in Canada and indicative of the company's growing stature.[18]

Just as the 1870s and 1880s marked the full-fledged emergence of French and American department stores, so did the 1890s mark the explosion of department stores onto Canada's retailing scene. During this decade the country remained overwhelmingly rural, with 3.3 million inhabitants living in rural areas compared to 1.5 million in cities and large towns. Nevertheless, Eaton's growing catalogue trade made department store shopping possible for people living in remote areas. Enhanced railway travel also made it easier for rural shoppers to reach such metropolitan department stores as Eaton's and Simpson's in Toronto and Morgan's in Montréal. Throughout the country, small and mid-sized department stores began to appear in towns and small cities, further enabling department store buying among rural and urban dwellers alike. On Vancouver Island, Welsh-born merchant David Spencer transformed his Victoria dry goods store, established in 1878, into a full-fledged department store. His new four-storey shop sold "clothing, shoes, furniture, books, china, stoves, drug sundries, kitchenware" and other items to a rapidly growing population, which reached 16,841 in 1891. In Vancouver in 1892, which then had a population of 13,709, Charles Woodward built a three-storey department store. By 1900, this former Ontario merchant was selling groceries, footwear, pharmaceuticals, and dry goods as well as conducting a mail order trade that serviced both British Columbia and Alberta. Albertans could also patronize Power and Brothers' stores, a Montana department store chain that opened in Calgary, Fort Macleod, and Maple Creek during the 1880s and 1890s. In Ontario, department stores appeared in several midsized towns, including St. Thomas, where Anderson's department store opened in 1896. In Montréal, two major department stores were created when Morgan's and Murphy's each relocated from their waterfront premises, where they had been expanding throughout the 1880s, to the uptown shopping district along St. Catherine Street. Morgan's, long considered Montréal's retail leader, retained that status with the 1891 opening of its new four-storey shop named Colonial House. With an exterior of red sandstone and an interior that boasted everything from sporting goods to luxury furs, it was Montréal's premier department store (Figure 1.1).

FIGURE 1.1   Morgan's Colonial House Department Store on St. Catherine Street in Montréal, 1891 | *Source:* McCord Museum, Montréal, Digital Image VIEW-2539.1. | Used with permission of the McCord Museum.

On Prince Edward Island, Holman's Department Store was emerging as a significant force. Established in Summerside before Confederation, this largest of PEI retailers underwent major expansion in the late nineteenth century, tearing down its older store and replacing it with a building that, as one newspaper stated, gave Summerside "quite a city appearance." At 134 by 105 feet, the building featured plate glass windows, grandiose staircases, and "ceilings of varnished spruce."[19] St. John's, Newfoundland, also became home to department stores, including Ayre and Sons, Knowling's, and Bowring Brothers, the latter having been established in 1811 as a jewellery store but transforming itself into a department store in the last decade of the twentieth century.[20]

Hudson's Bay Company department stores emerged during this period as well. Established in the seventeenth century as a North American fur-trading venture backed by British financiers, the HBC was in 1670 granted by King Charles II of England exclusive trading rights to the territory containing all the waterways flowing into Hudson Bay. The company's trading chiefs, or factors, acted as imperial governors throughout this massive region, which they called Rupert's Land, and which constituted 40 percent of contemporary Canada. When the Canadian government of the mid-nineteenth century made its interest in Rupert's Land known, the HBC agreed to sell most of it to the emerging Canadian state, retaining for itself small land parcels. The HBC continued operating in western Canada after this 1869 sale, managing trading posts as well as collecting sales and rents from its lands. As white settlement increased in the region, the HBC also began to recognize the growing importance of retail to the area's economy. It continued its fur and land operations, but it diversified into urban merchandising. In 1890, it built a two-storey store in Calgary, and in 1891 it purchased Baker's Fort Macleod, Lethbridge, and Calgary stores. The last of these was the biggest, employing nine workers in 1891. Much smaller than Eaton's or Simpson's Toronto stores, HBC Calgary was nevertheless southern Alberta's most modern store, offering organized departments and clearly ticketed merchandise. So successful was the HBC's Calgary venture that, in 1893, the company transferred its manager to Vancouver, where he oversaw the opening of another small department store. Three storeys high, HBC Vancouver offered a mixture of men's and women's clothing, carpets, and dry goods.[21]

If the 1890s were fortuitous for small and mid-sized Canadian department stores, they were even more so for Canada's largest. By 1893, Simpson's had reached department store status, selling not only apparel and dry goods but also carpets, wallpaper, footwear, stationery, books, food, and dinnerware. In 1894 this five-hundred-employee-strong company followed Eaton's in offering what became a cross-country mail order trade. Two years later, Simpson's became a joint stock company, and when Robert Simpson died in 1897, two prominent Toronto capitalists, J.W. Flavelle and H.H. Fudger, purchased his business. By the close of the century, Simpson's was earning $1.2 million in sales annually. It was the second largest retailer in Canada, surpassed only by Eaton's, which realized $5 million in sales in 1898.[22]

Calling itself "Canada's Greatest Store," Eaton's truly became a department store in the early 1890s. With merchandise as diverse as medication, bicycles, produce, meat, dinnerware, sewing machines, hardware, furniture, toys, paintings, menswear, fancy goods, carpets, women's dresses, and cosmetics, and with 2,475 employees by 1898, the company had earned its self-styled title. In the last few years of the nineteenth century, Eaton's bought property to house its delivery stables; it also acquired two nearby farms so as to supply its restaurants with dairy and eggs. By 1897, the Eaton store was over 326 thousand square feet, and the company's operations, which included manufacturing, sales, and mail order, covered a city block. Like Macy's, Wanamaker's, and Marshall Field's before it, Eaton's opened buying offices in London, Paris, and New York. By 1900, Eaton's was realizing larger annual sales than either Bloomingdale's in New York or Harrods in London. Yet, although Eaton's sales were approaching those of Macy's, which earned US$7.8 million in 1899, they were still lower than those of the Bon Marché, which made Fr123 million in 1906. And Eaton's still earned only half of what Sears, Roebuck, and Company made. Sears, a mail order company that had emerged in 1892, reported US$10 million in 1900 and became one of America's largest retailers. Only Wanamaker's, which had stores in both New York and Philadelphia, might have been bigger, but neither Wanamaker's nor Marshall Field's figures for this period are available.

Eaton's comparatively lower totals should be considered in light of the fact that in 1901 the population of Canada was 5.4 million while that of England and Wales was 32.5 million, and that of France was 40 million. In 1900 the population of the United States was 76.2 million. Alongside these numbers, Eaton's sales figures are significant. Regardless of Canada's small size, its population supported a department store whose sales totals neared, and in a few cases surpassed, the industrializing world's largest retailers. Eaton's comparative sales figures also reveal that Canada's retail market was more monopolistic than its counterparts in England, France, and the United States. Certainly not everyone in Canada patronized Eaton's, but if one considers Canadian spending at Eaton's on a per capita basis, then each Canadian resident spent 93 cents at Eaton's in 1898. In contrast, each American resident spent only 13 cents at Sears in 1900.[23]

This discrepancy in market shares between Eaton's, on the one hand, and America's largest stores, on the other, results from the countries' different retail situations. Between 1871 and 1911, the number of merchants in Canada rose from approximately 25,000 to 81,000, but almost 40 percent of these businesses were small "shoestring" operators. During this period, the United States had three of the world's largest department stores and two of the world's biggest catalogue operators. In Canada, however, Eaton's nearest competitors were Simpson's and Morgan's, each of which was earning about one-fifth of Eaton's sales. Eaton's grew so quickly that it simply eclipsed most other shopkeepers. Its cash-only policies, moreover, enabled it to accumulate more capital than could most other merchants, who continued out of neccessity to offer both credit and cash. Though many rural storekeepers were no doubt aware of the advantages of selling for cash only, many of their agrarian, hunting, fishing, and other non-industrial customers did not receive steady wages. Thus, rural merchants had to continue offering combinations of trading, credit, and cash. Small urban shops that catered to working people also provided credit, for many were situated in low-income neighbourhoods whose residents did not have access to ready cash. In contrast, as Morgan's, Simpson's, and especially Eaton's transformed their cash sales into deeper and deeper merchandise lines, these larger stores were able to obtain greater and greater discounts from their suppliers and were thus able to continually lower their prices. They were also able to generate a regular cash income: as they increased their stock turnover by holding regular sales, they were able to avoid seasonal trade slumps. Mail order was a final, crucial factor in the big Canadian stores' growth. By offering goods ranging from dresses to sinks to shovels at the lowest prices in the dominion, and by sending their catalogue to homes from outport Newfoundland to interior British Columbia, Simpson's and especially Eaton's set national standards in price, quality, and availability. Small-town merchants, independent craftspeople, and urban specialty stores could not compete with the Toronto giants' stylish products and bulk-purchased offerings. As Canada's rail system grew ever more sophisticated, customers all over the dominion could access these monopolistic retailers' goods. When the parcel post was introduced in 1914, it became even easier to partake of Eaton's seemingly limitless bounty.[24]

In terms of target consumer groups, Canada's retailing scene both resembled and diverged from that of other industrializing countries. France's largest and most successful store, the Bon Marché, was a solidly middle-class institution, catering to the nouveau riche and affluent provincials. Britain's department store scene was more diverse than that of its neighbour across the Channel. No major store dominated the country; instead, both mid-sized haute couture and popular stores existed. These included the upscale Harrods in London and the more down-to-earth Lewis's in Liverpool. America, too, had a combination of pricey and popular department stores, the former including Wanamaker's and Marshall Field's, the latter including Macy's. Late-nineteenth-century Canada did not have enough bourgeois consumers to support a massive upmarket department store, but there were enough affluent people in Toronto and Montréal to keep in business the mid-sized Simpson's and Morgan's, both of which targeted the carriage trade. In one sense, then, Canada's retail scene resembled that of France in that one major store – the T. Eaton Company – dominated the late-nineteenth-century marketplace. Yet, unlike the Bon Marché, Eaton's during this period was not middle-class. Instead, Timothy Eaton targeted urban spenders of lower-middle-class and upper-working-class status, as well as rural spenders of affluent, middling, and in some cases low-income status. In this way, like R.H. Macy before him, Eaton thus bypassed the affluent yet numerically weak bourgeoisie in favour of the lower income yet numerically strong lower middle class and working class. At the same time, he extended his market beyond Macy's. Though both companies ran large mail order operations, Macy's profits were hindered by intense competition from Montgomery Ward's and Sears. Woodward's and Simpson's offered Eaton's some competition, but not enough to challenge the latter's status as the dominion's largest catalogue operator. In ways unmatched by any other retailer in the industrializing world at this time, Eaton's captured both the urban petit bourgeois and working-class market as well as a wide-ranging rural market, which included customers of high, middling, and low socioeconomic status.[25]

Eaton's phenomenal late-nineteenth-century success was hence partly attributable to its founder's cash-only policies; his targeting of the numerically powerful lower, middle, and upper working classes; his emphasis on fast stock turnover; his excellent relationships with suppliers; and his policy of exponential growth. Yet Eaton's business acumen was not the only factor behind his big store's rise. Canada's increasingly complex railway network supported the store by enabling both people and goods to travel great distances. Not only did rail enable shoppers to travel to Eaton's downtown Toronto store, but it also carried manufactured goods from distant markets to Eaton's warehouses and transported commodities from Eaton's warehouses to customers across the dominion. To ease customers' shipping burdens, in 1906 Eaton's started paying the freight rates on orders over twenty-five dollars, and in 1907 it began covering rates on exchanges. In 1913, Eaton's began paying freight charges on orders over ten dollars. Also responsible for Eaton's success was tacit government support. Dominion, provincial, and municipal governments of this period were loath to interfere with the machinations of capital, preferring to let what was known as the invisible hand of the market drive the economy. Thus, although independent shopkeepers in the 1890s formed such organizations as the Retail Grocers' Association to lobby against what they perceived as unfair competition represented by mass retail, governments tended to avoid implementing any laws that would seriously curtail the emerging monopoly of Eaton's and, to a lesser extent, that of Simpson's, Morgan's, Woodward's, and the HBC.[26]

A growing propensity to consume among populations that had previously lived at or near subsistence levels was a final spur to the late-nineteenth-century rise of Eaton's and other mass retailers. As industrialization and capitalization accelerated not only in Canada but also in western Europe and the United States, money markets stabilized and wages became an accepted form of payment for work. Since industrial labour required workers' relocation to cities, where factories congregated, and since industrial work was extremely time-consuming, requiring twelve-hour days and more, employees did not have a lot of time to devote to household goods production, bartering, and trade. Factories employed primarily men but also some women and older children; those who were not employed in the factories had busy days taking care of younger children and maintaining households. Given these time pressures, workers began spending their wages in the consumer marketplace, acquiring food, clothing, and other important necessities. Timothy Eaton noted this tendency as soon as he set up shop in Toronto. Recognizing the potential that existed in a strictly cash trade, he targeted waged workers. During the early 1870s, for example, he became aware that Toronto's railway sector, the largest industrial labour force in the city, paid its workers on Thursday evenings. He responded by moving his sale days from Saturdays, the retail trade's traditional sale day, to Fridays. By the early 1880s, Eaton's "Friday Bargain Days" had become a weekly and much heralded event among the city's well-to-do working class.[27]

Certainly, not all of Canada's working people were able to buy goods from Eaton's or order from its catalogues. Prior to the mid-twentieth-century growth of the welfare state, people without access to adequate and steady paycheques had to rely on combinations of credit, bartering, and cash to make ends meet. Both urban and rural workers also continued to plant their own gardens and raise their own livestock. Selling crafts, taking in sewing and ironing, and renting out rooms were some of the other ways that economically disadvantaged households survived. Yet there are indications that, overall, Canadian spending increased during the last few decades of the nineteenth century. By 1889 in Ontario, Monod notes, "the consumption of non-essentials among the working class was a possibility for about half the ... wage-earning population and ... one in five [working-class families] enjoyed a substantial surplus income." At the turn of the twentieth century, "the average individual's annual pound and a half of currants and two bushels of apples were being supplemented by imports of bananas and pineapples and by the domestic manufacture of tinned pears and prunes."[28] Also indicative of rising Canadian standards of living was an increase in consumer goods production. Domestic clothing manufacturing increased in the 1880s, as did domestic food manufacturing in the 1890s, protected by Sir John A. Macdonald's National Policy, which was implemented in 1879 and which slapped increasingly high tariffs on imported goods. The domestic manufacturing of household goods, meanwhile, had increased throughout the 1870s, and the domestic entertainment industry expanded during the 1880s. Together with Eaton's phenomenal growth, these events indicate that consumer sentiment was growing among not only bourgeois but also petit bourgeois and upper working-class Canadians. Home ownership among working people also increased during this period, with the notable exception of workers in Montréal, who continued to rent their homes. This facilitated working families' ability to spend money on goods and services, as money that would otherwise have been spent on rent could be spent in the marketplace.[29]

A cultural orientation toward consumption accompanied this rise in spending. By the early 1900s, conservative Canadian intellectuals were lamenting what they perceived to be an increased dominion-wide materialism. Wilfrid Eggleston, Andrew MacPhail, George Parkin, and Arnold Haultain each bemoaned the abandonment of the nineteenth-century ideals of self-production and thrift, arguing that as Canadians acquired more goods, they become weaker and more vapid. Such rumblings, however, were not strong enough to stem the rising tide of consumption. As shopping became more convenient, as consumer goods and services became more affordable, and as standards became more reliable, Canadians all over the dominion sought out mass-produced goods.[30]

Consumers' motivations were many, and they are explored further in Chapter 5. It should be noted here, though, that time-consuming industrial labour, cramped urban living conditions, and the implementation of laws banning livestock within cities made it difficult for some families to produce their own garments and food. As well, when rural people moved to cities, they left behind stable communities in which social status depended upon kinship, and in which everyone had a clear place in the social hierarchy. In cities, new arrivals experienced anonymity and had difficulty sorting out their own and others' relative identities and social rankings. Consumption offered one way out of this conundrum. By assigning status to particular goods (prestige to expensive accessories, for example, and disgrace to agrarian-style clothing), urbanites made sense of their new social worlds.[31] Working people's need for respite was another factor behind the rise of consumption. After long days in the factories, offices, shops, and at home, many men and women – particularly young adults – sought fun and relaxation in Canada's growing entertainment venues, including dancehalls, soda parlours, theatres, and department stores.[32] Immigration, too, fuelled consumerism. Since modern European dress was a mark of belonging in British and French Canadian culture, immigrants wishing to avoid marginalization sometimes bought Western clothes to proclaim membership in the New World.[33]

Canadian Department Stores' Heyday: 1900s and 1910s

During the first decades of the twentieth century, the HBC, Simpson's, and Eaton's grew steadily. In western Canada the HBC continued its strategy of building department stores in emerging settlements, and when Edmonton's population reached seven thousand in 1904, it opened its first department store in that town. Simpson's, meanwhile, purchased Murphy's department store in Montréal in 1905; it also built a warehouse and women's wear factory in Toronto. By the next year, this mid-sized retailer had 1,800 Toronto staff members. Like its Yonge Street neighbour, Eaton's also opened its first branch store in 1905. It set its sights further afield, though. Recognizing that much of its catalogue trade came from the farms, towns, and cities rapidly being settled in southern Manitoba and southeastern Saskatchewan, Eaton's opened a colossal five-storey edifice in Winnipeg that year (Figure 1.2). Employing 1,250 workers and situated in a city whose population reached 90,153 in 1906, the Winnipeg store grew rapidly. Over the next few years, Eaton's added two more storeys, and by 1910 Eaton's Winnipeg factories were producing much of the region's consumer goods. Eaton's arrival in Winnipeg also precipitated the decentralization of Eaton's catalogue operations. The company established a mail order building and printing press in this major Prairie hub, making Winnipeg the centre of Eaton's western mail order trade.

Back in Toronto, Eaton's leadership continued. By 1904 it was printing 1.3 million catalogues annually and sending orders as far away as Mexico, Europe, China, and India. In 1905, Eaton's introduced the Santa Claus Parade, a successful annual public relations event that helped inspire the Macy's Thanksgiving Parade, which was introduced in 1924. By 1909

FIGURE 1.2   Illustrated postcard featuring Eaton's Winnipeg store, 1908 |
Source: From the personal collection of Andrew Cunningham. | Used with permission
of Sears Canada Inc.

Eaton's operations in Toronto covered twenty-two acres of downtown real
estate. The company had 11,700 employees spread over 125 selling and
17 manufacturing departments; it also had factories in Montréal, Toronto,
and Oshawa, which together employed 4,500 workers. By 1907 Eaton's
total annual sales had reached $22.5 million. It was much bigger than
Harrods, Great Britain's largest department store, which had sales of US$5
million in 1902. Eaton's had also grown bigger than Macy's, which earned
US$16.8 million in 1907. It was still smaller than the Bon Marché, which
earned Fr200 million in 1906, and mail order powerhouse Sears, Roebuck,
and Company remained North America's retail leader, bringing in US$50
million in sales in 1907.[34]

For the HBC, the second decade of the twentieth century marked a
turning point in company strategy. Recognizing the growing influence of
urbanization on Canada's west, in 1910 the HBC's principal shareholders
separated the company into three divisions: fur, land, and stores. It also
began shifting its focus from fur to retail. In 1912 the Stores Commissioner
stated that "the future policy of the company should be to develop departmental stores, both in Calgary and Vancouver and other principal
cities in western Canada ... at the present there is not a great deal of

competition, excepting the case of Winnipeg," where Eaton's had set up shop. In 1911 the company opened a modest department store in Manitoba's capital city, across from the company's Fur and Land Department. More extensive efforts were made in Alberta and British Columbia. After renovations to its Calgary site, in 1913 the HBC opened its new store to Calgary's growing population, which had reached 46,000 that year. With five acres of floor space, a children's playground, a library, and a restaurant, HBC Calgary was, the Stores Commissioner assured his superiors in London, "the finest store in western Canada." That same year, the HBC built a six-storey addition to its Edmonton store, giving the location 70,000 square feet of floor space. It also started construction on a six-storey store in Vancouver, which opened in 1920. With forty-seven merchandise departments and a restaurant serving "half a million meals ... annually," it was "a great community under one roof," as the HBC's publicity magazine put it.[35]

As settlement and urbanization expanded across western Canada, the number of department stores increased. In 1901, the total population of British Columbia, Alberta, Saskatchewan, and Manitoba combined was 598,169; by 1921 that figure had jumped to 2,480,666. The total number of residents in Canada's western provinces was not quite half that of Ontario and Québec, which together reached 5,294,172 in 1921, but it was sizeable enough to support the growing presence of mass retail. In British Columbia, which had a population of 524,582 in 1921, Spencer's was becoming a major operator. Through its mail order trade as well as its branch stores in Chilliwack, New Westminster, Nanaimo, and Vancouver, this Victoria enterprise could reach a substantial proportion of the population (Figure 1.3). With more than nine hundred employees in 1913, Spencer's Vancouver store was its largest. By 1923 Spencer's Vancouver location had 271,116 square feet of selling space spread over six storeys; it also operated a bank, a grocery warehouse, a furniture warehouse, a garage, and a storage facility. Of Canada's four western provinces, however, it was Saskatchewan that witnessed the most significant population increase, with numbers leaping from 91,279 in 1901 to 757,510 in 1921. Both Simpson's and Eaton's were quick to notice this growth, and in 1916 each established a physical presence in the province: Simpson's opened a mail order depot in Regina, and Eaton's built mail order buildings in Regina and Saskatoon. Independent stores also appeared in the area, including Cairn's of Saskatoon, which in 1911 established a five-storey department store that had 90,255 square feet of selling space.[36]

FIGURE 1.3   Cover of Spencer's Catalogue, 1928-29 | *Source:* Robert D. Watt, "Introduction," *The Shopping Guide of the West: Woodward's Catalogues, 1898-1953*, ed. Vancouver Centennial Museum (Vancouver: J. J. Douglas, 1977), ix. | Used with permission of Sears Canada Inc.

Unlike Canada's four western-most provinces, the dominion's three eastern-most provinces did not experience a rapid population surge between 1901 and 1921. Because of migration off the island, the population of Prince Edward Island actually declined from 103,259 to 88,615 during this period. Nova Scotia and New Brunswick underwent slight population

FIGURE 1.4   Holman's Department Store and Operations, Summerside, PEI, 1915. | *Source:* Wyatt Heritage Properties, Summerside, PEI, Digital Image 018.56. | Used with permission of the PEI Museum and Heritage Foundation and with permission of Wyatt Heritage Properties.

increases (Nova Scotia to 523,837 and New Brunswick to 387,876), and Newfoundland, which remained a British colony until 1949, also experienced gradual growth, reaching 263,000 in 1921. The total 1921 population of Prince Edward Island, Nova Scotia, New Brunswick, and Newfoundland was thus about half that of Manitoba, Saskatchewan, Alberta, and British Columbia combined and about one-fifth that of Québec and Ontario. In spite of its relatively smaller numbers, however, northeastern North America had enough purchasing power to support local department stores, including the Royal Stores Company in St. John's, Newfoundland (Newfoundland did not join Canada until 1949), and Vooght's in North Sydney, Nova Scotia. Established in 1902, the latter store employed thirty-three people by 1914. Meanwhile, Holman's in PEI remained one of the region's largest stores. In 1909 the firm launched what became a successful catalogue business, receiving orders not only from within PEI but also from Newfoundland, Nova Scotia, New Brunswick, and Québec. The firm built additions to its store throughout this period and by 1919 had grown sufficiently to employ two hundred islanders (Figure 1.4). Retailers in Saint John and Halifax, as well, operated both central and branch stores in New Brunswick and Nova Scotia during this period. Like their counterparts throughout the dominion, they had to contend with Eaton's and Simpson's, whose catalogues had been infiltrating eastern Canada and Newfoundland since the 1890s. A further challenge to Atlantic merchants was Eaton's and Simpson's decision during the First World War to establish a physical presence in Nova Scotia and New Brunswick. In 1916, Simpson's opened a mail order distribution centre in Halifax, and in 1918 Eaton's opened massive mail order depots in Halifax and Moncton, the latter employing 750 workers.[37]

Simpson's and Eaton's decisions to open catalogue warehouses in Saskatchewan, Nova Scotia, and New Brunswick were triggered by their determination to stave off competitors. In 1920, Simpson's earned $13.1 million in catalogue sales annually, while Eaton's made $60 million. Together, these two companies' catalogue trade represented 3 percent of total retail sales in Canada – an asset worthy of protection. Savings on parcel postage was another factor behind the big retailers' establishment of regional shipping depots. Just before Canada introduced the parcel post, Eaton's announced it would cover all shipping costs on orders over five dollars. By opening warehouses in strategic locations, the company could arrange bulk shipments from factories to regional warehouses and thus avoid onerous postal charges.[38]

Canada's most populous provinces similarly witnessed major retail expansion and change during the 1910s. In Montréal, Scroggie's emerged in 1913 and was purchased by Almy's in 1915. After the Montréal department store Carsley's went bankrupt, Goodwin's took over its operations. In Maniwaki, Québec, a department store called Hubert's was thriving, and in Ottawa, Ogilvy's (not related to Ogilvy's in Montréal) and Freiman's were making their names known. Other small and mid-sized stores included Robinson's in Hamilton and Goudie's in Kitchener. It was Eaton's, however, that experienced the most phenomenal growth of the period. In 1915 the company bought a knitting factory in Hamilton, and in 1916 it opened another Toronto factory. That same year, Eaton's built a new mail order building in Winnipeg, which added five more acres of warehouse space to its Manitoba catalogue trade. Three years later it added another factory to its Ontario operations when it bought the Guelph Stove Company. By the close of the First World War, Eaton's was operating

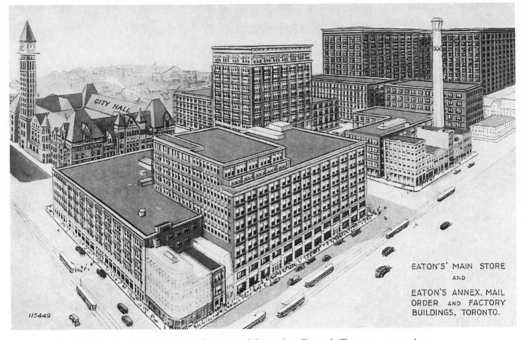

FIGURE 1.5   Eaton's illustrated postcard featuring Eaton's Toronto operations, 1920. | *Source:* Wikipedia, http://upload.wikimedia.org/wikipedia/commons/d/d4/ Eatonstoronto1920MainStore.jpg. | Used with permission of Sears Canada Inc.

buying offices in Tokyo, Manchester, Leicester, Belfast, Zurich, and New York, and it employed 16,000 people in Toronto alone. Two thousand of these worked in mail order, 6,400 laboured in manufacturing, and a further 7,600 staffed management and sales (Figure 1.5). In 1919, Eaton's annual sales totalled $123,590,000. Simpson's and the HBC, the country's second largest retailers, made only $33,444,765 and $14,865,000, respectively. Not only was Eaton's Canada's retail leader, but it was also a major contender on the international scene. In 1919, Macy's sales of US$35,802,808 rivalled Simpson's but were nowhere near those of the giant T. Eaton Company. Canada's largest store was still not North America's largest store, however. That title was still held by Sears, which earned US$235 million in sales in 1920.[39]

Competition and Challenges: 1920s and 1930s

Unfortunately for Canada's largest stores, the 1920s marked the start of a new merchandising era. The dynamics of Canadian shopping and retail changed during this decade, to the permanent detriment of department stores. During the 1880s and up until the First World War, individual spending on non-food consumer items had been directed primarily toward clothing and home furnishings, two of department stores' major product lines. Between the world wars, though, non-food consumer preferences shifted. Clothing and furnishings remained important, but a new sector was on the rise. Whereas only the very affluent owned automobiles in the pre-war era, survey of southern Ontario farmers revealed that 63 percent had automobiles in the early 1920s; a survey from the same period of Manitoba farmers revealed that 80 percent owned a vehicle. By 1930 automobile dealers were earning 13.86 percent of total consumer spending in Canada, surpassed only by department stores and mail order houses, which earned 16.39 percent, and food stores, which earned 22.33 percent. That same year, Canadian consumers spent 12.6 percent of each retail dollar on automobiles; only food products, on which consumers spent 29.01 percent of every dollar, and clothing and shoe products, which received 14.76 percent, earned more consumer money. As interwar Canadians began directing more of their income toward cars, department stores felt the pinch. Not only did they lose retail dollars to auto dealers, but they also lost mail order sales to in-store sales. Car ownership enabled rural customers to travel more quickly and frequently to regional retail hubs, where they could select merchandise in person. As a result, Canada's two largest mail order houses experienced a permanent slip in catalogue sales. Simpson's operations actually lost money in some years during the decade, and Eaton's mail order sales declined from their 1919-20 height of $63 million to $57 million annually through 1928.[40]

Also harmful was the emergence of the chains. In 1889 in the United States, only 2 chain businesses existed; by 1912 there were 177 chain retailers managing 2,235 outlets. By 1929 there were 1,500 chains in America operating 70,000 stores in total. Chains arose similarly rapidly in Canada during the 1920s, though on a smaller scale. Just a handful existed in the dominion prior to 1900, and in 1919 Canada's three largest chains, Loblaw's, Dowler's, and Carroll's, operated only 36 stores. Yet by 1924 there were 1,200 chain outlets across Canada, and by 1930 there were 13,287. Grocery stores were the most numerous, with Dominion's and Loblaw's dominating eastern and central Canada and Safeway's and Atlantic and Pacific doing the same in the West. Clothing chains included D'Aillard's and Tip Top Tailors, while shoes were most heavily represented by Agnew-Surpass. This decade also saw the expansion of the five-and-dime, or variety, chains. In 1912 there were two variety chains in Canada, Knox's and Charlton's, the latter American-owned. That same year, however, Woolworth's bought out both, adding "Knox's 108 stores in the United States and Canada and Charlton's 48" to its "expanding empire," which reached as far as Britain. By 1924, Woolworth's total sales were US$15 million, up US$12 million from 1912. They were much lower than Eaton's $125 million earned in 1922, but they were indicative of the rapid rise of chains during this period. By 1925 chains were earning the same percentage of the Canadian market as were department stores, and in 1930 they surpassed department stores' sales, bringing in $210 million net more, excluding $77 million net earned by catalogue operators, including those owned by department stores.[41]

The chain stores' rapid growth can be partially attributed to the inflation of the immediate postwar years. As department and independent stores' prices went up, chains deliberately kept their prices down, holding sales in advance of their competitors. They became known for their low prices, attracting customers seeking not only low prices but also standardized and familiar product lines, timely fashions, deep merchandise lines, and dependable quality. Chain outlets were also smaller than department stores and employed fewer people; they could construct and, if necessary, close branch locations more easily than could department stores. As rural and semi-urban North Americans acquired more cars, customers travelled to downtown department stores less often, preferring instead to drive to stores located closer to their homes. Building low-rent and low-tax stores in outlying urban areas, and offering better parking than department stores, chain stores profited from shoppers' increased mobility. A final reason for chain stores' 1920s ascension was an increased emphasis among retailers upon size. Recognizing that department stores' vast profits hinged on their ability to obtain deep buying discounts, affluent merchants responded by buying out smaller stores, increasing their sales volume and capital.[42]

During the 1920s, in response to not only the chains' advance but also to increasing rates of automobile ownership, several major department stores opened branch outlets and bought out smaller companies. In the United States, Marshall Field's opened a second downtown Chicago location and built suburban branches. Macy's expanded its flagship New York City location both outwards and upwards, making it one of the single biggest department store buildings in the world. Catalogue giants Sears and Montgomery Ward's also expanded. By 1929, Sears was operating 268 retail stores, along with its mail order enterprise, and Ward's was managing 532. In Great Britain, Harrods of London bought up smaller retailers and opened suburban stores. And Canadian department stores, too, devised ways to cope. Between 1925 and 1929, Eaton's brought its catalogue merchandise closer to its customers by opening a mail order branch in Moncton and a mail order showroom in Winnipeg. It opened branch stores in every province except New Brunswick, Prince Edward Island, and British Columbia, and it purchased the Canadian Department Stores company, a southern Ontario chain of twenty department stores. Not to be outdone by the food chains, Eaton's also launched its own food stores, dubbed "foodaterias."[43] Thus, in 1925, Eaton's opened a department store in Montréal; in 1927, Eaton's department stores were in Saskatoon, Red Deer, and Hamilton; in 1928, residents of Port Arthur and Halifax witnessed an Eaton's store arrival; and in 1929, Albertans saw Eaton's stores open in Edmonton, Calgary, and Lethbridge. So successful was Eaton's in the latter location that the previously dominant HBC branch closed in 1931. Eaton's first foodateria appeared in Regina in 1926; Medicine Hat saw one arrive in 1927; Prince Albert acquired one in 1928; and Edmonton and Dauphin each became home to Eaton's foodaterias in 1929. By 1930, Eaton's total regular workforce – excluding part-time and temporary staff – numbered 25,736. This one company therefore employed 11 percent of all full-time retail workers in Canada, an enormous figure, considering that there were 125,003 stores in the dominion in 1930. Eaton's also employed more than half the total regular department store workforce in Canada, a total of 45,810 people. By the Second World War, Eaton's had become the country's third largest employer, surpassed only by the federal government and the railroads.[44]

Eaton's sales were as massive as its workforce. In 1930 the total Canadian retail sales volume was $2.76 billion. Excluding its mail order division, Eaton's earned $225 million of this, taking in 58 percent of all department store sales as well as more than 7 percent of total Canadian retail sales. Together with Simpson's, Eaton's mail order took in a further 3 percent of Canadian retail dollars. In contrast, more than 75 percent of Canada's stores earned less than twenty thousand dollars in 1930; only eighty-six retailers sold over one million dollars of merchandise. By the dawn of the Great Depression, Eaton's was not only the key player in the nation's consumer market but it had also emerged as a major Canadian institution and was one of the biggest retailers in the world. It was much bigger than Marshall Field's, which earned US$1.7 million in 1931; it was also larger than Macy's, which had a full-time staff of 12,500 in 1928 and sales totals of US$99 million in 1930. Eaton's was still smaller than Sears, however, which realized US$400 million in sales in 1929.[45]

Eaton's rapid 1920s expansion was indicative not only of its aggressive stance but also of department stores' overall higher levels of national significance in Canada as compared to Britain and America during the interwar years. In 1930 department stores captured 14 percent of retail dollars spent in Canada. Eaton's, Simpson's, and the HBC alone took in 12 percent of these sales. That same year in Britain, department stores took in only approximately 4 percent of total national retail dollars. As well, Eaton's, Simpson's, and the HBC earned much larger proportions of national department store sales than did their counterparts in the United States. In 1930 these three companies earned 70 percent of Canada's department store business. In contrast, seventeen major US department stores earned only 34 percent of American total department store sales. Department stores, particularly Eaton's, Simpson's, and the HBC, were hence more important in the Canadian consumer market than they were in the British and American markets. During the 1920s these three companies might have faced increased competition from automobiles and chains, but their policies and activities continued to have a major impact on the character and direction of Canadian retail.[46]

In contrast to Eaton's rapid expansion, Simpson's response to the changing retail climate of the 1920s was to move slowly and carefully. Like Eaton's, in 1924 it opened retail sections within its Regina and Halifax mail order buildings, thus allowing the car-owning public in Saskatchewan and Nova Scotia to examine Simpson's goods before buying them. Despite this strategy, though, Simpson's mail order lost money throughout the decade, experiencing especial difficulty in western Canada, where its catalogue trade "failed to net more than a modest profit of 4 percent."[47] Perhaps because of these losses, this second largest Canadian retailer declined to follow Eaton's, Sears', and Marshall Field's examples of suburban and branch development. Instead, like Macy's, it invested in its flagship store. Between 1928 and 1930, Simpson's built a nine-storey addition in Toronto; it also created one of the world's largest store restaurants, the Toronto store's Arcadian Court, which seated 1,300. By 1929, Simpson's total workforce numbered 6,700, and the company had brought its Toronto store's sales up from $21 million in 1920 to $31 million in 1929. That same year Simpson's removed the Murphy banner from its Montréal branch and began operating it under the Simpson's name.[48]

Canada's third largest retailer, the HBC, also pursued a somewhat unique path. After Eaton's had established itself in Red Deer, Edmonton, Calgary, Lethbridge, Regina, Medicine Hat, Prince Albert, and Dauphin, the HBC could no longer claim to offer the lowest prices or best selection to Prairie customers. Eaton's incursion into the HBC's retail territory, coupled with westerners' increased automobile ownership, made the 1920s a trying time indeed. To offset these difficulties, this oldest of Canadian corporations pursued a price-slashing policy that, by the decade's close, threatened its very existence. Profits dropped dangerously, and by 1929 the company was losing four times the amount it had lost in 1924. In Edmonton, price reductions increased the store's sales from $1.5 million to $2.4 million between 1924 and 1928, but its losses actually grew from $86,000 to $130,000 during the same period. Despite such problems, the HBC continued to believe that expansion was its best policy, and in 1921 it opened a new store in Victoria, employing 350 people. It also purchased Cairn's Saskatoon store in 1922 and built a new store in Winnipeg in 1926.[49]

Other major department stores operating during this period included Woodward's and Spencer's, both headquartered on the West Coast. In 1926, Woodward's opened a branch in Edmonton, and by 1930 the entire Woodward's operation was realizing almost $10 million in annual sales. Spencer's, meanwhile, continued to operate its Vancouver, Chilliwack, New Westminster, and Nanaimo locations, earning an average total of $13 million in sales per year between 1924 and 1934. In Québec the Dupuis Frères was a major player. Established in 1882 as a dry goods store in a downtown French-speaking district in Montréal, this almost exclusively francophone store underwent constant diversification and expansion, becoming a department store by the First World War. In 1921 the Dupuis Frères diversified even more, launching what became a successful catalogue business serving French-speaking Québec. On Prince Edward Island, Holman's expanded its Summerside business to Charlottetown in 1923. As well, 142 smaller department stores also operated in Canada during this time. Tied to local regions, these merchants generally sold less than $100,000 of merchandise annually and had loyal, stable clientele.[50]

If Canada's largest stores found the 1920s challenging, they were even less prepared for the hardships of the 1930s. After the New York stock market crashed in 1929, investments shrank, production declined, and unemployment rose. Coupled with years of prairie drought, these conditions spawned what is rightfully remembered as a decade of deprivation. Yet, according to Statistics Canada, retail sales, excluding department store sales, increased by 28.5 percent between 1930 and 1941, jumping 49.8 percent between 1933 and 1939 alone. This seeming discrepancy between job and crop loss, on the one hand, and spending increases, on the other, is explained by the fact that the bourgeoisie and employed petite bourgeoisie continued to spend, even while unemployed workers and crop-less farmers became destitute. Regrettably for department stores, workers and farmers were key customers, and as the fortunes of these groups suffered, so did the fortunes of the big stores. From 1930 to 1941, department store sales increased by only 7 percent while their retail market share dropped to 10.3 percent. Not only did Eaton's, Simpson's, the HBC, and other stores have to contend with declining consumer spending, so did they have to continue competing with automobiles and chains. Making things even more difficult were huge overheads. During times of plenty, department store spending on maintenance, office staff, storage, and delivery was balanced by profits reaped from huge sales volumes. Yet, when sales diminished, department stores' overhead, much higher than that of independents and chains, became a burden.[51]

In contrast to the heady expansionism of the 1920s, especially exemplified by Eaton's, the 1930s saw Canadian department stores struggling to remain afloat. During the latter half of the 1920s, Eaton's and Simpson's had each undertaken major construction projects: Simpson's was renovating its chic Montréal store, and Eaton's was constructing a new, upscale house-furnishings store in Toronto. Each completed its task – Simpson's in Montréal reopened in 1931, and Eaton's College Street opened in 1930 – but neither Simpson's nor Eaton's launched any new construction during this decade. Instead, they sought to stem their losses. Since their catalogues remained unprofitable throughout the 1930s, each considered closing their mail order operations. They eventually rejected this idea, but Eaton's did begin sending catalogues only to those customers who had made recent purchases. Simpson's, meanwhile, closed several regional order offices. Woodward's, the HBC, and Eaton's also tried to offset losses through wage cuts and layoffs. In 1932 those Woodward's workers whose wages were below $30 weekly found their wages cut by 10 percent; wages over $30 weekly were slashed by 15 percent. Between 1930 and 1935, the HBC reduced its retail staff from 1,700 to 1,200. During the same period, Eaton's cut its sales staff by 15 percent, reduced salesmen's wages by one-fifth, and dropped saleswomen's wages by one-third. Unfortunately for all concerned, these reductions did not result in increased profits, largely because the stores' sales volumes continued to decrease. At mid-decade, therefore, Canada's largest retailers stopped tinkering with labour policies and instead began to raise prices. As Macy's in New York had discovered during the First World War, and as Marks and Spencer's in Britain had learned during the 1920s, department store profits could be boosted not only by increasing sales volumes but also by increasing price points. In 1934, Eaton's increased its markup to 44 percent. In 1939 the HBC's markup in Vancouver was 32 percent, while Simpson's markup in Toronto was 31 percent. Increased prices, together with the war-induced ending of the Great Depression, finally enabled Canada's largest retailers to regain their financial footing.[52]

If increased prices enabled Eaton's, Simpson's, and the HBC to survive the Great Depression, they also signalled the close of Canadian department stores' retail leadership. Between 1890 and 1920, Eaton's and Simpson's, and to a lesser extent the HBC, were icons of modern Canadian merchandising, introducing mass buying, one-stop shopping, unprecedented selection, fashionable styles, and low prices to the dominion's bourgeoning urban and rural populations. Into the 1950s, they remained Canada's largest and most influential stores, but beginning in the 1920s, increased interwar competition from automobiles and chains, combined with shrinking purchasing power among department stores' most important consumers, put these major retailers on the defensive. Once considered cutting edge, by the Second World War the department store had become stodgy, inflexible, and expensive. Plagued by high downtown real estate rates, significant overheads, and cumbersome sizes, massive department stores were more suited to the pre-automobile and pre-chain era than they were to the interwar and postwar years. As chains brought merchandise closer to suburban and rural customers, as cars changed consumers' spending choices and shopping patterns, as merchandise became more diverse, and as prices became more competitive, Eaton's, Simpson's, and the HBC – together with other major Canadian department stores, including Morgan's, the Dupuis Frères, Spencer's, and Woodward's – lost their position in the retailing vanguard.

Canada's department stores' fortunes foundered just like those of department stores internationally. In the United States, Marshall Field's and Macy's both made it through the Depression, even turning a profit in some years. Several British stores, too, survived; some, such as Lewis's, even prospered, buying up smaller independent and chain department stores. Yet by 1940 there was a general international retailing shift away from the traditional downtown department store form toward smaller stores built in outlying locations. Mass merchandisers continued to build department stores, but they began streamlining their stock, trimming their slow-moving merchandise such as books and musical instruments, and expanding their established lines, especially clothing, accessories, and small consumer durables. Automobiles and chains had done their work; beginning in the 1940s and continuing for the rest of the century, new mass merchandisers both internationally and in Canada were eager to bring their stores to their customers as well as to avoid stocking slow-moving goods, paying downtown real estate prices, and generating high overheads.[53]

CANADA'S LARGEST STORES appeared later on the world's stage than did large stores in Great Britain, France, and the United States. After they emerged, however, they grew rapidly, eventually overtaking many of the globe's largest stores in terms of size and sales totals. By 1920, Eaton's in particular had become a world class retailer, larger than Whiteley's in London, Wanamaker's in Philadelphia, Macy's in New York, and Marshall Field's in Chicago. During the first four decades of the twentieth century, Eaton's, Simpson's, and the HBC captured larger national market shares than did their counterparts in other countries, both through their aggressive catalogue operations and through their numerous branch stores. From their spectacular beginnings in the 1880s and 1890s, to their heyday in the 1900s and 1910s, to their diminishing ascendancy in the interwar years, Canada's largest department stores had a significant influence on Canadian economic, social, and cultural life. To fully appreciate their role in the creation of modern Canada, however, we must look beyond their cross-country expansion, their sales totals, and their business innovations. Through their publicity strategies, customer relations, and labour management techniques, Eaton's, Simpson's, the HBC, and a host of more regional department stores demonstrated to both their admirers and their detractors that a new era of Canadian consumer modernity had arrived.

2

Creating Modern Canada

If one wants to follow the evolution of civilization, perhaps he cannot do better than to trace the rise of the great Eaton store in Toronto.

– Eaton's advertisement, 1911

ENGLISH-SPEAKING CANADIANS often refer to the T. Eaton Company and the Hudson's Bay Company (HBC) as national institutions. When Eaton's closed in 1999, nostalgia dominated the mainstream press. David Hall, manager of a mall in London, Ontario, told the *National Post* that "Eaton's is a Canadian icon." The Eaton family had "screwed it up," and the loss of Eaton's "will be like the Toronto Maple Leafs disappearing."[1] The next year the HBC decided to capitalize on its own nationalist heritage. It launched "an aggressive marketing campaign ... to reposition the [HBC] stripes as a style icon that every patriotic Canadian should have in the home."[2] Fashion writer Deborah Fulsang followed HBC's cue, suggesting the HBC blanket is a "Canadian icon": "What Burberry's plaid is to London, the Hudson's Bay blanket stripe is to Canada in all its Far North glory."[3]

Exploring the relationship between department stores and Canadian nationalism, this chapter asks two questions: Why have many English-speaking Canadians come to see department stores, particularly Eaton's, as representative of their nation's identity? And what kind of nation did department stores help create? To answer the first query, the chapter investigates the history of the "Eaton's is Canada" idea, probing the factors that spurred commentators to express this notion. To answer the second, the chapter analyzes the content of department store advertising between 1890 and 1940. Certainly, advertising is not an accurate representation of reality; it is, rather, a biased medium created by ad workers whose goal is to sell goods and services. Nonetheless, advertising can provide insight into the cultures of the past. As Roland Marchand writes of the pervasiveness of advertising in the twentieth-century United States, advertising helped disseminate "incessantly repeated and largely uncontradicted visual clichés and moral parables." Thus, "Through repetition, bold display, and ingenuity, advertisements infused their images and slogans into America's common discourse" and in this way "played a significant role in establishing our frames of reference and perception."[4]

This chapter's investigation of advertising content, together with the conflation of department stores with Canadian identity, reveals that a critical reappraisal of the notion that department stores are national icons is in order. For more than five decades, it has been common to suggest, as Miaso Batts did in 1973, that "Eaton's and its catalogues" are "an expression of Canadian social history."[5] Journalists are not the only ones who articulate this perspective. Publicly funded heritage institutions also lend support to this idea. Today, Library and Archives Canada, the Archives of Ontario, and the Canadian Museum of Civilization maintain online exhibits that put department stores and their catalogues at the centre of the Canadian story.[6] These exhibits are correct to suggest that department stores influenced Canadian material culture. Yet because they do not offer critical evaluations of this influence, they bypass important analytic directions. This chapter argues that between 1890 and 1940 Canada's largest stores helped to construct a very particular kind of Canadian nation, one that perpetuated specific ethnic, race, and class hierarchies in Canada, as well as one that promoted retail and consumerism as quintessential features of Canadian life.

Advertising Mass Retail

Prior to 1850 advertising in Europe and North America was almost nonexistent. When it did appear, it was distributed primarily by carnivals and circuses and was perceived by the developing bourgeoisie as hokum. By mid-decade, though, advertising was becoming more prevalent. Early advertisements consisted primarily of newspaper notices placed by local businesses, as well as by pedlars of patent medicines and other goods, informing readers of services and merchandise. Such notices were word-heavy and, as William Leach puts it in his discussion of advertising in the United States during this period, "visually unappealing"; but they did constitute significant revenue for local newspapers, making up almost half of Canadian newspapers' total budgets.[7]

During the latter half of the nineteenth century, the advertising industry blossomed. As manufacturing output increased and as corporations grew, capitalist profits became more dependent on public goodwill and customer spending. Consequently, corporations began devoting more of their budgets toward publicity. To accommodate advertisers' demand for space, and to realize the revenue that advertisers and advertising represented, many newspapers and magazines expanded their operations. They lengthened their publications, distributed them more frequently, and invested in machines that allowed for specialized fonts and coloured printing. In 1872 not even half of Canada's households bought newspapers, but by 1900 "more papers were sold each day than there were families in the nation."[8] Comprising two-thirds of the content of each newspaper sold, advertising became Canadian newspapers' and magazines' single most important source of income, comprising almost three-quarters of publishers' total revenue.[9]

In the first half of the twentieth century, two of the most important groups of North American advertisers were manufacturers and mass retailers. Such major corporations as Ford, General Motors, Pears, and Campbell's were especially prominent. They placed in both Canadian and American publications visually appealing advertisements meant to spark interest and desire. Department stores advertised just as heavily as did the manufacturers. By the end of the nineteenth century, New York's "vast army of newspaper readers could hardly escape seeing a Macy announcement at least once a day."[10] A similar situation prevailed in Canada. By the 1870s, Eaton's, Simpson's, and Morgan's were placing "full-page advertisements, often a couple times a week," in their cities' newspapers.[11] By 1900, Eaton's and Simpson's were running full-page ads daily in Toronto, and Eaton's contributions appeared every day on the back page of the *Toronto Star*. Between 1900 and 1930, department store ads became even more ubiquitous, appearing in national, provincial, and local newspapers and magazines across the country. Department stores also advertised in more specialized venues. Eaton's advertisements appeared in all the major national and provincial dailies and weeklies, as well as in such publications as the *Christian Guardian*, the *Western Labor News*, the *Grain Growers' Guide*, the *Gateway* (a student newspaper at the University of Alberta), the *Woman's Century* (the magazine of the National Council of Women), and *Peg Leg* (the newsletter of Winnipeg's Junior League). Moreover, Eaton's did not restrict its advertising to English-language publications. In addition to advertising heavily in Québec's newspapers, it also took out ads in francophone newspapers across Canada, including *La Survivance* in Saskatchewan.

As extensive as their newspaper and magazine advertising was, department stores did not contain themselves to these media. To publicize their firms, goods, and services, they also circulated their own publications, many of which were extensive. Catalogues were commonly produced by both North American and European department stores, often including – as was the case with Eaton's, Macy's, and the Bon Marché – over 350 pages of illustrations and text. Eaton's printed its first catalogue in 1884; by 1895 this publication was reaching 75,000 homes across Canada, and by 1904 it was reaching 1.3 million. Other major Canadian catalogue producers were Simpson's, which distributed its publications nationally, and the Dupuis Frères and Woodward's, which were more regional. In addition to catalogues, European and North American department stores frequently distributed postcards, pamphlets, calendars, magazines and, during the interwar years, book-length store histories. All of these publications contained eye-catching combinations of illustrations and text, and all of them offered glowing descriptions of department stores' goods and services. In Canada, some of the store history publications included Eaton's *Golden Jubilee: 1869-1919,* Spencer's *Golden Jubilee: 1873-1923,* and Simpson's *Thumbnail Sketches* (1927).[12]

Department store advertisements in Canada between 1890 and 1940 were hence extraordinarily numerous and diverse, in both medium and message. It is possible, however, to determine some of their major themes. What follows is not strictly a content analysis, for as Valerie Korinek argues, content analyses of advertisements can often miss "the most compelling advertising fantasies" that corporations construct. By analyzing materials appearing at timed intervals, researchers might overlook "the more memorable ads" and the ones that "grabbed the readers' attention."[13] Rather than exploring a mathematically derived sample of department stores' advertising content, this chapter offers an in-depth examination of two types of materials. The first is a selection of advertisements preserved within department store archives and hence representative of advertising themes that the department store wished to keep for posterity. Indeed, department store archives are themselves a form of advertising, for through selective preservation and destruction of historical records they have constructed their own narrative history. The second type of advertising material examined is a sampling of ads that appeared in magazines, newspapers, catalogues, and books distributed throughout Canada between 1890 and 1940. Advertisements in this group were selected according to the clarity and ubiquity of their message.

Department stores' advertising messages can be divided into four categories: messages that were unique to individual stores, messages that were region specific, messages that changed through time, and messages that were universal to all department stores from 1890 to 1940. This chapter, given its aim to explore the national identity of Canada's largest department stores, concentrates on the fourth type of advertising message. It is hoped that future research will uncover other store-specific, regional, and temporal variations. At the same time, it must be remembered that, when investigating the history of advertising, the universal must not be neglected at the expense of the particular. As the case of Canadian department store advertising reveals, retailers' construction of themes that transcended companies, regions, and decades helped to create certain commonalities among a diverse population that shared the same national borders but that also had significant regional, ethnic, occupational, and cultural differences.

Agents of Canadian Progress
The idea that department stores were providers of essential goods and services underwrote all of the big stores' advertising for this period. Eaton's stated in 1919 that humankind has "five great intellectual professions relating to daily necessities of life ... The Soldier's profession is to defend it. The Pastor's, to teach it. The Physician's, to keep it in health. The Laywer's, to enforce justice in it. The Merchant's, to provide for it." Fortunately for Canadians, "Timothy Eaton cherished a high sense of the merchant's mission."[14] In making such claims, department stores drew upon an old shopkeeping service ideal. Since at least the 1600s, such western European merchants as Jules Savary, Richard Rolt, and Daniel Defoe had asserted that commerce was a divine activity that promoted peace and prosperity among humankind. European store owners who migrated to North America from the seventeenth through the nineteenth century brought this notion of providerhood with them. Shopkeepers such as Benjamin Franklin claimed that they served their communities not only by providing products but also by offering wages, benefits, and training to their employees.[15]

Department store advertisements offered pre-industrial claims, but they were also in step with their modern industrial and corporate environments. Capitalizing on the classical liberal economic belief that business growth spurred national development, Canada's largest retailers claimed that their very existence helped to bring about progress for humankind: "The department store is one of the great developments of the age [and] it will be counted among the great successes achieved in the progress of the world," asserted Simpson's in 1906.[16] Simpson's 1920 history book repeated this idea, suggesting that its Toronto operations were icons of enlightenment: "For almost a century, [Toronto's] Knox Church has stood as a monument of Canadian Presbyterianism. To-day, this landmark is going ... A new era has come. The Robert Simpson Company is expanding. When construction is completed ... Simpson's will ... occupy an entire city block of uniform height and design."[17] Eaton's made similar statements. Suggested the big store in 1924, the artist "looking for a subject" should go "to the corner of Yonge Street and Trinity Square, Toronto." Turning west, he "would see the grey old gothic church, dusky with shadows." Behind the church, "high into the blue sky," he would see "a pile of [Eaton's] factory buildings enveloped in sunlight." There, his eye would "rest approvingly," for "[a]gainst the foil of age in the Square below, their frank utility and rosy newness would arouse his imagination."[18] Using architecture as a metaphor, this advertisement implied that old codes of conservatism, humility, and divine authority, as represented by the gothic church, were on their way out. The twentieth century was one of bright "utility" and "newness," and department stores were doing their best to bring Torontonians into the modern era.

Department stores claimed to uplift humanity in general and individual communities in particular. In the examples above, Eaton's and Simpson's implied that Toronto was the lucky recipient of their improvement practices. Other stores made similar claims. In 1923, Morgan's told Montréalers that "the Morgan family have been closely identified with the progressive interests of the community ... They have not been content to remain self-centred in their business, but have taken part in every movement for the city corporate and the citizens at large."[19] Department stores further touted their regional contributions. Proud of its heritage, the HBC did not let customers forget it had helped create modern western Canada. Since 1670, *The Beaver* pointed out, the company's traders had "governed" Rupert's Land, "fed, clothed and supported the natives, and held the future Western Canada in trust for the British Empire."[20] As well, Woodward's called its catalogues *The Shopping Guide of the West* and referred to the company as "the Great Mail Order House of the West."[21] Though head-quartered in Toronto, Eaton's was similarly eager to identify with western development. In a Winnipeg advertisement distributed after the First World War, the company said, "the establishment of an EATON store in Winnipeg ... has meant much to the Canadian West, particularly in those lines which are manufactured in the EATON factories."[22] Claiming they helped to develop particular municipal and regional communities, de-partment stores hence constructed images of civic contribution. In this way they made themselves central to local and regional narratives of development.

If Canada's largest stores contributed to local and regional communities, so did they aid the progress of Canada itself. "In some avenues of com-merce and industry, Canada's progress has been slow," said Simpson's in 1906. Yet, "in the establishment and development of large retail stores, she has kept step fairly well with the rest of the world, thanks to a few energetic and enterprising dry goods merchants," including, it was im-plied, Robert Simpson. With the transformation of these merchants' shops into department stores, Canada's "larger stores [now] compare favourably with the larger stores of Chicago, New York, London and Paris."[23] *Thumb-nail Sketches,* a history of Simpson's published in 1927, also situated the history of the company in the context of the history of the Canadian na-tion. After discussing how both Simpson's and Canada had grown and prospered since Confederation, it concluded, "On the eve of Sixty Years since the Confederation of our beloved Canada, and fifty-seven since the inception of The Robert Simpson Company, Limited, we proudly point to the unparalleled development of Canadian enterprise and to Canada's position amongst the nations of to-day; to the corresponding growth of an outstanding Canadian merchandise organization, The Robert Simpson Company, Limited."[24]

Eaton's and the HBC, too, were proud of their contributions to national development. In 1905 one of Eaton's advertisements said that its past "reflects a series of successes ... the most satisfactory proof to us that we have succeeded is the tremendous growth of our business." Eaton's was "the biggest ... store of its kind in Canada" and was moreover "purely Canadian, not one dollar of foreign capital being invested in the busi-ness."[25] Three years later Canada's largest mass merchandiser made a similar declaration. Eaton's started out as a small business, one Eaton's pamphlet stated, "but the principles underlying it permitted of unlimited expansion, and year by year it grew until it became Canada's Greatest Store and a potent factor in reducing the cost of living in the great Dominion."[26] In contrast, the HBC pointed more often to its pre-twentieth-century contributions.[27] Nevertheless, the company did suggest its urban stores represented the next stage in Canada's march of progress. In his 1920 "Fur – and Further" in *The Beaver,* Sir William Schooling wrote, "Fur was the foundation of the growth of Canada, and in that further progress which the future holds in store the great Company that made the beginnings will continue to share."[28]

Some of Eaton's and Simpson's advertisements identified the stores with municipal and regional communities, but others suggested that these two retailers were national enterprises. During the 1890s they trumpeted their cross-Canada reach. In 1894, Simpson's said it was "Canada's Most Magnificent Store."[29] The cover of Simpson's 1896-97 Fall/Winter Catalogue assured readers that Simpson's was "Canada's Modern Departmental Store" with "No Equal in the Dominion."[30] The next autumn, Eaton's Christmas Catalogue featured a map of Canada over which was draped a banner with the words "Canada's Greatest Store" (Figure 2.1). In 1898, Simpson's published an advertisement so patriotic that it rivalled the nationalist pride that permeated the media during Canada's 1967 Centennial. Titled "A Canadian Enterprise!" the ad described Simpson's as Canada's premiere nationalist business. "Its capital is Canadian capital ... Canadians spin and knit, weave and sew for it. The food supplies it offers are largely the growth and product of Canadian soil ... This business is a commonwealth of Canadians, for Canadians, by Canadians."[31] This advertisement, prompted by rumours that Americans were going to purchase the R. Simpson Company, indicates Simpson's willingness to draw on national themes. Over the next thirty years, Eaton's and Simpson's continued describing themselves in nationalistic terms. Sometimes Eaton's broadened its self-definition, as it did around 1925 when it published a pamphlet called *Eaton's: Largest Institution of Its Kind under the British Flag.* The back of the pamphlet featured a map of Canada punctuated with Eaton's locations. Above the map were the words "Eaton's across the Continent."[32] By the Second World War, both retailers called themselves "Canadian institutions."[33]

Eaton's and Simpson's thus constructed themselves as municipal, regional, and national corporate citizens. Their advertisements suggested not only that they were participating members of communities both small and large but also that their activities promoted both local and national

FIGURE 2.1   Cover of Eaton's 1897-98 Fall and Winter Catalogue. | *Source:* T. Eaton Papers, Archives of Ontario. | Used with permission of Sears Canada Inc.

progress. For these two major retailers, then, local, regional, and national identities were not incompatible but, rather, connected parts of an integral whole. The determination of department stores to weave themselves into local and national narratives of progress no doubt played a role in the affection that Canadians across the country had for them, especially Eaton's. At the same time, this determination also contributed to a cross-country sense of a specifically modern Canadian community. By telling Canadians that their stores and catalogues served residents from coast to coast, department stores helped to create a national community of consumer citizens. Their advertisements suggested that if Canada's inhabitants read department store publications, shopped in department store buildings, and bought department store goods, they could share in a common narrative of consumption and retail. Department stores thus offered customers a way to claim membership in a broader national community, all the while retaining their specific local and regional identities.

According to their own publicists, Eaton's, Simpson's, and the HBC's catalogues, stores, goods, and services enabled many of Canada's inhabitants to become familiar with and proclaim membership in the growing consumer nation. Importantly, however, that nation was not ethnically inclusive. In fact, Eaton's and Simpson's department stores tended to broadcast messages specifically of English Canadian nationalism. In one national 1905 advertisement, called "Canada's Greatest Store," Eaton's conflated southern Ontario with Canada as a whole and portrayed Canada as the daughter of Britain. The brochure features photographs of "The Country We Live In," yet all the photographs are of southern Ontario, including "Moonlight Scene Muskoka," "Residential Street Toronto," "Yachting on Toronto Bay," and "Scenes on the Humber River Near Toronto." The song "The Maple Leaf" accompanies the pictures. With lines such as "In days of yore, from Britain's shore, / Wolfe the dauntless hero came, / And planted firm Britannia's flag / On Canada's fair domain!" the song expresses a British Canadian identity, nourished by the military conquest of French Canada and the subsequent English settlement of southern Ontario.[34]

Indeed, Canada's largest stores frequently and loudly proclaimed their loyalty to the "mother country." Eaton's 1919 history book declares that "in the [imperialist] Boer War, four men of the Eaton staff served with the Canadian Contingent in South Africa" and that "incidentally, it may be noted that their wages were paid to them [during] their absence" and upon the men's return, Eaton's sponsored a "concert in their honour" and "presented them with gold watches."[35] The Great War received Eaton's help as well. According to the *Golden Jubilee,* the company topped up the military wages of its 3,327 employees who joined the war effort; sent complimentary packages of food, knitted goods, and reading material to soldiers overseas; donated its facilities for war use; and raised money for military efforts. President John Eaton himself donated a machine gun battery, a canteen, and several thousand dollars. For his contributions, he received an English knighthood. Those Eaton's employees in active combat who received wage top-ups and gifts were understandably grateful to the T. Eaton Company. Many wrote letters to the organization thanking them for their gifts, and these were published in the history book.[36]

Canada's second biggest retailer was also keen to promote Britannia. At the turn of the twentieth century, Simpson's used a modified and illustrated British Ensign, with the words "The Robert Simpson Co. Ltd." printed on it, as a kind of banner for the store. This image appeared most often in Simpson's Toronto newspaper advertising from this period. Since the 1600s, the British navy and Britain's colonies, including British North America (BNA), had flown modified versions of the ensign. The Union Jack in the upper left quadrant was common to all, but their background colours differed; BNA's was red. Though Canada became a dominion in 1867, until 1965 many English Canadians continued to see what became known as the Red Ensign – which included the coat of arms of Canada in the right lower quadrant – as Canada's flag. Thus, when Simpson's inserted a modified ensign into its advertising, cheekily using its own name in place of the Canadian coat of arms, it was appealing to English Canadians' affection for their mother country as well as to English Canadians' sense of national pride. That it made this dual patriotic appeal in Toronto newspaper advertisements was logical, for this provincial capital was a stronghold of Anglo-Celtic culture.

Eaton's and the HBC also included the Union Jack within their advertising. Visits to Canada by British royalty prompted elaborate patriotic displays. When the Prince of Wales visited Toronto in 1919, Eaton's unfurled one of the "largest Union Jacks ever manufactured" to help celebrate his visit (Figure 2.2). During the coronation of 1937, not only Eaton's but also Simpson's and the HBC paid homage to Britain's monarchy. Decorating their buildings in flags, constructing display windows with royal paraphernalia, selling souvenirs of Britain, and printing special-issue pamphlets proclaiming the greatness of the British throne and Empire, the stores fuelled Commonwealth fervour. Other imperial occasions prompted similarly elaborate displays. In 1921 the HBC's Victoria store entered the city's Victoria Day Parade, held to celebrate Queen Victoria. Its prize-winning float featured "a young lady" dressed as England and "young ladies" posing around her "draped with" colonial flags.[37]

FIGURE 2.2   "One of the Largest Union Jacks Ever Manufactured." | *Source:* Edith MacDonald, *Golden Jubilee* (Toronto: T. Eaton Company, 1919), 287. | Used with permission of Sears Canada Inc.

Department stores did not always wait for special occasions to celebrate British royalty. In 1892, Simpson's secured the Countess of Aberdeen's endorsement of its "Irish Lace Department," which sold "a very select stock" of laces made by hand in Ireland. Its summer catalogue of that year contained a photograph of Lady Aberdeen alongside a description of

Simpson's laces.[38] Eaton's and the HBC also spoke about their owners' membership in English courtly society. After John Craig Eaton was knighted, Eaton's publicists frequently referred to the accomplishments of "Sir John."[39] *The Beaver,* meanwhile, noted in 1923 that "Prince Rupert, the Duke of York (afterwards King James II) and Lord Churchill (afterwards Duke of Marlborough) were the first three governors of the company in the seventeenth century; Lord Strathcona and Mount Royal was another distinguished governor of more recent times, and today the ancient company is presided over by Sir John Kindersley."[40]

British historian Bill Lancaster notes that department stores in the United Kingdom during the late nineteenth and early twentieth centuries viewed "draping the store in the flag" as a deviation from shopkeeping's traditional orderly standards. It was sentimental and gaudy and thus the "height of bad taste."[41] Yet, when former Marshall Field's manager Gordon Selfridge opened an American-style store in London in 1909, Harrods "panicked" and put on a "Diamond Jubilee festival to coincide with Selfridge's opening." This action was meant to strengthen customer loyalty and perhaps stir up some anti-American sentiment as well. Selfridge, however, had no intention of being labelled as unpatriotic. Each year his store held an Empire Day festival; he also used "external decorations to mark the death of the king and the subsequent coronation." Determined to be more British than the British themselves, Selfridge's overthrew London's High Street traditions of patriotic restraint in an attempt to win public support.[42]

Canada's three largest department stores' British Canadian publicity and advertising had similar objectives. Recognizing the pride in Britannia and Canada that dominated English Canada – particularly Ontario – at the time, they created flashy and sentimental expressions of patriotism so as to win public affection and customer loyalty. Unlike the United Kingdom's understated department stores of this period, Eaton's, Simpson's, and the HBC assumed that nationalist fervour was an appropriate way to sell goods. By associating their companies with British tradition and Canadian pride, they sought to appear respectable and trustworthy.

At the same time, department stores' nationalist advertising did serve other purposes. It promoted a specific form of Canadian nationalism, one that paid homage not only to Canada but also to Britain, the English language, and capitalism. It also helped keep Canadian attachments to Britannia alive and well. By broadcasting messages of empire to Canada's inhabitants both rural and urban, department stores implied throughout the period of 1870 to 1940 that it was normal and desirable to embrace England as Canada's mother country. In this way Canada's largest department stores helped to construct the Canadian consumer nation, and the nation they helped to construct was decidedly English-speaking and British.

Democratizing Luxury

In addition to building an English-speaking and British nation, department stores also promoted a democratic one. Integral to department stores' claims of aid to Canadian progress was the notion that mass retail democratized luxury. This assertion was not unique to Canada's stores; Sears and Macy's in the United States, the Bon Marché in France, and Lewis's in England had made similar declarations. As Simpson's 1896-97 Catalogue put it, "[W]e are earnest and busy with all the powers of capital, brains and distribution at our command in bringing you the best goods we can get at the least possible prices. Millions in merchandise. Cheapness unmeasured. They bring happiness."[43] Thirty-two years later, a Montréal store repeated this theme: "This new store of the John Murphy Company Limited will service practical ends of many patrons, and it will also contribute to the community reserve of comfort, convenience, and luxury."[44]

Of all the department stores' democratizing innovations, buying in bulk was the one mentioned most often. This practice allowed stores discounts on supplies, which they then passed on to customers in the form of low prices. As Simpson's said in 1906, "The merchant who can purchase a train-load of furniture is likely to get better terms than he who purchases only a carload."[45] According to Woodward's in 1912, "the buying powers of this huge business enables [sic] us to buy at the closest prices."[46] Emphasis on bulk buying persisted into the Second World War. In 1940, Eaton's asserted that "the buying power of the organization – buying in quantity sufficient for Store and Mail Order business throughout Canada" – provided customers a "money-saving advantage."[47]

Refusing to give credit to customers enabled merchandisers to build strong relationships with suppliers, which in turn meant savings and service for customers. Eaton's noted just before the First World War, "Buying and selling [for cash] saves money at both ends. The goods are bought at the very lowest prices, as the ready money is always a prime consideration to manufacturers; and, by selling for cash all the losses incurred by bad debts are avoided."[48] Not until the 1930s did Eaton's begin offering credit to

customers.[49] The stores also claimed that they had discontinued the ancient tradition of bartering because it gave merchants too much power
over shoppers. "That all should be treated alike was another [Eaton]
principle," stated Canada's biggest retailer: "It seemed unfair that one
person should pay more than another for the same article."[50] According
to another Eaton's advertisement, "Timothy Eaton saw plainly that it was
an unfair proposition for the merchant to pit his knowledge and skill
against the ignorance and the hope and faith of the buyer. His idea was
that the seller should be the attorney for the buyer, and he resolved that
he would be the friend of every customer he had."[51] Cash only and no-
bartering policies went against pre-modern shopping traditions, and
Eaton's publicity aimed to dispel criticism over these changes.

Sheer size was also democratizing. As Simpson's put it in 1898, "the
permanent success secured by the big departmental store with its many
hundreds of employees – its hundreds of thousands of dollars worth of
goods, all kept fresh and modern, by being completely and ruthlessly sold
out three or four times a year – its acres of floor space, and its mighty grip
on trade ... has demonstrated that where there is in command a general
instinct with the true spirit of the campaign which must be waged, the
departmental store marches only to victory."[52] Six years later, Eaton's
declared that "some people have made a wordy war against big businesses
such as this, but the modern ideal of retailing is what was demanded, and
Canada's Greatest Store – chosen by the people from all over the country,
supported by the people[,] you and we working together – has made and
established this new, improved, and better method of merchandising."[53]
This link between business growth and human progress explains an
otherwise curious feature of the stores' publicity: an obsession with magnitude. Like the McDonald's restaurants of the 1980s and 1990s, which
displayed on street signs the running totals of people served, department
stores referred endlessly to their enormous scale. One 1908 Eaton's booklet declared that there were "28 miles of [pneumatic] tubing throughout
the [Toronto] store"; the company also had a "massive electric churning
machine ... which turns out 1,000 to 1,500 pounds of the choicest creamery
butter ... daily."[54] Two years later a similar pamphlet boasted that "thousands are fed daily" in Eaton's Toronto Lunch Room and "a large Rotary
Press" "prints 1,600,000 pages per day."[55] When their declarations of size
and scale are considered in conjunction with their assertions of democ-
ratization, it becomes apparent that retailers assumed the bigger their
operations, the better they were.

In Canada and elsewhere, department stores turned to populist language in order to emphasize their innovative and democratic spirit. Lewis's department store in England, which by 1885 had branches in Liverpool, Manchester, Sheffield, and Birmingham, advertised its operations as "friends of the people."[56] Woodward's similarly declared in 1912 that it was "a *store for the people*. We are each year endeavouring to give better values, better service and improved store facilities to handle your business."[57] Yet Eaton's was far and away Canada's most populist merchant. In 1905 it claimed: "We made this the people's store – managing it directly in their interests. We were not hypocritical enough to talk of working for nothing, or of selling below cost all the time, but we allowed for the smallest possible margin of profit, did the best we could for everybody with household and personal wants to supply and made the burden of life easier by enlarging the purchasing power of every dollar ... we got what the people wanted and sold as they wanted to buy."[58] Eaton's mottoes reflected its populist approach. "The Greatest Good to the Greatest Number," conveying Eaton's democratic commitments, was borrowed from Jeremy Bentham (1748-1832), the utilitarian who famously stated that "it is the greatest good to the greatest number that is the measure of right and wrong."[59] No other motto, however, better communicated Eaton's populism than "A Square Deal to Everybody – the people we sell to, the people we buy from, and the people who work for us."[60]

Their populist rhetoric suggests that department stores were attuned to the democratic currents percolating throughout the industrializing and capitalist world. Where non-essential commodities had been the purview of the rich, they were now available to everybody. Department stores' populism also reflected turn-of-the-century ideas about standards of living. Although common today, the perception that people have standards of living is a fairly recent one. In a study of French sociologist Maurice Halbwachs' work on class and consumption, Judith Coffin shows that between the years 1913 and 1933, Halbwachs came to believe that the American culture of "getting and spending" led to more "democratic and egalitarian" conditions.[61] His work encouraged sociologists to measure people's relative social positions by examining their purchasing power, access to services, and numbers and types of possessions. "To talk about a 'standard of living,'" Coffin writes, "entailed conceiving, gathering, and evaluating social statistics in a different manner and creating new 'standardized' norms and measures with far reaching effects on concepts of social stratification and hierarchy."[62] Using populist language in their advertisements, department stores played to growing assumptions that equality and democracy depended on achieving greater access to goods and services.

Letters sent to their patrons serve to illustrate Canada's largest department stores' similar approach to customer relations. Eaton's open letter to the *Free Press Prairie Farmer* in 1934 expresses the folksy relationship it built with rural shoppers. "Some weeks ago ... we suggested ... it would be pleasant to hear just how many of our Western friends 'knew us when' we were young in the Mail Order Business ... We can't imagine anything more gratifying – or more inspiring – than the response we received ... From all over the West ... came letters from customers ... that was just about the biggest thrill an organization could experience! Old Friends, we thank you! ... We consider it a real achievement to have retained your good-will all these years."[63] Letters to individual customers conveyed similar sentiment. A 1935 Eaton's letter to Mrs. H.W. Hunt of Brighton, Ontario, stated, "We appreciate very much receiving your complimentary reply to the message contained in our Fall and Winter Catalogue 1935-36. We would like you to feel that our Catalogue has behind it a very human, personal organization, always anxious to give you the best values and service at all times."[64] Sent to millions of customers across Canada, Eaton's affable letters no doubt contributed to Canadians' views that Eaton's was a fair and generous organization.

A final indicator of Eaton's construction of itself as a family friendly enterprise was its sprinkling of evangelical rhetoric within its advertising. Timothy Eaton converted from Presbyterianism to Methodism during the 1850s and incorporated some of his Christian beliefs into his business. He kept his window display curtains closed on Sundays and, in support of temperance, refused to sell liquor and tobacco. Such policies publicized the founder's ardent Protestantism and were meant to appeal to Christian consumers. After Eaton died, his company's advertisements constructed an image of populist Christianity. A 1911 pamphlet describing the history of the T. Eaton Company reassured customers that at Eaton's, "Kindly helpful hands will reach out to you, and generous hearts will respond to yours." Emphasizing the emotional bond between staff and customers, this statement is reminiscent of Methodism's fervency. Another statement affirmed the store's Protestantism: "Faith, hope, human service, – and just a store after all. Such is Eaton's." Echoing the Christian motto of "faith, hope, and charity," but with the substitution of "human service" for "charity," Eaton's depicted itself as benevolent and religious.[65]

Civilizing the Nation

Eaton's, Simpson's, the HBC, and other stores claimed to offer a democratizing service to Canadians, that of making consumer goods affordable. Department stores were thus indispensable, they suggested, to the building of a democratic, comfortable, and enlightened Canadian nation. Yet Canada's largest stores' own democratizing assertions were contradicted by another component of their advertising rhetoric, that of civility. According to the giant retailers, by making their stores and commodities available in the farthest reaches of the dominion, they were performing a civilizing service for Canadians. Not only the stores' buildings but also their goods and services elevated Canada's inhabitants from a state of barbarity to a state of enlightenment. This message was similar to the stores' democratizing message in that it emphasized a transition from penury to plenty, but it was also different in that it set up class hierarchies among Canada's inhabitants.

To better understand this theme of civility, it is helpful to turn to John Kasson's explorations of nineteenth-century middle-class culture in America. Kasson argues that the attainment of prestige was a chief concern of this developing socioeconomic stratum. One method by which the middle class achieved status was by acquiring belongings that resembled those of the upper classes and by modelling their behaviour on the customs of the gentry rather than on those of the common folk. "The result was to make gentility increasingly available as a social desire and a purchasable style and commodity," writes Kasson. "For much of urban middle-class life the cultivation of bourgeois manners served as an instrument of inclusion."[66] Cognizant of this development, Canada's largest department stores deployed the power of social emulation to motivate Canadians to become consumers.

Between the 1890s and the First World War, department store advertisements were decorous and flattering. Canada's big stores portrayed themselves as knightly suitors who showered customers with flattery and finery. In 1910, Eaton's produced a booklet describing the store's achievements. The first page read, "Believing that a large number of our patrons throughout this great Dominion are interested in the constant growth of Canada's Greatest Store, we are induced to publish this brief sketch of our mercantile experience. On the strength of this prerogative we venture to represent it to you feeling assured it may render some small timely service and prove at least interesting enough to hold your attention to the end."[67] This excerpt exemplifies the civilizing tone taken by many department stores' early advertising. Casting itself as a suitor, Eaton's courted its readers' attention, thanked them for their indulgence, and reminded them of Eaton's importance.

Department store advertisements lost their decorous overtones during the 1920s, but in the interwar years the giant retailers continued to assure customers that their buildings were places of civility. A 1927 pamphlet for Simpson's American customers stated, "The atmosphere of Simpson's is that of quiet dignity. Here are reserved and mannerly patrons – no bargain-snatching and bustle so common with many departmental stores. The unaffected courtesy of its employees, resultant of natural good-breeding, will also impress you."[68] Drawing connections among gentility, refinement, and superior blood lines, this advertisement was aimed at those consumers who desired expensive and "above-the-fray" surroundings. By representing selling space as elite, advertisements suggested that shopping in department stores elevated patrons' status. Department store literature implied that crude people did exist in Canada, and that it was the department store's role to protect the genteel from the great unwashed. Department stores played on the middle-class fear of losing status and the middle-class desire for social mobility. By offering patrons refinement and dignity, department stores tried to build Canada's middle class.

Closely related to the department stores' declarations of civility was their tendency to draw upon narratives of imperialism in their publicity materials. In 1921 the HBC's advertising manager at Edmonton published an article in *The Beaver* about the history of Fort Edmonton, a former HBC fur trade post. After it was built in 1798, Fort Edmonton helped to "pacif[y]" the "savage Indian tribes," Jack Prest wrote. During the 1885 Northwest Rebellion, Fort Edmonton became "a refuge from the frenzied Indians and half-breeds for all the scattered settlers." At the turn of the twentieth century, and as white settlement increased, Fort Edmonton became a sophisticated retailing outfit. In the early 1900s, "[w]ell-dressed townspeople in the season's latest fashions" mingled at the HBC department store alongside "Indians gaily bedecked and painted." This presented "a striking contrast of past and present." As more whites arrived, "these customs gradually died out." Between 1905 and 1919, the company built several additions to the store. By 1921 the HBC had provided the expanding Edmonton settlement with "a thoroughly modern department store worthy of the largest eastern cities."[69]

Identifying First Nations customers with tradition and white customers with modernity, Prest suggested Edmonton's department store helped create British civilization in upper Alberta. Advertisements in *The Beaver* also supported this theme. Although members of the First Nations did patronize HBC department stores,[70] the company's advertisements mostly portrayed whites as customers. The back cover of the April 1922 *Beaver,* for example, featured a modern family dining at an HBC store restaurant (Figure 2.3). Although the father's complexion suggests that he might be of mixed heritage, his wife and children are clearly of western European descent. The father, moreover, is groomed according to modern standards, and is thus assimilated into urban white society. Looking happy and well mannered, he and his family represented the kind of customers the HBC wanted in its stores. It should be noted, as well, that the bottom of this advertisement contains an illustration of a French chef, along with the quote, "Ah! Zee Grand Satisfaction." During this period, western Europeans and their North American descendants viewed French cuisine as particularly refined; it was this assumption that spurred the HBC to include this chef in its publicity. Yet along with confirming links between French food and gastronomic satisfaction, this advertisement suggested that when francophones spoke English, their accent stood out, and was therefore humorous. Singling out French people in this way, the HBC suggested that it was not only whites, but specifically white anglophones, who were the true benefactors of modern Canadian consumer society.

The T. Eaton Company, too, portrayed itself as a civilizing force. A 1911 pamphlet proclaimed, "If one wants to follow the evolution of civilization, perhaps he cannot do better than to trace the rise of the great Eaton store in Toronto."[71] In 1919 the corporation stated that Timothy Eaton "reminds one of Cromwell smashing into the effete Parliament of Charles I; or of Cecil Rhodes founding a commonwealth among the savages."[72] Eaton's mail order was an especially powerful civilizing agent. By buying products through the catalogue, the company stated, rural customers could impose order on uncivilized territories. As late as 1969, a headline in a commissioned history asserted that Eaton's catalogue "helped to open Canada's new frontiers."[73]

Eaton's self-representation as an imperial factor is best revealed in its accounts of the 1905 opening of its Winnipeg store. Publicists portrayed the arrival of Eaton's in Winnipeg as the dawn of a new and progressive age on the Canadian prairies. Company lore has it that Sir John, when surveying his Winnipeg prospects in 1904, had a conversation with a newspaper boy. The lad informed him that "young Eaton's up here looking for a place to build a store." Further, if Eaton's *did* build in Winnipeg,

FIGURE 2.3   Back cover of *The Beaver*, April 1922. | *Source:* Library and Archives Canada. | Image courtesy of *The Beaver: Canada's History Magazine*.

the company would not be able to introduce "coppers" or pennies to Winnipeggers, nor would Eaton's be able to give its Winnipeg staff "Saturday holidays," as it did in Toronto.[74] Regardless of the boy's advice, over the next few months Eaton's erected a massive department store in Winnipeg. Located away from the downtown area, the Eaton's store lured Winnipeg's "retail traffic" away from historic Fort Garry, which used to be the starting point of the "old Indian trail to the far West."[75] The location of Eaton's in Winnipeg thus symbolized the birth of modern white civilization in the region. An early window display played up this theme. It took the "form of a Pageant of Western Progress, showing Indians, trappers, pioneer settlers, etc., etc., in their respective relations to the growth of the Prairie provinces."[76] Like *The Beaver*, whose pages erased First Nations people from Canadian modernity, this window pageant implied that First Nations belonged in the past and white modern commerce, especially retail, was the newest stage of evolution.

Particularly striking about department stores' claims to advance civilization was the belief that only white people were consumers. White people dominated Canadian department store advertising, as they did American advertising of this period.[77] Nonetheless, Canadian department stores did include racialized people in their advertisements. Continuing his discussion of the HBC's relationship with First Nations people, Prest penned two articles about the continuing loyalty of "full-blooded Indians" to the HBC: "[T]he white population of Canada" might prefer to deal with other firms, but the Cree near Edmonton give the HBC their "continued patronage." According to Prest, they did so because of tradition. In 1770, one of the "wise old chiefs" said that the HBC traders "are like the rock that cannot be moved and they give good goods and plenty ... If you are wise, you will go hence and deal with them." But while people with Aboriginal ancestry might buy things from the HBC, said Prest, they were not modern consumers. Their loyalty was simplistic and rested in practices developed during the fur trade.[78]

Prest's articles used the common stereotype of First Nations men as "noble savages": First Nations men were primitives and therefore both wise and innocent. A short lecture by Dr. John Maclean, featured in a 1926 catalogue, repeats this theme. Maclean describes a meeting he had with a First Nations friend named Calf Shirt, whom he had not seen for a while. Instead of telling Maclean he missed him, Calf Shirt "put his left hand upon his mouth, held out his right hand," and shook Maclean's. "[H]is face shone with delight" and "not a word escaped from his lips."

Maclean finds this an excellent greeting and uses it to criticize Europeans. "[T]he savage of the foothills was transformed and became as a little child, speechless with wonder and delight ... my Blackfoot savage ... has uttered a truth, deeper than he knew, and his sigh has become a symbol of the ages ... and rich in its fullness of meaning for all time."[79] Aimed at a white audience, this anecdote is significant in that it appeared in a department store catalogue advertisement. Through articles such as these, the HBC suggested people with First Nations ancestry existed outside modern time.

The HBC also depicted First Nations people as amusing and exotic. In *The Beaver's* June 1922 issue, the company included an article titled "English as She Is Wrote" and included "[a]n order written by an Indian and received by an H.B.C. Post":

As written:
1 pease 5 poin lard
20 poins bread frish bakin
1 pease tomatoes
...
As filled:
1 pail lard (5s)
20 lbs. breakfast bacon
1 can tomatoes.[80]

Highlighting the discrepancy between the customer's order and the HBC's translation was meant to be humorous; by suggesting the customer had difficulty with the written English language, the article underscores the perceived differences between the white consumer and the First Nations consumer. Similarly, in *The Beaver's* June 1925 issue, "A Summer Trip to the Arctic" included a snapshot of a fish, the midnight sun, and two of the HBC's northern vessels, as well as an unnamed "Eskimo belle." By including this latter photo in the collection, the HBC implied that the unidentified Inuit woman was not a member of Canadian society but, rather, a part of Canada's scenery.[81]

Representations of people of African heritage in department store catalogues made similar statements. Simpson's 1933 Christmas edition offered a "Happy 'Topsy'": The only black doll among a dozen whites, she was "a real lovable pickaninny" with a "roguish smile."[82] The term "pickaninny" is indicative of a paternalist attitude toward children of African heritage. They were perceived as adorable, happy, and innocent, but not

FIGURE 2.4   Excerpt from Woodward's 1912-13 Fall and Winter Catalogue. |
Source: From "The Great Mail Order House of the West – Catalogue No. 31," 87, reproduced in Vancouver Centennial Museum, ed., *The Shopping Guide of the West: Woodward's Catalogues, 1898-1953* (Vancouver: J.J. Douglas, 1977). Woodward's catalogues are located at the Vancouver Museum.

equal to white children. People of African descent appeared in catalogue illustrations of particular commodities. In its advertisements for cotton mattresses, Eaton's Moncton 1920 Spring and Summer Catalogue included illustrations of smiling black women carrying baskets of freshly picked cotton on their heads.[83] This oblique reference to African slaves' forced involvement in the American cotton industry suggests that Eaton's cotton mattresses are authentic because they are associated with African labour. Similarly, Asian people appeared in catalogue depictions of goods imported from Asia. Woodward's Fall and Winter 1912-13 Catalogue included a picture of a Japanese woman sitting among "Japanese Art Matting Squares" (Figure 2.4).[84] Asian people were also included in illustrations of Oriental rugs.[85] By incorporating Asian people in these advertisements, department stores established the authenticity and exoticism of Japanese matting squares and Oriental rugs. Yet, like Eaton's illustrations of black women carrying cotton, these images also served other purposes. They reminded readers that people of Asian ancestry were labourers. People of African and Asian descent were never depicted in catalogues as wearers of department store clothing, users of department store furniture, or readers of department store books. Instead their representation supplemented the value of the goods for sale. By portraying First Nations people as pre-modern, Africans and Asians as labourers, and whites as consumers, department stores suggested how mass merchandising helped to establish modern European civilization. This political economy drew upon imperialist legacies in its construction of race hierarchies.

The theme of civility within department store advertising hence followed two kinds of reasoning. Department stores implied that by making goods and services available to Canadians they were expanding modern British civilization, and department stores suggested their stores and commodities helped Canadians achieve more bourgeois lifestyles. In each line of argument, department stores portrayed themselves as enablers of Britishness, status, and distinction. According to the big stores, innovations in modern merchandising might have made commodities affordable to the masses, but white and affluent people remained the most important and privileged members of Canada's consumer citizenry.

Creating Canadian Consumers

Although reading department store publications and visiting the giant retailers' physical locations might familiarize Canada's inhabitants with the developing consumer nation, to truly proclaim membership in this polity one had to become a consumer. Since the existence of Canadian department stores depended upon Canadians' purchasing decisions, retailers went to great lengths to convince Canadians to buy their products. Like their American counterparts, by the early twentieth century Canadian department stores tried "not only to attract attention but to aggressively shape consumers' desires," as Jackson Lears puts it.[86] In their separate studies of US advertising of this period, Lears and Marchand find that advertisers portrayed their products as therapeutic. If consumers purchased commodities, promised advertisers, they would attain confidence and happiness. The corollary of this guarantee was, as Lears observes, "the threat" that the consumer's "well-being would be undermined" if a purchase was not made. Like American advertisers, Canada's largest stores followed a twofold strategy of provoking readers' fears and nurturing their aspirations. They exploited Canadians' hopes and concerns and tried to make consumption a natural response to anxiety.[87]

More than any other theme, status was a key element of department stores' commodity advertisements. What John Levi Martin says of 1920s American advertising applies equally to Canadian department store advertising between 1890 and 1940: "Far from indicating a turn toward hedonistic, self-fulfilling desire," it demonstrated "a turn toward obsession with social standing and sterility."[88] As central Canada became more industrialized and urbanized, people worried about the accompanying destabilization of traditional family and community relations. People who moved from rural areas to cities to take up new forms of work felt especially vulnerable. To assuage feelings of anonymity and volatility, Canada's largest retailers portrayed goods as signifiers of social position. Responding to the common assumption that ready-made clothing was a mark of vulgarity, Simpson's 1896 catalogue stated, "Let the ready-made clothing of this store convince you that money can be safely invested and all your ideas of taste, style and wear maintained ... We have set that as our aim, and judging by the satisfaction we are giving to the best class of people, we are about reaching it."[89] Such simple items as stationery could also reflect one's status. According to the HBC in 1904, its letter paper "indicates refinement and culture."[90]

Department stores also capitalized on the public's fear of unattractiveness, selling thousands of items designed to mould customers into images of conventional beauty. In most advertisements, the various uses of these beauty items appeared obvious enough. Nonetheless, department stores also used copy to emphasize their desirable results. Simpson's 1922 catalogue advertised a series of rubber devices designed to reverse the aging process by removing one's wrinkles and double chin.[91] Corsets were re-sculpting tools *par excellence.* An advertisement in the HBC's 1904 catalogue showed a distinguished-looking woman opening a door between two corsets. According to the copy, Royal Worcester Corsets were "the open door to correct dress for women" (Figure 2.5).

In department store advertising, the consumer's hopes for individuality were related to his or her fear of ugliness. Rapid urbanization during the late nineteenth and early twentieth centuries sparked feelings of anonymity and social estrangement among many. Although individuals in small towns usually enjoyed extended kin networks, in cities anonymity, isolation, and loneliness reigned.[92] Other contemporary developments also stimulated people's hopes for distinction. For example, photography,

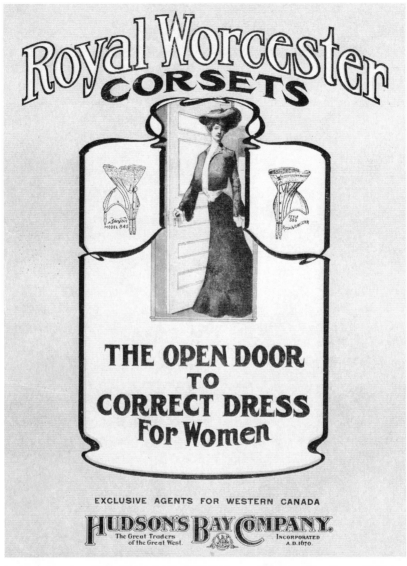

FIGURE 2.5   Corset advertisement in HBC Spring and Summer Catalogue, 1904. |
Source: HBC Spring and Summer Catalogue, 1904 (Winnipeg: Hudson's Bay Company,
1904), 4, Archives of Manitoba, MB 1.C9. | Used with permission of the Archives of
Manitoba.

unlike painting and sketching, was unforgiving of its subjects, highlighting
aspects of their physical appearance that they might otherwise prefer to
downplay. As women increasingly took on waged labour, their desire to
express their individuality also increased. In travel to and from work, and

at the workplace, women interacted with people outside their close family and social circles. Women used fashion and makeup to shape and express their identities and to create positive and lasting impressions.[93]

Especially in the interwar years, department stores played upon consumers' hopes for individual beauty. Sometimes they suggested that certain goods guaranteed distinction: Morgan's boasted in 1934 that its "evening gowns and dinner dresses" were "DIFFERENT! INDIVIDUAL! and IMPORTANT!"[94] At other times they provided lessons in beauty and style. Cosmetics lessons served an important function in this regard. In 1932 those attending "A Beauty and Fashion Review featuring the Personal Appearance of ELIZABETH ARDEN" in Simpson's Arcadian Court learned to achieve flair. According to one advertisement, "Miss Arden will give one of her fascinating talks on how to acquire a lovely skin. The clever Arden art of make-up will be vividly demonstrated with a parade of mannequins, when each costume colour will be shown with the correct make-up. An exhibition of rhythmic exercises by Arden exercise girls will show Toronto women the Arden way of achieving grace and slenderness."[95] As people who attended this event likely recognized, those who pursued the "Arden way" were not expressing their own creativity. Nonetheless, some might very well have wanted to learn cosmetics tricks that they could then use to highlight their own individuality.

Social acceptance played a major role in department store publications. A 1924 Eaton's advertisement for "middies" – sports shirts for girls – suggested that those who wore middies would win friends. Titled "How Five Girls Became Fast Friends: They Chose One Another Because All Had Middies," the advertisement featured illustrations of five happy girls playing sports. The accompanying copy declared:

> These five girls have been fast friends since school opened.
> During the long hours of that first day ... five pairs of very bright eyes roamed over the sun-browned little girls who sat at desks. And each of the Five insists that they all picked each other out as the very *nicest* in the room.
> "Because we all had middies and skirts on," explained Dot ...
> "Why, nice girls always have some middies and a pleated skirt for school."[96]

Playing upon the consumer's desire for social acceptance, this advertisement suggested that middies would spark lasting friendships. Another 1924 Eaton's advertisement depicted a young boy unsure about how to complete a blackboard exercise (Figure 2.6). According to the copy, "If

FIGURE 2.6   Advertisement in *Eaton's News Weekly*, Toronto, 1920s. |
Source: Library and Archives Canada. | Used with permission of Sears Canada Inc.

You Were a Boy And You Found Yourself in This Embarrassing Position
With All the Boys Grinning and the Master Looking Stern – You'd at least
be thankful that in the Christmas holidays, Dad had said to Mother – *"Better get the Boy one of these good-looking Eatonia Suits before he goes back to School."*
With the implication that an Eatonia suit would help a boy to achieve
educational success, this advertisement made explicit links between commodities and prestige.

If one believed the retailers' message, one might conclude that constant consumerism was the key to social success. Department stores often exploited the fear of being out of date. Simpson's especially marketed its wares as chic. In 1896 it played on the theme of obsolescence in an advertisement about "handkerchiefs, neckware, and veilings." Its stock of these goods was "pretty, tasty and stylish" as well as "adapted to the season ... there is no inconsiderable amount of newness in these lines, and we have everything."[97] Simpson's 1922-23 Fall/Winter Catalogue stated that its coats for women were "Following Fashion's Latest Dictates."[98] And in its Fall/Winter 1933-34 Catalogue, which marked a shift in Simpson's mail-order tone from soft selling to hard selling, the company ordered readers to "Keep stylish! Wear Simpson foundation garments!"[99] By telling customers what was stylish and what was not, department stores kept patrons abreast of fashion. Yet retailers' warnings about commodity obsolescence also served less altruistic purposes. The desire for newness, as Vance Packard pointed out in 1960, is one of the driving forces behind consumer capitalism.[100] Change, and the profits it fuels, keeps the mass market alive and well.

Fear and hope, then, were recurring undertones in department store advertising between 1890 and 1940. By insinuating that bad things would happen if people did not buy particular products, department stores attempted to create consumer dependencies and make ever-increasing numbers of commodities necessary for everyday life. By stimulating demand, they created profit, performed a service for the nation's economy, and encouraged people to see that the solutions to their problems lay in their consumer choices. In this way they ensured that both the ideologies and structured behaviours of consumer consumption became integral to Canadian life. According to advertisers, Canadians were consumers and Canada was a consumer nation – and for all the right reasons.

Responding to Department Store Messages

Department store advertisements might not always have provided accurate reflections of Canadians' lived experiences, but advertising and publicity did strike a chord with its audience. In 1907 a British journalist toured Eaton's in Toronto and subsequently reported that "only a great man" could have created Eaton's: "Mr. Eaton was one of the makers of the empire." Thirteen years later a customer sent Sir John Eaton a forty-five-year-old bag with pictures of Eaton's on it. Before signing her name to the accompanying letter, she wrote, "Hoping you will be prosperous, and able to continue your good works throughout the provinces for years to come, as in the past." Both of these statements echo themes present in Eaton's publicity. The 1907 statement suggested that Eaton's enterprise had helped build the British Empire; the 1919 letter pointed to a more domestic form of imperialism.[101]

In 1934 and 1937 in the *Free Press Prairie Farmer*, Eaton's invited "old-time" customers to send in their stories about Eaton's. Eaton's received replies from mail-order shoppers throughout Saskatchewan, Manitoba, and Ontario; many explained the reasons behind their loyalty to the store. Echoing Eaton's own advertising, they wrote of Eaton's trustworthiness, selection, return policy, merchandise quality, substitution practices, and fair prices. A few also mentioned Eaton's importance to the Canadian nation. Bessie McKillop of St. Thomas, Ontario, congratulated Eaton's for making it possible "for the people of this Dominion to get good things at a reasonable cost." R.J. Charbonneau of Ariss went further, stating, "The Pioneer Spirit of your Founder, the late Timothy Eaton, sloganned in 'Goods Satisfactory or Money Refunded', has long won for you a place in hearts and homes of our fair Dominion ... My slogan for Eaton's Store is 'Always buy "Made in Canada" goods from Eaton's where your dollar buys the best or your money refunded.'" Alluding to Eaton's role in the modernization of Canada, McKillop's and Charbonneau's replies reveal a familiarity with Eaton's own declarations of national importance and, further, suggest that they agreed with the company's self-assessment.[102]

If some customers agreed that Eaton's was crucial to Canadian develop-ment, others believed its catalogues represented ideal Canadian life. In 1937, G.A. Sims of Orillia, Ontario, sent in an essay about Eaton's 1937 Spring and Summer Catalogue to his local newspaper. It was rejected for publication by the paper, so Sims sent it to Eaton's advertising depart-ment. The company thanked Sims but said Eaton's would not publish it because it "comes too near propaganda."[103] According to the essay, every page of the catalogue demonstrated Canadian virtue. Sims applauds the illustrated women for being "smiling and very pretty," and the illustrated girls for making Shirley Temple and Princess Elizabeth look "like two cent stamps." Eaton's boys, too, receive praise. It "is refreshing to see that the one who wears the cheaper suit is smiling just as hard as the one garbed in the more expensive article. This is true democracy." Eaton's young men are admirable because they are clean-cut and wholesome boys who will never become "sit down strikers." Farmers are "handsome" and "happy, as though they really enjoyed doing chores." Pictures of industrious white-collar workers reveal that Canada will soon emerge from the Depression. Sims reserves his highest praise, however, for a particular scene of domesticity: Here, "we see Young Canada evidently just out of bed, and all over smiles ... We don't know whether it is the aroma of the breakfast bacon or mother scraping the toast, or the contemplation of another happy day in school. Any way it is a great example for boys of lesser breeds."[104]

Sims's words may be satirical. He might have intended the statement that "it is refreshing to see that the one who wears the cheaper suit is smiling just as hard as the one garbed in the more expensive article" to be ironic. In response to the sharpened class inequalities of the Depression, Sims might have decided to make fun of the images in Eaton's catalogue. Patricia Phenix argues just this point: "Clearly frustrated by the image of affluence Eaton's continued to project during the Great Depression," she writes, "a customer named G.A. Sims composed a searing page-by-page analysis of Eaton's Spring and Summer 1937 catalogue." Through it he "unravel[led] Eaton's version of the National Dream."[105] In the end, though, it is less Sims's own intentions than his conflation of Eaton's with Canadian heritage that is significant. His essay speaks to the growing belief that Eaton's was an important and benevolent Canadian institution whose advertising depicted modern Canadian life.

Customers' affirmations of Eaton's central role in the building of modern Canada, together with their conviction that Eaton's catalogues represented ideal Canadian life, indicated that Eaton's advertising helped many to articulate their beliefs about the character of Canadian modernity. As Miller also notes of the Bon Marché advertisements for France, Canada's largest stores' publications made modern ways of living "palpable."[106] Canadians' receptivity to department stores' messages about ideal Canadian life was indicated not only by their written statements attesting their agreement but also by the ways they used store publications. According to Dirk Hoerder, recent immigrants used Eaton's catalogues to learn English and decipher Canadian culture. Especially for those who came from pre-industrial or impoverished backgrounds, mail order catalogues "took the place of an encyclopedia." In addition, many people ordered goods from Eaton's to become more Canadian. Hoerder quotes a Galician Jew who "remembered his Canadianization in 1927 Saskatchewan": "Leafing through the Eaton's catalogue, I had decided to look more like a Canadian and ordered knee high boots and other western style garments."[107] Just as Macy's New York display windows showed "the newly arrived European about what the rank and file of Americans wore, something about their character and habits, and how they furnished their homes," so did Eaton's advertisements and catalogues instruct newcomers in the art of becoming Canadian.[108]

Department stores' promotion of national identities, combined with customers' acceptance of department stores' role in the building of modern Canada, eventually made self-evident the link between mass retail and Canadian identity. Eaton's especially appeared in nationalist narratives. In 1969, *Toronto Star* journalist John Brehl sounded a theme that reverberated for decades to come. "In Scotland ... children were reared on porridge and the shorter catechism; in Canada, on corn flakes and Eaton's catalogue." He also noted that "Eaton's special status lies in the way it has reflected, and, in some ways, helped shape, Canada." In autumn 1969 prevailing currents of nationalism compelled one woman in Massey, Ontario, to compose a poem and send it to Eaton's president: "'Twas right along with Canada that Eaton stores have grown. Integrity and truth have made the name well-known." In her accompanying note, she said she had just finished reading Eaton's 1969 company history, which the enterprise had donated to her local library. A boosterist book, it probably influenced her view of the corporation.[109]

Even Eaton's critics said the retailer was central to Canadian history. In 1970 the left-wing *Last Post* published an article about Eaton's. Responding to the oft-made connection between Eaton's and Canadian heritage, the authors agreed that Eaton's was a Canadian icon: "Eaton's is something that grew in a manner peculiar to Canada, and it stands as a Canadian institution, the highest development of Canadian capital."[110] Six years later there was a nation-wide outburst of Eaton's-related nationalism, prompted by Eaton's closure of its mail order. Eaton's received dozens of appeals to change its mind. T. Beauregard of northern Ontario wrote, "You tink [sic] that CANADA, his going to let you go ... Let say that you are resting and taking your second wind ... because knowing what you have accomplished, for the CANADIAN Nation, I would not expect, but to rise for greater hight [sic] for the good of our country! CANADA. for ever." After urging Eaton's to reconsider its decision, customer Cecelia Dickie wrote, "Eaton's has been a very important part of Canadian homes, Canadian life, Canadian history ... Canadians are concerned and interested in the future of the All-Canadian business, unique in its kind, which has helped to build Canada." In her letter, Dickie specifically mentions Eaton's "honesty," fair prices, "service, and reliable merchandise," thus indicating that wishes for simpler, more moral times pervaded her thoughts.[111]

Nostalgia has indeed permeated the last three decades of popular thought on Eaton's. In her 1972 essay, "Satisfaction Guaranteed: The 1928 Eaton's Catalogue," Fredelle Bruser Maynard offers a rosy interpretation of Eaton's past publicity. "Reading catalogue prose now is a little like sitting down to a large crockery bowl of old-fashioned porridge," she states. For rural Prairie women in the 1920s, the catalogue was "a friend in the city who knew your needs and could be trusted to serve them with absolute integrity." In contrast, the 1972 catalogue's captions "are saucy"; "older women, demoted to mid-book, wear modified junior styles and are elegantly slender"; and "the underwear section is all puffs of lace." She misses "the shy crudity of that fellow who used to write [Eaton's] touchingly sincere descriptions." For Maynard, Eaton's 1928 catalogue represents a time when older women were more respected and life was less hectic.[112] Eaton's customers, too, bemoaned the decline of the big store's glory. In 1983, for example, a customer reminisced about Eaton's overt Christianity: "If I remember aright, there was a time when your store-curtains were drawn on Sunday, and no tobacco was sold. Principles vs. profits. These things are not the style now."[113]

Certain customers' positive experiences with Eaton's services, workers, and products, discussed in detail in Chapter 5, no doubt contributed to their affections for the mass retailer. Yet shoppers were not alone in granting Eaton's an elevated historical status. In 1978, Mildred J. Young of the Canadian Library Association was happy to tell readers of *Canadian Life* that Eaton's catalogues "have been preserved in the Dominion Archives." The association, she stated, regards the catalogue "as one of our more interesting and accurate history books. Its line drawings and terse descriptions give a factual picture of Canadian life for the past hundred years." In Young's view, a look through Eaton's catalogues will allow one to "see how Canadians lived, what they wore and how much they paid for their goods for over four generations." That many Canadians probably could not afford Eaton's goods did not affect Young's view of Eaton's catalogue, nor did the fact that the catalogues portrayed Canadian consumers as white and predominantly middle-class. Instead, she suggested that Eaton's catalogues were accurate visual reminders of a bygone Canadian era.[114]

When Eaton's made its application for bankruptcy in 1997, the idea that the company was a Canadian icon was firmly in place. People's personal encounters with the store no doubt encouraged them to think about Eaton's as a national institution. As the largest retailer in the country, with stores in every province except British Columbia by 1940, and with catalogues that reached almost every home, Eaton's was a major presence in Canada's economy and culture. Yet Eaton's incessant broadcasting of its progressive, patriotic, and benevolent identity, together with journalists', heritage workers', and other cultural producers' announcements that Eaton's and Canadian development are intimately connected, also contributed to Eaton's iconic status. The view that Eaton's is representative of a simpler, more moral time in Canadian history speaks to a general distaste for the contemporary consumer marketplace and a yearning for more ethical retailing. At the same time, it is also suggestive of a need among some Canadians for a collective national memory. Canada's multicultural and bilingual status, together with its strong collection of regional identities, has made it difficult for post–Second World War Canadians to construct a common heritage. Such corporations as Roots, Canadian Tire, Tim Hortons, and Molson's have offered a capitalist solution to this vacuum. Inviting customers to identify with their brands and companies, these corporations have helped to create a consumerist Canadian nationalism that sidesteps questions of ethnicity, language, race, and region. By proclaiming to be loyal to these corporations, individual Canadians can broadcast their pride about their country. Canadian commentators began proclaiming their admiration of Eaton's more than one hundred years ago, but their affection for the company became even stronger after the Second World War. This sentimentalization is doubtless rooted in Eaton's ability to evoke a common national heritage. Its advertisements, books, and catalogues have been particularly well preserved. The visual power of Eaton's publications, combined with their ready availability, appeals to those yearning for a collective past.[115]

Canadian consumer nationalism may appear devoid of ethnocentrism, racism, and regionalism, but there is nevertheless a reactionary strain in nostalgia for Eaton's. In her discussion of nostalgia for early-twentieth-century downtown environments in the United States, Alison Isenberg argues that racism pervades some people's yearnings. Prior to the 1950s, blacks were not allowed to patronize "whites-only" downtown shops. They were especially not allowed to use whites-only washrooms and restaurants. Some people who desire older types of downtown environments are supportive of segregation; they believe this practice was simpler and better than integration. Isenberg is thus cautious about the politics of urban nostalgia. In Canada we should be similarly careful about nostalgia for old department stores. When people speak of Eaton's role in the building of the nation, there is a latent sense that the nation it helped to build was white and Protestant. Phenix hints at this sentiment in the concluding sentences of *Eatonians:* "Until almost the end of its existence," she writes, "Eaton's remained the biggest corner store in the country. From waitresses to delivery drivers," Eaton's employees "subscribed to the ideal 'one for all and all for one.' It was an ideal which ... had its roots buried deep in English Canada's Protestant soil." Indeed, when one considers the notion that Eaton's as a Canadian icon represents a Canadian golden age, one should query how that age is defined. As this chapter shows, Eaton's and other department stores not only wove themselves into the fabric of a modernizing Canada, they also defined that Canada as white, status-seeking, capitalist, materialistic, and Protestant.[116]

In a recent book on advertising in 1920s America, Simone Weil Davis acknowledges that it is impossible to establish whether "ads actually determine consumer decisions and choices." Indeed, perhaps "advertisers and their critics both overstate the powers of suggestion." Today's consumers, she acknowledges, "feel like well-versed readers, sophisticates [who] readily discern the manipulative ploys of advertisements." But then Weil goes on to state advertising's deeper significance: "Perhaps the thing is this, though: Ads *do* 'work,' but their primary function is not to lead a consumer to choose between brands. Rather, through inundation, ads serve to produce an all-around ambiance that encourages consumerism in toto, making it seem as desirable and natural as air."[117]

Between 1890 and 1940, the existence, magnitude, and increasing prevalence of department store advertising and publicity in Canada established the centrality of consumer capitalism to everyday life. The familiar presence of department store advertising, indeed all advertising, in Canada's cultural landscape made consumption seem normal and desirable. It universalized consumerism. Canada's department stores also helped promote a specific kind of Canadian nationalism and build a specific kind of nation. It is impossible to peer inside the minds of those who read department store publicity, but the fact that many commentators continue to conflate department stores with Canadian identity suggests that department stores were successful in their attempts to construct themselves as Canadian institutions.

Through their advertisements, department stores argued that they boosted economic, social, and cultural wealth, not only of the individual Canadian but also of the Canadian nation and the British Empire. Central to their publicity was the idea that department stores and their commodities helped Canadians attain social status and personal satisfaction. Department stores' notions of progress were thus middle-class and acquisitive. Moreover, their vision depended on hierarchical social categories. In department store literature, white Canadians were superior to non-whites. First Nations people were amusing primitives, and people of African and Asian descent performed the labour that made imperial consumerism possible. The Canada that department stores helped to build and represent was exclusionary and based on class and race privileges rooted in the social relations of empire and bourgeois class formation.

If department stores promoted race and class privilege, so did they advocate a consumerist orientation in life. Department store adworkers promised Canadians that commodities would alleviate their fears and help them to realize their desires. In an effort to create dependencies on consumer goods, department stores portrayed consumerism as natural. Since it was commonly believed that department store advertising represented Canadian life, department store portrayals of consumption as natural indicated that Canadians themselves were consumerist and that Canada was a consumer nation. Thus, not only did these giant retailers create the notion that department stores were Canadian institutions, they also suggested that Canadians were imperialist, racist, exclusionary, materialist, and consumerist. It was a potent set of assumptions, fusing national identity and the iconography of a particular kind of capitalism, one that worked constantly to prettify profit making, race and class privilege, and a materialism that promised to eradicate fear. Department stores indeed helped to make Canada in the years between 1890 and 1940, and they did so in ways that were far from disinterested.

3

Fathers of Mass Merchandising

Sometimes the question has been asked me, "Is it possible to keep a personal or family influence throughout a business as vast as Eaton's of Canada?"

– Lady Eaton, Memory's Wall, 1956

THOUGH HE DIED IN 1907, Timothy Eaton is still remembered fondly today. When his company collapsed in 1999, mourners visited his statues in Eaton's Toronto and Winnipeg stores, leaving flowers and notes at their bases. After the stores' doors closed for good, Canadians agreed the monuments were of historical significance. Following some debate over where they should be placed – people in St. Mary's, Ontario, argued one should be placed in their town because Eaton had lived there before he moved to Toronto – the Eaton family gave one statue to the Ontario Royal Museum in Toronto and one to a hockey arena in Winnipeg, built on the site of Eaton's original Winnipeg store. Today, those who pass Timothy's bronze likeness keep his memory alive by rubbing his left boot for good luck (Figure 3.1).

It is no accident that the memory of Timothy Eaton should be so well preserved. Indeed, Eaton's had mythologized him throughout the twentieth century. It was Timothy Eaton's hard work and innate genius, publicists claimed, that had turned his department store into a magnificent corporation. When he was alive, his Christian concern for his employees, his interest in his community, and his devotion to Canadians guided his actions. After he died, his sons and grandsons followed in his footsteps, ensuring his company remained an honest, fair, and civic institution. Such practices would have lasting effects on their intended audience. In 1976, an elderly female customer wrote the company to praise it for its "great contributions to charity," adding, "Too bad there are not more business

FIGURE 3.1   Bronze statue of Timothy Eaton, carved by Eaton's staff superintendent
Ivor Lewis on the occasion of Eaton's 50th anniversary, 1919. | *Source:* Edith MacDonald
[The Scribe], *Golden Jubilee, 1869-1919* (Toronto and Winnipeg: T. Eaton Company, 1919),
230. | Used with permission of Sears Canada Inc.

people with the same high standards, morally, as the Founders of 'The T.
Eaton. Co,' and their successors."[1]

Eaton's was not the only Canadian store to celebrate its founder's memory. Simpson's, Morgan's, Spencer's, Woodward's, the Dupuis Frères, and
a host of smaller stores paid lasting tributes to their original owners. In

this way they were similar to department stores in other Western capitalist nations. Between 1880 and 1940, leading department stores in Australia, France, the United Kingdom, and the United States made their founders' names, likenesses, personalities, and actions central to their images.[2] They did so to combat public criticism of their activities, and to put a human face on their otherwise massive, anonymous, and increasingly influential operations. As Roland Marchand argues, the growth of corporate capitalism at the turn of the twentieth century precipitated a "crisis of legitimacy" for big firms. "The traditional potency of the family, the church, and the local community," he writes, "suddenly seemed dwarfed by the sway of the giant corporations."[3] Department stores were especially troubled by criticism. Highly visible and well known to all, they became easy targets for anti-corporate angst. Chapter 7 demonstrates that small retailers, labour leaders, co-operators, and social reformers in Australia, western Europe, the United States, and Canada each blamed the giant retailers for everything from destroying local commerce to endangering the morality of the nations in which they operated.

Department stores were not the only firms to undergo criticism, but they did stand out among other corporations in their use of paternalism – which included the mythologizing of store founders – to counteract negative publicity. In ways unmatched by other corporate capitalists between 1880 and 1940, department stores throughout the industrializing world constructed images of themselves as fatherly providers that offered complete dedication, service, and protection to all who came within their purview. "The public face" of Marshall Field's, notes John Tebbel, the store's pre-eminent historian, was that of a "a big, happy family under the guiding hand of a great, all-wise father."[4] Department stores' paternalism was partly natural, for pre-modern shopkeeping was steeped in paternalist practices. As authoritarian but kind overseers of their businesses, which they called "houses," pre-industrial European merchants treated their staff and public as dependants in need of assistance and encouragement. They took in youthful apprentices and offered them shelter, food, and training. Paternalist treatment of customers was more subtle but present. David Monod writes, just "as they conceived of their workers as children, so too did retailers feel that they had a duty to teach and uplift their customers."[5] Yet if the paternalist approach seemed natural, it was also deliberate. Not only did modernizing department stores use paternalism to counteract negative criticism, they also employed it to create an overarching system of public, customer, and employee management that promoted admiration, loyalty, trust, profitability, and efficiency. As the world's largest department stores entered the twentieth century, they purposefully mobilized shopkeeping's pre-industrial paternalist past so as to construct some of the globe's most powerful and famous corporations.

During the first half of the twentieth century, department stores integrated several evolving business practices into their paternalist paradigms. Public relations, now known simply as "PR," rose alongside corporate capitalism; its purpose was to combat negative publicity and to promote particular companies. It remains a prominent business tradition, encompassing everything from institutional advertising (advertising that promotes specific firms rather than particular goods and services) to philanthropy to civic contributions to corporate sponsorship. Welfare work was also present in department stores. This movement saw large employers providing mostly white, youthful, female, and non-unionized workforces with benefits and programs so as to allay suspicion of the mistreatment of so-called vulnerable workers; it was also intended to promote workplace harmony and efficiency. The retail service movement, too, became incorporated into department stores' paternalist strategies. Related to the public relations trend, the retail service movement was intended to make mass retailers as attractive as possible to their consuming publics. Peaking between 1890 and 1930, the movement spurred department stores and other major stores, especially draperies, to offer such complimentary services as writing rooms, nurseries, coat checks, nurses' stations, concerts, art showings, and transportation arrangements.

There is a tendency among some labour and business historians to associate paternalism with pre-industrial labour relations and to designate public relations, welfare work, and the retail service ideal as more modern business practices. Yet department stores' image making, customer relations, and employee management strategies between 1890 and 1940 reveal that some of the world's most modern capitalist enterprises did not abandon paternalism even as they adopted PR, welfare work, and service ideal methods. In Canadian department stores especially, paternalism was all-pervasive. Eaton's – which as Chapter 1 shows was a world-class store – remained paternalist until its 1999 demise. Private ownership helped Eaton's maintain its fatherly image and its family-like atmosphere, but so did the constant efforts by managers and publicists to manage and represent the company in paternalist ways. For its entire existence, Eaton's behaved as an authoritarian *paterfamilias*, providing benefits to workers but also treating them as subservient beings dependent upon their employer for work and related favours. Eaton's paternalist treatment of the public and of customers, too, depended upon the assumption that the department store was a wise and masculine provider. Its benevolent and superior vision, maintained publicists and managers, enabled it to offer services, goods, and encouragement to all who entered its orbit – not only shoppers but also recipients of the giant retailer's philanthropic activities.

Canadian department stores' incorporation of PR, welfare work, and service within paternalist frameworks had some positive results. Eaton's, Simpson's, the HBC, Morgan's, the Dupuis Frères, Woodward's, and Spencer's were well-known philanthropist organizations; their wealth helped build many of Canada's leading educational and medical establishments. Free public events such as Eaton's famed Santa Claus parades, which started in 1905, entertained generations of Canadians; complimentary store services, especially lavatories, eased many Canadians' shopping expeditions. Employees, too, benefitted from department stores' paternalist and welfarist efforts. Employees without family or other support systems were grateful for department stores' familial atmospheres. And since many of Canada's social security programs did not come into existence until the middle of the twentieth century, many workers appreciated department stores' medical and welfare plans.

Yet Canada's largest stores' paternalist paradigms did not always translate into positive shopping and working experiences. As might be expected within a system of social relations that elevated the authority of the father, Canadian department stores treated female shoppers and employees as inferior to men, and in need of protection and guidance. These practices at times resulted in benefits for women, including private restrooms and extensive welfare programs, but they also created a range of sexist experiences and structures. Assumptions about feminine intellectual inferiority and women's inherent maternal roles meant that women rarely achieved management positions. Similarly, the notion that women were guided by their emotions, rather than their intellects, encouraged the staff to treat female shoppers condescendingly.

Canadian department store paternalism encouraged other forms of discrimination as well. Comfortable in their fatherly roles, owners and managers assumed complete authority over staff relations. They treated promotions, raises, and holidays as privileges to be earned through submissive and efficient behaviour, and they harassed and fired employees who showed even the slightest interest in collective bargaining. Ethnic and racial discrimination also occurred. Such discrimination was not caused solely by paternalism; it was, rather, the result of centuries of imperial activity, ethnic conflict, and xenophobia. Department store paternalism did, however, reinforce and exacerbate the dominant racial and ethnic hierarchies prevalent in Canada during this period. Just as it spurred owners and managers to treat women and workers in belittling and contemptuous ways, so did paternalism encourage white managers and employees to act condescendingly toward people of African, Asian, and Aboriginal heritage.

Paternalism's Origins

Paternalism in Canada's largest department stores originated in eighteenth- and nineteenth-century western Europe, where storekeepers had long behaved as authoritarian, fatherly providers. As industrialization and urbanization accelerated in that region, storekeepers' apprentices began immigrating to North America. Born in Scotland in 1819, Henry Morgan apprenticed in his father's store. At the age of twenty-five he moved to Montréal and opened a dry goods shop. By 1854 his firm had grown sufficiently to employ nine male clerks. To ensure their behaviour matched his own upright reputation, Morgan enforced strict rules, saying, "In case any employee is in the habit of smoking Spanish cigars, getting shaved at a barber shop, going to dances or other places of amusement, he will most surely give his employer reason to be suspicious of his integrity or all-round honesty." In addition, "Men employees are given one night a week for courting purposes and two if they go to prayer meeting regularly." Finally, after employees completed their fourteen-hour shifts, their "leisure time" could "be spent reading good literature." If clerks flouted these guidelines, they were assigned menial chores or dismissed.[6]

Timothy Eaton and Robert Simpson also transferred European shopkeeping traditions to the New World. Both men were born in 1834. Eaton worked at his uncle's general store in Portglenone, Ireland, while Simpson laboured at his father's general store in Inverness, Scotland. In the mid-1850s, both relocated to Canada West, where they started their own shops. Eaton moved to Toronto in 1869 and opened a dry goods store on King Street; Simpson arrived in the city two years later and opened a similar shop nearby. When Eaton's operations were still confined to the street level, Timothy Eaton followed the European practice of housing apprentices on the second floor. Every Christmas he treated employees to a dinner in his home, and he rewarded productive employees with prestige, favours, and advancement. He even once paid the interest on a favourite clerk's mortgage. Yet, as store father, Eaton also maintained a strict hold over store operations. When staff made mistakes, he responded with chastisements, revocation of privileges, and dismissals. According to one early employee, Eaton hired managers for "no other purpose than to veil and cloak the hand that held the whip."[7]

Only remnants of information about Simpson have survived. They indicate he was stylish and respectable. When Toronto "was very young," one 1949 advertisement stated, "the dignified figure of Mr. Simpson challenged tradition each business morning by driving, frock-coated and silk-hatted, in a victoria and pair, to [his] establishment on Yonge Street." Instead of staying behind his counter, this "courtly Scot ... moved ... among the customers to welcome them and make certain that their wants were satisfied."[8] Simpson took especial care with female customers. The *Toronto Star* reported in 1972 that in his early days Simpson placed a "huge tea urn" in his store, which "allowed ladies to sip and chat while examining female finery."[9] Toronto's business community respected both Simpson's success and his paternalism. Said the Toronto Board of Trade in 1893, "The store resembles one large beehive with everyone in it a worker and all loyal to their chief."[10]

Modernizing Familialism

As their businesses grew at the turn of the twentieth century, the world's largest department stores mobilized their paternalism to mask their increasingly anonymous and, some said, exploitative operations. The founders of Lewis's and Harrods in London, Farmer's in Sydney, the Bon Marché in Paris, Macy's in New York, Wanamaker's in Philadelphia, and Marshall Field's in Chicago had become national household names. In Canada the Dupuis brothers, the Morgan brothers, Robert Simpson, Charles Woodward, and David Spencer had achieved regional fame. Timothy Eaton, meanwhile, had become Canada's most well-known department store magnate.[11]

Department stores in Canada and elsewhere promoted their founders in corporate publicity. Advertisements, brochures, and company histories included pictures of owners, personal messages from owners, and hagiographic biographies. Making founders' names and personalities synonymous with their enterprises, publicists helped to generate for their firms an aura of reliability and personality. Spencer's *Golden Jubilee* of 1923 begins with a portrait of founder David Spencer, which is followed by a five-page article titled "Life Story of David Spencer and the History of the Development of His Activities."[12] After store owners passed away, publicists turned them into benevolent visionaries.[13] Eaton's 1919 history includes a biography of Timothy Eaton, which argues that Eaton's belief that "the world and all therein ... was made to increase the welfare of the individual man" led him to build "one of the greatest public service organizations in the world."[14]

Until after the Second World War, ownership of Eaton's, Morgan's, the Dupuis Frères, Spencer's, and other stores remained in founders' families. This "longevity," as Bill Lancaster notes of British stores, helped "cement the structure of department store paternalism well into the twentieth century."[15] Successors became public figures in their own right. Timothy Eaton's son, John "Jack" Eaton, was especially renowned. President of Eaton's from 1907 until his death in 1922, and knighted in 1915 for his war effort, he was a noted humanitarian whose good works included dispensing an entire medical staff, along with a train-car load of goods, to the survivors of the 1917 Halifax explosion. Eaton's publicists frequently portrayed Sir John as a "perpetual 'Boys Own'"; they also showed him as a national father figure. The Toronto *Globe* newspaper's 1907 Christmas edition included a two-page colour advertisement for Eaton's, in which a photograph of John Eaton figures prominently. Seated in front of a map of Canada, he presides over not only his vast business, but the entire Dominion. The centre of the spread includes two Red Ensigns, commonly considered by English Canadians to be Canada's flag. Dotted throughout the advertisement are photographs of the company's various operations and female employees. Provincial crests are also displayed (Figure 3.2). Through advertising images such as these, Eaton's suggested that its owners were committed to their employees' welfare, as well as the nation's. They also hinted that Eaton's was governed by a strong and masculine, and therefore trustworthy, provider.[16]

The transformation of store founders and their successors into public figures helped to craft a familial corporate identity. Other strategies were also integral to this project. For their 1905 opening day in Winnipeg, Timothy, Margaret, John, and Flora Eaton took the train from Toronto to the Manitoba capital. At their new store, they served behind counters and personally greeted visitors. They also hosted a luncheon for 325 guests, including Manitoba Premier Rodmond Roblin, Winnipeg Mayor George

FIGURE 3.2   Eaton's 1907 Christmas advertisement in the Toronto *Globe*. | *Source:*
Wikipedia, http://upload.wikimedia.org/wikipedia/commons/2/2d/Advertisement_for_
Eaton%27s_Department_Store_1907.JPG. | Used with permission of Sears Canada Inc.

Sharpe, and several members of the Legislative Assembly, as well as judges, lawyers, city council members, physicians, educators, Christian leaders, and newspaper editors. At the luncheon the Eatons declared their commitment to Winnipeg's development; they also, as the *Winnipeg Tribune* put it, "expressed the pleasure they ... experienced during their visit to Winnipeg," noting in particular their enjoyment of "the experimental farm" and the "Assiniboine valley." This visit did much to cement in Winnipeggers' minds an image of Eaton's familial goodwill.[17]

Department stores' familial imagery was even more direct when it came to employees. Worried about charges of labour exploitation, Canadian department stores joined other major European, Australian, and North American employers of women in the creation of genteel, homelike atmospheres. For department stores, the labour force as family metaphor had the added bonus of increasing efficiency and cohesiveness. Fostering corporate togetherness, familialism enhanced worker commitment. It also aimed at better customer service. Happy workers, it was believed, made excellent salespeople.[18]

Department stores' owners and managers referred to their enterprises in kinship terms. Eaton's called its Winnipeg branch the "daughter store," and Spencer's called its workforce the "big family." In keeping with paternalist tradition, owners invited employees to their homes. When their labour force grew so big that they could not invite the staff to their home for their annual Christmas dinner, Timothy and Margaret Eaton began having yuletide meals in the store. In 1898, 2,475 Eaton's employees sat down together for New Year's. Such executive-employee gatherings lasted into the interwar years. At all of Canada's department stores, employee picnics and dances were regular affairs. During the 1920s, Simpson's president, H.H. Fudger, who was not related to Robert Simpson but who nonetheless cultivated a paternalist persona, transported Simpson's female staff to his farm in Barrymede for a yearly "supper picnic."[19]

The Hudson's Bay Company was not family-owned, but it also had a familial atmosphere. Like Eaton's and Simpson's, it sponsored events that brought together executives and employees. To celebrate the company's 250th anniversary, HBC Governor Sir Robert Kindersley travelled to Canada from England to tour the firm's operations. Winnipeg managers held a banquet in his honour at the Fort Garry Hotel. Also present were the company's seven hundred Winnipeg store employees. Amidst the splendour of chandeliers and candlelight, the aristocratic Kindersley announced a new pension scheme. After explaining that the HBC was the "oldest company of its kind in the British Empire," he articulated the firm's paternalist views: "The record of [the HBC's] servants is one long story of adventures and unswerving loyalty to the company, and the history of the organization is very largely the history of Canada itself." This HBC banquet and speech together illustrated the HBC's paternalist ideal. Headed by a regal executive, the firm was composed of patriotic employees eager to serve their governor, empire, and country.[20]

Staff magazines were a final method by which the big stores fostered familialism. During the 1920s, Eaton's, Simpson's, Spencer's, the Dupuis Frères, and the HBC introduced newsy, informative publications for the education and entertainment of their employees. As at other Canadian and international companies that introduced such periodicals during this period, their overall purpose was to reinforce internal cohesiveness. Canadian department store magazines differed in size, format, and content, but all contained the message that individual workers belonged to a corporate family. Sections on employees' family news confirmed this message, as did sections on company-sponsored recreation, promotions, retirements, long-service staff awards, and special events. As Benson states of American department store publications, these magazines built up "a spirit of harmony and loyalty and ... promot[ed] team work."[21]

Providing for the Public

Department stores' familial imagery was only one feature of the big stores' paternalism. Central, too, were the giant retailers' providerhood personas. Drawing on their founders' established reputations for community devotion, department stores throughout the industrializing and capitalist world styled themselves as their communities', customers', and employees' generous benefactors.[22]

Philanthropy was one area in which this process was accomplished. As Canada's major stores grew, they became prominent corporate donors. Between 1912 and 1938, Eaton's Toronto store gave substantially to educational, religious, and social service organizations. These included the Girls' Friendly Society, the Salvation Army, the Children's Aid Society, the Federation of Community Services, the National Council of Women, the Canadian Social Hygiene Council, the Lord's Day Alliance, the Neighbourhood Workers' Association, and the Ontario Prohibition Union, to name but a few. Department stores' promotion of adolescent development also supported their benevolent images. The Dupuis Frères gave prizes for excellence in French, Eaton's sponsored week-long stays in Winnipeg for winners of Boys' and Girls' Club contests, and Simpson's gave away full university scholarships to essay contest winners.[23]

Department stores seized opportunities to showcase their providerhood. Canada's fiftieth birthday compelled Simpson's to distribute one thousand copies of its *The Confederation Story,* a collection of biographies about Canada's founding fathers, to politicians, school principals, university chancellors, newspaper editors, Kiwanis and Rotary Club executives, and religious leaders. This gesture communicated both the firm's nationalism and its largesse. Store birthdays similarly precipitated public offerings. For its golden anniversary in 1919, Eaton's published a 288-page company history and gave away copies to libraries, schools, and customers throughout the dominion. Elegantly written and lavishly illustrated, this book is still widely available in Canada today. Spencer's fiftieth anniversary in 1921 inspired a different kind of tribute. For one day, the company paid the full fare for all those wishing to ride Vancouver's streetcars. Taking advantage of this offer, schoolteachers cancelled classes and took children on field trips; one elderly resident even visited the resort town of Deep Bay for the first time in his life.[24]

Philanthropy, awards to schoolchildren, special books, and public relations events all contributed to department stores' reputations as community-minded institutions. Yet department stores' grandest public offerings were the stores themselves. As early as the 1890s, Leach writes, department stores "functioned as community social centers ... often filling many needs that other institutions were not responding to or saw no reason to fill."[25] All of Canada's big stores offered free attractions that demonstrated the stores' goodwill. In 1891, Timothy Eaton sponsored a complimentary concert in his store, at which "no goods" were "sold." By the mid-1920s, Eaton's Toronto and Winnipeg stores had at one time or another offered an indoor golf course, golfing lessons, an indoor picnic area, circuses with "live lions," and petting zoos. Every year, on the Winnipeg store's birthday, the company baked a huge cake, displayed it in the store windows and handed out pieces to visitors.[26]

Canada's largest stores styled themselves as gathering places for both men and women. Yet they viewed women as their primary customer base. In order to earn women's appreciation, they offered a host of complimentary services. Lavatories were especially appreciated. Prior to the late nineteenth century, women had difficulty finding facilities to relieve themselves while away from home. Erika Rappaport shows that suburban women who went shopping in West End London, England, could not relieve themselves until they arrived home in the evenings. Wealthy men had clubs that served this purpose, and men of modest means could – if the need became urgent – relieve themselves outdoors. People of both genders could also purchase meals and rooms in hotels and use these establishments' facilities. Yet women did not always feel comfortable in the available hotels, and many did not want to spend money for the sole purpose of urination. As more and more women ventured downtown, the need for lavatories grew. Affluent women solved this need by creating women's clubs. Conceived as comfortable gathering places for women, in which politics could be discussed, tea could be taken, and lavatories could be used, by the 1890s women's clubs had become popular resting places for female shoppers and sightseers. As Rappaport notes with regard to such clubs in Britain, however, many had "hefty fees" and exclusive memberships, and therefore not all women could partake of their offerings. For this reason many female sojourners continued to seek out alternative venues for relief and refreshment.[27]

Like their British counterparts, wealthy urban Canadian women created downtown clubs to edify, relieve, and refresh. Middle-class, low-income, and rural women, however, did not have access to such spaces. Department stores saw the need and filled the gap. Eaton's 1887-88 Toronto Catalogue contained an invitation: "Ladies, you come off the train ... you feel unrefreshed; you don't wish to beg anyone to allow you to make your toilet ... Listen! ... bring your parcels with you straight to Eaton's." Here, you can "leave your parcels ... send your telegrams, telephone, ask questions, leave your over garments, umbrellas, anything." One could also "find a nicely curtained waiting-room, a clean toilet room, with towels, soap, etc." Visitors did not have to pay for these services, nor were visitors pressured while using them: "These rooms are yours; we give them to you. Wash as often as you please; wait as long as you like." Simpson's and Morgan's late-nineteenth-century advertisements contained similar messages. By providing for women's bodily requirements, and not charging for such services, department stores turned themselves into downtown destinations for women.[28]

Other services were similarly aimed at securing women's custom. Unlike hotel saloons, store restaurants catered specifically to women, offering both "substantial meals and light lunches," as Simpson's put it in 1898. So common did it become to associate the big stores' restaurants with women that during the early 1930s a few experimented with eateries for men. Nurseries, too, were provided at the big stores. Eaton's Winnipeg store crèche was called Frolic Park; by 1905 it contained a sandbox, toys, and a merry-go-round. When consumer spending dipped in the 1930s, department stores began hosting free events for homemakers. A week-long afternoon cooking demonstration in Simpson's Arcadian Court in 1932 offered such door prizes as "aluminum ware, floor polisher and wax, [and] electric appliances." The grand prize winner took home an electric range.[29]

Through their services, department stores styled themselves as providers for Canadian women. Central to their image in this regard was the idea that retailers were masculine and that customers were feminine. In fact, Canada's giant retailers' publications sometimes took on the characteristics of a heterosexual interaction. In literature aimed at women, the stores portrayed themselves as concerned and fatherly overseers. Stated Simpson's in 1898, "the ladies are particularly well-provided for, having ... a special room ... where they may take their ease, write letters, and fill appointments with their friends."[30] Three years later, Morgan's announced that it had a "number of small rooms where ladies can examine the fit of a coat ... free from the gaze of curious eyes." By introducing fitting rooms, Morgan's enabled women to try on clothes in privacy. This gesture was not necessarily paternalist, but the language in which Morgan's announced its fitting rooms was. Suggesting they were shielding women from "curious eyes," the department store styled itself as a gentlemanly chaperone.[31]

At other times department stores portrayed themselves as female shoppers' courtly suitors. Before the Great War, department stores' advertising literature often depicted handsome salesmen serving women, imbuing their publicity with images of genteel courtship patterns. In fact, department stores' literature was filled with references to satisfying women. According to Eaton's 1887 Catalogue, at Eaton's "every desire that a lady may have concerning her dress can be easily gratified."[32] Department stores tempered their language of courtly desire in the first decades of the twentieth century, replacing it with less gendered statements. Thus Woodward's catalogue cover for 1929 claimed that its store was "Where Thousands of Satisfied Patrons Enter Daily."[33] Notes of heterosexual courtship continued to creep into the big retailers' press, however. Regarding its ready-to-wear section in Vancouver in 1923, Spencer's claimed that the "customer will find her desire in this department."[34] Suggesting that the big stores fulfilled women's wishes, department stores' adoption of courtship metaphors suggested that male stores were happy to provide pleasure for female shoppers.

Providing for Employees
Providerhood imagery might have been apparent in department stores' public and customer relations, but it was even more obvious in employee relations. In the late nineteenth century, department stores in Europe, Australia, and North America joined the bourgeoning welfare work movement. Like other companies with large and visible workforces, department stores began improving work conditions and employee benefits. Historians of corporate welfare show that these improvements served three main goals: they created a positive public image, they boosted employee efficiency, and they lessened worker dissent. Prior to 1990, labour historians generally believed that welfare work represented the modernization of labour relations and that it replaced the paternalism that preceded it. Newer analyses reveal, however, that some employers remained paternalist

even while introducing welfare programs. This was especially the case at workplaces staffed by white women. Worried that waged work damaged white women's reproductive capacity and morality, social reformers singled out employers of white women in their campaigns to uplift modern society. To combat images of female exploitation, paternalist employers of white women – including department stores – invested heavily in welfare.[35]

In the late nineteenth century, Canada's mass retailers began building what were among the best private welfare programs in the country. Health care was an early area of innovation. During the 1890s, Eaton's welfare office in Toronto "was empowered to extend ... extra financial assistance to employees especially in cases of sickness." By 1910, Eaton's and Simpson's Toronto stores had their own doctors, nurses, and hospitals; Eaton's in Winnipeg had similar facilities. By 1930, Canada's major stores offered employees "drugs at cost" and financial assistance for "medical and pharmaceutical bills," as one HBC pamphlet put it. Savings, loans, life insurance, pensions, paid vacations, profit sharing, and salary top-ups for male employees on active military leave were other innovations. In 1911, Morgan's even took twenty-seven long-serving staff members on a trip to Bermuda.[36]

Social and sports programs were other offerings. Susan Forbes writes that, by 1914, Eaton's Toronto and Winnipeg stores had literature, debating, photography, and sketching clubs. Eaton's sports teams included tumbling, soccer, baseball, and cricket for men and softball for women. During the First World War, Eaton's in Toronto purchased a YMCA building, which held a swimming pool, a cafeteria, a gymnasium, a library, and a sewing room. The company also bought land at Scarborough Bluffs, where it built a country club for young men. In 1923, Eaton's purchased a summer camp for female employees. Complete with sailboats, rowboats, baseball and basketball facilities, and a golf course, it charged nominal fees for weeklong and weekend excursions. In the 1920s other department stores also began standardizing their own social and sports programs. To oversee its employee recreation, the HBC created Amusement and Athletic Associations, later renamed Beaver Clubs. By 1931 the company had a clubhouse and tennis court in Winnipeg and an athletic field in Calgary.[37]

Health, vacation, and recreation benefits provided good publicity for department stores. They also boosted employees' physical health and therefore decreased absenteeism and low productivity. They further created cohesiveness. Employees who belonged to the same club often became friends, as did members of an Eaton's Winnipeg sewing group of the 1930s, whose friendships lasted into the 1990s. Bonding experiences outside the workplace smoothed job frictions, especially between entry level and managerial staff. Department stores in fact nurtured vertical employee friendships. Like Westclox in Peterborough during this period, department stores created clubs to help new, young workers network with older, more established staff. Eaton's and the HBC each operated Business Men's Clubs, whose members held banquets, learned selling and managerial techniques, and attended lectures on Canada's commercial, Protestant, and political environments.[38]

As in the Westclox case, department stores did not sponsor similar clubs for women. It was commonly believed that female employees' natural trajectory was to resign upon being married; mass retail's welfare work for women thus focused on their physical and moral health. As Tone notes of American welfare programs, Canadian department stores' recreation programs for women emphasized domesticity. The Toronto Eaton's Girls Club (EGC) was a particularly sustained effort. During the 1920s, as Forbes shows, it focused on "the attributes necessary for being a good wife, mother and housekeeper."[39] Sports received more attention during the 1930s, but the EGC's unofficial mandate remained respectable femininity. Unlike Eaton's Business Men's Clubs, which fostered training and promotions, the EGC promoted docility and compassion. As one 1932 motto put it, "The Eaton Girls' Club is a melting pot / Where each girl puts in the best she's got ... Put in friendship, the helping hand, / – or only sand. / The Eaton Girls' Club is a common pool / Which you have to stir with the golden rule."[40]

Sensitive to claims they were destroying feminine virtue, Canada's largest stores paid attention to female workers' respectability. After he opened his Winnipeg store in 1905, Timothy Eaton became aware that his female employees were "not pleased with the accommodation of the ordinary boarding places." He thus "purchased a large house to be used" as their residence. Similarly, during the Great War, Simpson's president bought a house in Toronto and transformed it into a residence for 160 female staff. Eaton's and Simpson's admonished their female staff to never speak to male shoppers unless it was necessary, and they provided chaperoned rooms in clubhouses where female employees could entertain male guests. In an attempt to safeguard their female employees' reputations, Canada's largest retailers hence acted *in loco parentis,* as Theresa McBride suggests of Parisian stores.[41] Through their paternalist guardianship of female employees, Canada's big stores behaved similarly to Penman's and West-clox, both in southern Ontario and both large employers of white women.[42]

Paternalism's Consequences

Canadian department stores' modernization of paternalism had some positive results. Their determination to prove their righteousness through philanthropy resulted in the creation of several worthy institutions, includ-ing the Woodward Library at the University of British Columbia. Depart-ment stores' sizeable donations to educational, medical, and social service organizations enhanced civic life; their military contributions to the Great War aided the Allies' cause; and their staging of countless amusements created enjoyment for many children and adults. By 1940 several Can-adians had expressed enthusiasm for department stores' commitments to charity and community service. As one shopper put it in 1919, Timothy Eaton had always been a "Christian gentleman."[43]

Department stores' paternalist approach to customer service was also beneficial. Eaton's well-known policies of "a square deal for all" and "satis-faction guaranteed or money refunded" encouraged shoppers to feel the store genuinely cared for them. In 1934 one customer stated, "It is quite a long time for a store to serve the public. The main thing is the honesty about it and the reliable goods." In 1937 another customer wrote that whenever she went shopping at Eaton's, she felt she was in the "home of an old friend."[44] Department stores' lavish in-house services were also appreciated. Female visitors to downtown areas who could not afford women's clubs' fees, and who did not want to enter male-dominated saloons, took advantage of department store lavatories, writing rooms and restrooms, parcel checks, and restaurants. Busy mothers left their children at department stores' complimentary nurseries, and mothers wishing to entertain their children for little cost brought them to department stores' toy sections, which often had free rides and games.

Finally, many employees valued department stores' paternalist approach to labour relations. For Catholic and francophone workers, "the family, faith, and nation credo" that pervaded the Dupuis Frères might have been more appealing "than the ideas in other job environments," particularly those operated by Montréal's anglophone bourgeoisie.[45] Eaton's, Mor-gan's, Simpson's, Spencer's, and the HBC's cohesive identities also offered a sense of security and belonging to workers who had little familial or social support. Even more appreciated were department stores' welfare benefits. Historian Joan Sangster finds that "a 1927 study done for the Ontario government on ... benefits ... revealed that many companies offered cheaper benefits like recreation and cafeterias, while fewer offered more costly employer paid vacations, sickness insurance, pension plans and so on."[46] Compared to benefits offered by other major Canadian employers, benefits at Eaton's, Simpson's, the HBC's, Morgan's, and Spencer's were substantial. Workers seeking health, retirement, and recreation packages would have been attracted particularly to department stores' welfarist offerings.[47]

Department stores' multifaceted paternalism is no doubt responsible for the ongoing affection that Canadians have for the big stores. Together with the giant retailers' nationalism, described in Chapter 2, this paternalism helped construct images of department stores as acting in the public's best interest. Nonetheless, paternalism at Canada's largest stores did have a host of negative consequences. One of the most significant was male dominance over female customers and employees. Since paternalism was modelled on the patriarchal family structure, female submission to male authority was expected in the department store. Stores' sales-training literature, which was published beginning in the 1920s, shows how this expectation structured sales floor interactions. Eaton's *A Little Chat about Selling* (1931) portrayed female shoppers as passive and malleable. Using the language of courtship, it instructed employees to notice what merchandise "stimulate[d] [the female shopper's] interest" and to describe to her the product's selling features. *A Little Chat about Selling* also implied that female shoppers were easily swayed. Employees should ignore the customer's price limit, it advised, and "explain the added value to her." For when she learns of the more expensive item's superiority, "she will nearly always buy." If a customer asked for items that were not in stock, salespeople were to "show her the nearest we have." This strategy often worked because the shopper usually did not know "what she want[ed]" and relied on salespeople to "tell her some of the facts." Trainers therefore viewed women as impressionable beings waiting to be persuaded to spend money. This depiction contributed to an overall store atmosphere of gentility and courtship, but it also suggested that female customers could not rely on their own intelligence or make their own choices.[48]

The perception that female customers were passive also implied that women were leisured beings who had all the time in the world to wait around while salespeople manoeuvred them into buying goods. These depictions contrasted with department store depictions of male customers.

As Wright demonstrates, Eaton's Toronto magazine chastised clerks for ignoring male shoppers' tight schedules. In 1935 it related that one male customer on his way to work stopped in and asked a clerk to get him an item, "whereupon the clerk began to tell of all the others they had in stock – other colours, other qualities, other prices." Too busy to listen to this "sales talk," he left without purchasing. This tale's lesson was that the seller should have recognized his customer was in a hurry.[49] Gail Reekie's research on Australian retail similarly finds that department stores portrayed male customers as efficient. This distinction between leisured women and busy men reinforced broader stereotypes, suggesting that men belonged to the important "public world of work," while women's less pressing responsibilities enabled them to spend their days being pampered in the shops.[50]

In her research on 1950s stove salesmanship, Joy Parr finds that experts "portrayed difficult customers as older, ugly, and overbearing." Pre-1940 Canadian department stores constructed similar images. In 1935 a male HBC employee in Vancouver sent a cartoon to his store magazine, which subsequently published it. Depicting a sales floor on the morning of a "Great Sale" with "Special Bargains," it features a salesman wearing protective armour. He is bracing himself against a crowd of angry-looking, older women about to burst through the department's doors (Figure 3.3). Unlike the compliant shoppers presented in staff training literature, these ones are assertive and dangerous. Disobeying department stores' genteel etiquette, these caricatures are the realization of trainers' fears. Instead of desiring high-priced goods, they desire low-priced ones. Instead of chatting amiably with salesmen, they intend to batter one down. And instead of presenting themselves as ambivalent or in need of guidance, they know exactly what they want. The cartoon hence turns bargain-hunting, assertive women into objects of derision. Rather than taking female shoppers' quest for low-priced goods seriously, it encourages employees to view independent female shoppers as debased. In the department stores' gendered hierarchy, assertive women were anomalies.[51]

Department stores' portrayals of the normal female shopper as docile and the deviant female shopper as crazed perpetuated stereotypes of the unrestrained female consumer. Such images downplayed the important economic function of shopping within Canada's capitalist economy and made women's consumer labour appear trivial. They also suggested that independent women were exceptions to dominant norms. Finally, department stores' twofold portrayal of the female shopper as both naive and

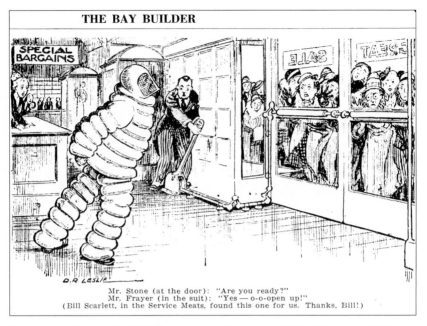

THE BAY BUILDER

Mr. Stone (at the door): "Are you ready?"
Mr. Frayer (in the suit): "Yes — o-o-open up!"
(Bill Scarlett, in the Service Meats, found this one for us. Thanks, Bill!)

FIGURE 3.3   Cartoon in HBC Vancouver staff magazine, 1935. | *Source: Bay Builder,* May 1935, 4, Hudson's Bay Company Archives. | Used with permission of the Hudson's Bay Company Archives.

domineering discouraged salespeople from treating female customers as intelligent. As Chapter 5 will show, between 1890 and 1960, hundreds of female patrons wrote to the big stores to complain about coddling, inefficient, and misogynous treatment.

Just as paternalism contributed to oppressive shopping experiences for women, so did it construct discriminatory environments for female staff. As Matthews notes of the Dupuis Frères, there was a "gender hierarchy ... that kept women in lower positions and enabled men to function in dominant roles." Sandra Aylward similarly demonstrates that at Eaton's prior to 1940 female employees had few opportunities to advance beyond entry-level positions. Indeed, Eaton's 1929 chart called "Supervisors, Group Managers, Heads of Departments and Assistants" shows that of the approximately 240 supervisory positions in Winnipeg, Regina, Saskatoon, Calgary, and Edmonton, only one was held by a woman. Women fared slightly better in the Department Head category, in which thirteen out of approximately three hundred positions were held by female employees. Male dominance permeated all levels of department store management. Lady Eaton herself fought for a place on the board of directors after her husband died. Yet even once she was accepted, she had little influence over decisions. Her activities were confined to restaurants and staff welfare, areas considered feminine.[52]

Department stores widely enforced the male breadwinner–female homemaker family model. According to one 1920 HBC article addressed to "H.B.C. girls," "whether she admit it or even believe it – the ambition of every business girl is – what the destiny of all normal women is – to find a husband that will tally to the measure of her ideal, provide a home for her and make her life really complete." Career-minded women chafed under department stores' unwillingness to support female talent. Working for Simpson's personnel department during the interwar years, one Toronto woman was frustrated by her job's tedium, monotony, lack of satisfaction, and low wages. Excerpts from her 1928 unpublished poem, "Ode To Personnel Person Persistently Pacifying *Wickens!* [her department manager]" express her dissatisfaction. "Art thou not disgusted with thy job / where thou dost labour for so cheap a sum? / ... just let [Wickens] rust / ... New York or bust!!!!!"[53]

Paternalist treatment of women led to the infantilization of female staff. When Timothy Eaton was in conversation with a customer, sixteen-year-old employee Emily Cowley relayed him a message. He called her "a little personage" and patted her on the head. A joke in Eaton's Toronto staff magazine is suggestive of Eaton's managers' view of youthful female workers: "Yes. It happened in a Toronto store, but NOT in EATON'S," it began. "A customer was looking at handbags. She fancied one with a smart modern metal ornament. 'I like this one,' she said to the salesclerk, 'but do you think the metal will tarnish?' 'Oh, yes, beautifully, Madam,' answered the helpful salesgirl."[54]

As the fatherly overseers of their stores, owners and upper- level managers ran the stores as they saw fit. They assumed total control over job security, pay, work schedules, benefits, and promotions. If managers were keen to cut expenses, believed certain workers were less entitled than others to pay and security, disliked a certain employee, or simply favoured one wage earner over another, workers suffered. Managers' twofold ability to smooth or make difficult employees' experiences caused workers to live in fear of dismissal and other punishments. When they received promotions, pay increases, or praise, they interpreted such things as favours, not entitlements. Lillian M. Poulter, who worked at Eaton's in Toronto from 1900 to 1952, said that when she was young, "Mr. R.W. Eaton once asked my manager ... what he paid me for as I [had] slipped up an order mistake." As a consequence, she feared "they were going to let me out." But her manager came to her defence: "he said if there was any firing to be done he would do it." Two weeks later she "caught a mistake" somebody else made, and "R.W. said that's the kind of people we want. So we just laughed." Poulter's description of these events is suggestive both of managers' power over workers and workers' fears of reprisals.[55]

Individualized treatment of staff affected both male and female employees, but women had the added burden of sexually charged favouritism. Some owners and managers flirted with female staff. Sir John Eaton was known among female employees as a playboy. He gave gifts of perfume to Eaton's mail order parcel girls and asked women to join him on excursions. In the early twentieth century, a group of employees cycled out to a co-worker's farm. John Eaton also went but took a horse and buggy. He asked a female employee to accompany him. She consented reluctantly, for she had promised another boy – her future husband – she would cycle with him. Recognizing the power disparity between Eaton and herself, though, she complied with Eaton's wishes.[56]

At times, individualized treatment of staff had tragic consequences. In March 1919, solicitor Edward Meek sent a letter to President Sir John Eaton. The letter related how, one morning in 1907, Eaton's Toronto salesclerk Josephine Rist had been unfortunately "shot in the face, eyes and arm" by a faulty shotgun, which a customer had returned to the store. She was knocked unconscious and carried to the store's hospital. That evening, John Eaton picked her up in his car and drove her to his home. He told her *"not to mention the accident to anyone,"* especially the press. After she recovered, the Eaton family purchased for her a one-way ticket to Winnipeg and arranged for a new job there. In Winnipeg, Rist's eyesight worsened and increasingly painful muscle damage in her back and arm prevented her from working properly. In 1919 she informed Winnipeg's manager of her difficulties, and he purchased her a ticket back to Toronto. Unable to work, her medical bills forced her into poverty. Though she finally contacted a lawyer, she continued behaving according to paternalism's script. As she explained in a letter to Lady Eaton, "I would not do or say anything further until I made sure that either Sir John or Lady Eaton ... knew the actual facts." For Rist, the individualized aspect of paternalism, along with its inefficiency, caused isolation, bodily harm, and eventual destitution.[57]

Paternalism, then, was a double-edged sword. When employees behaved according to management's wishes, they received so-called favours unheard of in similar workplaces. But if they asked for entitlements not supported by management, they were penalized. At no time was this aspect of paternalism more apparent than when employees organized to demand better working conditions. At Eaton's in the late nineteenth century, as Santink writes, "several company upholsterers who participated in one [Labour Day] parade were promptly dismissed." In 1900 the Vancouver local of the Retail Clerks' International Protective Association (RCIPA) told the Vancouver Trades and Labour Council that "certain large stores in this City had discharged or threatened with discharge their clerks for belonging to the Retail Clerks' Association." When approximately one thousand unionized Toronto garmentworkers, both men and women, struck against Eaton's in 1912, President John Eaton told the *Globe,* "When the union attempts to dictate ... it is utterly beyond its rights ... Now they are out, they are out the door for good ... if the rest go on strike, it will be safe for you to put into type that 2,000 will be out of work." Shortly after making this statement, Eaton's dismissed one thousand striking workers. Five years later Spencer's fired five Vancouver clerks for demonstrating interest in the RCIPA. And in 1934, Eaton's fired thirty-eight female factory operatives who had made contact with a union.[58]

Given department stores' anti-unionism, employees wishing to succeed in their jobs knew they had to be deferent. As Lady Eaton put it in her autobiography, "anyone who works for Eaton's is bound to be 100 percent *for* Eaton's ... The person who feels dissatisfied, and does not get this sense of oneness with the Company early, is seldom there for long." Employees who wished to regain their jobs after losing them because of union activity knew well the importance of playing the supplicant. After participating in the 1912 Eaton strike, John Levy visited the employment office several times to obtain his old position. Unsuccessful, he sent a letter to Sir John himself. In language echoing Rist's, he begged Sir John for reinstatement. "I am sorry that I deserted you, and hurt your feelings ... I beg and urge you to do fair play towards me."[59] Not only did department stores' paternalism discriminate against female employees, but it also established a top-down authoritative structure that demanded complete staff deference. Its individualized treatment of employees turned promotions and raises into favours that workers had to earn by appealing to managers. For some employees, department stores' encouragement of complete loyalty to the store family caused physical, financial, and emotional stress. Paternalism further ensured that workers could not organize to better their working conditions.

A final negative consequence of paternalism was its perpetuation of racism. During the late nineteenth and early twentieth centuries, most social institutions in Canada discriminated against anyone not visibly Caucasian. Department stores were no exception. In Vancouver in 1928, Spencer's, Woodward's, and the HBC joined 143 other businesses in a petition to the provincial government to "limit the number of shops owned by non-whites." As a result, the province created a Trades License Board that could "refuse licenses" to storekeepers "deemed against the public interest."[60] Department stores' support for white dominance in Canada between 1890 and 1940 in some cases resulted in open hostility, as in the example above, but it also manifested in other ways. During the interwar years, the HBC drew upon paternalism to suggest that Aboriginal people were inferior to whites. Thus in 1922 *The Beaver* announced, "The western Indian of to-day is still a child, literally speaking, and assimilation is slow." Aboriginal men especially had yet to modernize: the Aboriginal man "wears his hair in long plaits and loves bedecking himself in paint, feathers and other finery whenever occasion arises." Another *Beaver* article boasted of the HBC's aids to Aboriginal assimilation. Before Canada bought Rupert's Land, the company had "fed, clothed and supported the natives."[61] Through such paternalist statements, the HBC fostered a corporate culture that simultaneously romanticized and vilified Aboriginal people.

The HBC's view of Aboriginal people as childlike and primitive encouraged some employees to treat them with disdain. Winnipeg's 1935 *Bayonet* carried a poem by a male correspondence office employee that described an encounter with a male Aboriginal customer: "Standing before me, was a full blooded 'Injin.'" Though seeing the Aboriginal man frightened the poet, he still mocked the customer for wearing "feathers" in his hat. According to the writer, this customer had tried to civilize himself by wearing western accessories, but because he retained some Aboriginal elements, the effect was ridiculous. The author also stated that the customer "stroked my hair," which caused the author to believe he was going to be scalped. But all that the shopper wanted to do was to compare his hair with that of the poet, saying that whereas the author had short hair, he wore "braids." Despite the patron's peaceful intention, the poet instructed readers to keep their distance if they met an indigenous person; otherwise a "duel between tomahawk and gun" would occur.[62]

This employee's poetry articulated his views of Aboriginal men. Their racialized identity, he believed, made them relics of the past; it was impossible for them to modernize. To suggest that his Aboriginal customer did not dress himself properly likely bolstered the employee's sense of his own legitimacy and superiority, for presumably he himself had mastered Western fashion ideals. The poem thus implies that, prior to 1940, one's ability to conform to prevailing fashion norms marked one's membership in modernity. The employee's contribution further demonstrates that despite department stores' supposedly free-entry and service-for-all policies, racialized assumptions on the part of department store staff could create discriminatory shopping experiences for non-whites. Since *The Bayonet* saw fit to publish the employee's poem, it is likely that he was not the only employee at the HBC to hold such views.

Aboriginal people were not the only racialized group singled out for comment in HBC publications. One 1926 issue of *The Beaver* contained a section called "Nigger Humour," which featured twelve jokes about people of African heritage. Each joke portrayed people of African descent as dim-witted but endearing. "A negro woman of mammoth proportions and inky complexion," began one joke, "was brought unconscious to a hospital after a collision." After being told she could sue for "damages," the woman replied, "What Ah want wif damages? Ah got damages enough now. What Ah needs is repairs!" Within the framework of the joke, the woman's size, skin colour, and dialect marked her as unintelligent. Just as *The Beaver* portrayed people of Aboriginal descent as uncivilized, so it depicted people of African heritage as unsophisticated. Both stereotypes reinforced whites' presumptions about their own legitimacy and importance.[63]

Compared to Canada's other department stores, the HBC had the longest history of racialized paternalism. Other retailers did, however, publish paternalist portrayals of non-whites. In a special Eaton's flyer dating from 1930, a publicist reported on the opening of Eaton's College Street store. It was "one of the most representative gatherings Toronto has ever witnessed," proclaimed the flyer. It went on: "Didn't we see a precious little black pickaninny, about three years old, battered sailor cap cocked over one ear, stockings hanging down – o, while he dragged on the skirt of his mammy?"[64] In 1940, Eaton's again referred condescendingly to black children. Under a photograph of two African children in its Toronto magazine was the caption, "Two little fuzzy headed piccaninnies who attend a Mission Day School in Lutamo in the heart of Africa. It is recess time and what book do you think they are poring over? – EATON'S Mail Order Catalogue. Here's to you, fuzzy wuzzies. Perhaps we'll meet some day."[65] According to both the 1935 and the 1940 pieces, "pickaninnies," or children of African descent, were simultaneously cute and simplistic. Singled out because they were not white, Eaton's used their images in an attempt to inspire affection and amusement among white readers.

As EATON's, SIMPSON's, the HBC, and other stores transformed themselves into large, anonymous corporations at the turn of the twentieth century, they drew upon their paternalist traditions in order to appear righteous and benevolent. As paternalist providers and overseers of their communities, customers, and employees, they cast their founders as progressive visionaries and fostered familial shopping and working atmospheres. Several Canadians applauded these initiatives, and to this day many nurture affectionate sentiments toward Eaton's in particular. Paternalism did have a few positive consequences, including the provision of comfortable downtown spaces for sojourning middle-class women and the provision of fringe benefits for employees.

Yet department store paternalism also had more troubling legacies. Paternalism at Canada's largest stores promoted the views that whites were superior to Aboriginals and blacks, that womanhood was defined by "wifehood," that men were more intelligent than women, that the affluent were superior to the non-affluent, and that those of upper social stations had a duty to provide for the lower classes. Department store paternalism thus prolonged, articulated, and entrenched race, gender, and class hierarchies in modernizing Canada.

It also had more specific effects. Paternalism kept unions out of the department store labour force and crushed most attempts at collective workplace action. It fostered a selling environment that disparaged non-whites. It created a demeaning shopping environment for female customers. And it reinforced female employees' subordinate positions within the workplace. Since Eaton's, Simpson's, and the HBC were among the largest and most visible retailers and employers in Canada by the middle of the twentieth century, these consequences were significant. Because of their sheer size on the Canadian landscape and their effect on the lives of those they touched, department stores served as indicators of Canadian experience. That such influential enterprises could create and reinforce such inequitable conditions is a poignant reminder that, during this age of Canadian progressivism, not all pre-modern traditions were transcended.

4

Crafting the Consumer Workforce

She says her friends declare she is so thoroughly an Eatonian, they can almost see the diamond E on her face.

— *Eaton's, 1944, on the occasion of an employee's 35th anniversary*

ANYONE WHO HAS WORKED for a company that sells goods and services knows that consumer culture and image making are central to the work environment. As major corporations become more dependent on "optics" and public relations, they start going to greater lengths to ensure their workforce matches their image. Today, Google promotes a workforce culture of innovation and creativity, and WestJet promotes a culture of friendliness, good-natured humour, and patience. Future Shop employs savvy salespeople whom customers might try to impress or emulate, and the Gap employs preppy sellers that dress just slightly more fashionably than the company's target consumer group. Corporations also encourage employees to identify with their employer's images. By hosting parties and contests in which workers win company products, and by making it compulsory for employees to dress and behave according to corporate policy, companies attempt to craft workforces that fit their identity.

Scholars have explored management's turn toward image making. In her study of American flight attendants, Arlie Russell Hochschild finds that flight attendants are trained to behave artificially. Even when customers are being insulting or aggressive, they must restrain their responses. This causes burnout and alienation. In her work on cosmetics saleswomen in Taiwan, Pei-Chia Lan demonstrates that cosmetics workers must be youthful and attractive. The saleswomen Lan interviewed liked fashion and beauty, but they knew that they would lose their jobs "after getting pregnant or turning thirty." Researchers also note that corporations attempt to convince workers to become consumers. In her study of Westclox in Peterborough before 1960, Joan Sangster finds that its magazine portrayed workers as consumers not only of Westclox products but also of commodities in general.[1]

This chapter investigates how and why Canada's largest department stores incorporated advertising and consumption into workers' experiences between 1890 and 1940 and offers a historical analysis of image making and consumerism within the workplace. Building on research by international department store historians, the chapter suggests that these giant retailers pioneered the image-making and consumer-creating strategies, usefully referred to as commodification, that are now common in the consumer industries. The term "commodification" draws its meaning from the word "commodity," an object, service, or other entity that is perceived in terms of market value. Commodification, therefore, is the process whereby an object, service, or other entity, including a labourer, acquires value in the capitalist marketplace.

Like all employers, Canada's largest stores commodified their workers because they purchased their workers' labour. Yet commodification operated at these workplaces in other ways as well. Department stores viewed their workers as potential consumers. Workers possessed wages and, when exchanged for goods, wages became sources of profit. Department stores hence sought to coax wages out of workers by convincing them to acquire a consumerist ethos. Besides allowing the stores to recoup capital spent on salaries, workers' "propensity to consume" had other benefits as well.[2] Employees who actively sought, purchased, and used company products became advertisements for their stores. If they were enthusiastic about company wares, they would convince others to purchase goods. And if they displayed company merchandise in attractive ways during their leisure time, they would promote their company's products while off the job.

The inducement of consumerism was, however, only one side of commodification at Canada's giant retailers. Department stores also commodified employees by incorporating their appearances and actions into advertising and publicity. It is commonly understood that when workers sign employment contracts, they agree to provide certain services to employers. These include physical strength, productivity, and whatever identifiable skills the worker might possess. It is clear, though, that Eaton's, Simpson's, the HBC, and several smaller stores viewed workers' value in broader terms. Although these employers paid workers for only those services agreed to in the labour contract, they extracted additional services from them. Through hiring policies as well as welfare and training programs, Canada's major stores engineered workforces believed to enhance the stores' images and products. As well, through their formidable advertising and publicity departments, department stores made their employees' behaviours, bodies, and endeavours part of their marketing strategies. At Simpson's, the HBC, and Eaton's, workers' value was determined not only by their strength, skills, and commitment to productivity but also by their appearance, activities, and personality.

Canada's department stores' blend of paternalism, welfarism, and commodification was different from another management style that labour historians often associate with consumer culture. Researchers sometimes use the term "fordism" to describe a situation in which unionized workers relinquish control over the labour process in return for adequate leisure time and high wages. The word derives from the "five-dollar day" that Henry Ford introduced to assembly-line workers in Detroit in 1913. Concerned about worker dissatisfaction and low productivity, Ford reduced the work day from nine to eight hours and gave employees a raise in daily wages from $2.50 to $5.00. Productivity rose, and the "five-dollar day" did provide "solutions to the Ford labor problems." In recognition of Ford's dubious contributions to labour management, scholars today use the term "fordism" to describe the post-Second World War agreement that unionized workers made with the state and capital. They committed to high productivity and workplace quiescence in return for high wages, secure jobs, and adequate leisure time.[3]

As workers in de-industrializing countries move into non-unionized service jobs, employers are feeling less pressure to meet fordism's demands of high wages and job security. Especially within retailing and fast food, companies are practising the pre-fordist traditions of low wages, job insecurity, and individualized treatment of workers. Significantly, however, post-fordist employers are retaining a commitment to employee consumerism. They are also taking commodification to new heights. Recent television commercials by Bell Canada, McDonald's, and Walmart, for example, all portray employees as healthy, happy, and loyal. As corporations' advertising and personnel departments intertwine, it becomes imperative that researchers document the operation of workplace commodification.

Promoting Consumerism

Department stores' need to sell goods led to different forms of employee commodification, the first of which was the promotion of consumerism.

This consisted of convincing employees to be loyal, telling employees that goods would make their lives happier, and prompting employees to promote their employer's products. The paternalist practice of gifting was central to these efforts. When high-ranking employees married, Timothy Eaton furnished entire rooms in their dwellings. Both Eaton's and the HBC gave employees such gifts as gold watches, gold rings, gold cuff links, luggage sets, wool blankets, ivory hand mirrors, food baskets, tea sets, and dishes to mark weddings, retirements, and long-service milestones. During the First World War, Eaton's sent Christmas "boxes of goodies to each Eaton man in England and France" as well as monthly packages to employees who had been taken as war prisoners.[4]

Through gifting, Canada's department stores demonstrated appreciation, concern, and affection. Since gifts can represent a way of compensating someone for services rendered, gift giving also aimed at fostering obligation. Especially when gifts were given to mark events such as a male employee's marriage and long-service achievements, they became methods of extracting further productive service from workers. Gift giving also encouraged enthusiasm for company commodities. Home furnishings were meant not only to show appreciation but also to demonstrate and develop the pleasures of acquisitive consumption. Gold rings, gold watches, china, and silver dishes marked special occasions. Their very exclusiveness communicated importance. When gifts were presented to employees, it was usually done with fanfare, illustrating that the receipt of company gifts was a joyous event. Within company literature, stores reported positively on gifts employees received. At a "jolly party" in honour of Miss Morris, noted *The Beaver* in 1922, "Mr. Pout, on behalf of [his] department, presented Miss Morris with a handsome silver casserole, silver spoons and Madeira doilies. The evening was spent with dancing and music." The enthusiastic style of the article serves to create excitement for Morris and her receipt of the company's gifts, which almost certainly came from the firm's own stock.[5]

Privileges regarding goods were also aimed at convincing workers to consume. By 1910, Simpson's and Spencer's had employee discounts, and in 1920 the HBC started standardizing its discount policies. By 1935 each full-time HBC employee was entitled to two discount cards: one for himself or herself and one for an immediate dependant. HBC employees also had access to charge accounts and extra discounts on Christmas purchases. Special occasions such as the "employees' shopping evening" held at the HBC's Saskatoon store in December 1923 further promoted consumption.

FIGURE 4.1   Advertisement in Eaton's staff magazine, 1935. | *Source: Flash,* 12 August 1935, Archives of Ontario, T. Eaton Papers, Series 141. | Used with permission of Sears Canada Inc.

After a special-priced dinner and "group singing," employees went about the closed store, shopping, visiting, and buying. By 1933, Eaton's employees were entitled to 5 percent discounts on goods and could use a weekly payment plan. To ensure that employees did not leave their posts in order to shop during the day, Eaton's allowed its workers to shop between half past eight and half past nine in the morning. Eaton's Toronto employees were also permitted to take the morning bus between Eaton's College Street and the Main Store, during their working hours, so they could purchase goods.[6]

To further fuel consumerism, Canada's biggest stores advertised directly to employees. From at least the First World War, Eaton's included advertisements in workers' pay envelopes. For example, one 1926 insert read: "The Men's Hat Department of the Store is showing a most extensive selection this season of the new and smart hats for Spring. Select your Easter Hat now!" *The Beaver* carried advertisements since its inception in 1920. These were meant to appeal to the magazine's employee and non-employee readership. Canada's biggest stores also offered special employee discounts on goods and services. Simpson's staff magazine informed workers, "The Hairdressing department offers a manicure to employees until eleven o'clock for 25c." Figure 4.1 reveals that Eaton's magazines also advertised to employees.[7]

As Mary Matthews observes in her research on the Dupuis Frères, articles in staff magazines similarly encouraged consumerism. *The Beaver* praised the consumer ethic in an article titled, "What Are Your Wants?" "You may measure a man by his wants," declared the article, stating that the "poor plodder has few wants, expects but little, and generally gets no more than he expects." The "successful man," in contrast, "has many wants – good home, good clothes, good company, wealth, power and fame."[8] More usually, magazines informed employees about their stores' offerings and encouraged readers to become excited. A 1927 issue of Spencer's *Store Topics* reminded employees, "we have the finest hiking and outing boots in town. Why not have a look at them?"[9] Sales training sessions also encouraged employees to admire store merchandise. Trainers usually talked about commodities in an appreciative and breathless manner. In this way, employees learned about the composition and purposes of various goods at the same time that they were caught up in a sense of excitement and happiness. At "The Gingham Girl," a training fashion show staged by Eaton's Winnipeg's Dress Cottons Department in 1934, employees and customers learned "hundreds of fascinating new designs."[10]

Selling Employees' Activities

The consumer ethic was only one component of workplace commodification. In response to their critics' accusations, Canada's giant retailers seized every opportunity to demonstrate good treatment of staff. As Michael Miller writes of the Parisian Bon Marché, "the means by which the Bon Marché focused public attention on its [closely knit] internal community were nearly unlimited."[11] Eaton's and the HBC expressed their community involvement and employee contentment by hosting singing and theatre events featuring store employees. Eaton's weekly Toronto flyer frequently informed customers of Eaton's employees' chorale and drama performances. In 1935 the Hudson's Bay Choral Society in Vancouver staged a well-attended recital at the Empress Theatre, in conjunction with the Burrard Male Choir and the First Baptist Church Choir. The HBC's singing and dramatic performances often had an informal and relaxed air, but Eaton's events were formal and lavish. Such atmospheres communicated the firms' images to audiences. The HBC was a comfortable place to shop, and Eaton's in Toronto was an elegant merchandiser.[12]

The Eaton's Girls' Club (EGC) in Toronto was central to Eaton's attempts to profit from employees' activities. During the 1935 Christmas season, it staged a "Theatre Night" at the Margaret Eaton Hall. Eaton's transported guests from the Neighborhood Workers, the Aged Men's and Women's Homes, and the Christie Street Hospital to watch the show. Members of the EGC served guests ice cream and biscuits, and Eaton's drama troupe, the Masquers, performed a play. Also that year, the EGC – with help from Eaton's – put together two hundred Christmas hampers for "those in need." Creating friendly and entertaining moments in which workers interacted with members of the public, Eaton's and the HBC demonstrated that employees supported the goals of middle-class philanthropy and were therefore respectable.[13]

Eaton's and the HBC did not refrain from using worker-initiated activities as advertising opportunities. In June 1919 a group of Toronto employees rented the Armories so that they could stage a ceremony in honour of Sir John Eaton. Grateful for his New Year's Eve announcement of shorter hours – the firm would close every Saturday at noon and, during the summer, would be closed all day on Saturdays – these employees collected twenty thousand dollars from their co-workers and donated the money to the Toronto Hospital for Sick Children. They also pledged a cot, which they called the Sir John Craig Eaton Cot. Some rumours about this event suggested that employees grumbled about having to donate money, but it is true that formal presentations and employee gifts were part of paternalist employment relationships. As at other paternalist workplaces, celebrations and gifts marked employees' recognition of workplace concessions at the same time that they bound employers to their promises. Eaton's publicists, however, ignored employees' determination to ensure Sir John maintained shorter hours. Instead, they emphasized employees' "esteem" for Sir John and the harmonious nature of the event. "In the speech-making that followed," noted one Winnipeg newspaper advertisement in the late 1920s, the "Minister of Education for Ontario" said that Eaton's employees "had used a unique occasion to show loyalty, and at the same time to help one of the most Christ-like and helpful of institutions in the whole country." By publicizing this occasion, Eaton's appropriated its employees' activities, making them part of the company's general history.[14]

If Eaton's felt comfortable turning an employee gesture of goodwill into a public relations opportunity, so did Eaton's and the HBC consider it acceptable to report on employees' accomplishments in publicity literature. Eaton's 1919 company history proclaimed that male employees had received "ninety-four decorations" for their contributions to the Allies' cause in the Great War and included a chart showing the names of the decorations and the numbers of employees who received them. *The Beaver* often reported on employees' accomplishments. One issue informed readers that Robert Watson, Esq., was not only an accountant with the HBC but also a published novelist.[15]

Advertising Employees' Bodies

In the process of commodifying employees' activities, Canada's biggest retailers also advertised employees' bodies. Both types of publicity aimed to demonstrate goodwill and contentment, and both sought to enhance the stores' profit. Bodily commodification was different, however, in that it was a more explicit attempt by Canada's largest stores to transfer the market value generated by and represented in particular workers' beings to the value of the stores and their commodities.

The consumer standards movement that swept across the United States at the turn of the twentieth century influenced North American employers' portrayals of their workforces. Worried about impurities and safety, lobbyists pressed for higher standards and greater production transparency. In response, companies began advertising not only their clean working conditions but also their workers' respectability. "In food companies that sold goods to a mass market," Andrea Tone writes, "employers championed the superiority of their products by emphasizing the 'pleasing' attributes of the workers who made them." Workers' respectability could be proven by advertising their participation in sports and educational programs. It could also be illustrated by advertising their appearance. Tone shows that racist stereotypes crept into American welfarist employers' marketing strategies.[16]

In Canada ideas about race and class were crucial to this type of commodification. At the turn of the twentieth century, some English-speaking Protestants associated industrialization and urbanization with immorality and decay. Mariana Valverde shows that among social purity activists, the concept of "the city" became "intertwined with ... fears about racial, moral, and social degeneration." As she points out, many purity activists associated dark skin colour and working-class origins with urban deprivation. Similarly, in his study of Vulcan, Alberta, Paul Voisey reveals that many settlers constructed a new "western" culture in opposition to what they perceived were the main problems of the "East." These included the notions that it was "small, cramped, and crowded"; that it discouraged "enterprise ... independence ... straightforwardness and honesty"; and that it was rotting with "saloons and brothels [and] grimy factories and slums."[17]

In response to these beliefs, until the Second World War it was company policy at Eaton's, Simpson's, and the HBC to hire Canadian- and British-born white anglophones to staff customer-service positions. As a government investigation into unemployment observed in 1916, "There are few saleswomen of foreign extraction in Ontario."[18] Although the Dupuis Frères made a point of hiring francophones, the language of choice at Canada's other major department stores was English. So unilingual were most store employees that an HBC store inspector recommended in 1925 that the company's Winnipeg store hire "a few French salesclerks in order to cater to the French population in the city of St. Boniface, as none of our competitors specially cater to this trade."[19] Further, Canada's largest department stores rarely hired people who were not visibly Anglo-Celtic. In her history of Eaton's, Phenix recounts a story told her by "CBC newswriter Larry Zolf." To "pay Eaton's back for not hiring Jews or Slavs, he and a friend named Harold decided to steal wallets from the Winnipeg store."[20] Non-whites and non-Protestants were similarly rare in store workforces. As Cynthia Wright notes, "Jews and Roman Catholics were underrepresented" at Eaton's in the 1930s, especially when compared "with their numbers in the Toronto population."[21] Eaton's preferred to keep its white- and blue-collar labour forces Anglo-Celtic and Protestant, but it did hire small numbers of Jews and Italians to staff factory positions. The higher number of Jews and Italians in Eaton's factories compared to stores illustrates this company's preference to keep non-Anglo-Celtics out of customers' sight.[22]

To cultivate employees' purity, department stores offered a range of activities and programs designed to improve workers' bodies and minds. Sports were believed to create exuberant and attractive bodies, to uplift workers' hearts, and to generate store loyalty. Welfare workers also provided constant advice on how to maintain one's health. Throughout this period, welfare managers exhorted workers to eat nutritious food, get lots of rest, participate in wholesome recreational activities, dress properly, and even stand properly. In 1924, Eaton's inserted slips titled "Health Hints" into employees' pay envelopes (Figure 4.2). And at the 1926 annual meeting of the HBC's Vancouver Employee Association, "Dr. Ford, the Company's medical advisor," lectured attendants on "how to keep well, and how to get well after becoming sick."[23]

Department stores also followed a more direct route in their efforts to profit from employees' bodies: they advertised their workers' appearances. As early as 1905, Eaton's distributed a booklet titled *Eaton's Mail Order*

HEALTH HINTS

For the coming Winter we suggest the following rules of health which, if faithfully observed, should help to keep you well and safeguard the health of those about you, both at work and at home.

Rise in the morning in plenty of time to take a cold water sponge of the face, neck, chest and underarms. This will harden the skin and make you less susceptible to catching cold from sudden change of temperature in the house, street car, theatre, church, etc. Then eat a good breakfast. See that ankles and feet are kept warm and dry. Remember that fresh air and sunshine are nature's greatest health builders.

If you are subject to frequent cold, or have been suffering with one for some time, visit the Welfare Department.

ᵗʰᵉ T. EATON Cº. LIMITED

FIGURE 4.2   Insert in Eaton's Toronto employees' pay envelopes, 1924. | *Source:* Archives of Ontario, T. Eaton Papers, Series 171, Box 1. | Used with permission of Sears Canada Inc.

System, which explained the efficient and honest workings of its catalogue operations. The sixteen-page pamphlet contained seven photographs of groups of white male and female Eaton's employees, all neatly attired and working diligently in spacious, well-lit, and clean conditions. In department store illustrations, which represented ideals and not realities, Eaton's emphasis on workers' whiteness is especially apparent. Eaton's 1919 history book is filled with sketches of employees, and in each drawing, employees appear competent, attractive, efficient, and white (Figure 4.3).[24]

By advertising employees' "good breeding," as one Simpson's pamphlet for American tourists put it in 1931, department stores indicated their workers were wholesome and happy. As an Eaton's brochure stated in 1908, "Some people do not like the word 'factory' because they associate it with sweat-shop methods ... or with a constant whir of dust and noise. Our factories are simply gigantic work rooms where the best designers, cutters and operators ... gather every day in the pleasing occupation of making the very best of wearables." In 1911, Eaton's made department stores' rejection of racial and class degeneration explicit. In a booklet called *Evolution of a Store,* the company testified to its commitment to a

Figure 4.3   Illustration of male employees in Eaton's 1919 company history book. |
Source: Edith MacDonald [The Scribe], *Golden Jubilee, 1869-1919* (Toronto and Winnipeg: T.
Eaton Company, 1919), 199. | Used with permission of Sears Canada Inc.

particular kind of human progress. "The whipped-out, the tired, the de-
spondent, have no place at Eaton's. Store melancholia is a thing that has
never yet spread its microbes through this institution. Neither has it ever
had a labor strike." The pamphlet invited customers to "Note the air of
health, frankness and kindly self-reliance, coupled with a due deference,
on the faces of all workers." Eaton's claim of being strike-free is not entirely
accurate, for Eaton's Toronto printers did go on strike in 1902. Nevertheless, this pamphlet's suggestion that Eaton's workers were vigorous
and intelligent indicates the store's determination to prove its purity.
Evolution of a Store also announced that Eaton's buildings were equipped
with "light and good ventilation," which allowed the company's atmosphere to be "sweet and pure and wholesome." According to this booklet,
Eaton's employees were free of the cramped, dirty conditions associated
with metropolitan labour.[25]

Along with purity and docility, department stores emphasized employees' imperialism and nationalism. Before Eaton's male employees departed
for active service during the First World War, Eaton's Toronto and Winnipeg photography departments snapped their photographs and displayed
them in stores. According to Eaton's 1919 company history, the company
did this so that serving Eatonians would know they were "not forgotten."
Yet Eaton's was also conveying to shoppers that their employees were

FIGURE 4.4   Eaton's female employees' gymnastics event, 1919. | *Source:* William Stephenson, *The Store That Timothy Built* (Toronto: McClelland and Stewart, 1969), 81. | Used with permission of Sears Canada Inc.

fulfilling their proper patriotic duties. It thus attempted to extract value from employees' participation in the Great War. The HBC undertook similar actions. In the Christmas edition of the 1925 *Beaver,* it printed a two-page list of names of HBC employees who had aided the Allies' cause. Asterisks were placed beside those who had "died in the service of [their] Country." According to Jonathan Vance, this practice was common among Canadian businesses. Not only department stores, then, but other employers also attempted to profit from the bodily contributions that male workers made to the state.[26]

Female employees' bodies also appeared in publicity campaigns. After the war Eaton's hosted a public display of its Girls' Club members' bodies. The display occurred in an arena in Toronto, likely during an intermission of a male sporting event. The sports display would have featured male workers' virile and youthful bodies engaged in character-building activities. The female exposition also placed emphasis on virility and youth, but it also highlighted women's docility and ornamentality. In a dancing and gymnastics routine, Eaton's "girls" formed the words "For King & Country" with their bodies, to the appreciative applause of hundreds of spectators, including Eaton's dignitaries seated near the stage (Figure 4.4). Almost a decade later, Lady Eaton sponsored a similar event on her estate. She held a "May Festival," which was performed by youthful members of the EGC. Several spectators attended the "picturesque event," noted an Eaton advertisement. They witnessed "historic episodes of Spring from the time of the Druids ... in pageant, song and dance" and afterwards joined in "a song for England, and England's king and queen, as the players passed in procession" in front of them.[27] Both the "King & Country" event and the May Festival suggested Eaton's female workers were wholesome, dainty, and patriotic – visual embodiments of feminine purity and imperialist loyalty.

Department stores also used beauty contests and fashion shows to broadcast their female employees' attractiveness. *The Beaver* often reported that certain female individuals had been nominated by their department managers to enter local pageants. Underneath a photograph of four women, the February 1922 issue informed readers, "The above group of salesladies were selected to represent H.B.C." in the Edmonton *Journal* beauty contest. In this particular contest, prizes were to be awarded "to the group which the judges consider the best, not only for 'visibility' but also for [a] smart, business-like appearance." The HBC's entrants had a good chance of winning, claimed *The Beaver,* for they were "easy to look at and pretty hard to beat." By the interwar years, fashion shows had become staple components of the stores' public relations repertoire. Retailers occasionally employed professional models for these shows, but they more often featured their sales and clerical staff. As *The Beaver* wrote about a 1921 show, "The models who took part in the recent Fall opening ... have ... justified the reputation which the Edmonton branch holds for staging events successfully ... without going outside for talent ... In conversation with an Eastern manufacturer ... we had ... difficulty ... convincing him that the models were amateurs, selected from the sales-ladies of the store."[28]

The women who participated in beauty contests and fashion shows likely did so to have fun, to engage in creative forms of self-display, and to showcase their bodies and perhaps their sexuality. In this sense the contests and shows were inventive venues in which women workers took on alternative, and perhaps more exciting and glamorous, personas than those experienced in day-to-day life. Yet it must be remembered that department stores orchestrated these events and profited from the proceeds. They also promulgated the notion that women's success depended on attire and appearance. The titles and the scripts of the shows usually connected fashion and beauty with adventure and fulfillment, as did Eaton's 1934

Winnipeg show, titled "Windswept, Streamlined, and Going Places!" The shows did not challenge the presumption that women should display their bodies so that men could judge their appearance. Indeed, in a report on an HBC Edmonton fashion show, *The Beaver*'s editor offered the following: "New suits, hats, wraps, ... dresses and sumptuous Hudson's Bay furs were charmingly displayed by a bevy of pretty models chosen from among the girls of the store ... The girls ... captured the hearts of spectators."[29]

Commodification Epitomized: Salespeople

Of all department store employees, salespeople were the most commodified. Working at the heart of the commodity exchange, salespeople were under intense customer scrutiny. As early as 1908, Eaton's in Toronto was receiving regular complaints about its sales staff's demeanour, activities, and statements. Recognizing that sellers had the potential to influence browsers' opinions and purchasing decisions, Eaton's, Simpson's, and the HBC invested much time, money, and effort in ensuring that their sales forces appeared as attractive to customers as possible. In the nineteenth and early twentieth centuries, this responsibility fell to owners, department managers, and welfare workers. Often, owners posted lists of wrongdoings for which employees would be punished. A 1900 Eaton's poster, titled "Misdemeanors," was typical.

Assembling in groups of two or more for conversation.

Speaking with a salesman or saleswoman except on unavoidable business.

Striking a Cash Boy.

Reading Newspapers, letters or books, or writing letters.

Eating while at the counters or departments.

Loafing or spending unnecessary time ... away from your department.

Standing, sitting, or lounging on counters or shelves is particularly prohibited.

...

Cleaning or scraping the finger-nails while at the counters ...

Chewing gum or tobacco or spitting on the floor.

Driving nails or tacks about the counters ... scribbling on walls ...

Lighting matches in any part of the store ...

Ringing bells, or using speaking tubes without necessity ...

Mutilating or otherwise injuring ... property of the store.

Loud, noisy talk: fooling or quarrelling ...

The suppression of any fact that should be known to the Management.

The notice warned, "A deliberate careless, or willful violation of any of the above rules will render ... employees liable to an immediate discharge."[30]

Owners and managers also regulated salespeople's attire. It was mandatory for clerks at Eaton's, Simpson's, and the HBC to wear simple, chaste, and dark-coloured – preferably black – garments. This kind of garb helped customers to identify employees, but it also indicated that employees were respectful and respectable. *The Beaver* noted, "Customers Don't Like ... to see untidy people about the stores." Eaton's Winnipeg publication similarly declared, "Untidy clothes mean you don't care what [customers] think of your appearance ... But don't dress too well – that gives you an air of showing off." And an Eaton's training manual asserted, "A well-dressed business-like appearance is not obtained by wearing bright colours or extreme styles."[31]

Welfare workers were responsible for developing salespeople's pleasing appearance and behaviour. Through skills development classes, physical recreation programs, and regular medical evaluations, welfare workers tried to make customer-service employees polite, enthusiastic, intelligent, and physically attractive. In 1934, *Contacts* urged employees to "study the art" of cosmetics before applying makeup "since its proper use is of vital importance to those who would keep 'young and beautiful'– as well as those who would succeed in the business world." In 1937, Simpson's offered its employees a "Self-Teaching Course in Practical English and Effective Speech," intended to help workers "[learn] correct usage of English, and enlarg[e] their vocabularies." To further ensure salespeople's profitability, in the 1910s, Eaton's Toronto store created an Efficiency Department. Its experts provided "new employees with ... training in methods and merchandise." The department also paid for university extension courses in fields related to department store work. By the Great Depression, each of Canada's largest department stores was operating formal training departments. Like stores in France, these appeared approximately twenty years behind those in major US stores. Staff trainers held merchandising sessions as well as distributed booklets and magazines to sales employees, in attempts to perfect sellers' profitability.[32]

If employees' personas were regulated at the turn of the twentieth century, by the interwar years they were even more so. Within international sales-training literature, it had become a truism that shoppers judged a store's value, and hence its products, by evaluating salespeople's looks, attitudes, and capabilities. "In our manner, our speech and in our general bearing we are constantly making impressions on our customers," noted Eaton's *Employees' Book of Information* in 1933. Trainers bombarded sellers with messages on how to groom themselves and how to behave. Hands received especial attention. "Your hands – the two silent salesmen who are forever with you," Eaton's proclaimed in 1933, "often by their graceful and dainty manner convince the customer of the merits of the displayed merchandise." Since employees' hands had the power to enhance and diminish the value of a commodity, managers urged workers to "give oneself a home manicure." Eaton's recommended regimen included using "a strong nail brush every night," "shap[ing] the nail tips," "shap[ing] the cuticles," "apply[ing] the polish," and "massag[ing] the cuticle."[33]

Sales experts also taught sellers what to say. Winnipeg's Eaton magazine urged readers to use fifty-seven sentences that were sure to sell "a piece of merchandise *more times* than any other sentence." These included, "These ties will not wrinkle," "This tablecloth saves laundry bills," and "This dress is unusually slenderizing." Eaton's Winnipeg staff magazine also tried to guide employees' selling strategies. "Don't sell things ... *sell happiness,*" one article stated, and then continued: "Don't sell clothes – sell personal appearance and attractiveness ... Don't sell furniture – sell a home that has comfort and refinement and the joy of living. Don't sell toys – sell gifts that will make children happy ... Don't sell books – sell the profits of knowledge ... Don't sell radio sets ... sell the beauty of music."[34]

During the 1930s, driven by fears of declining profits, Eaton's trainers began applying principles of scientific management to the sales trans-action. They studied the selling process objectively and picked apart its various stages. Taking their cue from developments in US sales literature, they began telling salespeople that each sale had three steps: "1. Ap-proaching and greeting ... 2. Presenting the merchandise ... 3. Concluding the sale." Staff-training literature discussed each of these stages and broke them down into further categories. In one discussion of stage two, trainers gave advice on what to do when the customer asks for an article not in stock, when the customer does not state how much she is willing to pay, when the customer provides a price limit, when the customer asks for an item out of her price range, when the customer asks the price of an article, when the customer says "she" is just looking, when the salesperson is deal-ing with more than one customer, when the customer wants to see an entire line of merchandise and, finally, when a customer wants to see more than one type of product. By dissecting the sales transaction, trainers hoped to make customers and salespeople act according to a script, which they could then study further and modify.[35]

Breaking down the process of selling into smaller parts constituted a reification of salespeople's work. According to Georg Lukács, reification is caused by "the mathematical analysis of work-processes." When work is divided into the smallest units possible, "the inorganic, irrational and qualitatively determined unity" of goods and services is sundered. This sundering creates a reification – or a quantification and rigidization – of capitalist-dwellers' experiences. By choreographing sales floor life, Eaton's removed sellers' opportunities for creative skill development. It also made salespeople act artificially, opening up the possibility that they would start feeling alienated from their own intuitions and specific abilities.[36]

BETWEEN 1890 AND 1940, Canada's largest retailers used employees' activities, bodies, and appearances in advertising and publicity. They also saturated employees' experiences with encouragement to consume and reified the point of sale. Department stores paid employees for their time and skills, but they attempted to capitalize on much more, commodifying their activities, appearance, and propensity to consume. By using workers' beings to increase the worth of the store's product and image, and by selling goods to workers, department stores tried to gain more value from the employment contract than what had been agreed upon. Commodification was thus an unacknowledged form of exploitation.

As the appeal of fordism declines, it is imperative that scholars continue the inquiry into how employers' need to sell goods influences their treatment of workers. Between 1890 and 1940, Canadian department stores sought to create a workplace culture of consumerist loyalty. This culture would have pressured employees to consume in order to belong. They would have bullied employees to identify with their company and its products and hence to accept paternalism and avoid unionization. Department store advertising of employees' activities and bodies would also have had negative effects. It is likely that Eaton's, Simpson's, and the HBC's exhortations for employees to conform to particular body types and behaviours made some feel inferior and others feel angry. This would have been the case particularly for the minority of workers who were neither conventionally attractive nor white. As well, the stores' careful engineering of sales floor interactions prevented some workers from controlling their work process, which might have led to bitterness and despondency. Further, although the retailers' utilization of employees' behaviour and appearance in publicity materials might have made some employees proud, it could have made other employees feel their personal lives had been raided for someone else's gain. Finally, the retailers' bombardment of employees' lives with advertisements might have made some employees feel inadequate. Since the purpose of advertising is to create needs, those who absorbed their employer's message but who could not afford to constantly consume might have felt unfulfilled.

By hiring predominantly white workers who conformed to bourgeois expectations of working-class servitude and who were conventionally sexually attractive, department stores affirmed class, racial, and sexual hierarchies in modernizing Canada. They also demonstrated that those whose appearance matched prevailing race, class, and gender ideals had better chances of employment success. Today, this situation appears to have eased. Pluralism has made some headway in recent decades, and some retailers have made a point of hiring non-white workers. Nonetheless, it is true that whiteness remains an asset for people seeking customer service jobs. Class subordination likewise remains central to service work. Job seekers who present themselves as amenable to the goals of the bourgeoisie will have greater success in finding jobs than those who make potentially threatening views and behaviours known. Of course, if a retailer desires to portray itself as oppositional, it will hire people who dress and behave unconventionally. Yet if customer service workers today speak out against their employers, they usually find themselves fired or pressured to quit. Thus, whiteness, heterosexual attractiveness, and acceptance of class subordination remain factors in customer service employment.

5
Shopping, Pleasure, and Power

Those same catalogues make me long to be rich.

*– Female customer in a letter
to Eaton's, 1934*

WESTERN THINKERS HAVE LONG associated women with desire and lust. "Beginning with Eve," writes Elizabeth Kowaleski-Wallace, "*women* with appetites have had a special place in literary and popular lore." Yet it was only during the rise of consumer culture that the stereotype of women as ravenous consumers emerged. Women in eighteenth-century English literature "were assumed to be hungry for things – for dresses and furniture, for tea cups and carriages, for all commodities that indulged the body and enhanced physical life." As shopping became more prevalent, female retail patrons were caricatured as voracious consumers.[1] Canadian female shoppers did not escape this fate. In her 1912 novel, *House of Windows,* set in a fictionalized Toronto and featuring a fictionalized Eaton's, author Isabel Mackay confirms readers' suspicions. After a busy ribbons sale, one clerk says to another, "Did you ever see anything like that scramble for the sash ribbons ... At noon to-day three women had hold of the same piece. They fought for it like dogs for a bone."[2]

More recent commentaries on consumption have depicted female consumers as dupes of capitalism. During the 1960s and 1970s, some leftist theorists portrayed consumption as a tool of capitalist manipulation. Similarly, some second-wave feminists suggested that the glitziness of consumer capitalism made women blind to gender subordination. Portrayals of victimized female consumers rightfully highlighted the power of business to shape consumer culture, but they also depicted women and consumption as "dependent, manipulated, conforming, and captive."[3] Stereotypes of passive consuming women hence reinforced the equation of femininity with submission and irrationality. They also discouraged researchers from inquiring into other, more complex factors behind consumer motivation. Notes William Leach, the equation of consumption with acquiescence "cannot account for the way early consumer capitalism ... secured the loyalties of otherwise intelligent, resourceful, and thoughtful women."[4]

During the 1980s and 1990s, in response to images of women as spendthrifts, on the one hand, and victimized consumers, on the other, feminist historians conducted extensive investigations into consumption. Seeking to counter stereotypes as well as to understand when and why women became consumers, scholars now generally agree that consumption cannot be understood without attending to the rise of the West's gendered political economy. Until the Renaissance, European thinkers viewed luxury as vain and degenerate. Yet in the eighteenth century they began questioning this belief. Mercantilists argued that consumption, while distasteful, stimulated production. Consumerism was hence useful to manufacturing interests and crucial to wealth creation. In 1776, Adam Smith argued in *The Wealth of Nations* that consumption was "the sole end and purpose of all production." In Smith's opinion, the one stimulated "capital investment" while the other reproduced the "social system." Smith viewed the former as masculine and the latter as feminine. In *The Theory of Moral Sentiments* (1759) Smith had worried that manufacturers were producing irrelevant goods, "fitter for the playthings of children than the serious pursuits of men." Private consumption was a feminine activity, a necessary evil that threatened the moral health of the nation.[5]

As the market economy evolved, production and consumption became more distinct. *Laissez faire* capitalism depended on the belief that production and consumption were different economic realms, the former made profitable by the movement of commodities between them. Two further developments sealed the separation of production from consumption and made the gender of each explicit. The first, states Victoria de Grazia, was the "identification of wage labor with male labor." As men left the household to take up industrial jobs, production came to be associated with masculinity. Conversely, private consumption was connected with the household, and women were charged with acquiring goods. The second was the development of the civic sphere. The "commercial revolution" of the eighteenth century spawned such meeting places as "printing houses, markets and bourses, salons, and cafés," which were distinct from those sites that gave rise to "canons of courtly taste and religious authority." Ideals of liberal democracy and citizenship were born in this new sphere.

According to de Grazia, as "a civilizing politics of right out of which con-stitutional government and modern political systems eventually evolved," it "operated against [the older] moral economy ... ruled by a primitive politics of needs and desires." Women were identified with the older moral economy but excluded from the new public realm. Shepherdesses of the private, they fulfilled household needs and consumer desires. They ac-quired necessities and status-laden goods, the latter essential to the forma-tion of bourgeois class identity.[6]

Not only have feminist researchers gone some way toward revealing the roots of bourgeois women's consumer subjectivities, but they have also inquired into more recent motivations behind women's consumer actions. Historians now know that shopping emerged as a specifically female activ-ity in the middle of the nineteenth century. Whereas aristocratic women had long viewed patronizing upscale shops as pleasurable, only in the nineteenth century did browsing in shops become a source of sociability and leisure for women of the bourgeoisie and petite bourgeoisie. Depart-ment stores' free-entry and unlimited browsing policies, together with their additions of restaurants, lavatories, and nurseries, did much to popularize shopping. So did women's own growing desire to escape the confines of domesticity and to experience urban adventures. Shopping enabled middle-class women to appear in public, alone or with friends, without sacrificing their reputations.[7]

Feminist scholarship also provides insight into the consumption of domestic items. When working people moved into factory jobs in the mid-nineteenth century, less time was available for making food and cloth-ing. Concomitantly, workers' receipt of money wages encouraged them to spend their earnings on low-priced essentials in the consumer market-place. Middle-class women, too, purchased household requirements, not only for necessity but also for display. Yet for many women, domestic consumption was not only about necessities and status. It was also about "play." When postwar Canadian homemakers brought furniture into their homes, they "domesticated" it by incorporating it into their decorating schemes and assigning it the values of "stability" and "identity." In this way, consumption became a creative outlet, allowing women to express their identity.[8]

Drawing on recent feminist investigations, this chapter explores female customers' relationships with Canada's largest department stores between 1890 and 1940. It asks not only why women went shopping at Canada's largest retailers but also how they perceived department stores. In doing so, it corroborates other works that find that women's consumer roles must be understood in relation to their subordinate gender status, their household responsibilities, and their need to devote attention to their appearance. Yet this chapter also takes existing scholarship in new directions. In her analysis of male managers, female customers, and female employees in American department stores before 1940, Susan Porter Benson finds that managers' desires for productivity, coupled with views of female shoppers as capricious, created frustrating shopping experiences for women. Customers also had power on the sales floor, however. Writes Benson, "the microcosm of the department store created a more nearly equal balance of power" between men and women than could be found in general American society.[9] Unfortunately, and perhaps because of the extensive paternalist systems developed at Canada's big stores, female customers wielded less influence north of the Canada-US border. Because of the gendered hierarchies of Eaton's, Simpson's, the HBC, and other stores, managers treated female customers condescendingly. Many women's shopping expeditions to Canada's largest stores therefore resulted in disappointment, inefficiency, and anger.[10]

Canada's female shoppers experienced alienation in other ways, too. Sometimes going shopping and reading catalogues reminded patrons they could never afford the goods for which they longed. At other times, shoppers encountered wealthier customers than themselves, which caused them to feel inadequate. And sometimes department stores discriminated against customers of racialized and ethnic backgrounds. This chapter thus urges feminist historians of consumption to keep issues of power and oppression at the forefront of their research. Women who patronized Canada's largest retailers hoped to acquire goods and services necessary to sustain their families as well as to reflect their social status. They also hoped to fulfill more intangible aspirations, including desires for companionship, recognition, and social success. Yet because of consumer capitalism's enduring gender, racial, ethnic, and class hierarchies, shopping too often became a source of discrimination and disappointment.

Department Stores' Customers
The financial achievements of Morgan's, Simpson's, Eaton's, the HBC, and other department stores between the 1890s and the 1930s suggest that the stores' massive campaigns to capture Canadians' consumer dollars were successful. Yet who were the people that shopped at the giant retailers? In her dissertation on Eaton's, Wright argues that "the limitations of

the evidence available" make it difficult to determine "with any precision" Eaton's customers' "class, ethnic, and gender composition." At the same time, she notes that Eaton's College Street believed "the customer was most commonly assumed to be a woman, and in particular a well-heeled Anglo-Canadian woman." Wright also cites evidence to demonstrate that immigrants, low-income people, francophones, and men shopped at Eaton's stores in Toronto and Winnipeg.[11]

Canada's largest stores indeed reached a diverse market. Given that in 1930 Eaton's, Simpson's, and the HBC captured 12.7 percent of all retail dollars spent in Canada, this is not particularly surprising.[12] Customers' race, ethnic, regional, and class affiliations varied from store to store, though. In late-nineteenth-century Toronto, bourgeois women preferred Simpson's over Eaton's. Lady Aberdeen, wife of Canada's governor general, noted in her 1896 diary that Eaton's of Toronto was a "great cheap store," unlike Simpson's, which was "a beautifully arranged place with lots of air & light." As well, Morgan's in Montréal was known for its haute couture status. Non-affluent people considered it snobby, and working-class francophones avoided it altogether. Michel Tremblay observes in his novel *La grosse femme d'à côté est enceinte,* set in the 1940s, that women from Montréal's East End imagined many department stores on St. Catherine's Street, including not only Morgan's but also Simpson's and Ogilvy's, as "le grand inconnu: l'anglais, l'argent."[13]

Affluent people therefore constituted a significant portion of the department store market. Internal correspondence generated at Eaton's College Street house furnishings store in Toronto, built in 1930 and aimed at bourgeois customers, reveals that wealthy Torontonians spent thousands of dollars, sometimes monthly, on Eaton's interior-decorating services. Meanwhile, country-wide advertisements dating from 1890 through 1940 for such items as grand pianos, original artwork, designer clothing, one-of-a-kind "Oriental" rugs, and hardwood furniture suites – along with the complaints that department stores received regarding these items – also demonstrate that prosperous Canadians all over the dominion patronized the giant retailers.[14] Nevertheless, most of department stores' patrons came from more modest backgrounds. Before Eaton's achieved national stature, the company catered to working-class and rural people. To draw these women to his store, Eaton sold "small staples" like "buttons, gloves, bonnets, [and] underwear." In the early 1900s, he began holding "Limited Time Only" sales of skirts, each priced for a dollar. These sales were timed to coincide with railway workers' paydays, usually around the seventeenth

Figure 5.1   Shoppers waiting for Eaton's Toronto store to open on Friday Bargain Day, 1905. | *Source:* Archives of Ontario, T. Eaton Papers, Series 308, Item 401. | Used with permission of Sears Canada Inc.

of each month. The sales came to be known as the "Glorious 17th," and according to Eaton's archivist Dorothy Keene, they attracted so many people that customers fought over selections. Some even wore their acquisitions home. Non-affluent Toronto and Winnipeg women also looked forward to Eaton's "Friday Bargain Days," held at the turn of the twentieth century (Figure 5.1). Into the 1940s, Eaton's stores attracted price-conscious consumers. When conducting oral history research among women who lived through the Great Depression in Toronto, Katrina Srigley found that Eaton's "was undeniably the store of choice" among female wage earners. Similarly, in 1969, an elderly customer told President John David Eaton that his flagship Toronto store had been a lifelong destination of choice. She had enjoyed its "nice lunch and afternoon tea room."[15]

Mail order customers were especially budget-conscious. In 1968 a customer from Yarmouth, Nova Scotia, told William Stephenson that when she was a child, her mother and other "ladies" would gather at "a neighbour's house." Each one would "[put] in a little shopping[,] enough to make a twenty five dollar order." Since Eaton's paid freight on orders over twenty-five dollars, they were careful about the total price. They would even divide among themselves the price of the postage stamp. During the Depression one woman on the Prairies was "so broke" that in order to purchase clothing, she sent Eaton's whatever small coins she had – one time she sent eighty-seven cents – and asked the mail order department to look around for items that would match her budget.[16]

Despite many department stores' Anglo-Celtic image, not all customers were white and anglophone. Noted one customer in a 1963 letter to Eaton's, during the early twentieth century, "natives" in "north central British Columbia" made so many catalogue purchases from Eaton's in Toronto that their orders "swamped" the trains. Urban British Columbian shoppers, too, were of diverse backgrounds. According to the *Vancouver Province,* more than ten thousand people attended a 1908 damaged goods sale at Woodward's. Among the customers one could hear "English, French, German, Italian, Greek," and "Scandinavian" languages, as well as "the soft brogue of the Irish and the sharp twang of the Yankee, the broad vowels of Yorkshire and the aitchless snap of the Londoner." Chinese, Japanese, and Hindi were also being spoken. In Toronto during the interwar years, domestic servants of Finnish background patronized Eaton's College Street, as did working-class women of Italian and African descent. One African Canadian dressmaker even advised her clients to purchase dresses from Eaton's and to bring them to her for altering. And according to a 1943 newspaper article, all ethnicities of rural Manitoba were present on Fridays and Saturdays in Eaton's Winnipeg store's waiting room. "There will be plenty of Scotch ... One hears quite a bit of German, too ... Then there are the Ukrainians ... you will also find lively French-Canadians." The article also took note of customers' class affiliations. "There are prosperous-looking men whose wives wear fur coats and whose children are warmly and attractively clad. And there are the not-so-prosperous, those whose clothes are threadbare."[17]

If not all customers were affluent English-speaking whites, neither were they all women. The same *Province* article that described the 1908 Woodward's sale noted that "a surging mob of men and women" had crowded the store's opening on the morning of the event. Twenty-seven years later and across the continent, male customer W.T. Sands told the *Moncton Transcript* that he had been a loyal Eaton's catalogue customer since 1885. Letters to department stores also provide evidence of male patronage. In 1934, Charles Stephenson wrote to Eaton's to say that he had bought a pair of wool blankets from Eaton's in Toronto in 1898 and had used them "while prospecting and hunting in the Kootenays." Thirty-six years later they were still in "good condition." The HBC, too, received letters testifying to individual men's loyalty. In 1948, B.L. Williams of Vancouver, who had not yet received his complimentary annual calendar, wrote a letter to the HBC, saying he certainly deserved one as he had been a customer for "over forty years." And in 1953, Fred Paine of Alberta wrote, "I have lived in Calgary since 1905, purchasing from the Bay anything I needed."[18]

Yet, despite men's patronage of department stores, there was a widespread assumption that women, not men, belonged inside the giant retailers. After Eaton's opened in Winnipeg in 1905, the *Tribune* ran a full-page spread about the event. Noted the article, "It might naturally have been expected that the fair sex would form the great majority" of Eaton's opening day patrons, but "the crowd seemed to be about evenly divided between the sexes." After acknowledging men's interest in the store, the paper covered women's but not men's reactions to the new shopping space, underscoring the author's assumption that, despite men's apparent interest in the store, women were Eaton's natural customers: "How the ladies lingered over the departments where the beautiful dress goods, millinery, etc., were displayed."[19] Other English Canadian periodicals also typically portrayed department stores as feminine spaces. In 1927 the University of Alberta's student newspaper, *The Gateway,* printed a humour piece titled "Christmas Shopping," about a male student's trip to a department store to buy gifts. The humour of the article rests in the assumption that men did not belong in this shopping space. After passing the store "several times" and making "several false starts," the narrator "dashed inside." He instantly regretted it, for "the place was filled with women," and when they caught sight of him, "all eyes ... focussed on me." He eventually made it out safely, but not before experiencing a series of embarrassments that turned on his unfamiliarity with the feminine world of mass retail.[20]

If Canada's biggest stores were presumed to cater to women, there was also a belief that English-speaking Protestants were their preferred customers. References in complaint letters indicate that some Canadians appreciated the stores' English, Protestant images. Two years into the

Second World War, Eaton's Toronto store received a letter from Stuart Somerville of Ottawa. It was a letter of congratulations, and also of warning: "It is refreshing to peruse your catalogue without the insult of Bi-Lingualism," he wrote. "The french language is the Roman Church's expression in Canada. It must not get too good a hold, if we want unity." When the Eaton's employee who opened it forwarded Somerville's letter to management, he observed that Somerville was certainly "not aware of our French Catalogue!" The HBC also received letters from anti-Catholic customers. In 1950, Vancouver customer Doris Ashdown wrote a complaint to the general manager. She believed the recent "discourtesy of employees" in the store could be attributed to the fact that "the [store] manager and a number of executives are R.C.'s."[21]

Department Stores and Domestic Labour

Whether they approved of Canada's largest stores' English Canadian and Protestant image, women all over Canada did patronize the big shops. Between 1890 and 1940, they were in fact department stores' most numerous clientele. The nineteenth-century emphasis on domesticity, combined with husbands and sons increasingly choosing to earn wages in the industrial and commercial sectors, left wives and daughters responsible for their households' domestic labour. The influx of wages into households, the increasing availability of low-cost domestic items, and the growing tendency to conflate status and fulfillment with material goods all encouraged wives and daughters to forego aspects of domestic production and secure household products in the marketplace.[22]

When buying domestic goods, Canadian rural, working-class, and petit bourgeois women balanced conflicting demands of affordability and quality. Budgeting had become women's responsibility in many parts of Canada in the late nineteenth and early twentieth centuries. Some rural and working-class women preferred shopping at local retailers because they could obtain much-needed credit and they could trade farm products for factory ones. Others, though, began patronizing the stores that offered competitive prices. These women generally had access to more income than poorer women, as stores with low prices often sold for cash only. Poorer women continued to seek out shops that offered credit. Nonetheless, working-class and rural women of all income levels did begin shopping at low-priced retailers. It is therefore significant that Canada's largest department stores, especially Eaton's, offered the lowest prices on household staples across Canada. They also offered a range of styles and a quality of goods that independent retailers could not match. Department stores' return policies were also competitive, making them appealing to budget-conscious shoppers.[23]

Left-wing critics and independent merchants grumbled that working-class and rural wives and daughters who patronized department stores destroyed the livelihoods of craftspeople and independent merchants. Yet most female shoppers did not heed these concerns. As Dana Frank also notes with regard to working-class women in Seattle between 1919 and 1929, Canadian working-class and rural wives were responsible for securing affordable and high-quality goods for their families. Their quest for such items encouraged them to patronize merchants who promised the best deals. They therefore passed up local shops in favour of mass retailers. As Mrs. F.E. Horwood of Riverside, Ontario, told Eaton's in 1941, "I have always found your goods superior in quality to what I could get at the same price anywhere in town."[24]

When assessing quality, shoppers looked for both durability and style. Major department stores offered commodities that were long-lasting and aesthetically pleasing. Conceptions of style, of course, were relative. Better-heeled shoppers looked down on the merchandise offered by Eaton's catalogue. A wealthy Port Arthur, Ontario, customer informed the company, "the Catalogue things are usually rather cheap, + when I want better ones, I frequently write [to Eaton's personal shopping service in Toronto]." Yet other customers believed Eaton's catalogue merchandise to be fashionable. Vera McIntosh of Duntroon, Ontario, felt that Eaton's styles were "graceful" and that "the whole catalogue [was] made up of the latest styles in everything." For McIntosh, style was irrelevant if goods were not durable or affordable. The "quality of [Eaton's] goods make them last so much longer and yet they stay lovely, till they're worn out ... The prices are low enough to let each individual have many frocks or suits which they admire."[25]

Since they placed a premium on durability, budget-conscious shoppers spent money at stores that offered long-lasting goods. Eaton's archival records are sprinkled with letters from customers who wrote to congratulate the company on the resilience of its merchandise. Throughout the twentieth century, people wrote to Eaton's to inform the corporation that items purchased twenty, thirty, even fifty years previously were still in mint condition. Once in 1939 and once in 1982, two different customers informed Eaton's that drapes they had purchased from the company were still being used. The 1939 customer's drapes were seventeen years old, and the 1982 customer's were fifty years old. Other customers living in villages and farms in Ontario, Manitoba, and Saskatchewan wrote to congratulate Eaton's on the quality of a twenty-one-year-old iron stand, a twenty-one-year-old toaster, a twenty-one-year-old cream separator, a thirty-five-year-old set of parlour furniture, a thirty-five-year-old dining room set, and a forty-four-year-old set of framed prints, all of which were still in use at the time. Like the female shoppers in Parr's study of postwar Canadian consumption, these customers made longevity central to their purchasing decisions. This conservationism was not radical, but it did go against the interests of retailers and manufacturers, who encouraged frequent purchasing and who promoted accelerated capitalist accumulation through their practice of commodity obsolescence.[26]

When making consumer choices, women factored in the attitudes of particular retailers. Many preferred to shop at Eaton's because they believed the company was fair. "I have dealt with you ever since you built the Winnipeg store," Mrs. Thom T. Nixon of Wapella, Saskatchewan, told Eaton's in 1934. She had "come to depend on the goods so much" that she "scarcely" bought "dry goods from any other place." Eaton's policy of substituting out-of-stock goods with goods of superior quality was legendary. Remembered Mrs. E.R. Reinhardt of Asquith, Saskatchewan, in 1969, "You always sent a better dress for the dress sent for. It was often the one I really wanted but didn't think I could afford!" Christian customers associated Eaton's policies with its founding family's religiosity. Mrs. William Lees from Kisby, Saskatchewan, shopped at Eaton's in Toronto prior to her late-nineteenth-century migration to the Prairies. Thirty years later she was still loyal. "I dealt with Mr. Timothy Eaton when he had the little store," she told the Winnipeg manager, "and I knew him personally as a Christian gentleman."[27]

Employees' attitudes were just as important. In 1920, *The Beaver* published the results of a survey of 197 households regarding their reasons for no longer spending money at particular stores. Forty-seven responded that the "indifference of salespeople" was their major motivation. Another eighteen responded that "errors" caused them to switch retailers. Sixteen stated "over-insistence of salespeople" was the chief factor, sixteen decided "insolence of salespeople" was key, and six replied that "ignorance concerning goods" was a primary reason. More than half of the survey's respondents stopped shopping at certain retailers, then, because they found employees' behaviour disagreeable. Letters to Eaton's also indicate the importance placed by customers on courtesy, intelligence, and efficiency. Stated Alice H. Rogers in 1940, "I appreciate tremendously also the very kind and efficient help given to me by saleslady no. 617. She went to a great deal of trouble to satisfy every detail of my order." Agreeable salesclerks were welcome, but disagreeable ones were not. Mrs. Georgina Leonard of Sault Ste. Marie liked shopping by catalogue better than going to the store. As she explained in a letter to Eaton's, "there [are] no clerks breathing over my neck, expecting me to hurry and pick something out or move on."[28]

Mail order was the preferred method of shopping for many Canadians. Mothers with small children used catalogues to purchase what were deemed to be essentials because catalogues were convenient. Rural women appreciated catalogue services even more. Houses in a logging camp at Claydon Bay, British Columbia, were all built on rafts. During the interwar years, women in this community "bought all our groceries, and dry goods, as well as hardware" from Woodward's catalogue, as one former resident explained. Rural dwellers east of the Rockies usually patronized Toronto-based mail order companies. In 1968 one woman from Pugwash, Nova Scotia, remembered her parents' orders to Eaton's. "My Father moved here with my Mother and Family in 1904. We depended on Eaton's at that time for nearly every thing, we would send for a $25.00 order, Groceries, & Clothing ... We bought Coffee beans, lye laundry soap."[29] Rural wives liked catalogues because they could shop from home and because they could buy everything they needed at once.[30]

Housewives were responsible for cooking, cleaning, clothing the family, and decorating. Department stores offered affordable and high-quality goods that aided all of these tasks; they also provided reasonably efficient, generous, and convenient services. Wrote one Grand Falls, New Brunswick, customer in 1958, "I got all my good from eaton [sic], from clothes to furniture most of it on budget, I been doing business with Eaton for 35 years since I got marry, and I had eight children. Everything I have in the house except, singer sewing machine, and frigidair, it come from Eaton." Consumption of prepared foodstuffs, ready-to-wear clothes, and factory-made textile products such as curtains and tablecloths increased throughout the twentieth century. Yet, into the Second World War and beyond, Canadian women also purchased raw materials to make household products. In the spring they purchased chicks from Eaton's, and in the fall they slaughtered the fowl to feed their families and earn money in local markets. Seeds were bought and turned into gardens. Yarns and threads became sweaters, socks, blankets, curtains, tablecloths, and doilies. Textiles and notions became clothing.[31]

Correspondence reveals that some women did not enjoy being full-time homemakers. In a 1976 letter, prompted by the closure of Eaton's mail order, Mrs. Daisy Waddell described her childhood in interwar prairie Canada. When she was growing up, she wanted to become "a great artist." Yet her parents discouraged her: "I was told it would be better if I aspired to be an artist in making apple pies – (which incidentally I did become!)." As Waddell's letter reveals, many women perceived homemaking to be their only financial and cultural option. To make their lives more enjoyable, some Eaton's customers turned domestic labour into a creative activity. One young woman who had grown up in southwestern Ontario moved with her new husband in 1913 to rural Saskatchewan, where she subsequently experienced loneliness and displacement. She comforted herself through sewing. Recalled her daughter, "The first year mother was married she raised turkeys and with the money she bought herself a beautiful new 'seamstress' sewing machine [from Eaton's] ... how delighted she was with it ... oh the dresses, aprons, petticoats it turned out!" Like the women in Parr's study, these women made mandatory domestic labour more enjoyable by turning it into an outlet for creative expression.[32]

As a component of domestic labour, shopping was a respectable social activity in which homemakers could engage. Travelling by themselves, with friends, or with their children to department stores, women could purchase household goods and enjoy relatively worry-free and inexpensive hours away from their homes. Department stores' merchandise departments offered socializing opportunities, for in them women could interact freely with other shoppers; they could also engage in limited conversations with store employees. Department store nurseries enabled women to enjoy quick breaks from child-minding responsibilities, and department store restaurants gave those who could afford them some refreshing moments of respite. Noted a Woodward's advertisement in 1903, "Shoppers who desire a cup of tea or other light refreshment can simply take the elevator to the top floor [and] have their lunch." Photographs of customers in Eaton's Toronto Cafeteria and Grill Room in Toronto in 1910 attest that women with small and large budgets alike took advantage of the company's dining options. Whereas the cafeteria customers wear modest coats and hats, the Grill Room patrons are lavishly dressed (Figures 5.2 and 5.3). Especially before the 1920s, department stores played an important role

FIGURE 5.2　Eaton's Fifth Floor Cafeteria in Toronto, 1910. | *Source:* T. Eaton Company Papers, Series 308, File 2304. | Used with permission of Sears Canada Inc.

FIGURE 5.3　Eaton's Grill Room in Toronto, 1910. | *Source:* T. Eaton Papers, Series 308, Item 2319-i. | Used with permission of Sears Canada Inc.

in women's downtown excursions. Not only were they among the only buildings to offer free lavatories for women, but they were also among the only places, besides costly members-only clubs, where women could dine alone or with female friends. Saloons did offer meals, but these establishments catered primarily to men. Upscale hotel restaurants were more welcoming of women, particularly middle-class white ones, but most women did not feel comfortable entering these premises without a male escort.[33]

In addition, women from towns and rural areas used shopping expeditions to cities as opportunities for adventure. Eaton's archive contains an early-twentieth-century letter from a wife to her husband, Charlie, written on the free stationery that Eaton's had provided in its Toronto Writing and Rest Room. "I arrived safely and got to my boarding place about 2 o'clock and went straight to Eaton's," she assured her spouse. After writing about dining sets offered by Eaton's and other stores, she related, "I have not been to Simpson's yet am ... going this evening. The Y.W.C.A. is very nice and easy walking distance to Eaton's. I called up at J.C. Wells last evening," she wrote, adding "Love to the girls." This shopping trip enabled the writer to fulfill homemaking tasks while also taking a short vacation from domestic obligations. Not only individual female out-of-towners but also groups made special excursions to department stores. During the 1931 annual convention of the Woman's Christian Temperance Union in Toronto, for example, delegates could choose to join "specially organized shopping tours and luncheon[s] at T. Eaton Co., and Robert Simpson Co."[34]

Some women used department store catalogues not because they enjoyed them, but because their children did. Rural Canadians treated Eaton's catalogues as entertainment for their offspring. Children made paper dolls and clothes from catalogues, used catalogues as colouring books, and clipped household items to decorate miniature houses. Some youths invented their own games involving the catalogue, including flipping the pages and describing what they would do with various items. Catalogues kept children busy, providing breaks for their caregivers. Nellie McClung, in her 1910 novel *The Second Chance,* offers an excellent example of how catalogues were used as distractions for children. The main character, Pearlie Watson, an adolescent in an impoverished family, cheers up her younger brother by "telling him that when he grew to be a man he would keep a big jewellery store." As part of his preparation for this role, she had him "cut watches and brooches from an old Christmas catalogue."[35]

Even as catalogues aided in daily child care, it must be noted that they had questionable long-term effects. Children learned to look at Eaton's fondly and to expect the ideal domestic life to involve the consumption of countless commodities. Catalogues not only catered to needs that already existed, then, but they also expanded children's sense of what was a necessity. As Irene Stewart of Minden, Ontario, recalled, "We were not able to afford to send for many items but we spent hours poring over the pages and many colored prints which often infiltrated our dreams." According to Thelma Hayes of rural Manitoba, when she was growing up, she and her sister so desired catalogue objects that whenever they earned any money, they sent orders to Eaton's.[36]

Fashion and Beauty

Just as it was women's responsibility to provide domestic labour, so was it their duty to appear ornamental. During this period women were considered objects of sexual attraction. It was a man's entitlement to choose and seduce a woman; it was a woman's responsibility to either accept or deny the man's advances. Since women were objects of desire, the individual woman's ability to conform to conventional images of attractiveness helped define her social and economic status. Women who men found attractive had better chances of finding and keeping a husband than women who were not considered attractive. Marriage was the most common avenue by which women achieved financial security, and so many women expended much time, effort, and resources to appear attractive. It was this pressure upon women to achieve conventional beauty that caused department stores to offer fashion and beauty goods and services. Many women, in turn, looked to department stores to assist in their appearance creation.[37]

Fashion and beauty research did not require much spending. By the interwar period, Canadian women could learn about fashion trends by watching Hollywood movies; reading international periodicals, including *Vogue;* and browsing domestic women's magazines, including *Chatelaine.* As Josephine Burge, a character in Robert Stead's 1926 Manitoba novel, *Grain,* stated in her defence of wearing pants instead of skirts, "In a ladies' magazine ... it says they're quite the thing, but of course the people around [here] don't know that, yet." Like magazines, department stores offered affordable ways to discover what was *au courant.* Taking advantage of the big stores' advertising and merchandising, and using the stores' principles of free entry to their advantage, women all over the country studied department stores' window displays, browsed new merchandise, and read flyers and catalogues to learn about grooming and beauty trends. Women also employed department stores' return services for fashion purposes. According to former catalogue customer Jean Louis Perron, women in rural French-speaking Manitoba "took advantage of [Eaton's] refund policy. Clothing, gloves, shoes ... would be returned after being used." Some "ladies ... had a different hat every Sunday [at church], because each was returned after it was worn." Yet it was not only women who returned used merchandise. Even "articles for the farm," bought by men and women alike, were used and returned.[38]

A desire to attract the male gaze might have been one factor in determining a woman's aesthetic and fashion interests, but many women did not make this conformity their top priority. For some women, keeping up with style was a way of demonstrating success. In a 1969 letter to Eaton's, Mrs. Reinhardt said that during the 1920s in small-town Saskatchewan, "Saturday night was what everyone waited for." Farm dwellers "went to town in their model 'T's' to show off [their] new clothes." Jean Louis Perron, a participant in the Museum of Civilization's oral history project on Eaton's, said that rural Manitobans saw fur coats in Eaton's catalogues and then desired them for themselves. He remembered, "some of the wealthier farmers' wives [wore] mink stoles with three, four or even five heads hanging down. Often Christmas was the time for these women to show off their furs." Because fur was costly, those who wore it communicated their wealth and success.[39]

Fashion was connected to status, but it was also pleasurable. Women who attended Eaton's dollar skirt sales might have found them stressful, for they sometimes fought over sale offerings. Yet they also had fun. Shopping for fashion bargains enabled women to use two acceptable feminine skills, namely, the construction of ornamental appearances and their consumer expertise, to purchase goods that made them attractive, proclaim their membership in the fashion world, suggest their distinctiveness, and brighten their days. During one of the worst years of the Depression, Simpson's held a low-priced dress sale in Toronto. In its coverage, *The Globe* announced, "Women are still buying dresses, some of them two and three at a time." Simpson's "placed on sale 10,864 dresses ... Thousands of women attended the opening of the sale."[40] By lunchtime almost all the dresses were sold. This large turnout suggests some women had looked forward to the sale. When household budgets tightened, wives spent their days looking for ways to economize and get by. They often sacrificed their own needs so their husbands and children could be fed and clothed. Thus, when a department store offered a low-priced dress sale, thousands of women attended.[41]

If sales offered respite from strain, so did they offer opportunities for same-sex leisure. In 1911 the *Grain Growers' Guide* of Winnipeg printed a poem called "The Shopper's Philosophy." About a group of "debonair" women who are wearing "gowns" as well as "fluffs and feathers," and who are "hasting with speed" toward a sale, it suggests the women are relishing every second of their shopping journey. Tripping merrily," they are excited about the bargains they might find. In this poem, fashion presents an opportunity for female bonding. Wearing fashionable clothes and travelling together toward a sale, it suggests, was just as much fun as the sale itself.[42]

Fashion shows, too, provided socializing opportunities. At fashion shows at Eaton's, Simpson's, Morgan's, the Hudson's Bay Company, and Spencer's, women learned new styles, mingled with other women, and enjoyed what were often complimentary tea and biscuits. Some shows, such as those at Spencer's and the HBC, were informal, held in store departments and featuring employees as models. Others, especially those presented to Simpson's, Eaton's, and Morgan's customers in Toronto and Montréal during the interwar years, were more extravagant, held in store restaurants and theatres. Fashion mavens presided over these latter events, providing commentary on clothing worn by professional models. Canada's largest stores also lent clothing to bourgeois women's sororities, clubs, and charities. Armed with stylish garments, these groups held fashion shows to raise money. They charged money for attendance, raffled off fashion items, and sold refreshments and snacks. The Women's Undergraduate Society of the University of British Columbia held such an event in 1930. The HBC lent most of the clothing, and proceeds went to the Undergraduate Women's Union Building. Always ready to capitalize on its civic spirit, the HBC included an article about it in the next issue of *The Beaver*.[43]

Fashion shows constituted good public relations for department stores and turned women's groups into participants in the fashion industry's spectacle. Not only did fashion shows broadcast stores' newest fashions and aim to convince consumers to buy new garments, but they also made fashion and retail even more integral to Canadian life. Yet bourgeois women also benefitted from the fashion industry. They raised money for charitable purposes, and they extracted pleasure and status from fashion events. During the 1930s, for example, the Junior League of Montréal held an annual fashion review at the Blue Bonnets horse race track. Held on racing days, the shows took place when the stands were full of spectators. Models for the shows were not professionals but rather members of Montréal's Junior League who wore clothing donated by Morgan's. Playing out their roles as sexual ornaments in a patriarchal culture, these elite young women declared themselves masters, not victims, of modernity, consumerism, and beauty.[44]

Fashion and beauty were hence complex phenomena. At times, women wanted to appear stylish because it helped them achieve success and distinction. Thelma Hayes, born in 1913, best articulated this aspect of fashion when she told the Museum of Civilization's staff what she had done in her adolescence, after seeing someone at school wearing an Eaton's dress that she had dreamed of owning: she went home and ripped the page with the dress out of Eaton's catalogue.[45] Besides evoking feelings of spite, though, fashion and beauty also enabled some women to enjoy themselves, to socialize, to utilize skills developed during their everyday experiences, and to channel creativity. Given the limited opportunities available for women during this period to achieve these ends in the more formal realms of education, politics, and employment, it must be concluded that despite fashion and beauty's limited scope for progressive empowerment, they did constitute important outlets for the aspirations and fulfillment of women of many classes and regional affiliations between the late nineteenth century and the Second World War.

Experiencing Shopping

If many women enjoyed fashion and beauty shopping particularly, so did many enjoy shopping generally. The 1904, 1912, and 1914 diaries of Manitoban Beatrice Brigden (1894-1977), who became a socialist activist after the First World War, reveal that for some young women, department stores were a constant feature of an otherwise changing life. As a girl on the rural Prairies, Brigden received books and other items from Eaton's; they had been ordered by her parents through the company's mail order. Then, when Brigden was a student at the Toronto Conservatory School in 1912, she regularly went to Eaton's and Simpson's to have lunch, browse the departments, and escape the rigours of scholarly life. At twenty, Brigden was hired by the Methodist Department of Social Service and Evangelism as a sex educator for girls; in that capacity she journeyed across North America and on such trips would visit department stores, partly to pick up the clothing and accessories required for public appearances and partly to take breaks from work. In Chicago she visited Marshall Fields, where she "bought a dress and a lot of things." In Toronto she "rushed down to Simpsons and rescued a pair of velvet boots from a sale"; on another day in that same city, she spent her "morning in office," "had lunch at Eaton's!" and afterwards rushed off to a meeting. For Brigden, Eaton's was a link between her childhood and adulthood in that she procured goods from the same store during both life stages. Brigden's writings also reveal that during the pre-First World War years, some young Canadian women considered department stores to be places that offered stylish, affordable items. They further viewed the big retailers as convenient and comfortable resting stops in which people on limited budgets could enjoy solitary moments of respite.[46]

In addition to providing goods and relaxation, department stores offered pleasure. A woman born in 1882 phoned Eaton's archives during the 1960s to relate her mother's lifelong affection for the store. According to the archivist who recorded their conversation, "her mother used to do all her shopping at Eaton's. They had a big chest in their home and called it 'little Eaton's,' where she put purchases." So much did this woman look forward to shopping at the store that her husband teased her by singing, "Ta-ra-ra-boom-de-ay / It's Eaton's Bargain Day."[47] Other women particularly liked department store catalogues. In 1934 a woman near Birch Hills, Saskatchewan, wrote that the catalogue proved that someone "took an interest [in] some of these lonesome farm women." Mrs. F. Grieve of Radcliffe, Alberta, echoed this sentiment. In her letter to Eaton's mail order division, she wrote, "Five years ago my husband passed [on] ... My needs are not so many now as I have almost reached the three score years and ten. It's nice to think and know I still have my old friend The T. Eaton's Catalogue to refer to in time of need."[48]

Many women remarked that catalogues enabled them to pass away long hours. Of Eaton's catalogue, Georgina Leonard stated in 1976, "I was able to do a lot of serious shopping, also 'window shopping' when the days were long, lifting and brightening my mood many times." People confined to their homes found catalogues particularly important. "Being a rheumatic invalid for some years," Mrs. W.P. Lister of Verdun, Québec, told Eaton's in 1939, "you would hardly credit the pleasure one may derive from, being able to order by mail." She "wondered how many invalids and shut-ins, in our vast dominion, would greatly appreciate a copy of your catalogue even for a nominal charge – it would help pass many a leisure or wearisome hour, perusing their pages, in other words, 'window shopping at home.'"[49] What made looking at catalogues so pleasurable, in addition to passing the time, were the promises of fulfill-ment this activity held out. Many women knew they would not acquire consumer goods, but they enjoyed thinking about the possibilities that commodities represented. As Rosalind Williams argues, "From earliest history the human mind has transcended concerns of physical survival to imagine a finer, richer, more satisfying life." With the advent of modern consumerism, "goods, rather than other facets of culture, became focal points for desire." Window shopping, whether done on the street or in the pages of a catalogue, was a way in which women imagined more ful-filling lives. Lonely or depressed women who went shopping felt happier because catalogues and store displays represented vague promises of social transformation.[50]

Some customers also associated department stores with childhood contentment. Memories of Eaton's Santa Claus Parade and Toyland illus-trate the connections women drew between innocence and department stores. In 1977, Eaton's asked Toronto customers to send in letters describ-ing memories of Eaton's at Christmastime. Several women responded, thus inadvertently indicating that many of the female children in the massive crowds that gathered to watch Eaton's parades cherished their experiences long into adulthood (Figure 5.4). Writers recalled affection for parade characters, especially Peter the Clown, who made an appear-ance before the 1920s. They also described the sense of awe they had felt when going upstairs to meet Santa Claus, guarded by elves and ensconced in Eaton's toy department. One female Toronto customer even sent a poem. After describing "the grand parade," the "wonder windows," and children's enjoyment of the holiday season, she stated that Eaton's was part of her family's Christmas traditions.[51]

Eaton's and other department stores were proud of the fondness that female customers directed toward them. It justified their own supposedly benevolent existence and constituted good public relations. It was for these reasons that department stores preserved customers' letters in the first place. They wanted future researchers to find out just how wonderful the department stores had been and the important roles they had played in Canadian development. Nevertheless, not all women in Canada loved shopping, and not all shopping experiences were as enjoyable as depart-ment stores claimed. Much as Canada's largest department stores wanted the public to believe their buildings were safe, for example, dangers lurked within. The worst shopping fate to ever befall a Canadian woman occurred

FIGURE 5.4 Eaton's Santa Claus Parade in Toronto, 1918. Santa has just arrived at
Eaton's flagship Toronto store and is ascending the ladder to his headquarters in
Toyland, Eaton's toy department. | *Source:* Archives of Ontario, T. Eaton Papers, Series
308, Item 794. | Used with permission of Sears Canada Inc.

in 1906. While purchasing Christmas presents for her relatives, a forty-
five-year-old married customer with four children took the elevator in
Eaton's Toronto store. The elevator had no doors, and her skirt caught
on an outside wire. When the elevator started its ascent, she was pulled
out of the car. She fell three storeys to the shaft floor and was killed instantly. Eaton's staff identified her by her "transfer card," which she was
"clutching."[52]

Deaths in department stores were fortunately rare. Injuries, however,
were not. For legal purposes, the big stores kept track of shoppers' accidents. Most records from the 1890s to the 1930s have been destroyed, but

documents from the 1940s indicate that injuries were routine. Revolving doors at HBC Winnipeg were treacherous; elderly women fell while going through them, fracturing legs, hips, and arms. HBC employees who pushed carts piled high with merchandise ran into shoppers. And women eating in HBC's restaurants found themselves at risk. One female diner, twenty-seven years old, "choked on a piece of glass," which slashed the inside of her throat. More rarely, the stores also became places of violence. Miss F. Goodman found this out in 1944. While washing her hands in a restroom at Eaton's Main Store in Toronto, a "girl" smashed Mrs. Goodman's head with a pipe and tried to steal her purse. Goodman's injury was severe enough to require a nurse to change her bandage daily for a week.[53]

Shopping could also be irritating, and Canada's largest stores received complaints daily. Customers especially resented poor treatment by staff, but they also complained about faulty merchandise, price discrepancies, refund problems, delivery issues, personal account charges, goods shortages, inefficient operations, and other wrongdoings and inconveniences. Simpson's had received enough complaints by 1910 that it began offering standardized forms for customers to fill out. Before the First World War, Eaton's in Toronto published a "Complaint Column" in its weekly magazine, which provided responses to shoppers' grievances. One 1908 issue answered letters about "goods getting wet in transit," slow service in lunch rooms, crowded facilities, a lack of seats for tired customers, and Eaton's confusing store layout. Most complaints, however, were about customer service. Four complaints attacked salesclerks' indifference, lack of knowledge, and snobbery; a fifth was directed against management. One customer complained that Eaton's managers pretended to care about customers, but whenever shoppers lodged grievances, managers ignored them.[54]

Canada's department stores destroyed most of the complaints received from the 1870s through the 1930s, but Eaton's and the HBC did preserve complaints written during the 1940s through the 1970s. Together with sparse documentation from the earlier years, they provide glimpses into customers' subjectivities. Customers who wrote complaints implied that the ideal relationship with a retailer was convenient, efficient, pleasant, and rewarding. They were busy people and had many responsibilities. They did not want to wander around looking for items, searching for clerks, locating places to pay for items, and waiting in queues. They also did not want to waste time waiting for clerks to get back to them, obtaining adjustments on purchased goods, exchanging faulty or wrong merchandise, fixing damages made by inept interior decorators and workers, sending merchandise in to get repaired and then waiting for months to get it back, being passed around from clerk to clerk on store telephone systems, and travelling downtown to buy merchandise that was out of stock. They hated waiting around all day at home for deliveries that failed to arrive, they became exasperated with misleading advertisements, and they expressed anger when department store prices were higher than those of competitors. Most of all, customers detested condescending attitudes. At least half of the preserved complaints document instances of staff snobbery and other mistreatment, including blatant lying.[55]

Shoppers who penned complaint letters suggested they budgeted carefully, had limited time to spend on shopping, and directed their energies to buying products not only for themselves but also for husbands, children, and relatives. One Toronto customer told Eaton's in the early 1950s that a poorly constructed sofa bed had cost "$228.50 – a considerable price for a working woman to pay." In her opinion, "when in good faith an A-1 price is paid for anything, surely one is entitled to A-1 efficiency and ... service." In 1947, Theresa Falkner of Toronto wrote, "I am a very busy woman ... and I can not spend time worrying about my purchases. I want service." And in 1945, Mrs. Margaret Moslen of London, Ontario, was nervous about her husband's return from active war service. To ease her worries, she bought a lamp for the first time in her life to "add to the home and help make my living room a cosy place for when my husband came home from overseas after serving five years." Price, efficiency, and a desire to make one's home comfortable were uppermost in shoppers' minds.[56]

Poor service also rankled. Employees who ignored customers, offered false information, spent too much time looking around for stock or invoices, or who failed to show up for appointments caused customers to waste time. One woman sent a complaint to Eaton's because she had waited at home all day for workers to install her linoleum. Shoppers found poor service irritating because it indicated a lack of respect. One female shopper who had waited outside a lamp department manager's office for twenty-five minutes until he got off the phone "felt more embarrassed by the moment." A minority of customers also felt they were superior to employees, and so demanded deference. Joan Rumney of Toronto was patient with Eaton's incompetent staff during wartime because she knew there were severe labour shortages. After the war, however, she felt purchasers might "hope for some small measures of courtesy from your junior clerks. They are becoming increasingly indifferent to the point of insolence." Most complainants, however, stated they deserved to be treated respectfully not because they were inherently superior to clerks but because they were spending money at department stores. Their purchasing power entitled them to courtesy. After being given the run-around on her drapery order, Mrs. J. Lorna South of Toronto stated in 1950, "You would think the store was doing me a favour allowing me to spend money there!"[57]

Even when encountering rude behaviour, most shoppers remained sympathetic to workers. They recognized that harsh complaints against employees might spur employers to fire them. Purposefully, many complainants did not reveal the identities of offending staff members. When employees trespassed the boundaries of decency, though, shoppers did take action. Medical doctor Gladys Munroe of Toronto informed Eaton's that after she had bought a furniture set from a saleswoman named Mrs. Boyd, a salesman named Mr. Case had removed the sold tag from the set and sold it to someone else. Munroe informed Eaton's that she had instructed her "lawyers, Hamilton, Campbell and Opper ... to take legal action in this matter if my money is not refunded this week."[58]

A few customers took poor treatment to heart, nursing grievances for years. Doris Ashdown informed the HBC in 1950 that in 1946 an assistant manager in Vancouver had "chewed gum and was most rude." Customers were especially troubled when they felt employees had judged them to be of a low class. In her study of Toronto's working women during the 1930s, Srigley found that many women ensured they received good treatment by dressing up to go shopping. Yet even this did not prevent mistreatment. At Eaton's College Street cake counter in 1958, waiting customers were assigned numbers and served sequentially. After reaching the front of the line, customer M. Hill, who had number 52, was interrupted by "A beautifully & richly dressed woman ... having #55." This customer "asked [the saleswoman] if she had to wait for her parcel – she had telephoned an order." The "saleslady left me to attend to her – and she got other items as well as what she had ordered." Then, when number "54 was called the saleslady asked another one to finish my order." M. Hill was insulted. "I know I am not richly dressed," she wrote, "but at least my coat was an Eaton's product – and I do feel I was very shabbily treated by the saleslady." Palaces of consumption, department store displays, and inducements to buy suggested that wealthy consumers were the world's most important people. When they went shopping, then, customers became all too aware of gradations of affluence. Sensitive to her own mid-dling status, this customer was hurt by the saleswoman's snobbery. As her complaint reveals, department stores might have promised to democratize luxury, but hierarchies of class pervaded the big stores' atmospheres.[59]

Shoppers complained about both male and female employees' behaviour, but there were differences in how they interpreted employees' actions. Female employees were castigated for ignorance and snobbery, and male employees were criticized for acting aggressively, presumptuously and, worst of all, misogynistically. These differing interpretations of sales-people's actions reflected the dynamics of class and gender on the sales floor. Saleswomen sometimes asserted class superiority over shoppers, but salesmen sometimes asserted both gender and class superiority. An incident described in a 1957 letter reveals that some male employees believed female shoppers deserved to be mistreated. The writer informed Eaton's superintendent that she "would like to call your attention to one of the most disgusting exhibitions I have ever seen ... which happened last night at Eaton's College Street Drapery Dept." Just before a sale due to start at seven o'clock, the department managers "cleared off one of those low display bunks that are just off the floor and ... brought these curtains out and threw them over the people's heads on to the floor." The women attending the sale "had to stoop over to grab the curtains and it was such a small area the people behind knocked the others all over the floor." As he watched this spectacle, the "The Manager stood back with his arms crossed laughing." In the writer's view, this behaviour was no "laughing matter." She wrote, "there could have been a much better system for those few curtains, rather than throwing them on the floor like bones to a bunch of dogs."[60]

Department stores promised to make women's lives easier and more satisfying, but they often fell short of their targets. For many Canadian women, shopping was irritating, time-consuming, and degrading. Although some suffered inefficiency and mistreatment in silence, others took action to rectify their grievances. Some took legal action, some shopped elsewhere, and some spread bad publicity about the stores. These actions indicate shoppers did not passively accept poor treatment. They also show that consumers knew their power lay in their purses. At the same time, however, customers' responses to poor treatment remained individualized. Writing complaint letters to department stores, engaging in individual boycotts, and spreading bad publicity did not threaten the stores themselves. If anything, these actions helped the mass merchandisers recognize their failings and work to develop stronger customer-relations skills. Yet these expressions of dissent remain significant. They point to a widespread frustration with mass retail that existed among women in Canada.

If complaint letters underscored women's dissatisfaction with retail's organization of twentieth-century consumption, so did shoplifting. By 1897, Eaton's considered shoplifting a significant enough revenue loss that, in tandem with the Toronto police, it established store constables. Instead of pressing formal charges, which would cause bad publicity, Toronto's stores sought confessions and promises not to reoffend. Department stores' shoplifting records have not been well preserved, but notorious cases were reported in the press. In 1912 a married woman from western Canada "from a very respectable family" was visiting her ill mother in Toronto. Taking a break from her duties, she visited Eaton's and stole a diamond ring. She might have wished for a little excitement, or perhaps she simply desired the jewellery. Whatever her motivation, her actions subverted the number one rule of retailing: shoppers must pay for goods received. Even though store advertising and displays promised a better life through consumption, their "consumer democracy" was not available to all. Shoplifting was one method by which consumers could express disagreement or dissatisfaction with the social and financial expectations of consumption.[61]

A vague sense of frustration indeed pervaded many shoppers' experiences. Several customers expressed disappointment and anger at their inability to buy goods. As Wright observes, "longing had a central place at the heart of working-class and immigrant experience of department stores."[62] During the Depression, Eaton's received several letters from customers who lamented their shrinking budgets. Harriet Bateman of Pierson, Manitoba, hoped that "times may soon improve so that more parcels may be sent for." Her family lived in the "dried out and hopper infested southwestern part of Manitoba, and conditions with us are very bad." One woman reminded Eaton's of her long-term loyalty and asked the company to give her a gift of the "feltol rug no. 25X101 in your sale cat. size 7½ X 9." She had purchased one "some time ago and badly wanted another but have never been able to afford it." In her view, long-time support of Eaton's entitled her to a few gifts when times were hard. Another woman asked if Eaton's would buy an old catalogue from her; she would use the funds to buy "clothing in your store." Woodward's customers also felt the Depression pinch. Laura Chase, whose family lived in a logging camp, ordered goods every few weeks from the store. She kept a list of everything she wanted, and by the time it was ready to send the order in, she had to "cross off" all the "extras" and "frills," as "something more important would have to be bought."[63]

These women's desires for goods, along with their inability to acquire them, are suggestive of the disillusionment inherent in consumer capitalism. Department stores' displays, advertisements, and catalogues promised fulfillment through consumption, and it was all but impossible to ignore their persuasion. Not only did the big stores advertise in most newspapers and magazines across the country, so did they attempt to send their catalogues to every home in the dominion. Gladys McGregor, who had grown up in northern Saskatchewan, told Eaton's in 1976, "Next to our Bible the T. Eaton catalogue was our most prized possession, and I fear it was read much more than the sacred word." Children who grew up in such homes were deeply familiar with the desire and disappointment that catalogues engendered. As Elizabeth Bilash informed Canadian Museum of Civilization employees, "it was wonderful just looking at [Eaton's] dolls but she knew she couldn't have any of them. There just wasn't that kind of money." By the time these children reached adulthood, they were fully aware that the fruits of consumer capitalism could be achieved only through upward mobility and financial success.[64]

Some contemporaries recognized the longing and disappointment that accompanied the rise of mass retail. Mary Quayle Innis' short story, "Holiday," published in the *Canadian Forum* in 1932, takes capitalist consumer culture as its theme. In the story, Nettie Samchuk, mother of four and wife of an unemployed "foreigner," travels with her baby to a department store. It was a vacation, an escape from her daily chores and pressing financial concerns. She and her family were "on the Charities," and Samchuk wanted to enjoy the store's luxury. Although she had no money, she knew that "a store was for everybody." Samchuk visited every department. In Ladies' Dresses, she ogled a "blue velvet one with a cream lace vest ... the skirt swept out in deep blue folds right to the floor." In the Garden Department she eyed the "tempting" sight of "hammocks and swings." Growing weary, she sat down "on a huge sliding couch covered with striped denim." She thought, "If you had a couch like this you'd have a swell garden to put it in with grass and flower beds." Her store visit would have been perfect if rude employees and customers had not interrupted.

In the elevator, "A woman in a big brown fur stared at her." While resting on a stool in Infants' Wear, a "salesgirl" asked "icily" if she needed assistance. When she sat on a couch, a floorwalker told her to move along. In Groceries, a woman handing out samples ignored her. And as she was leaving the store, a "tall, horse-faced woman" criticized her for bringing an infant out in public. Samchuk stood her ground during each confrontation. After the run-in with the snobby salesclerk, she "got off the stool with dignity and walked away slowly to show that she was as good as anybody."[65]

Portraying Samchuk as a "decent, respectable person," Innis vilifies those who assume outward appearances express one's inner character. Innis also offers a sympathetic portrayal of working-class women's consumer desires. To alleviate her own hardship, Samchuk takes a holiday at her local department store. She cannot afford anything, but she derives pleasure from the store's displays. Yet Innis also criticizes the department store's classed splendour. When fantasizing about the merchandise, Samchuk feels pangs of sadness. While in Ladies' Dresses, she realizes her husband "hadn't seen her look nice since the year they were married." Her own dress is "faded to a bilious yellow." In Millinery, the new hats remind her that her own is second-hand and "out of shape." After looking at the "cakes iced with roses and 'happy birthday' in pink" in Groceries, she "sighed and leaned against the glass case with a sudden horrible empty feeling." Through such statements, Innis suggests that consumer capitalism is unequal. Though all were entitled to browse the department store and dream about its goods, only the affluent could purchase them. Department stores existed for the bourgeoisie, and they helped them purchase items that would keep them apart from the less privileged.[66]

In her 1987 autobiography, Gabrielle Roy also explores the link between poverty and consumer alienation. In a chapter about shopping, she describes the path from hope to alienation that characterized her mother's trips from their rural francophone community to Eaton's in Winnipeg during the interwar years. "We almost always set off in high spirits and full of expectation. Maman would have ... heard ... that Eaton's was having a sale ... Always, as we began these shopping expeditions, we were drawn by the hope that so warms the hearts of poor people, that of turning up a real find at the bargain counter." Roy's mother was excited about the possibilities awaiting her. "[S]he'd talk to me about the things she'd buy if the discounts were really big. But she always let herself imagine much more than our means would allow, thinking perhaps of a rug for the living room, or a new set of china." After a day of shopping, however, her hopes would dissipate. Despite being on sale, most commodities were out of her price range. Shopping at Eaton's thus reminded Roy and her mother of their marginalized financial status. "[T]hough we crossed the bridge on the way out with our heads full of plans as if we were rich, we never re-crossed it feeling anything but poor, three-quarters of our money having slipped through our fingers, very often without our being able to say where it had gone."[67]

By offering low prices, a vast array of merchandise, and generous service policies, department stores might have made consumer goods more accessible. Yet as Roy's autobiography demonstrates, they did not democratize retail. Eaton's in particular claimed to enrich the lives of all Canadians, but in practice it served only those citizens who could afford its goods. Eaton's and other major anglo-Canadian retailers also divided Canada's inhabitants into different racialized and ethnic groups. Eaton's, Simpson's, and the HBC might have declared public devotion to all of Canada, but actual instances of customer service tell a different story. When recounting her mother's trips to Eaton's, Roy recalls being embarrassed because her mother was francophone. If Eaton's few French-speaking salespeople were not available, Roy's mother would be forced to "'bring out'" her English. Anglophone staff would hover around, trying to understand her mother's requests. "These confabulations were intended to solve our predicament," Roy writes, "but to us they were pure torture." To escape saleswomen's "rescue" efforts, Roy's mother once opened an umbrella and dashed down the aisles. Unfortunately, Roy writes, anglophone discrimination toward francophones was not restricted to Winnipeg. After moving to Montréal later in life, Roy "found things no different in that city's west end department stores," which would have included Morgan's, Simpson's, and Eaton's. Since Québec was predominantly francophone, she "began to feel there was no cure for the misfortune of being French Canadian."[68]

Eaton's public declarations of being "Canada's Greatest Store," together with its massive catalogue trade, encouraged both native-born Canadians and newcomers to perceive this mass retailer as a symbol of Canadian identity. As such, racialized and ethnic minorities' experiences of ethnic discrimination at this big store symbolized these groups' marginal status not only in retail but also in Canada itself. A "working-class southern Italian woman interviewed by Franca Iacovetta 'recalled crying all the way home after being laughed out of a department store one day in 1949 when she could not make herself understood by the saleswomen."[69] As well, during the 1950s, Eaton's New Canadian committee found evidence of employee mistreatment of recent immigrants. According to one committee report, "Eaton's saleshelp ... lack courtesy in their treatment of [immigrants] and are impatient with them because of the language difficulties and the reluctance of a New Canadian shopper to make up his mind as quickly as a Canadian."[70]

Despite department stores' images of benevolence and fairness, their internal practices encouraged staff to treat low-income, racialized, and ethnic minorities in a discriminatory manner. Unfavourable descriptions of racialized and ethnic minorities in employee magazines especially encouraged prejudice. Spencer's and the HBC's magazines both included derisive jokes about black people. The HBC printed anecdotes that depicted First Nations people as ignorant and amusing; and Spencer's published jokes that showed Jewish and Chinese people to be dim-witted and amoral. In two instances, the "humour" of these tales lay in the fact that Chinese and First Nations customers had difficulty writing in English.[71] By including such content in staff publications, department stores encouraged racial and ethnic prejudice toward non-anglophones and non-whites. Their advocation of discrimination was not solely responsible for the mistreatment of customers by salespeople, but it did help encourage such behaviour.

BETWEEN 1890 AND 1940 department stores portrayed themselves as havens for women. Offering complimentary lavatories, coat and parcel checks, nurseries, and writing rooms, and catering to their every need, department stores promised female patrons shopping experiences filled with ease and pleasure. For a variety of reasons, Canadian women of diverse backgrounds and geographical locations answered department stores' calls. Balancing concerns of affordability, durability, style, and good service, they purchased goods at the big stores. Behind their shopping expeditions was their position within the gendered division of labour. As wives and mothers, it was their duty to take care of their households, raise their children, purchase goods that proclaimed their household's status, and appear sexually attractive to suitors and husbands. Since they offered merchandise and services that aided women in these endeavours, department stores captured Canadians' spending money and reaped unprecedented financial rewards.

This chapter agrees with the general feminist premise that the gendered division of labour is what causes many women to become consumers.

Responsible for household production, social reproduction, and attractive appearances, Canadian women bought goods that assisted them in these responsibilities. This chapter also supports the argument that consumption can be a site of pleasure and fulfillment. Women in this study attempted to make shopping enjoyable and satisfactory. They took pleasure in their consumer skills, and they used shopping as an excuse to venture outside the household.

At the same time, this chapter reveals that historians must continue inquiring into consumption's oppressive and alienating aspects. It is important not to portray female consumers as victims of capitalist machinations, but it is crucial to remember that class inequality is fundamental to consumer capitalism. Similarly, male managers' desire for power over women, employees' use of snobbery to gain power over customers, ethnic prejudice, and department stores' prioritizing of profit meant that many customers experienced shopping as irritating, frustrating, and dehumanizing. Finally, evidence of female customers' attempts to rectify store mistreatment, whether through small boycotts, legal action, or spreading bad publicity, reminds us that not all women revelled in their consumer experiences. Though most customer dissent was individualized, historians must not dismiss their actions. They point to a widespread dissatisfaction with consumer capitalism, one that likely still exists.

6

Working at the Heart of Consumption

*Who could have foreseen the mighty stream of business women
pouring, day in day out, into office, bank or store?*

– *E.M. Knox*, The Girl of the New Day, 1919

"IT'S NICE WHEN YOU discover the job is as good as the coffee," stated a
Tim Hortons placemat in 2003. "Flexible shifts," a "fun, fast-paced environment," and a "comprehensive training system" were among the restaurant's
advertised attractions. What the placemat did not mention were the long
hours of standing, the hot ovens, the occasionally grumpy customers, the
late evening shifts, and the low wages. The placemat was trying to attract
workers, but it was also intended to counter rumours about poor conditions. As anyone who has worked in the customer service industry knows,
entry-level jobs offer camaraderie and flexibility on the one hand and
insecurity and financial hardship on the other.

For more than a century, service work in Canada has been characterized
by this positive-negative binary. Such major department stores as Eaton's,
Simpson's, and the HBC were among the first Canadian employers to
develop entry-level service work's now common characteristics. Susan
Porter Benson's description of saleswork in American department stores
before 1940 applies equally well to work in Canada's largest stores. It "was
an intricate patchwork of the best and the worst, the most deadening and
the most challenging, the worst-paid and the most lucrative to be found
in the world of women's paid employment ... At one pole, toil, tedium,
and poverty; at the other, glamour, fulfillment, and financial security."[1]

Not only were department stores pioneers of contemporary service
work, so were they among the first North American employers to hire
white women to staff service jobs. Prior to the rise of the department store,
retail positions were believed best filled by men. Apprenticeship tradition

158

held that employees were in training to become shopkeepers; thus men belonged behind counters. More than this, male employees were thought to be more skilled than female employees. Yet, as department stores modernized, they began hiring more and more women. They did so partly because they believed customers were more likely to purchase from a woman, but also because they wanted to keep labour costs down. Women's wages were lower than men's; by hiring girls and women, department stores saved money and turned profits.

Despite the low wages and meagre advancement opportunities offered to women by the largest department stores, women applied for work by the thousands. Eaton's, Simpson's, Morgan's, Spencer's, Woodward's, the Dupuis Frères, and the HBC were among the only major employers in Canada to offer white-collar positions to women. More than this, department stores had developed respectable reputations; to work for Timothy Eaton or Robert Simpson was to work for a reputable retailer. In this era, when women were believed to belong in the home, this was no small consideration. By the interwar years, more than half of Canada's total department store labour force was female. It was also almost entirely white. Because of prevailing notions of white superiority, department stores refused to employ non-white personnel for customer service positions.

Once employed, women gained first-hand knowledge of department stores' twofold positive and negative working conditions. Some quietly accepted their fate, but others tried to make their workplaces more equitable. Like the American saleswomen studied by Benson in her groundbreaking investigation of US department stores, Canadian department stores' female employees countered expectations of efficiency and servitude by developing their own workplace customs. And, in ways not studied by Benson, they complained about their employers to municipal, provincial, and federal governments and organized collectively against them. During the first three decades of the twentieth century, female retail employees across Canada went on strike and tried to unionize in order to make their jobs more enriching and their employers more accountable.

Rise of Retail Employment

Sales and office jobs grew steadily in the first half of the twentieth century. In 1891 these sectors comprised 5 percent of the Canadian labour market, and in 1921 they comprised 12 percent. This figure remained steady into the Second World War. In 1891 only 10 percent of the sales and clerical workforce was female, but by 1921, 33 percent of sales and clerical workers were women. By 1941 fully 41 percent of all Canadian sales and clerical workers were women. Because sales and clerical work was concentrated in urban and semi-urban locations, between 1891 and 1911, most female sales and clerical workers lived in Canada's largest centres, including Montréal, Toronto, Winnipeg, and Vancouver. During the 1920s and 1930s, when smaller places like Saint John, Québec City, Ottawa, Saskatoon, Regina, Edmonton, Calgary, and Victoria reached larger proportions, they too became home to thousands of female sales and clerical employees.[2]

Prior to the twentieth century, sales and clerical positions were considered masculine. Boys usually apprenticed in shops and offices, where they learned how to become shopkeepers and bookkeepers. The growth of corporate capitalism during the 1890s through the 1920s, though, made the future of shop and clerical apprentices precarious. Large corporations gained monopolies in retail, finance, insurance, and utilities; within their bureaucracies they created white-collar hierarchies. Instead of leaving to start their own businesses, men in these industries began competing for promotions and climbing the corporate ladder.

By the turn of the twentieth century, financial, insurance, utilities, and retail corporations employed young men and women to perform entry-level work. Within these hierarchies, male workers were expected to advance, while girls and women were expected to stay in entry positions. Employers justified this framework by stating that women were going to leave once they got married. They also said that women were less competent than men. Managers funnelled women into routine, menial tasks that, as Graham Lowe shows, male employees were supposedly "unsuited" for and "unwilling ... to perform." By the 1920s these practices precipitated the feminization of entry-level white-collar work. It became a female-dominated job ghetto, or pink-collar sector, characterized by low pay and a lack of upward mobility.[3]

Presaging his reliance on female labour in the century to come, when Timothy Eaton opened his Toronto shop in 1869, he employed one man, one woman, and one boy. Eaton employed more men than women during the next decade, but he did hire a few women to staff low-priced counters and sewing rooms. Some also attained low-level supervisory positions. When Eaton devoted his entire first floor to millinery, mantles, and skirts in 1878, he put Miss Annie Murdock in charge. She hired Miss Haldane to run errands and Miss MacDonald to cut and make mantles. For "a time," remembers one employee, "Miss Murdock had the oversight of the whole floor, and ... was the sole saleslady." When Eaton's became a department store in the late 1880s, women were a familiar presence. By 1893 the company had 200 female buyers, and by December 1896, Eaton's employed 308 salesmen and 463 saleswomen. By 1900 there were two thousand saleswomen in Toronto, and it is likely that more than half of them worked for Eaton's and its largest rival, Simpson's.[4]

As Canada's department stores expanded, their female workforces grew apace. Male clerks' unions began making overtures to Woodward's and Spencer's female workers early in the century. Spencer's 1923 *Golden Jubilee* brochure refers to three female Victoria department managers with fifteen to twenty-five years of service. In Québec by 1910, l'Association des employées de magasin, organized by the Fédération nationale Saint-Jean-Baptiste, claimed 973 members, 107 of them active; the Federation's l'Association des employées de bureau claimed 1,675 members, 125 of them active. On the eve of the Great War, the University Women's Club of Winnipeg found that 2,432 women laboured for Eaton's, the HBC, Robinson's, and Carsley's in their city. The 1916 *Report of the Ontario Commission on Unemployment* similarly found that of the one hundred seventy-five thousand working women in the province, between twelve thousand and eighteen thousand were saleswomen.[5]

Comprehensive statistics on retail became available in 1930. After surveying all retail and service enterprises in Canada, the Ministry of Trade and Commerce reported, "Male workers in retail merchandise trade formed 9.28 percent of the gainfully employed males in the provinces, while female workers formed 14.66 percent of the gainfully employed females." As sales levelled off during the Depression, however, stores began trimming salaries, hours, and staff. Like other jobs, retail positions became difficult to retain. In letters to her brother in New York, a secretary in Simpson's Toronto employment office described the daily lineups outside her door. "[O]ffice gets busier every day – heaps of bodies out o' work and very few jobs to give them," she wrote in 1930. Nevertheless, by the Second World War, department stores were still employing more women than men. In 1939, Eaton's had 4,962 men and 5,981 women on its regular Toronto payroll. It also had 355 male and 1,200 female employees who worked on Saturdays only.[6]

When hired, female applicants were funnelled into a variety of occupations. Youthful women worked as "parcel girls," "messenger girls," "stockgirls," cashiers and, at the HBC, elevator operators. From these positions, employees sometimes advanced to selling, filing, and related positions. Other placements were mail order letter writing, switchboard operating, telephone order taking, sewing, finishing, cleaning, waitressing, food preparing, and nursery minding. Selling positions were among the stores' most lucrative and sought-after jobs. In Winnipeg's four department stores in 1914, messengers, parcellers, stockgirls, and cashiers received between five and eight dollars weekly, while saleswomen received between six and twenty-five dollars weekly, with the average weekly sales wage without commission being around ten dollars. Inexperienced saleswomen were assigned positions in low-priced goods departments. Skilled saleswomen worked in departments that sold high-priced goods, including jewellery, prestigious fashions, and furs.[7]

Clerical work had the highest status of all non-managerial positions (Figure 6.1). Typists, for example, were treated as more responsible than other female employees. An Eaton's Toronto employee remembered that during the interwar years typists did not have to wait for the bell to ring before they went home, like other store employees. They left when they finished their tasks. If they applied themselves, argued one advice book for women, clerical workers could "receive promotion to the position of private secretaries and book-keepers." Considered the highest rungs of the secretarial ladder, these positions gave women autonomy and status.[8]

Other opportunities beyond entry-level jobs included nurses in store hospitals and sickrooms. Then, when welfare departments expanded in the 1910s, retailers hired trained welfare workers. In the 1920s, recreation specialists and social workers were added to staff. Some managerial positions also opened up. As early as the 1870s, women occupied "supervisory positions in some merchandise classifications." One Simpson's president recalled that Florence Parsons, manager of the Toronto Cash Office during the 1910s, "was one of the best women managers [he] ever knew." A few saleswomen, as well, were promoted to buying positions. Miss Louise Black started at Eaton's as an office worker in 1914. She moved to the Ribbon Workroom, where she began "selling on the floor during busy noonhours." She was transferred to the dress department and after several years "went out on the market as a buyer."[9] Eaton's and the HBC staff literature is peppered with reports about female buyers travelling to Toronto, Montréal, New York, Paris, and London.[10]

FIGURE 6.1   Photograph of women working in Spencer's general office in Vancouver, 1923. | *Source:* David Spencer, Ltd., *Golden Jubilee* (Vancouver: David Spencer, 1923), 25. | Used with permission of Sears Canada Inc. and the City of Victoria Archives.

Women did not become managers and buyers in departments stereotyped as masculine. Toronto Eaton's 1940 list of managerial personnel listed approximately 20 female department heads and approximately 125 male heads. The female heads were in "feminine" departments such as millinery, foundation garments, fancy goods, misses' and women's clothing, restaurants, and the Wedding Bureau. Even within feminine-typed departments, women rarely attained well-paying, broad supervisory positions. Violet Ryley, an esteemed dietician who became the general manager of all of Eaton's Toronto restaurants in the 1920s, was a rare exception.[11]

Attractions of the Big Stores

Canada's largest stores constantly received more applications than they required. Wrote Canadian feminist Adelaide Hoodless in 1900, "The supply of female labour in shops ... exceeds ... demand." By 1916 there was an oversupply of saleswomen in Ontario and British Columbia. Throughout the 1920s, demand among women for department store work remained steady. During the Depression it increased. Former Eaton's employee Olwen Robinson recalled, "Eaton's or the Bay were about the only places you could get work" during the 1930s in Winnipeg. Even still, one had to stand "in long line-ups ... day after day" before obtaining even casual employment.[12]

Financial need was the most common factor behind girls' and women's decisions to apply for employment. Some worked to supply themselves with money to be spent on non-subsistence goods, but most worked to support themselves and their families. In Vancouver in 1914, 90 members of Spencer's 360-member female workforce did not live with their parents. Girls who did live at home contributed their wages to their family's' collective income. Some parents, usually mothers in need of cash, took their daughters to store employment offices and requested they be hired as messengers and parcel girls. Other daughters lied about their age so they could get work. "There are lots of [girls] in the stores under age," a member of the Vancouver Local Council of Women told the 1914 British Columbia Labour Commission. "The prices of food and living are so high that [their parents] are glad to get the few dollars a week."[13]

Women with dependants but without husbands also worked in the big stores. Annie Hyder obtained work in Eaton's Toronto Despatch Basement Office in 1899 because her parents had died and she needed to support herself and her sister. In 1925, Marjorie Cowie started working full-time in Eaton's Toronto shoe department to support herself and her young son. She remained there for at least twenty-five years. In 1930, Elizabeth Brown, who held a university degree and later obtained work with the United Nations, accepted the position of employment manager's assistant at Simpson's in Toronto. Her mother had recently separated from her father, and she, her younger brother, and her mother had moved into a new apartment. Brown's mother needed her assistance, and Brown became the household's chief breadwinner.[14]

Between 1890 and 1940, most female wage-earners in Canada were young and unmarried. Department store employees were no exception. Managers believed that most women would eventually leave their jobs and become full-time wives and mothers. In 1914 the Ontario government found that sales work is "spoken of as a young woman's occupation ... There seems to be a tendency ... to prefer the young girl as a saleswoman." The Winnipeg University Women's Club found the same year that most female wage earners in department stores were youthful. Store policies underscored the division between independence and wage earning, on the one hand, and wifehood and mothering, on the other. In interwar Winnipeg, Eaton's stipulated that if a full-time female employee married, she was either to drop to part-time status or to resign. In contrast, male employees who married received a pay raise.[15]

A minority of mature female employees retained both their independence and their jobs. In 1923, at Spencer's in Victoria, the head cashier, the head of the Alteration Department, and the head of the Millinery Workrooms were all single women who had been with the company since at least 1908. Eaton's in Toronto was also known as a place where single women could attain lifelong employment. After her parents died when she was "quite young," Miss Margaret O'Meara obtained work as a waitress in Eaton's Toronto restaurant in 1906. She retained her position until she retired in 1945. Single mature women could also be found among Eaton's Winnipeg staff. Born in Ontario, Miss Margaret Kerr moved to Winnipeg in 1908 and found work in Eaton's Corset Department. She retained this position until she died in 1933.[16]

Married women also worked in some of the big stores. Eaton's in Toronto and all the HBC's locations retained senior saleswomen and buyers after they married. During the 1920s the policy of Eaton's in Toronto was to employ "for part-time work married women who were merely supplementing their incomes rather than single women who would find it difficult to live in comfort on the wages earned for part-time employment." Widows, too, found employment in retail. There were only "one or two" widows in Toronto's stores in 1892, but by 1939, 9 percent of Eaton's regular Toronto staff were widows.[17]

When deciding what stores to apply to, some girls and women factored in advice received from acquaintances. In 1899 one girl asked for a job at Eaton's in Toronto because her mother's friend, who was the forelady of the Lace Department, encouraged her to do so. Others had relatives and friends who had been successful in finding jobs in certain department stores, so they, too, tried their luck. In 1925 three sisters from Manchester, England, applied successfully for jobs at Eaton's in Toronto, which they had heard about from "Canadian visitors." They so liked their new homes and positions that they convinced a fourth sister to apply at Eaton's.[18]

Women from Britain especially regarded Eaton's as a place to obtain secure, lifelong employment. In the late 1940s, Eaton's Toronto staff magazine began publishing biographies of long-service employees. Some described women born in Canada, but many detailed lives that had begun in Scotland, Ireland, and England. Many of these employees eventually moved beyond their entry-level posts and attained supervisory and secretarial positions. Since Timothy Eaton hailed from Ireland, some employees believed that the firm was more tolerant of immigrants than were other employers. It must be remembered, however, that Eaton's tolerance did not extend to people of southern European, Asian, African, or Aboriginal backgrounds. People who were not visibly Anglo-Celtic rarely attained work at Eaton's or other department stores.[19]

For those who met department stores' preferred racial and ethnic profiles, shared backgrounds created a sense of belonging. Matthews demonstrates that the Dupuis Frères blended Catholicism, French Canadian nationalism, and paternalism to create employee loyalty.[20] A similar process occurred at the HBC and Eaton's, though in this case Protestantism, English Canadian nationalism, and paternalism made up the mix. At Eaton's club meetings and other gatherings, speeches by prominent English Canadians appeared on programs alongside patriotic songs and Christian prayers. Store magazines included religious sermons, passages from the Bible, hymn lyrics, and news about the British royal family. In many cases such content was intertwined, giving readers the impression that loyalty to one's company was but one part of one's commitment to Canada and the British Empire. When King George VI ascended the throne in 1937, Eaton's staff magazine in Calgary ran front-page photographs of the King and Queen, along with the headlines, "God Save the King!" and "God Bless the House of Windsor!" Underneath this text was the message, "the approaching Coronation" makes "Calgary no less than London, conscious ... of a loyal regard for the persons of our British Royal Family." Continued the article, "May we translate this in a practical way right in this local Eaton family, by a unity of work and good feeling."[21] Workers who supported employers' religious and imperial identities would have found commonality at the big stores, but it is important to note, first, that the few non-Christian and non-European workers at the big stores were marginalized by the stores' ethnocentrism and, second, that notions of Christian and British superiority promoted prejudice toward minorities.

Until 1921 domestic service was the largest sector of female employment in Canada. Since it was located in private homes, reformers believed it the best type of labour for young women. Domestics, however, chafed under its restrictions. Many detested their servile status and had difficulty securing time off. Those who lived with employers disliked their lack of privacy. In contrast, factory, shop, and office work offered set hours, and when the factory or shop assistant's "work [was] over," one observer noted in 1892, "her time [was] her own." Girls and women turned to domestic service when times were hard, but white women – who did not face the same race barriers as black, Asian, and Aboriginal women – seized opportunities to leave domestic service. After the Bolshevik Revolution, a group of White Russian refugees in Canada were placed as domestics in Ottawa. Within months, five had quit their jobs, moved to Toronto, and obtained department store employment.[22]

Of all Canadian retailers, department stores offered the best hours. By the Great War, Morgan's, Eaton's, and Simpson's were all closing by six o'clock during the weekdays. Eaton's and Simpson's were also offering half-holidays on Saturdays. In 1913 organized store clerks in British Columbia pressured the provincial government to legislate similar work schedules. "In Montréal a large departmental store introduced a system of not keeping open late during Christmas week. Previous to that they had kept open until nine," reported the secretary of the Retail Employees' Organization of British Columbia. In 1938 employees of chain stores pressured the New Brunswick Fair Wage Board for shorter hours. Their goal was to achieve schedules set by Eaton's.[23]

Some girls and women associated department stores with respectability. In 1886, at the age of sixteen, Emily Cowley of Toronto went against her parents' wishes and obtained paid employment. She decided upon Eaton's, not only because it was one of the few firms that paid wages to apprentices but also because "'clerking' was one of the very few respectable positions available to a young lady." To understand why women believed department stores would protect their ladyhood, it is important to recognize that between 1890 and 1940 many white Canadians assessed a woman's respectability by judging her sexual virtue. If a woman remained virginal until marriage, she was considered pure. If she engaged in sexual or even suggestive behaviour, or if rumours circulated that she did so, then she was sinful. Women without male breadwinning partners were especially regarded as morally endangered. Their low wages, love of fashion, and desire for amusement, it was believed, caused them to trade sexual favours for gifts and money.[24]

To defend their reputations, many women desired jobs considered respectable. Unlike most domestic, factory, and restaurant positions, retail kept women free from dirt, grease, and sweat. Department stores allowed office workers to wear whatever they liked, as long as it was businesslike. Sales floor dress was more constrained. Salesclerks could wear their own clothes, but the clothes had to be either black or navy. Eaton's did not relax this policy until the 1960s. Dark clothes made salespeople easy to distinguish from customers, but they also emphasized their subordinate status. Whereas customers in the big stores could wear whichever clothes they chose, employees had to conform to their employers' strict dress standards. Nonetheless, as historians Alison Prentice and colleagues point out, sales jobs "were seen as a step up for many young working-class women, for as sales clerks they could ... work in a clean environment compared to women in factories. Their work was less isolating than domestic service [and] less menial."[25]

Along with department stores' clean working environments, their paternalism enhanced workers' reputations. Simpson's, Morgan's, Spencer's, the Dupuis Frères, the HBC, and Eaton's all acted as doting fathers toward their female employees. By admonishing them never to speak to male customers unless absolutely necessary, they protected their employees' virtue. Well-equipped, lavish restrooms for women workers also boosted employees' gentility, as did department stores' participation in the early-closing movement. Smaller stores stayed open until ten and eleven o'clock, but department stores in Toronto closed at six o'clock in the evenings, ensuring their workers went home at a decent hour.[26]

Department stores' sociability, too, made them appealing. In 1963 a male employee told Eaton's archives staff about what the company's mail order department in Toronto was like in the 1880s. "A more unsatisfactory state of things could not be imagined," he wrote. There were "girls talking and gossiping, sitting down behind counters, in each other's depts., lazy, saucy, impudent, coming in and out at all hours." Slow periods enabled employees to chat with co-workers; saleswomen could chat further with acquaintances who came into the stores. To avoid creating an appearance of informality, retailers frequently had to instruct sales staff to "avoid gossiping and do not allow your friends to consume your time by visiting you." Employees were also not to "indulge in conversation when upon opposite sides of the aisle. Going "about the store arm in arm" was especially to be avoided.[27]

According to Benson, the "time-honoured rituals of women's culture" were integral to American saleswomen's experiences. Staff newspapers "reported scores of showers and parties to commemorate engagements, marriages, and births." Canadian female wage earners enjoyed similar rituals. In 1925, *The Beaver* reported on a typical shower. "Rose Reading and Pearl Young entertained at a shower at the latter's home, in honour to Edith Mills, a bride-elect of November. Gifts were presented in an umbrella, prettily decorated with pink and white crepe, by little Madge

Empey. Edith Mills has been a member of the store for many years. She left the Company's employment October 31st, and was the recipient of a silver cake plate, a silver casserole and six coffee spoons, from her co-workers." Showers were feminine events that celebrated women's passage from single status to wifehood. They enabled women to support their co-workers; they also helped them with purchases one person alone might not have been able to make.[28]

A culture of heterosexual romance pervaded Canada's giant retailers. The magazines of the Dupuis Frères and the HBC, which sometimes carried staff contributions, were rife with flirtatious innuendo. In December 1928 a male employee published a jokey article in *Le Duprex* that lamented, according to Mary Matthews, "the frivolous nature of women's conversations, their focus on their love lives, clothing, teas and dances." Since the article's author "had a reputation as a playboy," most of the women who responded ... were quite flirtatious."[29] Both at work and away, department stores offered opportunities for heterosexual mingling. Woodward's secretary told the 1914 British Columbia Commission on Labour that girls "meet boy companions" while at work. The boys "generally wait for them outside." Welfare and recreation departments also included mixed-gender activities. Eaton's Winnipeg camera club of the early twentieth century brought men and women together, as did the dances, picnics, and parties that department stores hosted (Figure 6.2). Not only did such activities provide enjoyable leisure opportunities, so did they also help employees meet potential marriage partners. A man and woman in Eaton's Winnipeg camera department got married in 1936, and Mabel Reid, who worked in Eaton's Toronto shirt factory from 1914 to 1949, married one of Eaton's carpenters.[30]

If some women found marriage partners in the big stores, others remained single and laboured at department stores until retirement. Some of these employees relied on department stores' familial atmosphere for emotional and social support. Employees without relatives were especially drawn to the stores' paternalism. When asked by Eaton's archivist what she considered to be the most exciting experience in her career, Lillian Poulter, a salesperson in Toronto from 1900 to 1952, responded, "The quarter-century garden parties at Col. Eaton's and R.Y. Eaton's and the dinners and get togethers." Other employees remarked upon Timothy Eaton's practice of "shaking hands to the staff at the foot of the light well in the Main Store," a tradition "carried on by Sir John and Lady Eaton." Miss E.M. Giroux looks "back with Gratitude and Happiness over the years

Get Your Table Reserved for the

Beaver Club

Christmas
Party

The Greatest Social Event
of the Season

ON THE STAGE
A Spectacularly Beautiful
Christmas Programme

ON THE FLOOR
New and Novel Cabaret Acts

Rhymthical Dance Music by
LEN ACRE'S ORCHESTRA

THURSDAY, DEC. 27th
CRYSTAL GARDENS
Reserve Your Table Now

Admission 50 Cents.   Table for Four, 75 Cents.

FIGURE 6.2   Notice of upcoming HBC party in Victoria. | *Source: The Bay Window,*
December 1934, Hudson's Bay Company Archives. | Used with permission of the Hudson's
Bay Company Archives.

I spent with the T. Eaton Co. and can only say that I would want to do the
same thing over again."[31]

Besides offering emotional solace, department stores' paternalism had
concrete benefits. When one of Eaton's employees contracted typhoid in
1892, the firm sent a nurse to her residence, paid for her transportation
to the General Hospital, funded her five-week stay there, and then funded
another three-week stay at the convalescent home. In this age before
state-funded medical care, such support was crucial for employees' health.
Recreation programs also enhanced workers' well-being. Not only was
Helen Smith of Eaton's Toronto Mail Order Adjusting Department a
member of Eaton's Chorale Society, but she also "carried off several gold
medals for her singing and ... won great honours for her radio work."

THE BAY WINDOW, NOVEMBER, 1934

GIRLS HOOP TEAM OPENS SEASON

Above is the Hudson's Bay Girls' Basketball Team as they appeared when they opened the season under the coaching of Laurie Wooster (the gentleman with the tinted toe-nails). The players, in the order of proximity to Mr. Wooster are Irene Esler, Winnie Ford, Florence Anderson, Irene Stewart and Gladys Cook. Hilda Booth, captain of the team, was not present when this picture was taken.

FIGURE 6.3   Female basketball team, HBC Victoria, 1934. This clipping from the front page of HBC's staff magazine in Victoria reveals that some female employees enjoyed the athletic opportunities provided by department stores. | *Source: The Bay Window,* November 1934, Hudson's Bay Company Archives. | Used with permission of the Hudson's Bay Company Archives.

Eaton's famous drama troupe, the Masquers, gave women an outlet for creativity and provided travel opportunities. Other employees found fulfillment in sports. The HBC reported that during a 1934 women's basketball game in Winnipeg, "Hilda Booth, tall, fair-haired skipper of the team, stood out with her sensational playing in all phases of the game" (Figure 6.3).[32]

In 1919 Canadian social commentator E.M. Knox reflected on why women worked for wages. Women of earlier generations, she said, had "felt the helplessness of the weaker type of finishing schools of a half a century ago, the painting on velvet, the ... 'getting in and out of a carriage.'" They therefore now want "something which would give them a chance of working for themselves, examination tests, gymnastics, sports, anything, everything which would make them physically, mentally, and spiritually able to press forward in the battle of life."[33] Aside from the general need to earn money and the various attractions of department store work, girls and women proved the veracity of Knox's statement, for some evidently perceived department stores as workplaces where they could develop skills and achieve fulfillment from productive, creative, and socially esteemed labour.

Abilities that were considered to be natural to women were those that department stores most strongly supported. Thousands of store employees worked in service jobs, and many derived pleasure from honing interpersonal skills. Eaton's and the HBC magazines frequently printed letters from customers congratulating certain workers for their helpfulness and intelligence. Wrote one Toronto customer, "I just wish to express my satisfaction and appreciation in ordering from your department, particularly in regard to Miss Summers, the clerk who always takes my order." The letter continued, "She has taken my orders for some time now and I cannot speak too highly of her ability and attention."[34] Simpson's telephone clerks received similar accolades. According to a document in Simpson's archives, "A very neighbourly feeling seems to grow up between [Simpson's] telephone saleswomen and their customers. It is the proud boast of some of the older operators that they have supplied many Torontonians with practically all their clothes 'from their christening sets to their wedding outfits.'"[35] Waitresses, too, developed strong service abilities. Of Mrs. Margaret McBride, a long-time server in Eaton's Toronto Managers' restaurant, Eaton's archivist wrote, "Cheery 'Mac' has been a bright spot in the Managers' diningroom. She has made many friends."[36]

Food preparation, another ability considered feminine, offered women outlets for creativity. Around 1958, Miss Margaret O'Meara, a long-serving worker in Eaton's Toronto upscale restaurant, remembered her contribution to Canadian culinary life. "To celebrate the official opening of the beautiful GEORGIAN ROOM, I worked hard and succeeded in mastering the Art of making up attractive Chicken and Lobster Salads," she recalled. "Begorra – thereafter THEY became known as 'MARGARET'S SPECIAL CHICKEN AND LOBSTER SALADS.' For the LUNCHEON given in Honour of THEIR MAJESTIES, THE KING and QUEEN, in the Great Hall of HART HOUSE [1939], I was requested specially to make up "Margaret's Special

[Salads]. I received a letter of thanks." O'Meara treasured the letter for years afterwards.[37] This passage is a good example of one female employee's feelings of loyalty to both Eaton's and the British Empire. It also indicates that department stores provided women with (albeit limited) recognition of their specialized skills.

Girls and women who worked as salespeople also experienced a modicum of fulfillment. Tending to customers, as well as making them feel happy about themselves, required product knowledge and empathy. Employees who developed such skills were much appreciated by shoppers. In 1939 one customer wrote to the manager of HBC Vancouver to "praise Mrs. Bradford of your Millinery Department." She noted, "Never anywhere, London, New York, Paris, included, have I found such a treasure." The letter writer had "for some years been faithful to one make of hat," but Mrs. Bradford persuaded her "to try something just a bit different for a change." She "put the most becoming blue silk" on her head and the customer "immediately approved! [and] thanked her for my new personality."[38] Other HBC saleswomen were also praised for courtesy and knowledge. An article in the HBC's Winnipeg publication related that the "large personal following" of Mrs. Carter of the Drugs Department stems from her "interest in every customer's needs." Miss Minnie Muir of Hosiery, meanwhile, "knows how to DISPLAY her merchandise," and Miss Vickers of Furs has "a real knack for putting herself in the customer's place ... she doesn't try to high-pressure the customer ... in fact she doesn't appear to sell at all." And the popularity of Mrs. Torrens in Ladies' Dresses is due to her knowledge of "just what lines they have and what they will do for the figure."[39]

Understanding customers' desires was also necessary for one of the department store's most prestigious occupations: buying. Successful buyers were familiar with international markets and local tastes. Born in Trenton, Ontario, Miss Kathleen Duggan started at Eaton's in Toronto in 1914 as a clerk in Infants' Wear. Her manager promoted her to section head a year later, in which capacity she started buying for the department. During the war she bought merchandise in New York, and in the 1920s she made buying trips to London, Leicester, Manchester, Paris, Brussels, and Zurich. According to Eaton's Toronto magazine, "She has a strong artistic flare [and dresses] the showcases in the Infants' wear ... Besides her duties as a buyer, she sends out merchandise information to the branch stores." Duggan was also "fond of interior decorating and occupies herself with needlepoint when opportunity occurs." Hence, Duggan managed to parlay the feminine-typed interests of children, fashion, and decorating into a demanding and often adventurous career. She was still a full-time, respected buyer in 1948, when she celebrated her thirty-fifth anniversary at Eaton's.[40]

Unlike most other jobs open to female wage earners, department stores offered opportunities, however slim, for advancement. Moving up the retail ladder sometimes entailed losing touch with one's co-workers, but it enabled women to exchange menial positions for rewarding ones. As Marjorie MacMurchy relates, girls who started as apprentices could sometimes advance to secretarial, management, and buying positions, "which carry with them great responsibility, and correspondingly large wages."[41] Biographies of long-serving employees in staff magazines attest to patterns of career mobility. In 1925, Miss Verona Hibberd obtained a job in the Gloves and Hosiery Department Office; by 1935, she was head of the Stock Control Office.[42] Some women enjoyed aspects of managerial work. Miss Emily Caine, who worked in Eaton's Toronto restaurants from 1907 to 1946, proudly told the Eaton's archivists that she had been sent "to Hamilton when the Pansy Room was opened to train dining room personel [sic]. Also to Stratford to the Green Arden Room." When asked which job gave her the most satisfaction, she replied, "When I was in charge of College Street Luncheonette[, I] worked there for eleven years and had a grand staff of girls and also met some lovely people who came daily to eat with us."[43]

Drawbacks of Department Store Work

Department stores offered better conditions for women than did many other employers, but this did not mean "that they conform[ed] to any advanced standards of employee welfare," as a federal report on retail labour put it in 1938. Despite their employers' images of benevolence, girls and women at Eaton's, Simpson's, the HBC, Morgan's, the Dupuis Frères, Woodward's, Spencer's, and smaller Canadian stores all experienced financial hardship and inadequate working conditions.[44]

As in the United States, Europe, and Australia, Canadian saleswomen's earnings varied widely among retailers and within individual stores. In 1914 the members of Winnipeg's University Women's Club Civic Committee interviewed Eaton's and the HBC's managers on the thorny subject of wages. To the committee's delight, it found salaries were "much better" than "popularly believed." Exceptionally skilled sellers, buyers, managers, secretaries, and professional employees received commendable earnings.

According to the Women's Club, one saleswoman was "earning $50.00 a week and there are probably half a dozen others approximating this point." Yet even this sympathetic organization had to acknowledge that "for the great mass of saleswomen the high point is probably $20 a week and the general average of the experienced and efficient first rate clerk may be found between fifteen and eighteen dollars." Female employees "of average efficiency" earned "nine dollars per week" and female apprentices earned "five, six, seven and eight dollars a week." That same year the Victoria Council of Women argued that a living wage for a single woman was fifteen dollars weekly. Even allowing for cost-of-living differences between the two cities, Winnipeg's department stores' pay rates would have allowed only a minority of sales employees to live independently. Nevertheless, Winnipeg's saleswomen did make more money than their Vancouver counterparts. According to the Local Council of Women of that city, in 1914 "the wages of women clerks in this City range from $3.00 to $25.00 per week ... the very low wage is paid to the very young girls, and ... $25.00 is received by very, very few. In between we found many girls receiving from $6.00 to $10.00 per week." Given that the cost of living for a single woman on the West Coast during this period was fourteen dollars weekly, Vancouver's saleswomen's wages were meagre indeed.[45]

Under constant pressure to reduce labour costs, managers relied on cheap and flexible female labour. Often department stores referred to female employees as "girls," "apprentices," or "juniors." In the nineteenth century, following apprenticeship traditions, some shops did not even pay wages to juniors. It was thought retailers were doing junior employees a favour by giving them the opportunity to gain experience. In the 1890s department stores started paying their apprentices, but their salaries never approached a living wage. In Toronto's big stores, wrote Jean Thompson Scott in 1892, "girls sometimes ... start as check and parcel hands at $1.50 and $2.50 a week." Unfortunately, "inexpensive room and board at the YWCA cost $2.50 a week." Such necessities as "weekday lunches, shoes, repairs, and toiletries," as well as medical expenses and clothes, were beyond the reach of junior employees. Despite this gap between earnings and the cost of living, department stores encouraged apprentices to regard their salaries as generous. In 1897, *Saturday Night* published an anonymous letter that stated, "Girls [in department stores] who receive $3 per week are given to understand that they are very fortunate in receiving such a large salary, inasmuch as their employer, did he choose, could discharge them, and get others to fill their place at two dollars per week."

Drawing on paternalism's tendency to treat wages as privileges rather than entitlements, department stores' false inflation of wages discouraged employees from challenging their meagre pay. Despite their own portrayals of wages as generous, though, department stores knew full well that such salaries could not support those who lived independently. As the superintendent of Spencer's told the 1914 British Columbia Commission on Labour, "We won't employ young women who are boarding ... If she can't earn what we think she should have [to live] we don't want her."[46]

Low apprenticeship rates persisted in the first half of the twentieth century. The 1914 BC Commission on Labour revealed that in most Victoria stores, "cash girls and little girls in the haberdashery departments" received about four dollars weekly. At the HBC in Vancouver, female apprentices were usually fourteen or fifteen years old; they started at three dollars and were usually "messengers or cash girls." Spencer's paid fourteen-year-old girls "just coming from school the first four weeks $2.50; after that $3.00." Aware that employers were using apprenticeship traditions to justify the existence of a permanent low-waged workforce provincial wage boards during the 1920s created laws stipulating the lowest tolerable wages for female apprentices and defined the number of months that should constitute the apprenticeship period. To get around such regulations, the HBC moved juniors from one department to another. After personally experiencing this practice, HBC employee Daisy Gibson complained to the Saskatchewan Minimum Wage Board. "From July, 1936, til July, 1937 I was employed at switchboard, post office, and library work," she stated. "During that period I was a minor and received $10.00 a week ... this is sufficient according to minimum wage orders." When she reached the date of "11th January, 1938," she became "experienced and entitled to $14.00 a week if and so far as my former experience counted." However, the HBC continued paying her apprenticeship rates until she quit in June. In her opinion, "I should have received $14.00 and ... the difference ... should be paid me." The board decided the "claim was figured at $73.20" and ordered the HBC to give Gibson her missing wages.[47]

One might assume that long-serving employees were exempt from department stores' skimping but, unfortunately, the opposite was true. Knowing that mature single women and female breadwinners had scarce employment opportunities, managers did not peg women's salaries according to marital status and experience, as they did for male employees. Instead, they paid them close to the same salaries they had earned when they were hired. As a result, new employees sometimes received higher pay than women who had served for many years. This was particularly frustrating for Miss C. Fullerton, a saleswoman in Simpson's Toronto basement. After being hired in the mid-1920s, she received two raises, bringing her total earnings to fifteen dollars per week. During the Depression her wages were cut to the legal minimum of $12.50 per week, as were most Simpson's female employees' salaries. By 1942 she had received a raise of a dollar. Believing she deserved more, she asked her manager for an increase, explaining that she had only taken two half-days off work in her entire twenty-four years of service and was a dedicated worker. Her manager ran it by his managers and eventually reported that her new salary would be $14.50 a week. Fullerton was incensed. In a letter to the American Federation of Labor she stated, "If I wasn't a good hard conscientious worker *I would have been out long ago* ... there are dozens, and dozens of Employees like me in this store, and newcomers are given the same wages, or more, to start with as we get, and we can do nothing about it."[48]

Department stores' unwillingness to provide monetary assistance beyond that which was legally required led to straightened economic circumstances. In 1904, at the age of thirty-seven, Timothy Eaton's private secretary Margaret Hoskins retired from the company, citing "nervous strain." After a month of "stock-taking which [she] supervised," her mother became ill. They moved to Scotland, where in 1907 Hoskins became the primary caregiver of a second dependant, her late sister's son. The company granted money to Hoskins upon her retirement, but by 1931 she found her savings insufficient. At the age of sixty-three, she appealed to the company again for money, which it provided. Sometime during the next ten years, she had a stroke, and a friend's daughter took her in. In 1944, Hoskins' nephew appealed to Eaton's for more money on her behalf. After Hoskins died in 1945, her friend wrote to Eaton's to again request money. The funds Eaton's provided over the years, she stated, fell short of meeting Hoskins' living expenses. This once valuable Eaton's employee survived through the kindness of her friends, on whom she was entirely dependent.[49]

If financial remuneration could be unattractive, so could hours of work. Eaton's and Simpson's in Toronto had enviable working hours, but clerks in other stores and cities were not so lucky. Montréal's stores closed later than Toronto's, and saleswomen throughout Québec, as Micheline Dumont and colleagues relate, "often spent twelve hours a day on their feet serving customers." In 1914 all of Vancouver's department stores remained open until nine and even ten o'clock on Saturdays. This forced full-time sales-women to work from eight o'clock on Monday morning to late Saturday evening. "Lots of shop people are absolutely fatigued on Saturday night and it takes all Sunday to get over it," J.E. Wilton told the BC Commission on Labour. All department stores, including Eaton's and Simpson's, of-fered extended hours during Christmas and other sale periods. In prov-inces that regulated female workers' hours, department stores had to apply for special permission to stay open late during these times. Eaton's in Winnipeg paid double-time for working after supper and gave workers special discounts on suppers. Other stores, though, used every means possible to avoid paying overtime. During the 1930s the HBC in Saskatoon held sales during which workers had to stay at the store until late, some of them until midnight. After the sales the time card manager recorded employees' shifts in pencil and later "erased" workers' extra hours.[50]

Long hours are exhausting in any job, but they are especially exhausting in retail because workers are unable to sit down. As in other Western countries, turn-of-the-twentieth-century Canadian feminists pressured governments to force department stores to provide seats for saleswomen. As provincial Shop Acts went into effect in the 1890s through the 1910s, department stores did put chairs behind counters. Because they were always supposed to look busy, though, managers discouraged sellers from sitting. As Mrs. William Forbes MacDonald told the BC Commission on Labour, Spencer's has "seats for the girls, but if a girl sits down to rest the shopwalker tells her she had better get busy." Working in sales was espe-cially tiring. An excerpt from a poem titled "A Lament," written by a salesperson at the HBC in Calgary, describes the pace of work on busy days. "[H]ere come the crowd / Boy! Are they loud! / People push and grab, crowd and crab."[51]

Expectations of good service could also be wearisome. The Winnipeg University Women's Club said saleswomen suffered from "nervous strain" from talking to customers, filling out slips, getting out goods and measur-ing them, and giving parcels to customers, all at a speedy pace. Even when tired, sellers had to "keep in mind that [they] should please the customer and not expect the customer to please [them]." As Eaton's reminded them, "It is your duty to serve."[52] In this way, selling was akin to domestic service. Hired to help, clerks had to remain respectful even when custom-ers were rude, lying, unreasonable, and uncaring. "Customer's Complaint," a poem by a Winnipeg employee, captures salespeople's frustration. It begins by quoting a fictitious customer. "'I bought a little hot dog / Down at your little stand / and when I went to chew it / 'Twas like a rubber band. / Your store is famed for quality, / I ask you what is this? / I paid a nickel for it / Expecting hot dog bliss. / I want to see the manager, / and Superintendent too.'" The clerk replies, "'O madam, here's your nickel; that hot dog we do rue. / Thank you for telling us; / It is so sweet of you.'" Yet in her mind the author thinks differently. "(And I was really thinking / had you nothing more to do?)."[53]

It is true that Canada's largest department stores were among the cleanest, most well-ventilated, bright, and fire-proof workplaces. Owners wanted customers to feel safe and content while shopping, so they made their stores comfortable. This did not mean, though, that employees enjoyed lavish surroundings. In Eaton's early-twentieth-century Toronto workrooms, desks for parcel girls were "high up on the wall and not very easy to ascend," as one employee recalled. Prior to the 1920s, Eaton's Toronto basement cash offices were dank and dim. Pneumatic money tubes glittered under artificial basement light and caused sore eyes; they were also loud. As late as 1914, the Vancouver HBC did not have restrooms for employees. Before the 1920s, women who worked near large store windows in Winnipeg endured draughts of cold air. And in 1927, as Mrs. Arthur Gibeault informed readers of *La Bonne Parole,* women in Montréal's department stores suffered from "les conditions hygiéniques déplorable." Dangers specific to sales work also plagued employees. Eaton's Toronto employee Lillian Poulter remembered that early in the twentieth century she "was knocked out by a customer pulling a roll of oilcloth down just as I was passing. It hit me on the head." Eaton's was unwilling to provide compensation, and it "took me 6 months to collect 3 days pay."[54]

Some saleswomen, buyers, and other female employees might have earned wages well above average, but from 1890 to 1940, most women found it difficult to advance beyond entry-level jobs. Women's difficulties in attaining promotions arose from the widespread beliefs that women were not breadwinners and that women were not as skilled as men. Yet retail's glass ceiling was also due to managers' efforts to keep labour overhead low. Department store profits, as Joy Santink notes in her study of Eaton's, depended on constant vigilance over payroll expenses. For this reason, "wages for the large percentage of the Eaton work-force" were kept low. Drawing on the widespread assumption that women were transient wage earners, department stores deliberately kept women at entry-level salaries.[55]

Faced with low-paid lifelong employment, many female department store employees opted for marriage and motherhood. One former Eaton's employee's conversation with Barry Broadfoot about her experiences in the store's Toyland Department in Toronto during the Depression captures this reasoning: "We worked, well we had to be there at 8.30, door opened at nine, and sometimes we were on our feet for 14 hours a day except for half an hour lunch." She continued, "For seven dollars a week. They really didn't give us anything for nothing. I never knew a girl who wasn't glad to leave that place. Girls used to marry fellows they didn't even care for, to be free of Eaton's."[56]

Finally, sexual objectification occurred in the big stores. Contributors to department stores' interwar magazines frequently remarked upon female workers' appearance. In 1923, *The Beaver* published a photograph of HBC employees at a track meet titled "A Bevy of H.B.C. Girls at the Sports," suggesting women's attractiveness was more important than their athleticism. Just before the Second World War, the HBC's Winnipeg staff publication, *The Bayonet,* ran a similar article. The company had "A Bevy of Beauties to Smooth Customer's Ups and Downs," declared a front-page headline. Underneath a photograph of ten young women, posing together with one male manager, was an article that read, "We're mighty proud to present this heart-stirring array of loveliness to our readers ... No doubt all you fellows are quite envious of Mr. H.C. Collins, around who the young ladies are pivoted."[57] Eaton's and Spencer's staff magazines also portrayed female employees as pleasing and docile objects of male attention and affection. In an article about the Ladies' Swimming Club Life-Saving Class, which included a collage of photographs of eleven women wearing bathing suits, the contributor stated, "Almost our last official act in the interests of this high-minded journal was to 'cover' the presentation of awards" to Eaton's female swimmers. "The reader will readily understand, if he glances above, that we found this assignment very much to our liking, and we spent a most enjoyable evening."[58] And in 1927, Spencer's of Vancouver's *Store Topics* included a snapshot of four women who worked in the produce department. Each woman was holding an imported fruit, and the photograph's caption read, "Some Peaches from Department 64."[59] Together with the HBC's and Eaton's publications, Spencer's staff magazine implied that men were store magazines' readers and that women were displayed in such serials for men's gratification. The easy comfort with which magazine writers reported on women's bodies reflected the gendered power differential within department stores. Men were decision makers and supervisors; women provided the submissive labour – and the ornamentation – that kept the retailers functioning and pleasant.

Responding to Poor Working Conditions

Eaton's, Simpson's, the HBC, Morgan's, the Dupuis Frères, Woodward's, Spencer's, and other major Canadian retailers between 1890 and 1940 offered certain advantages to female wage earners, but their workplaces were by no means a collective panacea. Low wages, difficulties in advancement, exhaustion, and objectification characterized many women's experiences in the big stores. In response to these unfavourable circumstances, Canadian female retail employees developed a variety of coping mechanisms. Some of these were private tactics that enabled workers to cope with daily irritants, and others were organized responses designed to make retail labour more rewarding and equitable.

Keen to maximize profits, department stores urged employees to behave efficiently at all times. Employees, though, developed their own work rhythms. Department stores' instructions on proper behaviour are suggestive not only of managers' preferred routines but also of how seriously workers took employers' exhortations. In 1900, Eaton's informed employees that "reading Newspapers, letters or books, or writing letters" was grounds for dismissal, as were "eating while at the counters or departments" and "chewing gum or tobacco or spitting on the floor." As in the United States, Canada's department stores often berated employees for "huddling," or gathering in groups and chatting. "Gossiping, loitering, standing in groups, talking loudly, or making unnecessary noise either in or around the building is strictly prohibited," Morgan's advised its employees in 1912. Eleven years later, Eaton's staff was told not to whistle or sing. Owners and managers grew particularly irked when they heard clerks "call one another by first names, heard "a pet name or slang name used," saw salespeople "listless or half asleep," and noticed "them leaning against the store fixtures." In the 1930s a cartoon in *Contacts* visually illustrated the ways in which employees engaged in their own forms of acceptable behaviour (Figure 6.4).[60]

Huddling, whistling, and leaning against fixtures were not direct challenges to department stores' authority, but they do indicate that workers had their own ideas about when it was appropriate to exert energy and appear professional. Full-time employees usually had only one daily break,

Sure it was a swell game—but in the meantime this would-be customer aims to catch a train!

The Back-to-the-Land movement is a worthy object, but the back - to - the - counter movement doesn't help anybody.

Of course they're good friends —but need they stroll hand in hand through the Store to prove it?

While the "sprawl stance" may be comfortable—it's not pretty to see nor yet safe for passersby.

Finishing a bit of gossip while waiting on her customer. The latter feels of small consequence.

Engineers assure us the building doesn't need reinforcing at noon hour.

All "gummed up" and going places.

The "leaners"—with a yawn or two for good measure.

A little bit late—but hoping to be noticed soon.

FIGURE 6.4   Eaton's Winnipeg magazine's illustrations of good and bad sales floor behaviour. | *Source: Contacts,* April 1935, 18, Archives of Ontario, T. Eaton Papers, Series 141. | Used with permission of Sears Canada Inc.

which lasted between forty-five minutes and one hour, so they seized moments throughout the day to engage in conversation and rest, and to put aside their professional demeanour. This informality suggests that some employees did not identify with their employers' quests for profit and efficiency. Younger employees in particular might have viewed their jobs primarily as vehicles for socializing and earning money, as Santink notes.[61]

Attitudes of informality also challenged expectations of servility. Writes Benson, "saleswomen shared with millions of American workers an ethic of independence: they would work but they would not serve."[62] Women in Canadian department stores similarly viewed subservience with distaste. To assert their importance on the sales floor, they developed notions of turf. Around 1920, Eaton's Winnipeg trainers told sellers, "You will use the word 'we' instead of 'I' in all cases other than those of a strictly personal nature, as 'We have it in three styles,' not 'I have it in three styles.'" By claiming stock as their own, clerks also claimed a higher status. Rather than being unskilled, low-status employees, female employees viewed themselves as skilled arbiters of taste who controlled stock turnover. To demonstrate that they were on an equal social footing with customers, salespeople sometimes ignored them. In 1933, Eaton's in Toronto felt it necessary to tell sellers, "If you are busy on some other work ... do not appear indifferent and give the customer the impression that you are too busy to attend." Employees disliked having to use employee entrances and elevators, rather than those designed for customers, and the big stores constantly reminded employees to use staff facilities. In a further assertion of social standing, saleswomen used informal expressions when interacting with customers. *Contacts* had to remind staff that when a shopper looked like she needed assistance, salespeople were not to ask, "What is it, dear?" Rather, they were to politely inquire, "May I help you?"[63]

Recognizing that both managers and customers viewed them as insignificant, it appears that female employees used their knowledge of merchandise to assert their power. In conversations with customers, sellers let it be known that they, and not the shoppers, were expert consumers. According to *Contacts,* "a good way to drive a customer out of the store is ... to take on superior airs ... You cannot serve satisfactorily if you have a pronounced feeling that you are a better judge of style than your customer and let her know it by telling her exactly what she wants." Saleswomen also broadcasted their status by wearing elaborate clothes and hairstyles. Girls and women who laboured in manufacturing, domestic service, and other occupations wore fashionable clothing, but saleswomen were among the most stylish of Canada's female workforce. In Isabel Mackay's 1911 novel, *The House of Windows,* one character applies to a dowager, Mrs. Torrance, for a position to read books to her. Torrance and her maid mused about Brown's possible social status. "Oh she's got airs and graces

FIGURE 6.5   Photograph of staff of one of Spencer's selling departments in Vancouver, mid-1920s. The women's attire indicates an awareness of youthful fashion trends, including the wearing of men's ties. | *Source: Store Topics,* Spencer's staff magazine, MSS 1495, 945-0-1, File 2, City of Vancouver Archives. | Used with permission of Sears Canada Inc. and the City of Vancouver Archives.

enough!" she said. "But you never can tell. Shopgirls are getting very dressy, these days." In her discussion of this passage, Lindsey McMaster rightfully suggests that it demonstrates that saleswomen used the tools of consumer culture to challenge the middle-class notion that women who worked for wages were not respectable. Photographic evidence from the interwar years also indicates that young female department store employees dressed confidently and stylishly (Figure 6.5).[64]

If some saleswomen dressed fashionably, others dressed elaborately. Evidence from store-training literature suggests that trainers believed assertive and stylish saleswomen were purposefully trying to intimidate customers, who might have had less confidence than did saleswomen about their personal appearance (Figure 6.6). Drawing connections among stylishness, snobbery, and inefficiency, Eaton's told its employees that "ladies will avoid all extreme styles of hairdressing, particularly that of covering the ears and forehead. We prefer a ... businesslike arrangement of the hair. You will not wear ribbons, velvet bands, fancy combs or pins." A 1921 poem titled "Ode to Our Flappers," written by a publicist at HBC Edmonton, is further indicative of salesgirls' attention to appearance:

A young lady at business keeps her dress simple and inconspicuous—not like this!

FIGURE 6.6   Illustration in Eaton's Winnipeg magazine showing incorrect attire for female employees. | *Source: Contacts,* October 1933, 5, Archives of Ontario, T. Eaton Papers, Series 141. | Used with permission of Sears Canada Inc.

"Her tiny ears are covered, / With her hair of golden brown, / ... Her ankles [are] trim and graceful, / ... [She is] "A thing of youth and beauty, / As she gaily trips along. / With her laugh and with her giggle, / And her little snatch of song. / ... There is Ethleen McEwan, / And pert little Alice Wright, / There's vivacious Bessie Ogilvie / And cute Ruth Williamson, / There are scores of other heart breakers, / Employed at Edmonton." With its implication that flappers were sexually confident and potentially immoral, this poem is indicative not only of salesgirls' interest in fashion but also of moralists' fear that wage-earning women – so clearly enjoying their sexuality and femininity – were disrupting middle-class norms.[65]

If girls and women did not always behave with servility and chastity, neither did they always accept that women were primarily interested in marriage and motherhood. From 1890 to 1930, Eaton's recreational offerings included elocution, sewing, and cooking lessons that, as Susan Forbes writes, had "one purpose – to help Eaton's female employees make the transition to middle-class domesticity."[66] Eaton's was never able to attract to such programs the desired numbers of participants. In the late 1920s, the company's female recreation program expanded to include softball, bowling, basketball, badminton, and swimming – and women enrolled in record numbers. Their participation indicated they were more interested in athleticism than in becoming genteel housewives, or at least in letting Eaton's teach them how to become so. Similarly, when the Dupuis Frères started publishing *Le Duprex,* women questioned the magazine's masculine focus. In an article called "Féminisme," a female employee complained that "depuis que ce journal existe on n'y a pas lu un mot uniquement consacré à notre sexe, c'est peu galant, je dirais même, ce n'est pas galant du tout!"[67]

Neither did all girls and women labouring for Canada's biggest retailers accept long hours and low wages. As today, their most popular expression of dissatisfaction was to quit. Turnover was high in the big stores, and it is likely that girls and women held a series of jobs throughout their wage-earning careers. Such was the case with Elvina Ralph, who by the Depression had worked in several offices and stores in Saskatoon and surrounding towns. Quitting was usually an individual response to unsuitable conditions, but sometimes groups of women quit en masse. After British Columbia established minimum wage laws for women in 1918, the HBC discontinued paying its female clerks wages around eight dollars weekly, plus commission. It cancelled women's capacity to collect commission and started paying them the minimum wage of nine dollars per week. Male clerks "continued to receive both a salary and a commission." Enraged by their loss in pay and by their loss of status, a "number of female clerks [in Vancouver] quit their jobs in protest." This action did not cause the HBC to change its policy, but it did demonstrate a willingness among women to engage in collective, labour-identified action.[68]

To obtain redress for unsuitable conditions, some girls and women enlisted government assistance. In early 1897 a group of Eaton's saleswomen approached "a member of the provincial legislature about the problem of lunchtime accommodation." They were using the customers' cafeteria because they felt the employees' lunchroom was inappropriate. Management informed them they had to use the employees' lunchroom, so the women asked an Ontario minister to help them obtain a better place to eat. The minister of agriculture was placed in charge of the grievance, and he forwarded the matter to Timothy Eaton, who responded that all workers should use the employees' lunchroom. The minister, agreeing with Eaton, let the matter drop. Through the next century, employees continued to bring grievances to governments. In 1918 a group of women informed Toronto's City Hall that the air was stale in Eaton's basement, and in 1931 an unidentified worker sent the following telegram to the federal Royal Commission on Price Spreads and Mass Buying: "There are thousands of employees of the two big Toronto stores looking to you for help in obtaining shorter hours better pay and a weekly half holiday don't let them down."[69]

In rulings on labour issues, governments tended to side with department stores. In 1906, Israel Mintz brought Eaton's to court because the company, upon hearing he was a labour sympathizer, refused to hire him in its factory. After it was established that Eaton's was in need of operators, and that the Eaton family did keep lists of strikers, the judge ruled that "there was no offence in refusing application" of any worker, striker or not. During the late 1920s, the provincial inspector of women's workplaces, John Cairns, acted in the HBC's interests, against female staff. During his reign, the board received several complaints about the HBC's Beauty Salon. People claimed that workers did not receive overtime pay, were not paid higher than apprenticeship wages, had to pay for the laundering of their smocks, and had to purchase supplies out of their pockets. After inspecting the salon, Cairns informed the board that nothing was amiss. Cairns was also notorious for telling the HBC's managers the names of those who complained.[70]

Most salespeople who lodged formal complaints did so anonymously. As one woman informed the Saskatchewan Minimum Wage Board, "For obvious reasons, I do not wish my name mentioned in any investigation so must write under a nom-de-plume which is ... Fair Play." Unwilling to jeopardize their positions, very few women talked to people investigating labour conditions. Most of those who did, such as a group of Eaton's female garment workers in 1934, did so after they had stopped working for their employer. As a member of the Vancouver Trades and Labour Council told the BC government in 1912, "The great difficulty about getting information ... with regard to seating accommodation and lavatory accommodation in Department stores is that the girls ... are afraid that if they gave the information they would lose their occupation." When employees did testify against their managers, they knew their employers would scrutinize their remarks. Only a couple of saleswomen gave testimony to the BC minimum wage hearings, and when they did their manager sat right beside them.[71]

At Canada's biggest stores, striking and joining a labour union were grounds for dismissal. It is true that the Dupuis Frères had a union, but it was operated by management. Retail employees did not have to look very far to find examples of store workers who had lost their jobs because of collective action. At Eaton's in the nineteenth century, notes Santink, "company upholsterers who participated in one [Labour Day] parade were promptly dismissed."[72] In 1900 the infant Vancouver local of the American-based Retail Clerks' International Protective Association (RCIPA) told the Vancouver Trades and Labour Council that "certain large stores in this City had discharged or threatened with discharge their clerks for belonging to the Retail Clerks' Association."[73] When approximately one thousand unionized Eaton's Toronto garment workers, both men and women, struck against Eaton's in 1912, President John Eaton told the *Globe*, "When men are engaged for us, they must remember they are paid by us not by the union ... Now they are out, they are out the door for good. Not a single man will be reinstated ... if the rest go on strike, it will be safe for you to put into type that 2,000 will be out of work."[74] John Eaton held fast, and shortly afterwards over one thousand workers were dismissed.[75] Five years later Spencer's fired five Vancouver clerks for demonstrating interest in unionizing.[76] Again in 1934, Eaton's fired thirty-eight Toronto female factory operatives who had made contact with a union.[77] Even when department stores simply suspected that employees were unionizing, managers monitored their activities. In 1917 one manager loitered in front of the Vancouver Labor Temple "to see if any of his clerks were attending a ... meeting."[78]

Perhaps Eaton's most sustained anti-labour activities occurred during the six-week Winnipeg General Strike of Spring 1919. More than five hundred Eaton's workers walked off the job, causing Sir John Eaton to publicly "threaten" to close the Winnipeg store, as the *New York Times* put it in its coverage of the strike, "for a year if the strikers win."[79] Probably because of Eaton's advertising clout, Canada's major papers made no mention of this statement, but it did reach readers of major US papers, including both the *New York Times* and the *Chicago Daily Tribune*.[80] Eaton's other anti-union actions included placing classified advertisements for employees in the *Strike Editions* of the *Winnipeg Telegram:* "Sorters and Trimmers for Amateur Photo Finishing Department," "6 Experienced Furniture Packers," "1 Experienced Finisher," "1 Experienced Cabinet-maker," "Three Experienced Furniture Polishers," and "Waitresses,

Kitchen Help and Male Cooks for Grill and Lunch Rooms."[81] In calling for workers in these occupations, Eaton's revealed its determination to stave off unionization among craftworkers, for whom the process and philosophy of unionization were traditionally strong. It additionally revealed that Eaton's kitchens, where both men and women worked, were pro-labour strongholds. Eaton's also gave employees time off to attend anti-strike demonstrations, and it was rumoured that the company paid workers for participating in anti-labour parades. When the Winnipeg General Strike ended and Eaton's strikers returned to work, nobody was surprised when the company fired more than three hundred of them.[82]

Such blatant anti-unionism would have prevented many of Canada's largest stores' employees from unionizing and striking, but it was not the only factor that inhibited collective labour action. Drawn not only from working-class families but also from petit bourgeois and agricultural families, some girls and women who obtained jobs in department stores were unfamiliar with organized labour. In her letter to the Saskatchewan Minimum Wage Board, a woman from a small Prairie town revealed she did not know what to do about the HBC's refusal to pay adequate wages. Instead of contacting a labour organization, she "appealed to the Y.W.C.A. and was advised to write direct to you." Eaton's participation in the early-closing movement, along with its provision of half-holidays on Saturdays, might have further tempered workers' desires for organizing. In the late nineteenth and early twentieth centuries in the United States, France, and British Columbia, clerks' primary motivators for unionization were the achievements of hours and benefits like those established by Timothy Eaton and Robert Simpson. In 1887 saleswomen at four Pittsburgh department stores went on strike successfully for holidays and shorter hours.[83]

Recognizing the increasing presence of women in clerking, some male clerks' unions, usually composed of salesmen from small stores, tried to include women in their ranks. In 1900 a group of retail clerks in Vancouver formed Local 279 of the Retail Clerks' National Protective Association, which soon changed its name to the Retail Clerks' International Protective Association (RCIPA). In 1904 some retail clerks in Victoria also joined the RCIPA. Formed in 1835, the RCIPA was a male union that, as Benson writes, "was at best paternalistic and often outright hostile to the organizing of saleswomen." The RCIPA was strongest in tight-knit independent shops, where feelings of solidarity were more easily created than in big stores. Despite such difficulties, a handful of female workers did join the

Vancouver and Victoria locals. They might have derived a sense of solidarity from their membership, but they also might have experienced gender discrimination. According to historian David Neufeld, "the RCIPA locals in British Columbia held many traditional ... notions about the role of women in society." In the words of the Victoria local, women had to "conserve their health and strength [because] they are the future mothers of the race." The BC RCIPA locals viewed women as mothers first and workers second. At the end of the Great War, the RCIPA in Victoria wanted to see women receive a minimum of fifteen dollars weekly, and men to receive a minimum of twenty-five dollars.[84]

Surveying the odds against unionization, Benson comments, "it is remarkable not how little but how often saleswomen tried to organize."[85] In fact, 485 female employees of Canada's largest department store joined the largest general strike to ever occur in Canada: the 1919 Winnipeg General Strike. Some were blue-collar workers from mail order and factory departments, some were white-collar staff from sales and clerical units, and some were from the so-called grey-collar departments of hairdressing and waitressing. When the strike came to a close, the second vice-president of Eaton's sent a letter to each Winnipeg staff member who did not walk off the job. He wrote,

> With the hearty approval of Sir John C. Eaton this letter is addressed to you. Times such as we have just passed through test the loyalty and the devotion to duty of our boys and girls.
>
> During the past six weeks you have given a fine example of these qualities. You have given your time so unsparingly and have done everything asked of you in excess of your regular duties so willingly, that you have helped us to carry on successfully.
>
> For your untiring efforts the Company wishes to express to you its most hearty thanks. While we do not attempt to place a money value on such service we trust the enclosed will in a measure express the Company's appreciation.

This correspondence re-established the paternalist relationship between Sir John and his "boys and girls" and rewarded employees financially for their loyalty. Also following the strike, Eaton's staff superintendent arranged interviews with the women and men who had participated so as to determine whether they were likely to cause further trouble. He allowed 272 strikers to return to their positions, and he fired 343. In a letter to Eaton's vice-president he noted, "The strike was in some respects, a blessing in disguise, as we have been relieved of a number of people who were nothing but a load to carry." Such a statement well describes Eaton's attitude toward workers who questioned the company's style of labour management.[86]

Female retail employees do not appear in most recorded descriptions of strike and union activity before the Second World War. So far, Eaton's employees' participation in the Winnipeg General Strike is the largest and most sustained known example of such collective action prior to 1943, when hundreds of Simpson's female employees in Toronto voted to unionize. Importantly, though, women in other kinds of retail outlets did launch strikes. In 1917, again in Winnipeg, women who worked at the discount chain Woolworth's went on strike for higher pay, "union recognition, and a half-day holiday." Woolworth's refused to recognize the union, and most striking women lost their jobs. Women who were hired afterwards, though, did receive higher wages. Given this record of female retail employees' determination to better their conditions, it is possible that further research into the experiences of female department store workers will reveal other instances of collective workplace action.[87]

THE TWENTIETH-CENTURY RISE of mass retail helped create the entry-level customer service labour force so familiar to Canadians today. Through its investigation of developments in department stores between 1890 and 1940, this chapter explores female retail employees' experiences. It shows that pink-collar department store workers came not only from working-class backgrounds but also from petit bourgeois and agricultural backgrounds. Most of them had secondary education and were English-speaking, native-born, and Anglo-Celtic. Several were young, single, and lived with their parents, but some were married and lived with their husbands. Some were breadwinners for their children and siblings, and some were mature, single, or widowed and independent.

Girls and women chose to work for Canada's biggest stores for various reasons. Most compelling was the need for money. Other considerations included department stores' respectability, hours, sociability, welfare programs, and opportunities for skills development. Compared with domestic service and factory work, department store employment offered the possibility, however slim, of glamour and occupational mobility. Nevertheless, department store work did have negative aspects. Sales floor workers were on their feet all day, often dealing with difficult customers. Their daily lives were shaped by expectations of servitude, assumptions of inferiority to men, and less than ideal wages. Department stores were also intensely paternalist. Female employees faced objectification and other forms of sexism, and all employees were subject to arbitrary authority, job insecurity, and an intolerance of unions. Such conditions made it difficult for girls and women to launch organized grievances. It is therefore unsurprising that much employee resistance took the form of individualized protest, including quitting, foot dragging, thieving, and behaving rudely toward customers.[88] A few female retail employees did, however, organize and protest collectively. Most dramatically, more than five hundred women at Eaton's walked out during the Winnipeg General Strike.

Ideals of respectable femininity shaped wage-earning girls' and women's activities. Some applied for jobs in department stores because the stores allowed women to remain ladylike. Salesgirls and businesswomen at Eaton's, the HBC, Simpson's, Woodward's, Spencer's, Morgan's, and the Dupuis Frères dressed in elaborate, feminine, and stylish fashions because such attire allowed them to showcase their femininity and their social status. Given unionism's association with masculinity, it is possible that some women's desires for respectability prevented them from associating with this form of workplace protest. Many of the individualized, even cautious, forms of resistance in which many girls and women did take part did not directly challenge their ladyhood.

Even more central to pink-collar girls' and women's lack of unionization, though, was the power their employers exerted. Department stores were among the largest and most visible enterprises in the country, and they went to great lengths to prevent their workers from organizing. Those who laboured for Eaton's, Simpson's, and Canada's other large department stores between 1890 and 1940 risked instant dismissal if they demonstrated interest in unionization. Department stores' hostility to unionism was hence ultimately responsible for non-unionization.

Even in the face of employers' resistance, pink-collar women at the Dupuis Frères, Eaton's, Simpson's, the HBC, Woodward's, and Spencer's did not always accept their jobs' expectations of servitude, docility, and quiescence. They engaged in a range of protests, formal and informal, against owners, managers, and shoppers. While their struggles are only now being recovered, further research might reveal more retail workplace action. For now it is important to note that department stores' female employees were proud not only of their femininity but also of their labour. They endeavoured to shape their working environments into settings that recognized their entitlements, both as women and as workers. Their willingness to challenge the limits of patriarchy and capitalism illustrates that today's customer service workers have a rich heritage of struggle, solidarity, and achievement.

7

Criticizing the Big Stores

[There are] not only members of all trade unions which the T. Eaton Company has endeavored to crush, but besides there are the shopkeepers [it] has undersold, druggists [it] has undercut, whole towns and cities [it] has manipulated.

– *International Ladies Garment Workers' Union, 1912*

ONE TUESDAY MORNING IN April 1935, a group of seven hundred unemployed people entered the Hudson's Bay Company's [HBC] department store in downtown Vancouver. They occupied the entire main floor, blocking aisles and ignoring managers' requests to leave. Demanding "food and shelter" from the city, they had originally planned to occupy Spencer's, Vancouver's largest store, but managers had seen the marchers coming and had locked the doors in advance. Rather than sending a negotiator to the store, the city and federal government together sent over three hundred police officers. In response, the demonstrators began "kicking in showcases, smashing perishable goods," "throwing other articles to the floor," and causing thousands of dollars' worth of damage. Officers responded by beating six rioters unconscious, themselves receiving "cuts and bruises." The protesters left the HBC and joined 1,300 other unemployed people in a park ringed by fifty provincial police, "two truckloads" of Royal Canadian Mounted Police (RCMP), and thirty-five RCMP astride horses. This demonstration was interrupted when Mayor G.G. McGeer climbed a podium and read the Riot Act. Under threat of attack, the unemployed dispersed.[1]

As this book reveals, between 1890 and 1940 Canada's biggest retailers became symbols of Canadian democratic consumer modernity. They marketed themselves not only as public spaces that all Canadians could enter but also as providers of comfort, luxury, and success to all Canadians. That the unemployed sit-down strikers chose first Spencer's and then the

HBC to hold their demonstration is therefore significant. By occupying a large department store in downtown Vancouver, the demonstrators drew attention to the irony of their poverty. In a country and city that could produce such monuments of consumerist democracy as department stores, which sold everything from cakes to books to pianos, it no doubt seemed to the protesters absurd that large segments of the population should live without food and shelter. Thus, when the police descended upon the strikers and ordered them to disperse, it is unsurprising that many of them chose to smash display cases and ruin the goods for sale. After having experienced destitution and joblessness, the demonstrators would probably have perceived display cases and price tickets as powerful reminders of their own inability to attain material security.

The 1935 HBC riot was a dramatic event, born of the desperation caused by the Great Depression and by the state's intransigent response to such desperation. And yet as Chapter 5 demonstrates, many other Canadians between 1890 and 1940 felt similarly frustrated at the class inequality that permeated the rise of Canada's supposedly democratic consumer society. Indeed, the 1935 incident was not the only occasion between the late nineteenth century and the Second World War that Canadians publicly criticized the giant retailers. Throughout this period attacks upon Canada's largest retailers were made by a range of groups, including merchants, co-operators, labour activists, and women's rights activists.

This chapter explores these attacks and reveals that the concerns voiced by Canadian department store critics echoed statements made by critics in other industrializing countries. Like commentators in France, Great Britain, and the United States, department store critics in Canada viewed department stores primarily as threatening to more desirable ways of life.[2] Central to commentators' understandings of retail's threats, moreover, were ideas about gender. As did critics in other countries, Canadian commentators used images of the victimized and greedy female shoppers and employees to prove their point. The appearance of these figures in such commentary lends credence to the feminist observation that deep-rooted concerns about gender and sexuality pervaded urbanization, corporate monopolization, and the rise of consumer culture in the late nineteenth and early twentieth centuries.[3]

Small shopkeepers, moralists, philanthropists, feminists, and the labour and co-operative movements have all received attention from Canadian historians. This chapter draws on their work but at the same time extends existing research by revealing similarities among these groups' beliefs, as well as by offering analyses of hitherto unexamined archival and published materials. Considering not only what critics said about department stores but also what critics did to alleviate mass retail's negative influence, the chapter suggests that those concerned about the future of Canadian society believed department stores to be emblematic of modern inequality and depravation. As well, this chapter probes the efficacy of various attempts to rectify department store injustices, and it proposes that two factors prevented these attempts from being successful: first, critics never adequately addressed the complex motivations behind people's decisions to patronize Canada's biggest shops and, second they were never able to convince the federal and provincial governments to take decisive action against the giant retailers.[4]

Unfair Competition

As soon as they emerged, department stores aroused small merchants' anger. As Santink remarks, the rise and success of department stores in the late nineteenth century "drew the scorn and wrath of those who could not compete with this new manner of doing business." Some historians have chalked up shopkeepers' resentment of department stores to an unwillingness to participate in modern mass merchandising.[5] According to Monod, though, small merchants were willing to embrace change, but they were hampered in their efforts because, once department stores became established, it became difficult for small merchants to compete with mass retail's low prices, large selections, and convenient services.[6] By 1897, Ontario merchants' anger about department store tactics had crystallized sufficiently to result in the formation of the Retail Merchants Association (RMA), based in Toronto but including merchants from ninety-two Ontario towns as far east as Ottawa, as far north as North Bay, and as far west as Parry Sound. The RMA grew throughout the early twentieth century, becoming by the 1930s a major national lobby group instrumental in bringing about the federal 1934-38 Royal Commission into Price Spreading and Mass Buying, as well as such provincial campaigns as a 1937 attempt in BC to have Victoria legislate against mass retailers' practice of pricing items below cost.[7]

During the RMA's inaugural year, the Toronto weekly *Saturday Night,* a mid-brow magazine offering news items, thought pieces, poetry, and fiction, ran a series of articles called "The Barnums of Business." Sympathetic to the RMA, the series was authored by printer and journalist Joseph T. Clark, who went by "Mack"; it aimed to drum up anti-department store sentiment.[8] "Barnums" was named after a New York showman who had become famous forty years earlier for his funhouse and circus offerings, including P.T. Barnum's Grand Traveling Museum, Menagerie, Caravan and Hippodrome, as well as for coining the phrase "There's a sucker born every minute." *Saturday Night*'s choice of title for its anti-mass-retail series was apt, for "Barnums of Business" argued that department stores' success derived entirely from their ability to trick the public into buying their wares. As Mack put it, department stores were managed by "shrewd and unscrupulous men" who "have cleverly mixed retail storekeeping with the tricks of the circus, the lottery, the junkshop and the confidence man."[9]

"Barnums" offered several examples of department store "trickery." Foremost among them were descriptions of department store items that appeared to be of high value but were actually of low value. Mack informed readers that department stores' seed packets were cheaper than those sold elsewhere because there were fewer seeds per package, that department stores' inexpensive candy was made with glucose rather than refined sugar, that department stores' pill boxes contained fewer pills than did boxes sold by drug stores, that tea dust was mixed into department stores' premium teas, and that department stores' spools of silk appeared bigger than usual because the wooden spools were rounded on each side rather than being straight. The series also portrayed loss leaders – items priced below cost and heavily advertised so as to draw customers into the stores – as dishonest. "Barnums" also contained several discussions about the negative consequences of mass retailing. Depicting department stores as "evil" threats to vibrant communities, the series suggested that by drawing customers' money away from shops in urban neighbourhoods and rural towns, department stores ruined the economic sustainability of individual, vibrant communities. In contrast to "honest" and "fair" independent shopkeepers, department stores did not pay local taxes, employ local workers, offer credit to locals in need, or participate in local initiatives. Customers who gave their money to the giant retailers, then, were supporting a depreciation of local real estate values, a rise in local unemployment, and a destruction of local communities.[10]

"Barnums" was inventive, using poetry and images in its campaign. In one instalment, a humorous, six-stanza poem by Ernest E. Leigh, called "The Departmental," appeared. Suggesting that Satan himself approved of the "scooping" done by mass retailers, the poem mimics department stores' advertising language, saying that after Lucifer fell he resolved to sell "'hot bargains' at 'rock bottom.'" He "rack'd his brain" for "centuries"

MONOPOLIZED.

FIGURE 7.1   Illustration suggesting that department stores are hogs at the trough of consumer trade. | *Source:* Reprinted from *The Ram's Horn* and featured in Mack, "The Barnums of Business," *Saturday Night,* 17 April 1897, 8. Copyright expired.

on how to do so, and was finally inspired by "the departmental": "'Hurrah!' he said, and swish'd his sting; / 'Hurrah, thou blatant, bloated thing!' / An all his imps, with swagg'ring swing, / Yell'd, "bargain Day's next Friday!'"[11] In another issue "Barnums" included an illustration of a hog that represented department stores, sitting in the trough of "trade." The caption reads, "Monopolized" (Figure 7.1). In addition, "Barnums" ran advertisements for fake department stores, lampooning their hyperbolic language and promises of great amusements and deals. Under the banner "Ketchem, Skinem & Cookem's Mammoth Department Store," one advertising parody stated, "We shoe horses, run threshing machines, repair clocks, mend umbrellas, grind scissors, doctor furniture, peddle pills, keep a livery stable, conduct funerals, dig wells, sell cemetery lots, pull teeth, and sell some goods. We want to do all the business on earth."[12]

Despite "Barnums" tongue-in-cheek approach, it was serious in its efforts to curtail department stores. It reported with fanfare on the first meeting of the RMA; it also discussed the RMA's provincial lobbying efforts.

Unfortunately for "Barnums," and despite the RMA's best efforts, the Ontario legislature paid lip service to the RMA's claims of unfair competition but did nothing during "Barnums" run to regulate mass retail. Not to be deterred, *Saturday Night* printed a petition to reform postal regulations, which readers could cut out, circulate, and mail to the postmaster general. According to the petition, the regulation that allowed for the free circulation of newspaper had enabled department store advertising to flourish, for department stores could now send out free "fake newspapers" whose sole intent was to advertise. The petition also asked for reform of the law that permitted all parcels to be distributed at equal price, arguing that heavy parcels shipped by department stores over long distances represented an unfair tax burden on the tax-paying citizenry. In addition to the petition, *Saturday Night* reprinted its "Barnums" series in pamphlet form. Selling for six cents each, the booklets were popular among merchants, who bought them to give to customers. Finally, "Barnums" reprinted sympathetic letters from its readers. James Symon of Wharton wrote to say, "I believe that your article will do an immense amount of good," while George Watson of Toronto not only congratulated *Saturday Night* for the series but further suggested that retail merchants should, "as a matter of justice, patronize another," rather than taking their own private business to the big shops. Another "prominent citizen of Toronto, and a retail merchant" added his thoughts, arguing that shopkeepers should require certification to sell their particular line of products, and that no one shopkeeper should be allowed to "sell more than one branch of goods in one store." Such letters demonstrated that "Barnums" was having an impact on readers, creating a community of anti-department store thinkers and perhaps activists. Some of them, such as the one that argued for certification, also revealed that small merchants took pride in their product knowledge and specialization and believed their expertise set them apart from the big stores.[13]

Other late-nineteenth-century periodicals also criticized department stores. According to the *Monetary Times*, "The existence and increase of enormous concerns such as Eaton's, Simpson's, Walker's, which are no longer dry goods shops alone, but bazaars which trench upon the business of druggists, booksellers, crockery men, picture dealers, are a growing menace to the small retailer. The system is eating up the smaller men, many of whom can no longer pay their former rent, if indeed they can continue in business at all."[14] Yet between 1890 and 1940, the "Barnums of Business" was probably the most sustained press campaign against

Canadian department stores to be published. As department stores' advertising budgets increased, the giant shops wielded growing power over the mainstream press. According to Mack, at one time both the Toronto *World* and *Globe* had reported, "with much truth and feeling," on the "ruin that was being done in Toronto" by the big stores. By 1897, though, they had "dropped the fight, and instead began to publish the big advertisements of these all gobbling monopolies."[15] Labour sympathizers also noted department stores' influence. In 1904 the *Toronto Trades Union Guild and Mercantile Directory* called department stores a "modern octopus," stating, "By their advertising revenues they control the press."[16] In 1912, Toronto feminist and labour activist Alice Chown concurred, noting that despite her frequent efforts to publicize an Eaton's garment workers' strike, the newspapers "were all afraid to publish any account of the strike, because the firm carried a large amount of advertising matter."[17] Indeed, during the First World War, President John Eaton owned 11.7 percent of the stock in the *Toronto Star* and suppressed articles he disliked.[18]

Even during the hearings that took place in the 1930s as part of the Royal Commission on Price Spreading and Mass Buying, some newspapers were reluctant to criticize department stores. Editors refrained from comment, and newspapers that did report on the commission's findings did so in a tone of impartiality. "Hudson's Bay Co. Growth Reviewed" noted one *Vancouver Daily Province* headline. Significantly, however, when the commission found that department stores' practices were driving down wages, some newspapers did quote directly from testimony presented to the commission. When in June 1934 the commission found that buying competitions between Eaton's and Simpson's were causing cuts in garment workers' pay, the *Globe* ran a front-page article titled "Big Stores' Bid for Trade Cuts Wages of 10,000." The author himself did not criticize Eaton's or Simpson's, but he did note that "Samuel Factor, Toronto Liberal, pointed out that 630 of the overcoats mentioned [in one advertisement] cost less than $15 and were sold at $25" and that "Norman Sommerville, K.C., of Toronto, counsel for the committee, said the initial mark-up cost when the coats went into the store ranged from 13 percent to 98 percent." During this period of financial crisis and widespread wage and job cuts, this *Globe* article demonstrated that some newspapers were willing to lose advertising revenue in their attempts to cover the consequences of the economic downturn. It also indicates that as department stores' market shares decreased, newspapers became bolder in their coverage of the giant retailers' activities.[19]

With or without mainstream newspapers' support, small merchants continued their fight against department stores. At times they achieved modest success. In 1897, and in response to a druggists' complaint, Judge Dugas of Montréal "fined two department store firms $25 each for selling patent medicines." Between 1895 and 1907, independent boot and shoe merchant Isaac B. Johnston of Toronto brought a number of complaints to the Court of Revision. Stating Eaton's taxes were too low, he persuaded the city to increase taxes on Eaton's, on an almost annual basis.[20] Meanwhile, RMA lobbying on tax issues inspired Ontario to pass a new business tax in 1904. Containing a special clause for department stores, the bill stated, "Every person carrying on the business of what is known as a departmental store ... or in connected premises where the assessed value of the premises exceeds $20,000," is accountable for a "sum equal to 50 percent of the assessed value of the said land and premises in addition to the full assessment of said land and premises."[21]

As department store catalogues moved into rural areas, rural merchants joined their urban counterparts' fight. One shopkeeper in a small Ontario town wrote to "Barnums of Business" to say that employees who receive municipal wages should not be allowed to shop in department stores, for the "taxes paid by local merchants" help pay municipal salaries.[22] In Gimli, Manitoba, a shopkeeper ripped up an Eaton's hat that a customer had just received in the mail. As Jean Bruce and Eleanor Thompson of the Canadian Museum of Civilization record in their summary of an interview with a former Eaton's catalogue customer, "the shopkeeper chastized the woman for ordering this hat and told her she had better hats in her store for less money. She then proceeded to rip up the hat and handed her customer a big woman's hat that wouldn't have fit her daughter, and said, 'now take this to your daughter, this is a much nicer hat with red ribbons.'"[23] To further beat mail order competition, shopkeepers destroyed Eaton's catalogues. General country merchants, as William Stephenson relates, "who usually acted as postmasters ... 'lost' or destroyed copies of the hateful [Eaton's catalogue] which made them seem like customer-gouging scoundrels."[24] So opposed were rural Saskatchewan merchants to department stores that during the 1930s they lobbied for – and secured – state protection of their businesses. In 1937 the province ruled that relief recipients could not spend clothing allowances on out-of-province mail orders, and it further stipulated that municipalities could order recipients to take their clothing orders to local merchants.[25]

Small shopkeepers were the most vocal defenders of their cause, but they did receive support from independent commentators. Most did not support small merchants per se but rather felt that when small-town buyers sent their money to distant corporations, they lost opportunities to enrich their own communities. According to a sermon delivered by Reverend R.A. Burriss of Bowmanville, Ontario, in 1897, "Our merchants rent stores, pay taxes, keep up our schools and churches." For these reasons, "People who spend their money elsewhere should be sent along with it, for they are more than useless to our town." According to an anonymous letter sent to a Toronto newspaper in 1904, Canadian citizens should not "be taxed for a parcel postage, which benefits so largely the Babel stores of the great cities, to the injury of local trade." Fiction writers also criticized department stores' inroads. In Lucy Maud Montgomery's *Anne's House of Dreams* (1917), set in Prince Edward Island, the opinionated Mrs. Lynde says that "too much money [is] going out of this Island to ... Eaton's." Politicians, too, got involved. Shortly before the First World War, the Conservative government of Ontario awarded Eaton's a contract to print all provincial primary school textbooks. The Opposition was against this decision, arguing that it would destroy local communities. Since Eaton's offered consumers 20 percent discounts if they bought the primers through Eaton's instead of local stores, Eaton's was effectively ruining the primary textbook trade. This bothered the Opposition: "We want a little for the Province outside of the city of Toronto."[26]

Shopkeepers' criticism of department stores became an issue of public debate during the Depression. As profits dropped and belts were tightened, commentators blamed factories' and retailers' markups for the imbalance between production and consumption. Conservative member of Parliament Herbert Stevens decided to use these sentiments to increase his profile. In 1934 he convinced Conservative Prime Minister R.B. Bennett to launch a Royal Commission on Price Spreads. Its purpose, as the report states, was to "investigate the causes of the large spread between the prices received for commodities by the producer thereof, and the price paid by the consumers therefore; and the system of distribution in Canada of farm and other natural products, as well as manufactured products." Commissioners were particularly to look at "the effect of mass buying by department and chain store organizations upon the regular retail trade of the country, as well as upon the business of manufacturers and products" and the "labour conditions prevailing in industries supplying the requirements of such department and chain store organizations."[27] The government invited Canadians to appear before the commission and send the commission their letters. "Day after day," writes Monod, the commission "revealed the way that the chains and the departmentals had ruthlessly slashed salaries and wages, how they had cancelled spillage and wastage allowances, and how efforts had been made to cheat unknowing customers out of their hard-earned pennies."[28]

Business owners took an immediate interest. Retail associations, independent merchants, and sympathizers across the country sent in their thoughts. It was unanimous: department and chain stores were responsible for devastating independent shops. Their buying power, advertising might, and ruthless opening of branch stores brought down labour conditions, lowered product and service standards, and ruined local communities. The Independent Retail Merchants of the City of Yorkton sent an especially descriptive letter: "We .... Hereby resolve that ... the Local Retail Trade has and is suffering the consequences of being unable to compete with the existing method used by Large Mail Order Houses and Chain Departmental Stores in buying and selling." In members' opinion, "protection for [independent] merchants is vital for them to survive." In fact "the greatest existing evil in modern merchandising [is] Chain Department Stores." Eaton's, Simpson's, and the HBC "do not stay with General Store merchandise ... when they see an opportunity for further profit." Department stores trounce on small businesses' terrain, "[posing] as chemists, optometrists, hardware merchants, jewellers ... using only the 'best sellers' of these places – Their bread and butter lines, and [cutting] in price to act as 'bait.'" Department stores' low prices make the small shopkeeper "appear as an overcharging rogue, not to be trusted ... because he must be fleecing the public." Although the local merchant "keeps the community going," his customers consider him "much inferior to a highly advertised and highly capitalized corporation."[29] In this letter, the Independent Retail Merchants of the City of Yorkton portrayed small merchants as virtuous and community-minded. Customers' preferences for department stores were considered but quickly passed over. Instead of taking customers' quests for low prices and stylish merchandise seriously, and their own inabilities to meet these demands, the Yorkton retail merchants depicted their predicament as akin to that of David facing Goliath. Take away the evil department stores, the association suggested, and customers will happily patronize local dealers.

In their complaints, small retailers spelled out how department stores counteracted civic goals. C.P. Moore of C.P. Moore Limited, Heavy and Shelf Hardware in Sydney, Nova Scotia, stated, "local dealers, even though they may not do a very large business, are the men who pay the local taxes, take an interest in local affairs, and are ... the back bone of the Community in which they live. In contrast ... the big Department Stores, of which we have three on our street ... have no interest in our city affairs, beyond their own immediate stores."[30] In Moore's view, local merchants sustained local communities. Department stores, in contrast, drained money from local coffers and channelled it toward metropolitan regions. J.E. McCurdy, of McCurdy and Company, Direct Importers of Exclusive Ready to Wear, Knitted Wear, Children's Wear, and Millinery, also in Sydney, agreed with Moore. Department stores, he wrote, "endeavour to squeeze everything they possibly can out of the community and put nothing back. All their interest is wrapped up in grinding out money and sending it out of the community .... Their main object ... is to ride everybody else into destruction, using for ammunition, their mass buying power."[31] Given the similarities between Moore's and McCurdy's complaints, it is probable they attended the same business meeting prior to writing their letters.

Some letters went into detail regarding department stores' destructiveness. J.M. Ferguson, Manager of Ferguson and Co., General Merchant and Hardware in Ruthilda, Saskatchewan, related,

> A few years ago anything required could be got in our Village now a good many lines cannot be got at all. We had built a fine church, school, community hall &c, now I understand our minister is leaving in June as we cannot support him ... there is talk of the school likely to be shut ... and the community hall ... is not used for anything now ... it looks more like a barn than a hall ... While these conditions cannot all be blamed on the patrons spending their money in the mail order houses, still I am certain a good deal of it can be traced to that.[32]

E.F. Chesney of Wolseley, Saskatchewan, had similar grievances.

> At one time a certain portion of the wealth produced in a district circulated in the district. The trading supported local institutions, like a good school, clean sport and all other activities that made the home town a place with some community life, and a place which the resident was proud of, and fully satisfied with and a good place to live and rear his family in. Now the trading

is enticed to the large City where massed Capital is able to dictate to Manufacturers, prices at which merchandise will be bought for, and are then in a
position to offer for sale at prices less than the small business man can buy."[33]

Angry at the difficulty of maintaining a vibrant small town on the modernizing Prairies, Ferguson and Chesney blamed department stores for drawing consumer dollars from their districts.

Farmers, too, were unhappy. In 1934, J.W. Harris sent a telegram to
W.L. McQuarrie of Saskatoon, to be forwarded to the commission: "Mass
buyers particularly harmful to farmers within Saskatoon District stop they
can buy potatoes at less than price retailer pays local farmer and undersell
retailer who is forced to continually cut down price to farmer to compete
stop Saskatoon consumes approximately twelve thousand bushels each
month and local farmers could raise all requirements if reasonable price
was maintained."[34] By selling at lower costs than local retailers who purchased local goods, department stores hurt both local shopkeepers and
local producers.

Letters sent to the inquiry portrayed department stores as rapacious
corporations that victimized virtuous distributors and producers. Merchants called for government regulation of department stores so as to
level the retail playing field. They were not critical of profit seeking per
se; rather, they suggested department stores were not following rules of
gentlemanly business conduct. A begrudging acceptance of consumers'
desires for low prices and quality goods lurked within their complaints.
Retailers knew customers would seek out the best deals. In order that
customers would continue to find the independent shop competitive, it
was necessary for the state to weaken the mass merchandiser. This position
was not overly sympathetic to consumers. Although local merchants
claimed they were interested in civic values, they ignored the wishes of
their own community's citizens for affordable, quality merchandise. Since
women tended to shop more frequently than men, the merchants' unwillingness to seriously consider consumers' motivations hints at a gender
blind spot within their arguments.

Whatever the shortcomings of small retailers' complaints, they were, in
the end, moot, for the Royal Commission on Price Spreads and Mass
Buying did not secure long-lasting legislative reform. Stevens resigned his
position as chair of the commission before the commission's report was
even written. Due partly to Prime Minister R.B. Bennett's disinclination
to blame retail for price spreading, and partly to strong relationships

forged during the Depression among Eaton's President R.Y. Eaton, Simpson's President C.L. Burton, and the Conservative cabinet, the report only made mild recommendations. As Monod states, it "urged a maintenance of the old combines approach, a fairly minor revision to the Criminal Code, and an only half-hearted form of codification."[35] The state's unwillingness to interfere in Canada's retail landscape ensured department stores could, and would, continue their decades-old traditions of undercutting small competitors, offering better merchandise, and drawing money out of local communities.

Unfair Labour Practices

As department stores grew, criticism of their labour practices emerged alongside criticism of unfair retailing strategies. In Canada and elsewhere, the long hours store clerks worked was one of labour's earliest grievances against the big retailers. From the mid-nineteenth century onwards, labour and reform groups pushed for shorter store hours so clerks could enjoy leisure time and worship.[36] Closing Societies targeting store hours appeared in the United States as early as 1835; these societies became antecedents to the Retail Clerks National Protective Association (RCNPA), established in 1890.[37] Interestingly, shop owners supported early-closing efforts. They believed shorter hours would curb late-hours competition, lessen overhead expenses, and make them appear labour-friendly.[38] In the 1870s in Montréal, proponents of Saturday half-holidays, along with members of the Nine Hours Labour League, convinced the city to make the closing hours for large stores earlier. In the 1880s the Dry Goods Store Clerks in Montréal began supporting what became known in Canada as the Early Closing Movement.[39] During the 1880s, Timothy Eaton began shortening the operating hours of his Toronto store. This move strengthened his reputation for benevolence and invited workforce loyalty. It also allowed him to cut heating and electrical expenses.[40] By the early twentieth century, Eaton's boasted the shortest work week of all major retail stores in the dominion. Eaton's Toronto clerks worked from 8 o'clock to 5 o'clock on weekdays and until 2 o'clock on Saturdays. At the end of the First World War, Eaton's in Toronto cut its hours further. Its regular staff worked eight-hour days during the week and received Saturdays off during July and August. Saturday half-holidays were granted throughout the remainder of the year. Canada's business press applauded Eaton's leadership in the Early Closing Movement, suggesting that it had a number of benefits. Noted Canada's leading business newspaper, *The Financial Post,* in 1919,

Eaton's schedule "demands admiration" because it will attract "the best available help," increase workers' energy and therefore "efficiency," and have a "good effect on public opinion."[41]

Retail clerks' groups composed almost entirely of male members also praised Eaton's involvement in the Early Closing Movement. In cities where department stores continued to close after sunset, retail clerks' organizations pressured merchants and municipal governments to reduce shop assistants' working hours. West Coast shop clerks, a number of whom had been active in the British labour movement before moving to Canada, were especially vocal. In 1899 a group of male Vancouver clerks formed Local 279 of the RCNPA, which soon began calling itself the Retail Clerks International Protective Association (RCIPA).[42] Local 279's primary goal was to shorten retail employees' work week. In 1902 male retail clerks in Victoria established an additional RCIPA local. In 1913 another male retail clerks' association, called the Vancouver Retail Employees Association (VREA), formed on the Mainland. The main objective of both the Victoria RCIPA local and the VREA was to reduce working hours.[43] As D.W. Poupard, executive of the VREA, told the BC Commission on Labour in 1914,

> There is a general unrest among those ... in the retail trade, they feel that they are working under conditions which compare unfavorably with those enjoyed by most others ... Most workers employed in the crafts and trades work only eight hours per day and receive a half holiday each Saturday.
>
> In the case of the retail employee the hours worked are often very excessive and the conditions of labor are mostly monotonous and confined.

In Poupard's opinion, shorter hours were necessary so workers could "study" and "play games or sports" on days other than Sunday.[44]

Like their US counterparts, BC's organized male retail clerks took a peacemaking, conservative stance when liaising with employers and governments. Not wishing to put his supporters' precarious job security in jeopardy, Poupard assured the BC labour commissioners, "We feel that the large majority of the employers would welcome the introduction of a measure whereby a weekly half-holiday and a limitation of hours could be secured."[45] This unwillingness to create employment instability, combined with international developments in labour politics, influenced the RCIPA's relations with Canadian unions. In 1919 the left-leaning One Big Union (OBU) invited British Columbia's RCIPA locals to join its movement, but they refused. Affiliated in the United States with the more conservative American Federation of Labor, which was against the OBU, the RCIPA locals also withdrew from the Vancouver Trades and Labour Council, which supported the OBU.[46] Though RCIPA members were critical of department stores, they did not represent especially serious threats to mass merchandising.

Besides the push for shorter hours, other labour causes also spurred critics into action. At times the response to department store exploitation proved tragic. In 1899, Timothy Eaton decided a strike in his garment factory was imminent. He tried to circumvent the looming event by arranging for several New York garment workers to journey to Toronto to labour at Eaton's. Their contracts stipulated they had to work for Eaton's for a period of six months. If they quit earlier, the cost of their transportation would be deducted from their pay. Eaton did not inform the New York workers that their purpose was to keep Eaton's factories running in the event of a labour stoppage. When Eaton's Toronto garment workers did walk off the job in July 1899, Alexander Reder, a New York cloak maker, was devastated. He did not know he was going to be a strikebreaker, and he told his friends he would rather starve than "scab." He quit working at Eaton's but was unable to pay his way home. He decided instead to fill his pockets with rocks and drown himself in Lake Ontario. At least that is the official story told of his death. According to Phenix, at the inquest that followed, the judge "imposed nothing harsher than a verbal reprimand on Timothy Eaton."[47]

Department stores often portrayed their staff as loyal and content. In fact, some employees engaged in militant protests against the big stores. The best-known examples of organized labour activity at the retailing monopolies between 1890 and 1940 occurred at Eaton's in Toronto. It is important to note, however, that more research into retail history might reveal further instances of organized dissent. As Chapter 6 points out, although one thousand Eaton's employees walked out during the Winnipeg General Strike, labour historians have not yet examined this participation. Fortunately, labour disturbances at Eaton's in Toronto prior to the Second World War have received historians' attention. Scholars have examined a 1902 printers' and bindery girls' strike, in which Eaton's workers refused to print catalogues until Timothy Eaton matched wages and hours with prevailing conditions in the unionized printing trades.[48] A 1912 garment workers' strike has also been studied. In this strike, one thousand employees walked out to protest speed-ups and Eaton's attempts to take away some female workers' sewing jobs. A 1934 garment workers' lockout, in which thirty-eight female employees lost their positions because they had consulted with a union, has also been the subject of scholarly study.[49]

Although the 1902, 1912, and 1934 actions were among the most organized and militant campaigns against department stores, they did not achieve significant reforms. Seven months into the 1902 strike, Eaton's printers accepted one of Timothy Eaton's proposals. He would pay union rates, but printers had to work the same hours as other Eaton's employees. Eaton, moreover, would not recognize his printers' union.[50] Five months after Eaton's garment workers went on strike in 1912, President John Eaton (Timothy's son) offered to re-hire some employees. He offered no concessions; he also stipulated that if union leaders wished to return, they would have to suffer salary cuts.[51] And in 1934, Eaton's never let the locked-out female garment workers return to work.[52] Eaton's anti-unionism is discussed in Chapter 3 and needs no further exploration here. It is important to note, though, that because the state did not assist Eaton's workers, it tacitly supported Eaton's unwillingness to bargain with its employees. Nativist sentiment against "foreign" workers also played a role in the 1912 strike. As Frager argues, since the "vast majority of the Eaton strikers were Jews," some labour sympathizers, activists, and clubwomen saw the Eaton's strike as a Jewish strike. Many were thus less willing to support the strikers than might otherwise have been the case.[53]

The 1902, 1912, and 1934 actions occurred in industries with strong unions. During each event, several unions offered their support, often substantial, to striking and locked-out workers. Middle-class feminists also got involved in the 1912 and 1934 incidents. They were interested in helping Eaton's female wage earners. During each action, interested onlookers drew attention to the gap between Eaton's philanthropic image and its poor labour practices. In 1902 the *Typographical Journal* criticized "the disreputable methods pursued by Tim [Eaton] and his departmental trust to defeat and prostitute the principle he and his psalm singing sycophants so earnestly put forth to the gullible section of the community." The journal observed, "To save his dividents, poor old Tim had better put his philanthropic endowments to that of paying living wages to those who create his wealth."[54] During the 1912 Eaton's strike, the muckraking journal *Jack Canuck* similarly observed that President John Eaton "gives immense amounts of money to hospitals and other institutions to take care of the sick and indigent, and apparently tries very hard to keep these institutions supplied with patients by overworking and underpaying his employees."[55] Unionist Jimmy Simpson, who later became mayor of Toronto, concurred. "We want to lick Eaton good and we are going to lick him good ... These monuments, hospitals and buildings are donated by the oppressors of the people and paid for with sweat money."[56]

Feminist Alice Chown offers an astute explanation of Eaton's tendency to portray itself as benevolent while providing low wages and poor working conditions. In her 1921 fictionalized account of the 1912 strike, she describes how Eaton's "pulled down the blinds of the big show windows on Sunday, so no one would be tempted to break the Sabbath by gazing on desirable goods." She also remarks that Eaton's "carried on extensive welfare work for the employees, and gave handsomely to civic causes." She further observes that the company's board members "were rated as good citizens, loyal supporters of the Methodist church and its various causes, [and] were fêted by both church and national authorities." She is "sure that the members" were proud of their philanthropic tendencies. All the same, Chown also suggests that Eaton's directors would never "share" their "authority" with their employees. She recognizes such a proposition would have made them "sorrowful," for they "had great possessions and power."[57] Unlike other middle-class feminists who applauded Eaton's philanthropic efforts, Chown observed that Eaton's directors chose philanthropy over a greater sharing of wealth because charity did not require a fundamental redistribution of power.

By exploring comments made during the 1902, 1912, and 1934 actions, as well as during other moments in which critics spoke out about retail labour practices, it is possible to identify specific grievances held by labour sympathizers and employees. That department stores paid "starvation wages," as *Jack Canuck* claimed about Eaton's in 1912, was a widespread criticism.[58] Although the main concern of "Barnums of Business" was to show that department stores' merchandising policies compared unfavourably to those of independent shops, the series also touched upon the effect that department stores had on wages. According to Mack, not only did the giant retailers pay insufficient wages to their own employees, but they also drove down wages in all other industries. Their strategy of forcing discounts from suppliers through their bulk purchases also forced suppliers to lower their wages; moreover, when independent shops closed, neighbourhoods lost internally generated revenue. As a result, local workers experienced wage and job reductions. In one advertising spoof, "Barnums" made clear its stand on department stores' wage policies. Noting that the Trades and Labour Council endorsed newspapers that contained

Mephistoph, Eat'em & Co.

EVERY DAY IS BARGAIN DAY IN WORKINGMEN

We Manufacture These Bargains Ourselves by Selling Goods Below Legitimate Cost

What the Workers Must Come to if They Support Departmental Stores

How would the Trade and Labor Council like to see the following advertisement in one of the papers which publish the "news" of bargains in these Departmental Stores, which they have endorsed:

500 Bricklayers, worth	$3 00	per day, reduced to			$1 25
500 Stonecutters, worth	3 50	"	"		1 35
500 Carpenters, worth	2 50	"	"		1 00
1000 Builders' Laborers, worth	1 50	"	"		55
5100 Tailors, worth	1 50	"	"		65
2500 Dressmakers, worth	1 00	"	"		35
3500 Sewing-girls, worth	75	"	"		25
4000 Counter-girls, worth	50	"	"		15
4500 Messenger Boys, worth	35	"	"		10

OUR BOOKKEEPING BARGAINS

50 Bookkeepers, worth	$20 00	per week, reduced to			$5 00
500 Asst. Bookkeepers, worth	10 00	"	"		2 99
1500 Heads of Departments, worth	15 00	"	"		3 98

PULPIT BARGAINS

100 Preachers, worth	$2,000	per year, reduced to			$350 00
1000 Preachers, worth	2,500	"	"		399 00

PRINTERS' BARGAINS

395 Dozen Printers, worth ....$12 00 per week, reduced to................$5 00
(No reserve.)
200 Job Lot of Editors, Reporters (bought of newspapers busted by Departmatal "ads.") reduced to 25c. (the price of removing).

The Labor Bureau can have this pointer to go into business as a departmental store, and do quite a business.

FIGURE 7.2   False advertisement lampooning department stores' advertisements. Rather than offering bargains in goods, it offers bargains in "workingmen." | *Source:* "Mephistoph, Eat'em and Co.," *Saturday Night,* 10 April 1897, 3. Copyright expired.

department stores' advertisements, it hinted that it was time for labour sympathizers to recognize the deleterious effects that department stores were having on the work force (Figure 7.2). By printing hypothetical daily wages of particular labourers employed within and without the big stores, it suggested that department stores' bargains were not in merchandise but in labour costs.[59]

During the first half of the twentieth century, critics continued to rail against department store labour policies. In 1904 the Toronto *Trades Union*

Guild and Mercantile Directory claimed that the monopolist stores "lower clerks' wages" everywhere. In 1921 Chown repeated a common claim when she wrote, Eaton's "pay[s] less wages than trade union wages."[60] And during the Royal Commission on Price Spreads and Mass Buying, the belief that department stores paid low wages surfaced often. Prior to conducting hearings, in fact, commissioners hypothesized that department store profits were achieved not only through markups but also through low wages.[61]

Department stores' anti-unionism was another thorny issue. During the Winnipeg General Strike, the *Western Labor News* frequently mentioned Eaton's and the HBC as being among the most anti-union firms in the city. "There are some who think that trades unions are acceptable to the whole mass of employers today," stated the publication, but "this is not true." Unions are "defied by such men as Barrett, the Eatons, the Hudson's Bay, the Deacons ... and hundreds of others."[62] Given the *Labor News'* anti-Eaton's stance, it is hardly surprising that Canada's largest store pulled its advertising out of the newspaper during the Winnipeg General Strike. Yet, apart from Eaton's and the HBC's strikers themselves, the *Labor News* was not the only anti-department store element active in Winnipeg in 1919. Throughout the strike Eaton's continued sending delivery orders out on trucks, and since Winnipeg's transit system was shut down, it also drove scabs to their job sites. The sight of Winnipeg's department stores' delivery vehicles carrying both merchandise and strikebreakers angered many. On 6 June in the working-class area of Weston, frustration erupted among pro-labour housewives, who attacked three delivery trucks owned by department stores. They "smashed" the trucks' wheels, destroyed the vehicles' merchandise, and drove one of the rigs into "a ditch." They also "assaulted" the trucks' drivers and the "special policemen" who had accompanied the trucks as guards, issued verbal threats to the "shop girls" who were riding the trucks as a means of getting to work, and told the drivers they would "murder" them if they again attempted deliveries. When Winnipeg police arrived on the scene, the situation was so tense it was impossible to conduct an investigation. A few days later, several of the activists were charged with disorderly conduct and assault; some were also fined twenty dollars apiece. In keeping with most mainstream publishers' policy of not naming advertisers within news stories, the *Tribune's* report of this incident did not state the name of the department stores under attack. Since the trucks were carrying female strikebreakers, though, it is likely they were Eaton's trucks. Although hundreds of female Eaton's employees walked off the job during the strike, hundreds also continued working at the big store. As previous chapters reveal, Eaton's offered both "carrot" and "stick" incentives for them to do so, including two-dollar raises for those who did not strike, complete with an accompanying confidential letter communicating the Eaton family's appreciation of the employee's loyal services, and, for those who did strike, threats of job termination. Not only did many white-collar female employees have limited knowledge of unionism, but many also feared for their jobs. In this context it is understandable that many chose to continue working for Eaton's during the strike.[63]

In addition to criticizing department stores' anti-unionism, anti-retail activists in Canada condemned department stores for their refusal to offer job security. In Chown's account of the 1912 Toronto strike, a female striker states, "when each man makes an application for work, he signs an agreement that he can be discharged without notice ... They want work so badly they sign, hoping they will escape [being fired]."[64] In Vancouver one witness told the 1914 provincial labour commission that, "during the Christmas season," one department store stayed open every night until "between nine and ten o'clock." But then on Christmas Eve, "nearly two hundred employees were handed their discharge slips." Among those fired were "forty children fagged out with the strain of extra hours." Upon receiving their notices, "several broke into tears."[65] Job insecurity at the stores became infamous during the Depression. According to the report of the price spreads inquiry, "the decline in business from 1922 to 1933 has caused quite large reductions in the staffs of most department stores and mail order houses, and many of the employees who were retained have not been able to secure a full year's employment."[66]

To retaliate for poor conditions in the big stores, some Canadian labour activists promoted boycotts. In 1897 the Cigarmakers' Union of Hamilton began fining "any member either by himself or through any member of his family" who was "found patronizing" department stores.[67] During various job actions at Eaton's in Toronto, unionists also used boycotts to rally support. To support the printers' strike, people marched along Yonge Street carrying signs that urged "Don't buy at Eatons."[68] In 1912 the International Ladies Garment Workers Union asked supporters to boycott the firm. One poster announcing a "Mass Meeting" about the strike noted that "the Women of the City who control the purchasing power are specially invited" (Figure 7.3).[69] And in 1934, as Frager notes, "Union leaflets that were issued to publicize the dispute called on all women to support

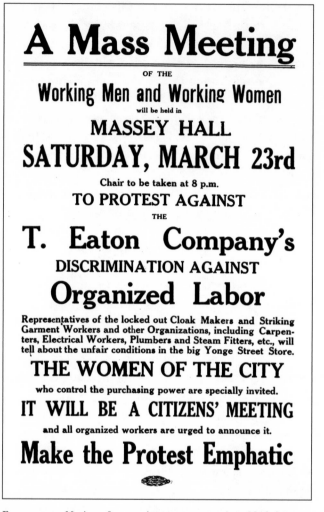

FIGURE 7.3   Notice of upcoming protest meeting, 1912. | *Source:* Archives of Ontario, T. Eaton Papers, Series 162, Oversized Scrapbook. Copyright expired.

the female strikers and declared that before any woman buys a new dress, she should make sure it was made under fair working conditions."[70] Calling for boycotts of Eaton's goods, and urging male labourers and family members to buy commodities made and sold by union members, unionists highlighted links between working people's earning and spending interests.[71]

In her analysis of labour-oriented consumer activism in Seattle, Dana Frank notes that consumer strategies depend on pro-union husbands convincing their wives to shop in ways conducive to unionism's goals. As she writes of 1920s consumer campaigns, "Male union members were quick to demand unionized shopping from wives who they kept out of the movement but whose workload would be increased by seeking out union products and services."[72] However, since working-class housewives were responsible for managing tight budgets that included expenditures for shelter and food, they tended to shop at stores that offered the lowest prices, whether or not they were unionized. Labour's consumer campaigns against stores and manufacturers whose customers included working-class women therefore usually met with half-hearted responses. Calls for boycotts of Eaton's achieved similarly mixed results. In a collection of memories about Eaton's sent to the company's archives, one manager recalled that although printers urged people to boycott the firm, "the wives of the strikers ... continued to buy at the store."[73] It is possible that calls for politicized shopping were more effective when organizers drew on ethnic as well as class solidarity. During the 1912 strike, one labour publication reported that "Jewish patrons of Eaton's" had "transferred their custom to the Robert Simpson Co."[74]

Small shopkeepers' and labour activists' positions hence dovetailed around many issues, including that of consumer spending. Both wanted to change department stores' actions but were unable to convince purchasers to stop patronizing the giant retailers. Because they enjoyed consumer support, department stores were thus able to ignore small merchants' and labour protesters' sentiments. Labour activists' concerns also resembled those of independent merchants in that they were ineffective in sparking state action. As we shall see, particular concerns about women's working conditions and wages resulted in the passing of provincial protective legislation, but this legislation did not seriously hamper department stores' oppressive labour practices. Importantly, though, lobbyists' inefficiency was not responsible for state inaction on labour policy. Rather, federal and provincial governments did not intervene in department stores' labour policies because they rarely interfered with mass retail at all.

Co-operative Alternatives

Merchants and labour activists were the most vocal of Canadian anti-retail activists, but other groups also emerged. Among the most prominent of these were co-operators. Believing that business enterprise should not be owned by the few but rather by the many, they condemned department stores for monopolizing profits and urged individual producers and consumers to form their own marketing and buying organizations. "The co-operative commonwealth," said a 1931 article in the Winnipeg co-operative journal *The Scoop Shovel,* "is an economic and social system under which all the activities in which the people are engaged will be carried out with the object of the mutual benefit of all the people." Unlike Canada's present capitalist system, "in the co-operative commonwealth, every activity connected with the production and distribution of goods ... will be carried on not for the profit of any individual or group, but for the benefit of all."[75] This passage resembles the 1933 Regina Manifesto of the Co-operative Commonwealth Federation (CCF), an emerging social democratic party.[76] Anti-monopolist co-operators and CCFers both wanted to eliminate profiteering and foster active citizenship. Yet, while the CCF believed the state should take more control of the economy, co-operators took a different tack. They believed economic rather than social reform was the best path to fulfillment. Rejecting both communism and democratic socialism, co-operators argued, "Our co-operative system offers the only effective alternative to ... competition and private profit."[77]

Department stores occupied a significant place within co-operators' vision. Unlike small merchants, co-operative activists did not complain about department stores' bulk buying practices, low prices, convenient services, or broad selection. Instead, they were aggrieved that department stores were managed on a monopolistic basis. As H.H. wrote in a letter to the Winnipeg *Grain Growers' Guide* in 1915, the "profits from [a co-operative store] are divided amongst many, while from a [traditional] store only one receives all." Given their preference for member-owned businesses, co-operators were not sympathetic to small merchants' complaints. In his 1915 letter to the *Guide,* J.R. Rowe of Chaplin, Saskatchewan, noted that the small merchants' "plea that money sent away for goods injures the town is a specious one." If he "spent a dollar with a local merchant he [the merchant] sends that part of the dollar away to the wholesaler which he paid for the goods, retaining only the profit." Rather than proposing that independent stores were solutions to department store monopolies, co-operators suggested that people should form member-owned department stores. Stated J.W. Ward in 1911, "If all the farmers doing business at any town in Western Canada" created a co-operative organization, they could "easily maintain a well stocked and up-to-date department store," in which they would always be sure of getting the best goods and reasonable prices." As this statement suggests, co-operators were not against mass retail's practices of bulk buying, wide selection, and low prices. Rather, they felt that if these practices were implemented by a co-operative society, its members would reap the benefits.[78]

Between 1900 and 1940, consumer co-operatives sprang up throughout the country. Ontario, New Brunswick, and Nova Scotia saw co-operators build successful retail stores during the 1910s.[79] Designed to offer lower prices and better goods than both independent shopkeepers and mass merchandisers, co-operators aimed to replace both styles of retailing. More consumer co-operatives emerged in the 1920s and 1930s, enjoying particular success in the eastern part of Nova Scotia; the Ontario cities of Brantford, Hamilton, and Toronto; and the southern half of the Prairies. Central to consumer co-operation in all these regions was the idea that citizens should be educated about the uplifting economic and moral potential of member-owned enterprise. Working with the labour movement, the Ontario stores further sought to educate citizens about how, with their low wages and job insecurity, mass merchandisers exploited not only consumers but also labourers. Both the Saskatchewan Co-op and the United Grain Growers (UGG), meanwhile, sought to offer alternatives to department store catalogues. As Canadian co-operative historian Ian MacPherson puts it, Prairie consumer co-operatives of this period "were strongly opposed to the impersonal large stores associated with the major cities."[80]

From its origins to the Second World War, men dominated the Canadian co-operative movement. Some women did join, including Agnes MacPhail of the United Farmers' of Ontario, and some feminists supported co-operation.[81] Yet, though co-op leaders tried to interest women in co-operation, they did not have much success.[82] As Rusty Neal finds in her research on co-operatives in Nova Scotia, "feminism was almost impossible in co-operatives, as were equality, equal rights and freedom for women."[83] Indeed, co-operators did not always act with homemakers' interests in mind. Like small merchants and labour leaders who urged boycotts of department stores, their philosophical arguments about co-operation's benefits rarely mentioned such topics as budgeting, convenience, or fashion. Given that all three were important to most homemakers when they went shopping, co-operators had difficulty securing female spenders' support. At the same time, it is also important to note that some women ran their own co-operatives. During the Depression, writes Mac-Pherson, "Buying clubs emerged in Windsor, London, and Ottawa and at least three consumer groups appeared in Toronto." One of the Toronto groups was founded and managed by women. Called the Toronto and District Wholesale Society, it operated between 1930 and 1932. After its closing, the same group started another buying club, the Toronto Rochdale Co-operative Society. It remained open until the late 1930s.[84]

Defending Women Workers

With the notable exception of the women who attacked strike-breaking shopgirls in Winnipeg, critics of department stores usually had much sympathy for retail employees. Labourist, journalistic, and reformers' diatribes against the big stores often emphasized department stores' rapacious treatment of women workers. They acknowledged that both male and female retail employees suffered from poor conditions, but they reserved special condemnation for how the big stores treated their female staff. In making such criticisms, their intent was to drum up support for anti-department store positions. Yet emphasizing women's poor working conditions also had other effects. Most importantly, this emphasis suggested that department stores' female employees were defenceless creatures who required moral protection and even, perhaps, removal from the labour force.

In the late nineteenth century, Toronto's *Daily News* printed a letter from a wholesaler that attacked mass merchandisers. Angry that Eaton's had withdrawn its patronage, the author portrayed department stores as corrupt. Unlike department stores, wrote the author, wholesalers pay "fair salaries." Moreover, "Our business is not carried on by a staff of shop girls at two dollars a week." This writer's grievance was not that Eaton's employed women, but that it had withdrawn its business. Yet he referred to Eaton's employment of poorly paid women to underscore Eaton's destructiveness. Good businesses, implied the author, paid their staff decent wages. Into the twentieth century, Toronto's newspapers condemned department stores' treatment of working women. After criticizing department stores for gobbling up property, driving taxes down, taking away business from shopkeepers and wholesalers, and lowering wage rates, an early-twentieth-century publication criticized workers for patronizing the big stores: "Do they ever consider the poor girls and women who work and weep, on the verge of starvation, sewing and making up wear for men, women, and children, which is sold there?" Toronto unionists, too, were critical. Female employees, stated one commentator during the 1912 Eaton's strike, "can earn only Five, Four or even less Dollars per week

[and] girls are forced at times to take 'homework' to do at night, after the long day in the factory."[85]

During the Royal Commission on Price Spreads and Mass Buying, female victims again took centre stage. Before the commission even started, Herbert Stevens revealed his conviction that downtrodden female employees would make powerful weapons in the war on mass merchandisers. He told the congregation of Toronto's Trinity Church that Jesus Christ himself would condemn Eaton's for forcing "women and girls" to work "under conditions that ... shame ... self-respecting people." During the same period that the inquiry was gathering evidence, Eaton's locked out a group of its female dress workers, and these women agreed to be interviewed by the commission. Investigators inquired not only into Eaton's piece rates but also into the women's constitutions. After being asked about the physical consequences of Eaton's working conditions, one employee replied that because of production speed-ups, she had gone "into hysterics several times and I had to go to the hospital and the nurse said, 'What is the matter? You girls are always coming here.'" Her answer provides evidence of Eaton's exploitation of women workers; indeed, at least two historians of Eaton's have used this employee's testimony to demonstrate the company's poor labour practices. Yet her words also support prevailing ideas about women's fragility. Eager to condemn her employer, she portrays herself in a way that demonstrates to the public the extent of Eaton's depravity at the same time that it exemplifies her own supposedly inherent feminine delicacy.[86]

Special criticisms of department stores' labour practices came from commentators involved in Christian reform movements. They believed that industrialization and urbanization corrupted Canadians' morality, and in their pursuit to reform the nation, they focused on young female wage earners. Some of these critics were members of the National Council of Women of Canada (NCWC), which was a predominantly English-speaking, Protestant organization that strove to better women's working conditions in Canada. Others belonged to the Fédération nationale Saint-Jean-Baptiste (FNSJB), which was similar to the NCWC in terms of its ideals and practices, but most of its members were French-speaking and Catholic. Members of the Young Women's Christian Association (YWCA) and the University Women's Clubs also voiced concern over female retail employees' working conditions, as did individual activists, professionals, and reformers, including midwives, lawyers, and wealthy philanthropists.[87]

A fear that store employment impaired women's reproductive systems lurked within reformers' portrayals of endangered women. In 1881, Montréal midwife Charlotte Fuhrer published her memoirs, *The Mysteries of Montreal.* They contained the lurid tale of Esther Ryland, who had worked at Morgan's before marrying a wealthy tailor. When the couple tried unsuccessfully to have a baby, Ryland began to believe she was infertile. Hoping to obtain an unwanted baby and pass it off as her own, she sought assistance from Fuhrer. The midwife refused, and in *Mysteries* she discussed the reasons for Ryland's barrenness. When she had been a shopgirl, Ryland had not been allowed to sit down for more than fifteen minutes per shift. Not only did she have to serve customers "incessantly," but during the Christmas season she had to "shorten her dinner hour," as Constance Backhouse states in her analysis of this passage. Since shopkeepers were not going to voluntarily change their working conditions, Fuhrer urged the state to make seats for salesclerks mandatory.[88]

In the late nineteenth century, Canadian feminists joined their European and American counterparts in lobbying for seats for salesgirls. By 1888, Canadian feminists had successfully pressured the Ontario government into passing a Shops' Regulation Act. After stating that "children and young persons" could not work in a shop more than seventy-four hours per week, the act mandated that all shops employing women must provide chairs. Similar acts followed in Manitoba and British Columbia in 1901. To ensure department stores made seats available, reformers took it upon themselves to conduct inspections. After visiting Eaton's in the early twentieth century, the Toronto Humane Society sent a complaint letter to Timothy Eaton and the inspector of morals of the City of Toronto. The letter stated that Eaton had failed "to protect the welfare of young women by not placing stools throughout his store." Into the interwar years, the shop seats issue remained salient. Madame Arthur Gibeault told readers of the FNSJB newsletter in 1927 that although provincial legislation made shop seats mandatory, saleswomen rarely made use of them because they were scared of being fired. Yet it was imperative that saleswomen have opportunities to rest. Long hours of standing caused varicose veins among women, she wrote. Standing also caused "des désordres organiques très graves," which compromised "les maternités futures et cause souvent des accidents à la colonne vertébrale."[89]

Activists who viewed female employees as morally endangered sometimes claimed that saleswomen's low wages led to prostitution. Noted Reverend Mr. Eaton of Toronto – who might or might not have been related to the department store family – in an 1897 sermon, the department store "devil" forced saleswomen to sell their bodies: "In large cities ... departmental stores are the tombs of virtue," and "When one considers the dreadful nervous strain, the appearance that must be kept up, and the extremely low wages that obtain in these stores ... one can see that it is simply impossible for the average girl to escape contamination." Fifteen years later, when presenting evidence to the British Columbia Commission on Labour, one member of Victoria's Local Council of Women hinted at similar consequences: "I think we may well stop and ask ourselves what this question of low wages means ... Ladies, you know the answer as well as I do, and knowing it, shall we blame the girls who find some other way of satisfying their natural desire for a little amusement, candy, or some other small luxury?" Ignoring independent working women's need to pay rent, food, and transportation, this speaker imagined female wage earners as "girls" in pursuit of "small" luxuries. Her statement betrays her own middle-class sensibilities, which were unable to view wage-earning women as workers with material needs.[90]

Reformers believed store women were particularly susceptible to the "social evil." They wore stylish and, some said, provocative clothing. They worked in public spaces, where men could flirt and arrange secret meetings. During the 1912 Eaton strike, *Jack Canuck* "repeatedly stressed that the company's employment policies led to 'the social evil,'" Frager notes. On the eve of the Second World War, stories about clerks becoming prostitutes continued to resonate. A 1939 edition of the Toronto-based *National Tattler* ran a provocative front-page headline: "Eaton's Girls Shamed!" The story was accompanied by an illustration of a seductive woman, presumably a saleswoman who prostituted herself (Figure 7.4). According to the tabloid, "Girls working in Eaton's and other huge department stores throughout Canada are resorting to many things to supplement a meagre income." The article's purpose was to condemn violations of the Minimum Wage Act, but the *Tattler* used the image of saleswoman-turned-prostitute to grab readers' attention.[91]

To safeguard young working women from physical and sexual exploitation, feminist reformers pressed for protective legislation. In 1897, after the Provincial Council of Women in Ontario had sent it a petition calling for shops inspectors, the Ontario government appointed such inspectors. Over the next decades, maternal feminists, social reformers, and similar parties continued lobbying for better conditions for female department store employees. Their activism helped bring in the Shops Acts, instituted

What are the poor girls supposed to do? Here is a **REAL** problem
for economists and parliamenticians!

FIGURE 7.4   Illustration in the Toronto *National Tattler,*
showing a fictional Eaton's saleswoman forced to prostitute
herself, 1939. | *Source:* "Store Girls Are Forced to Shame Selves,"
National Tattler (1 February 1939), 3, Archives of Ontario, T. Eaton
Papers, Series 37, Box 21, File: Tabloids 1939. Copyright expired.

and amended in several provinces from the 1890s onwards. After the First
World War, lobbying encouraged provincial Minimum Wage Boards to
adopt specific apprenticeship guidelines. To stop stores from paying low
apprenticeship wages, the Québec Minimum Wage Board of 1934 stipulated that only 25 percent of an employer's total labour force could be
apprentices.[92]

In reformers' lobbying efforts, ethnocentrism and racism were some-times visible. Just before the First World War, members of the Vancouver Local Council of Women (LCW), the Vancouver Trades and Labour Council, and the Vancouver Board of Trade met to discuss saleswomen's conditions. Together, they drafted a list of proposed amendments to the British Columbia Shop Act. Recommendations included "regulat[ing] the hours of assistants," "women assistants 20 years of age and over shall receive not less than $16 per week," and "in no cases shall Caucasians be permitted to work in the same establishment as Asiatics." To the LCW, the Trades and Labour Council, and the Board of Trade, the presence of Asians in shops symbolized poor working conditions for women, just as did long hours and low wages.[93]

Some middle-class activists established clubs for wage-earning women. Headed by reformers who believed that working girls needed solace, friendship, supervision, and religious support, they held parties, teas, meals, reading classes, and other get-togethers. In the 1890s, YWCA activist Bertha Wright borrowed a room from the Woman's Christian Temperance Union in Ottawa. After asking "employers in hotels, department stores and government departments for permission to invite their employees" to meetings in the room, she started a Sunday afternoon club. There was initially little turnout, but eventually the club attracted enough members to build a structure that housed "domestic science classrooms, a dining room, rooms for meetings, offices, [a] living room, [and] sleeping accom-modation for about 50." The FNSJB similarly involved itself in working women's associations. With the support of the Catholic Church, it created clubs in Montréal for employees of stores, factories, offices, and telephone companies. Headed by *les femmes d'affaires*, they fostered leadership and responsibility among wage-earning women. By 1921 the groups were holding annual meetings, studying economic issues, and discussing work-ing conditions. The store employees' club was concerned with shorter hours and shop seats; it also had elocution lessons and a choir.[94]

A few society women had intimate relationships with store magnates and were hence able to influence their treatment of staff. During the Great War, Elizabeth Fudger, wife of Simpson's President Harris Fudger, convinced her husband to purchase a boarding house for Simpson's fe-male employees. In interwar Montréal, wives within the Dupuis family nominated themselves patronesses of the FNSJB's store employees' as-sociation. Sir John Eaton's wife, Lady Flora Eaton, took a special interest in Eaton's female employees. In the 1960s she explained her concern to

Eaton's official historian. Before she had created Eaton's welfare department in 1918, she related, the twelve thousand girls and women on staff had suffered from poor housing, low pay, a lack of hygiene, debt, sexual exploitation, unwanted pregnancies, botched abortions, and illnesses. Like many of her contemporaries, Lady Eaton thought youthful female workers were in moral danger. The irony of Lady Eaton's perspective, of course, was that the Eaton family was responsible for the company's low wages. Yet, instead of pressing for higher wages, Lady Eaton believed welfare programs were the best path toward the betterment of Eaton's female workers.[95]

When it came to criticizing department stores, middle-class feminists tended to focus on how they treated white female employees, particularly saleswomen. If such treatment was satisfactory, they usually left the big stores alone. In fact, many bourgeois feminists cultivated professional relationships with mass retailers, hosting fundraisers and other events within their domains. During the 1920s the Local Council of Women of Toronto held an Empire Shopping Week tea at Simpson's, which showcased goods for sale that had been produced within the British Empire. It also held an "International Night" at Eaton's College Street's upscale restaurant during the same decade. Organized, middle-class Canadian feminists thus tended to treat mass retail more positively than did their counterparts in the United States, where the National Consumers' League, founded by "a group of upper-middle-class white women in the Northeast," as Dana Frank puts it, lobbied for better working conditions for labourers producing consumer goods. Not only were they worried about young working women's employment conditions, but they were also "concerned that germs would enter their own houses on the threads of garments sewed by impoverished workers with tuberculosis and other diseases."[96]

If some feminist critics of mass retail claimed that department stores' female employees were exploited victims, a few took this view even further, suggesting that department stores should not employ women at all. A minority of feminists believed that women whose economic circumstances forced them to earn their living should enter domestic service. As household servants, they would enjoy the protection and security of a middle-class dwelling and, ideally, a charitable employer. Mrs. Mitchell of the Victoria Council of Women argued in 1914 that the province should fund "an industrial institution" for orphaned girls that would train them in "good, clean service." She cited the example of a motherless girl whose salary at the Fifteen Cent Store was too low to allow her to pay rent regularly. She therefore drifted in and out of employment. Yet, if she became a servant, she would stay off the streets and earn "an honest living." For Mitchell, domestic service was the solution to the independent salesgirl's poverty.[97]

Other critics, most assuredly not feminists, were against the employment of women in retail entirely. The presence of women in retail, so the argument went, undercut the male breadwinners' right to living wages. Seeking to mobilize working men against department stores, one early-twentieth-century Toronto writer asked rhetorically, "Where will the toilers be if children and young women are going to monopolize all the work attendant to business?" When Canadian hostility toward girls and women in the labour force generally peaked during the Depression, activism against department stores' employment of women also increased. In Montréal a group of men angry at rising levels of unemployment formed an organization called *collets blancs*, which urged the replacement of white-collar female workers with men.[98]

In this context of hostility, it is noteworthy that a minority of retail's critics argued that department stores' female employees were not defenceless innocents but rather assertive, independent, and hard-working. Unlike most journalists and reformers, these commentators did not make moral judgments about women's presence in the Canadian labour market. Instead, they accepted women's decisions to work for money and advocated improvements in women's working conditions, particularly in hours and pay. Women in garment workers' unions and women sympathetic to left-wing thought were among the most prominent adherents to this perspective. To support the women who walked out of Eaton's Toronto factory in 1912, the International Ladies Garment Workers Union sent organizer Gertrude Barnum. Arguing for better treatment, "Barnum especially worked to promote the boycott of the T. Eaton Company," writes Frager. During the 1934 lockout, left-wing activists again came to the defence of Eaton's female employees. Socialist feminists Rose Henderson and Jean Laing publicized the strike in CCF publications, held strike rallies, and raised money by holding dances.[99]

Independent feminist Alice Chown also viewed female retail employees as entitled to a living wage. After trying to obtain prominent feminists' support for the 1912 Eaton's strike, she came away disappointed. "The common, everyday longings for better conditions, for a life that would provide more than food, clothes, and shelter," she wrote, "were not recognized as justifying a strike." Instead, her middle-class counterparts wanted to hear stories about individual girls' exploitation.[100] Fiction author Isabel Mackay would have understood Chown's frustration. After moving to Vancouver in 1909, Mackay "wrote a number of novels, primarily romantic in tone," notes Lindsey McMaster.[101] Her *House of Windows* (1912) is about three sisters who lived together in Toronto. Following dime-novel convention, the sisters are dainty and pretty. Sister Celia's hair "was wavy and soft," and her eyes "were clear and pleasantly serious." Ada Brown's "sweet and simple" voice was full of "purity." Christine, the heroine, had hair that "flashed like a ray of sunshine" and a nature that was "gay and bright." The sisters' income was meagre, but they kept a tasteful home. According to one visitor, "There was a round table with a moss green cloth in the centre of the room; the old-fashioned chairs were upholstered in green; a green rug half covered the floor, which was painted to match, and the paper was pretty and quite in keeping." The sisters' decorating testified to their respectable femininity.[102]

The Brown sisters were not only virtuous, they were hard-working women entitled to every penny they earned. Mackay presents a sympathetic view of saleswomen. Their hours were long and their work exhausting, but they were nonetheless cheerful. During a bargain sale in the Ribbons Department, the clerks rush around until closing time; afterwards, they revive each others' spirits by discussing customers' less-than-worthy qualities. "Did you see the gay one in green try to sneak a bolt out of the fifty-cent division?" asks Miss Twiss. States Miss Eden, "All their eyes look alike ... Greedy, I should say!" Mackay uses her novel to publicize unfavourable working conditions. She denounces women's lack of upward mobility and low wages, and highlights customers' poor treatment of clerks. Finally, Mackay's book suggests that although department stores wanted bright, attractive saleswomen, the stores' long hours, fast pace, and low wages were injurious to employees' health. When Christine tells Celia she wants to work at the department store, Celia responds, "If you must work, wait until you find something else. You have youth, health, beauty and courage. That is what the Stores want. They'll take it all, day by day, week by week, year by year, they'll take it all! ... And then when these are gone they take what's left and ... I don't know just what they do with what's left."[103]

Their specific perspectives differed, but Gertrude Barnum, Rose Henderson, Jean Laing, Alice Chown, and Isabel Mackay all portrayed female department store workers as entitled to (but not receiving) fair wages and adequate working conditions. In their view, female wage earners were hard-working, independent, and assertive; they deserved comfortable lives, good jobs, and respect. Such perspectives suggested female wage earners were empowered beings with the capacity to work toward bettering their conditions, despite the oppression they faced. In contrast to those who used the image of the downtrodden female employee to advance other causes, these activists and writers put the interests of female retail employees at the top of their agendas. Given the poor conditions in which female retail employees laboured before 1940, it is unfortunate that their views were in the minority.

Rationalizing Consumer Activity

Holding up victimized female employees as emblems of department store depravity, critics of mass retail tended to ignore women workers' own attempts to better their working conditions. They also reinforced widespread assumptions about working women as helpless and defenceless. Similar difficulties ensued when critics tried to understand consumers' subjectivities. Instead of taking seriously consumers' preferences for low prices, good service, convenience, and reliability, critics frequently portrayed consumers as ignorant and gullible. According to some, department stores' flashy merchandising tricked Canadians into spending money. As the *Dry Goods Review* reported in 1897, department stores engaged in "schemes," such as putting loss leaders at the front of stores, "devised" to "lure" shoppers. These worked the customer into such "a state of mental fatuity that he or she [did] not know whether the full price [was] paid or not." Thirty-seven years later, the Independent Retail Merchants of Yorkton stated that the "highly trained merchandising expert" employed by department stores "is able to fool a gullible public, who is not trained in true economy and thrift, and therefore get a major part of their earnings."[104]

Just as critics employed the image of the victimized female worker to underscore department store depravity, so did they employ the image of the victimized female customer to highlight department store corruption. Santink notes that the "Toronto *World* ... published highly emotional letters" about women who became ill and died after incidents involving Eaton's and Simpson's drug departments. One letter was dedicated "To the memory of dear little Jane," whose death "was attributed to the fact that 'departmental stores would not supply needful medicine at night time.'" Another article carried similar themes: one woman filled a prescription at a department store where the clerk accidentally mixed up the labels; luckily, the customer went to her doctor to verify the prescription, and he discovered that her pills contained "a dangerous poison." The moral of this story is evident in its conclusion: "Now the physician stipulates that patients must have prescriptions filled by qualified druggists."[105]

Stereotypes of female shoppers as capricious and gullible also figured in critics' attacks. The popularization of the clothing fashion industry in the late nineteenth century, combined with the advent of seasonable ready-to-wear items, encouraged middle-class female consumers to become more discerning in their clothing and accessory purchases. Scorning the slow-moving stock of the independent retailers, many turned to department stores. This caused small shopkeepers no end of frustration. To shopkeepers, the modern female customer was "little more than a 'gambler' whose 'speculations' led her to 'prowl around the stores' ... 'What she wants, in the way of weaves, colours and other details, [was] the great question.'"[106] According to *Saturday Night,* it was women's naivety, and not their whimsy, that caused them to patronize department stores. In a mock Eaton's advertisement, the magazine condemned women's supposed interests in novelty: "Thousands of ladies visit our store every day, brought here by our cunning advertisements ... The ladies – bless 'em – are our game. If it wasn't for them we couldn't make the thing work at all. Men are not so easily caught, but the women just fall into our trap by the thousand ... darling woman! It is you that makes the department graft a possibility."[107] As Cynthia Wright notes, this piece blamed the "gullibility of the woman shopper" for the big stores' rapaciousness.[108]

Moralist denunciations of vanity further tinged criticism of female consumers. In *Anne's House of Dreams,* Montgomery pokes fun at such views. On the subject of the Eaton's mail order service, the elderly Mrs. Lynde "indignantly" intoned, "as for those catalogues of theirs, they're the Avonlea girls' Bible now, that's what. They pore over them now on Sundays instead of studying the Holy Scriptures."[109] Whereas Montgomery suggested religious condemnations of fashion were too puritanical, others took them seriously. In a collection of sermons called *Fighting the Devil's Triple Demons,* Robert J. Moorehead included a piece called "Mrs. Grundy against God Almighty." Directed toward young women, the piece was about style and personal appearance. In "this modern whirl we call society, with its panoramic splendours and lewd dances, fashion's decrees have displaced the Ten Commandments," Moorehead claimed. "Not only ninety percent of the average woman's talk, but fifty percent of her time is taken up with the all-absorbing topic of what she shall put on, and wherewithal she shall be clothed." This was dangerous for Christians everywhere. Fashion "wastes the time ... of countless multitudes, who might be engaged in noble and ennobling service. It "destroys physical grace, and wrecks the health of her adorers." And, through the encouragement of corset wearing, it kills unborn children. Moorehead's sermon illustrates that women who participated in fashion challenged Protestantism's feminine ideal.[110] It thus unwittingly supports William Leach's argument about the liberating aspects of consumerism. Shopping and women's increased interest in consumption at the end of the nineteenth century, he notes, helped them escape the confines of the "domestic frontier."[111]

Bolstered by moralists, merchants blamed women's interest in fashion and beauty for the demise of the independent retailer. When they were being completely honest with themselves, though, many knew that department stores' conveniences and low prices enabled them to capture consumers' dollars. In his letter to the Stevens commission, N.A. Baillieul of Port Hawkesbury admitted that he could "hardly blame many for buying from the mail order houses ... even for the difference of a few cents."[112] Fed up with being criticized for their shopping decisions, consumers themselves waded into the fray. In June 1910, *Red and White,* the student newspaper of St. Dunstan's University on Prince Edward Island, printed a lengthy defence of mail order shopping, notable not only for its recognition of the critiques of mail order but also for its assertion of shoppers' dignity and for its list of reasons that shoppers use department store catalogues. In words echoing Joseph Clark of *Saturday Night,* the article acknowledged that mail order's critics had "adopted the Barnum axiom that people like to be humbugged." The author took issue with that perspective, arguing that PEI's inhabitants were not fools but instead were "shrewd dealers" who "know the value of money" and are "not a class who will submit to being gulled year after year." After defending PEI consumers' intelligence, the article went into detail about their shopping preferences. Unlike local businesses, "the large houses" have a "one-price system which eliminates 'beating down' and bantering"; thus, the "buyers feel they all are being treated alike and saved the displeasure of asking for bargains." Many islanders, as well, lived far from any town and therefore had to "drive ten or fifteen miles to do their shopping," an onerous chore since the island's roads were usually "paved with a generous depth of good soft, red mud of home manufacture." Taking the train was worse, for schedules were made with "no wish to serve" shoppers, allowing only a "few hours in the city." Those who attempted the train, moreover, had to wait until it was accepting passengers, for it alternated between human and freight cargo. Add to this the "miserable hour" waiting in one of "these well-ventilated sheds that so often do service for a station," it was obvious why many islanders chose to "have goods delivered by mail." If PEI's merchants were truly committed to bringing in local business, the article concluded, they would have to revise their own practices. Elimination of haggling and marked-up prices, together with some effort to secure "better roads and train arrangements," would go a long way toward convincing shoppers to "buy their goods near home."[113]

Customers in other areas of Canada would have agreed with the *Red and White*. During the same year that the PEI article appeared, a resident of Port Arthur, Ontario, criticized the town's merchants in a letter sent to the local *Evening Chronicle*. Responding to shopkeepers' claim that they deserved local business because they paid local taxes, the letter reminded readers that the "consumer has taxes to pay as well as the merchants," and that there "are hundreds of consumers to one merchant." In this writer's opinion, "Mail order houses may be pernicious things but they are a blessing when the consumer is militated against by the local merchants who have combined in order to keep up prices." Indeed, "self-preservation" was "the first law of nature"; it was more important to be loyal to "one's self and family" than to local merchants. According to this writer, then, local merchants were not as virtuous as they claimed. Recognizing they marked up goods, the author rerouted small merchants' charges of mail order profiteering toward their own doorsteps.[114]

Letters sent to Eaton's during the Great Depression reveal that Prairie shoppers, too, felt that local merchants gouged their customers. John Dewell of Alameda, Saskatchewan, wrote, "we could not live if we didn't send to Eaton's. The stores here were charging two prices without much choice of goods, so it was a regular thing to make out a big order every fall for our winter supplies. When we were raising our young family of four boys we used to send big orders to Eaton's ... This was in the 1890's and later." According to James Day of Rothwell, Manitoba, "I have dealt pretty steady with you ever since you came to Winnipeg [in 1905] ... They have knocked the mail order houses pretty hard as spoiling local trade, but I firmly believe that if you hadn't been in Winnipeg the half of us could hardly have lived, as the local storekeepers are not any better than they might be." Although local merchants portrayed themselves as keeping their community's interests in mind, these customers' letters suggest that their town shopkeepers' high prices went against local people's interests.[115]

Despite consumers' sustained defence of their dignity and shopping decisions, small merchants believed the righteousness of their cause to be self-evident. Due in part to some independent stores' unwillingness to offer viable alternatives to department stores' prices and conveniences, and even more in part to their inability to compete with mass retailers on these fronts, they were never able to fully convince purchasers to stop spending money in department stores. Leaders of labour and reform organizations also had difficulty curbing department stores' actions. Not only were they unable to convince shoppers in general to stop patronizing the big stores, they were also unable to convince members of their own groups to do so. Remarking on Eaton's successful targeting of working-class customers, one Toronto journalist stated in 1907, "The trades union people have the chance of a life time to act consistently. Those who establish a living wage for themselves should not spend the money thus earned in building up a place which is crushing the life out of trade and out of so many of their struggling fellow beings in store and factory and driving hundreds of honest tradesmen with honest goods who are also employing labor to the brink of bankruptcy." Unionism would never be successful, in other words, if members spent their money at stores that undercut places that offered fair wages and conditions.[116]

According to the manager of the HBC in Victoria, not only working people but also leaders of reform and labour movements patronized department stores. During his testimony to the 1914 BC labour commission, Thomas Lockyer was on the defensive. After being grilled on wages paid to women workers, the potential immorality of his staff, and the hours his employees worked, he had had enough, declaring critics of department store policies to be two-faced. Although reformers wanted department stores to shorten store hours, he had personally "seen clergymen and leaders of social movements and leaders of labor movements very largely in our stores on Saturday night. How do you account for that?" he asked. As Lockyer made clear, Saturday evening shopping was popular. If hours were to be shortened, critics had to give up their weekend night expeditions to the stores.[117]

BETWEEN 1890 AND 1940, Canada's largest stores found themselves under attack. One of the most dramatic anti-department store demonstrations occurred in 1935, when a group of unemployed men destroyed property inside the HBC Vancouver store so as to express their anger at the state's refusal to help them obtain food and shelter. Yet throughout the 1890 to

1940 period, a range of groups expressed dissatisfaction with aspects of
the big stores' policies. Shopkeepers, co-operators, and labour leaders
believed department stores were greedy monopolists bent on destroying
local economic viability. Co-operators, sometimes in tandem with labourists, attempted to build community-minded alternatives to the big stores.
Working with department stores' own employees, labourists supported
strike actions and unionization attempts. Middle-class feminists, often
with the support of unionists, sought to protect white female employees'
health and morality. Many feminists would have liked women to leave
store employment and take up domestic service, but failing that they lobbied for protective legislation that monitored women's hours and abilities
to sit down while working.

Independent merchants, labour leaders, co-operators, and sympathetic
onlookers would have preferred to see customers end their patronage of
Canada's largest stores. Yet no large-scale boycott ever occurred. Supporters of these movements grudgingly recognized that customers valued superior selection, convenience, and affordability more than they could be
drawn to shopkeepers' claims of civic spirit, co-operators' anti-monopolistic
intentions, and labour leaders' arguments of unfair labour practices.
Department stores' size and strength made it impossible for small retailers
and co-operators to offer the same advantages as the giant retailers. At
the same time, merchants tended to downplay customers' motivations for
shopping at department stores, preferring instead to portray themselves
as virtuous and customers as vain, gullible, ignorant, and stubborn. This
tendency no doubt hampered their ability to construct successful alternatives to department stores. Further, because they did not address women's
daily concerns of budgeting, convenience, and style, labour-led boycotts
and co-operative alternatives to mass merchandising never achieved re-
sounding success.

Nevertheless, the federal and provincial governments' disinclination to
intervene in matters involving mass merchandising was an even more
important factor. Although the two levels of state together introduced tax
reforms on big business, protective labour legislation, some anti-combines
laws, and minor revisions to the Criminal Code, these measures did not
prevent department stores from opening branch stores or buying in bulk.
They also did not prevent them from paying non-union wages and firing
workers who went on strike and attempted to unionize.

Some critics of department stores had progressive goals. Co-operators'
efforts to create producer, distributor, and consumer organizations

managed and owned by collectives with common interests were ultimately intended to eliminate profit seeking and alienation from modern society. Labourist attempts to mitigate employer paternalism and improve wages and working conditions strove to better employees' material and cultural circumstances. Other activists' objectives were more questionable. Small retailers' arguments sprang from their own hopes to profit from commodity distribution. They wanted to enjoy the same advantages of department stores, just on a smaller scale. Moralists and bourgeois feminists, meanwhile, wanted to regulate working-class women's morality. Believing sales work threatened white women's sexual and moral health, and therefore the future of white Canada, they advocated stronger welfare measures – not higher wages – for white women.

Co-operators' attempts to create community-owned alternatives to mass merchandising failed, but they remain significant. As profit-seeking mass retail continues to dominate the Canadian consumer landscape, it is important to consider its consequences. Do the majority of Canadians patronize mass retailers simply because there is a lack of convenient, affordable, and stylish options? If progressive co-operatives existed that offered these amenities, services, and qualities, would Canadians patronize them instead? It is difficult to imagine a Canada without mass retail. Nonetheless, it remains important to keep alternative visions alive. The pre-Second World War retailing practices of inadequate working conditions still prevail. Critics between 1890 and 1940 did not condemn mass retail's equation of industrial and material expansion with progress, but we now know that these circumstances also have negative consequences, particularly environmental ones. We should disagree with some past critics' assumptions and actions, but it is important to keep their oppositional spirit in mind. Today, more than ever, we must remain skeptical of mass retail's claims to infallibility and progress, understanding that there is another world of sales that is possible.

Epilogue
Canadian Institutions?

"HEAR YE, HEAR YE! Canada for sale! Caaaaanaada for saaaale!!!!!" So posted R. Stevens to the comments section of a 2008 CBC News online article announcing the sale of the Hudson's Bay Company to American firm NRDC Equity Partners. Over two weeks, visitors offered 210 comments on the article, a significant but fairly typical sum for the website. Disappointment at the loss of what posters referred to as a "Canadian icon" pervaded the forum. Even while acknowledging that the HBC had been owned by American Gerry Zucker since 2006, readers suggested that the HBC was symbolic of Canada's past. "While it isn't Canadian ... it's still historical," said Raincity. MercuryBlue agreed. "It's not about the Americans ... It's about Canadian people wanting to hold onto Canadian business and tradition."[1]

This notion that department stores are integral to Canada's heritage has a long history. Since the 1890s Canada's largest mass retailers have proclaimed that they have been uniquely positioned to make particular contributions to Canadians' economic, social, and cultural development. Eaton's was among the most successful in convincing its publics of its national stature. When the company closed its mail order in 1976 and declared bankruptcy in 1999, many Canadians were saddened by the loss of what they viewed as a symbol of their national identity. Such sentiments linger today. The CBC online article was about the HBC, but it also triggered posts about Eaton's as well as its main competitor, Simpson's. "Well kiss another Canadian icon goodbye," wrote Dave Miles; "Eaton's and Simpsons are gone," and "It's all Sears and Walmart now." Claire Beatty took a slightly different tack, noting that, in her opinion, "Most Bay stores look like a junkyard." She "still mourn[s] Eaton's, though. THAT was a Canadian institution to be proud of."[2]

Public perception of Eaton's, the HBC, and Simpson's as national icons has been influenced by department stores' own publicity, which, as Chapter 2 reveals, was incessantly patriotic. Yet promotions and advertising were not the only spurs to the big stores' climb to national heritage status. Between 1890 and 1940, Simpson's, the HBC, and especially Eaton's were among the largest retailers in the world, and compared to UK, French, and US department stores' market shares in their respective nations, they captured much larger proportions of their country's consumer dollars. Their flagship locations aided them in this endeavour, but so did their massive mail order operations and their far-flung branch stores. By 1930, Eaton's, Simpson's, and the HBC were receiving twelve dollars out of every one hundred spent in the dominion; Eaton's alone was receiving seven of that total. Even if they did not spend money at the big stores, most Canadians knew of their existence, if only because their neighbours patronized the retailers or because they themselves received Eaton's and Simpson's catalogues.

Individual Canadians' relationships with the big stores hence also contributed to the construction of Eaton's, Simpson's, and the HBC as national icons. Browsing these stores' advertisements, shopping in their departments, lunching in their restaurants, and taking advantage of their lavatories and nurseries, thousands of residents all over Canada incorporated Eaton's, Simpson's, and the HBC into their daily lives. They did so for several reasons, including their pursuit of stylish, affordable, and reliable goods; their search for convenience and quality service; and their desire for low-cost and safe relaxation and entertainment. Together with the big stores' advertisements, these everyday practices – especially engaged in by women – helped to make Eaton's, Simpson's, and the HBC symbols of a common modern nationhood.

Advertising and daily activities alone were not solely responsible, however, for the construction of Canada's largest mass retailers' national heritage status. If thousands of Canadians shopped in the stores, thousands more laboured for them. By the end of the Second World War, Eaton's was, after the railways and federal government, the country's third largest employer. Whether or not department store employees approved of their employers' massive paternalist efforts – and several did – many of them did enjoy skills development as well as platonic and love relationships at the big stores. For many individuals, such activities would have contributed to the creation of a sense of commonality, one that pertained to one's individual store, but also to the many other stores that constituted their employer's retailing empire.

And yet, despite department stores' own claims to national greatness, and despite Canadians' everyday buying and working practices, it was not inevitable that Eaton's, Simpson's, and the HBC would become national icons. To fully understand why these three stores became so intricately linked to many Canadians' sense of heritage, the widespread yearning for a collective identity in English Canada between 1890 and 1940 must also be acknowledged. After Ontario, Québec, Prince Edward Island, Nova Scotia, and New Brunswick became provinces within the new Dominion of Canada in 1867, after the federal government purchased Rupert's Land in 1869, and after British Columbia became a Canadian province in 1871, Canada became a coast-to-coast political entity encompassing a vast array of geographies and cultures. As the federal government spread its institutions outwards from southern Ontario to the Atlantic, Arctic, and Pacific oceans north of the United States, residents of northern North America became aware and in many cases angry that they were now within the boundaries of a new and enormous state. Those who were against the Canadian project, including many French-speaking and Aboriginal groups, did not feel any need to participate in Canada's national development. Those who were more receptive to the idea of Canada, however, began to cast about for markers of common identity. By identifying these markers, and then by identifying *with* them, they could make sense of what it meant to belong to the new dominion. They could also claim membership and pride in this collective.

Through their massive advertising efforts, Eaton's, Simpson's, and the HBC tapped into this yearning. And by providing opportunities for shopping and working experiences that had some regional differences but that also remained remarkably consistent from Victoria to Halifax, department stores gave those who longed for a sense of national belonging something that could be identified as specifically Canadian. By reading Eaton's, Simpson's, and the HBC's advertisements, and by patronizing and working for the giant retailers, people throughout the Dominion of Canada could perform their membership in this broader federal polity. Canada's largest mass retailers between 1890 and 1940 hence played an integral role in the building of a modern Canadian nationhood, one that was forever linked to capitalism and consumerism. They did so not only because their advertising and branch stores reached more residents than did that of department stores in other nations, but also because members of department stores' publics came to identify shopping in and working at the big stores as specifically Canadian activities.

In their comments on the CBC's article on the sale of the HBC, posters most often mentioned the HBC and Eaton's as nationalist enterprises.

They did, however, suggest that other corporations, especially Roots, Molson's, Canadian Tire, and Tim Hortons, were similarly emblematic of Canadian culture. Some such comments were critical – "It's sad when we consider 'Canadian identity' a donut shop and a former fur-trading company," said Olivia P – but most were favourable toward the chains. "Let's hang on for dear life to Canadian Tire," suggested Josephus HAP, proud not only of Canadian Tire's nationalist identity but also its Canadian ownership.[3] In her exploration of what she calls Roots nationalism in the 1980s and 1990s, historian Catherine Carstairs takes up the question of why, over the past twenty years, English Canadians have associated certain branded goods with Canadian identity. During the 1950s, 1960s, and 1970s, she argues, a civic nationalism took root among English Canadian intellectuals, one that viewed Canada's bilingual, multicultural, and artistic heritages as a strong basis for Canadian national pride and identity. Yet, because of fallout from the 1980 Québec Referendum, the 1990 Meech Lake Accord, and the 1990 Oka crisis, that particular dream faded away. Nationalism among English Canadians did not, however, as was evidenced by the immense popularity of Molson's "I am Canadian" campaigns, the widespread adoption among middle-class English Canadians of Roots as their apparel of choice, and the ongoing association of Tim Hortons with Canadiana. Carstairs argues that this new form of "branded nationalism" is different from earlier civic nationalisms in that it evades questions of ethnicity, artistic production, and language.[4]

Branded nationalism might have been potent in the last two decades of the twentieth century, but its history stretches back to the 1890s, as this book's explorations reveal. Identifying Eaton's, Simpson's, and the HBC as national institutions is different from purchasing Roots, Molson's, or Tim Hortons goods, but the association of capitalist enterprise with Canadian heritage remains the same. Because of this similarity, it can be concluded that the conditions that exacerbated branded nationalism in the 1980s and 1990s did not create it. For over a century, individual Canadians have been identifying particular companies as national symbols, and they have been doing so for a variety of reasons, including their own everyday shopping and working relationships with the companies, as well as their own desire for a sense of collective belonging. When Roots, Tim Hortons, and Molson's nationalism emerged in the late twentieth century, it thus had a long heritage on which to build. Moreover, despite branded nationalism's skirting of ethnic differences, it must be said that there are some similarities between the ethnic characteristics once attached to

Eaton's, Simpson's, and the HBC and those attached to more recent Canadian-identified firms. Between 1890 and 1940, customers of a range of ethnic, racialized, and class backgrounds did patronize the giant retailers, and they continued to do so for decades more. Nevertheless, Eaton's, Simpson's, and the HBC's advertisements, together with their practices of employing Anglo-Celtic customer service personnel, did give many onlookers the impression that Canada's biggest retailers were white, Protestant, and anglophone. Carstairs' research indicates that Roots' imagery carries similar connotations. The company bases its brand iconography on middle- and upper-class summer camp experiences among southern Ontario urbanites; as well, "Roots' presence in Québec was proportionately smaller than it was in the rest of the country." These findings indicate that although the Roots brand is frequently touted by the company and customers alike as Canadian, it is actually more reflective of a certain kind of Canadian nationalism, one that is white and English-speaking, and one that is receptive to iconography that purports to be national but is rooted in bourgeois Ontario.[5]

Since many historical and recent forms of branded nationalism in English Canada have essentialized a particular ethnic identity as quintessentially Canadian, it follows that we must remain suspicious of claims that certain companies and products are representative of true Canadian nationhood. We must also ask ourselves if we want capitalism and commodities to represent Canadian culture. Notes Carstairs, branded nationalism serves the purpose of increasing Canada's international profile, as was the case when Roots' apparel designed for the 1998 Olympics received global acclaim, but it also encourages exhaustion of the earth's resources through "over-consumption" as well as leaves Canadians "with little sense of Canada's history or values."[6] Rather than associating particular corporate symbols with Canadian identity, we should encourage a broader sense of collective belonging, one that depends not upon retail, upon consumerism, or even upon nationalism, but upon respect, equality, and diversity.

Fortunately, in our efforts to question Canadians' long conflation of consumerism with nationalism, we have a rich past on which to draw. As Eaton's, Simpson's, and a host of smaller stores climbed the rungs of Canada's retailing ladder, they ignited a storm of discontent. For some, such as the seven hundred unemployed activists who attempted to stage a sit-in at the HBC in Vancouver in 1935, department stores represented class privilege and thus all that was wrong with consumerist modernity. Independent shopkeepers, for their part, claimed department stores were unfair competitors who destroyed local businesses and communities. Organized labour was also critical. Sometimes labourists repeated small retailers' arguments about how mass retail destroyed community life but more often they concerned themselves with department stores' influence upon working people, stating that since stores did not recognize unions nor pay union wages, they threatened unionized workers and forced employees to live and work in substandard conditions. Co-operators, too, were skeptical. Believing department stores cared about neither local communities nor workers, they called for the elimination of corporate concentration. And finally, middle-class feminists condemned the big stores' treatment of female employees. They tended to see young, white, female wage earners as ripe for exploitation and corruption, and they monitored department stores' treatment of female employees and lobbied for protective legislation. Anti-retail activists would today rightly reject the racial and protectionist impulses of these feminists' concerns, but they would nevertheless do well to continue monitoring mass retail's treatment of workers. In this pursuit, they should pay especial attention to retail's tendency to exploit the view that women are responsible for domestic labour and child care and are thus expendable labourers who are happy to work for little pay and no benefits.

Even as they chose to shop at the big stores, customers also expressed dissatisfaction. Female customers complained that department stores were crowded, chaotic, unorganized, and dangerous. When department stores failed to deliver efficiency, quality service, respectful treatment, and good merchandise, customers sent complaint letters, discontinued their patronage, spread bad rumours, and pursued legal redress. Similarly, although women chose to work for department stores – albeit often forced into such choices because of economic need and a lack of alternatives – many expressed discontent. Long hours, draconian rules, low wages, job insecurity, and other workplace conditions were criticized. Foot dragging, quitting, rule breaking, and being rude to customers occurred, as did striking, unionizing, and contacting government officials. Female employees of Canada's largest stores confronted formidable obstacles in their efforts to better their conditions, but their willingness to challenge the big stores indicates they did not always agree with their employers' portrayals of themselves as benevolent.

When past critics' actions are considered together with the contemporary difficulties associated with branded forms of nationalism, it becomes apparent that the affection Canadians continue to heap upon department stores is unwarranted. We should not be surprised that Eaton's, Simpson's, and the HBC made nationalism integral to their public image, but we should question the continuing belief that Canada's largest department stores made positive contributions to the development of this nation. It is true that many Canadians have fond memories of these giant retailers, but this should not prevent us from seeing department stores as institutions that perpetuated Anglo-Celtic, male, and class privilege in Canada, that exploited wage earners and consumers, that helped to destroy co-operative alternatives to mass merchandising, and that conflated consumerism with Canada's national identity. There is no doubt that department stores contributed to the making of modern Canada. Yet we must ask, What kind of Canada did department stores help to create?

Notes

Introduction: Canadian Consumer Society

1 Theodor Adorno and Max Horkheimer, "The Culture Industry: Enlightenment as Mass Deception," in *Dialectic of Enlightenment*, trans. John Cumming (New York: Continuum Publishing Group, 1976), 120-67; Betty Friedan, *The Feminine Mystique* (New York: Norton, 2001 [1963]). Mica Nava provides a good overview of the consumer-as-passive trajectory in "Consumerism Reconsidered: Buying and Power," *Cultural Studies* 5, 2 (May 1991): 157-73.

2 Ellen Willis, "Women and the Myth of Consumerism," *Ramparts* (1969), http://fair-use.org/ellen-willis/women-and-the-myth-of-consumerism; as quoted in Cynthia Wright, "'The Most Prominent Rendezvous of the Feminine Toronto': Eaton's College Street and the Organization of Shopping in Toronto, 1920-1950" (PhD diss., University of Toronto, 1992), 26; Joy Parr, *Domestic Goods: The Material, the Moral, and the Economic in the Postwar Years* (Toronto: University of Toronto Press, 1999), 7.

3 Parr, *Domestic Goods*, 7; Susan Porter Benson, *Counter Cultures: Saleswomen, Managers, and Customers in American Department Stores, 1890-1940* (Urbana and Chicago: University of Illinois Press, 1988); Kathy Peiss, *Cheap Amusements: Working Women and Leisure in Turn-of-the-Century New York* (Philadelphia: Temple University Press, 1986); Kathy Peiss, *Hope in a Jar: The Making of America's Beauty Culture* (New York: Owl Books, 1999); Nan Enstad, *Ladies of Labor, Girls of Adventure: Working Women, Popular Culture, and Labor Politics at the Turn of the Twentieth Century* (New York: Columbia University Press, 1999).

4 See Erika Diane Rappaport, *Shopping for Pleasure: Women in the Making of London's West End* (Princeton, NJ: Princeton University Press, 2000). The quotation in this paragraph is taken from page 13 of that publication.

5 Parr, *Domestic Goods*, 10.

6 Victoria de Grazia, *Irresistible Empire: America's Advance through 20th-Century Europe* (Cambridge, MA: Harvard University Press, 2005), 13.

7 The Cohen text is *A Consumer's Republic: The Politics of Mass Consumption in Postwar America* (New York: Alfred A. Knopf, 2003).

8 Karen Dubinsky, *The Second Greatest Disappointment: Honeymooning and Tourism at Niagara Falls* (Toronto: Between the Lines, 1999); Craig Heron, *Booze: A Distilled History* (Toronto: Between the Lines, 2003); Suzanne Morton, *At Odds: Gambling and Canadians, 1919-1969* (Toronto: University of Toronto Press, 2003); Jarrett Rudy, *The Freedom to Smoke: Tobacco Consumption and Identity* (Montréal and Kingston: McGill-Queen's University Press, 2005); Steve Penfold, *The Donut: A Canadian History* (Toronto: University of Toronto Press, 2008); Parr, *Domestic Goods*.

9 David Monod, *Store Wars: Shopkeepers and the Culture of Mass Marketing, 1890-1939* (Toronto: University of Toronto Press, 1996), 102-3.
10 *Oxford English Dictionary Online*, 2nd ed., 1989, http://www.oed.com.
11 When exploring such topics, researchers would do well to begin with Michelle Comeau, "Les grands magasins de la Rue Sainte-Catherine à Montréal: Des lieux de modernisation, d'homogénéisation et de différenciation des modes de consommation," *Material History Review* 41 (Spring 1995): 58-68; Lorraine O'Donnell, "Le voyage virtuel: Les consommatrices, le monde de l'étranger et Eaton à Montréal, 1880-1980," *Revue d'histoire de l'Amérique française* 59 (Spring 2005): 535-68; John Willis, "Cette manche au syndicat – La grève chez Dupuis Frères en 1952," *Labour/Le Travail* 57 (Spring 2006): 43-51; Joan Sangster, *Transforming Labour: Women and Work in Post-War Canada* (Toronto: University of Toronto Press, 2010), 108-44.

Chapter 1: Rise of Mass Retail

1 Margot Finn, "Sex and the City: Metropolitan Modernities in English History," *Victorian Studies* 44, 1 (Autumn 2001): 25-26.
2 Claire Walsh, "The Newness of the Department Store: A View from the Eighteenth Century," in *Cathedrals of Consumption: The European Department Store, 1850-1939*, ed. Geoffrey Crossick and Serge Jaumain (Aldershot, UK: Ashgate, 1999), 68.
3 David Monod, "Bay Days: The Managerial Revolution and the Hudson's Bay Company Stores Department," 4, unpublished paper, 1990, Hudson's Bay Company Archives (hereafter HBCA), PP 1986-10; Joy L. Santink, *Timothy Eaton and the Rise of His Department Store* (Toronto: University of Toronto Press, 1990), 222; H.H. Stevens, *Report of the Royal Commission on Price Spreads* (Ottawa: J.O. Patenaude, 1937), 207; Statistics Canada, *Department Stores in Canada/Les grands magasins au Canada, 1923-1976* (Ottawa: Statistics Canada, 1979), 16-19.
4 Dominion Bureau of Statistics, *Seventh Census of Canada, 1931,* vol. 10: *Merchandising and Services Establishments – Part I: Retail Merchandise Trade* (Ottawa: J.O. Patenaude, 1931), x.
5 Tomoko Tamari, "Rise of the Department Store and the Aestheticization of Everyday Life in Early 20th-Century Japan," *International Journal of Japanese Sociology* 15 (2006): 100; Marjorie Hilton, "Retailing the Revolution: The State Department Store (GUM) and Soviet Society in the 1920s," *Journal of Social History* 37, 4 (Summer 2004): 939-64; Evan Roberts, "'Don't Sell Things, Sell Effects': Overseas Influences in New Zealand Department Stores, 1909-1956," *Business History Review* 77, 2 (Summer 2003): 265-89.
6 Margaret Conrad and Alvin Finkel, with Cornelius Jaenen, *History of the Canadian Peoples: Beginnings to 1867,* 2nd ed. (Toronto: Copp Clark, 1998), vol. 2, 332-35; Santink, *Timothy Eaton and the Rise of His Department Store,* 5, 29.
7 Jan Noel, "Defrocking Dad: Masculinity and Dress in Montreal, 1700-1867," in *Fashion: A Canadian Perspective,* ed. Alexandra Palmer (Toronto: University of Toronto Press, 2004), 78.
8 Margaret Atwood, "Introduction to *Roughing It in the Bush*," *Moving Targets: Writing with Intent, 1982-2004* (Toronto: Anansi, 2004), 36-37; Jacqueline Gresko, "'Roughing it in the Bush' in British Columbia: Mary Moody's Pioneer Life in New Westminster, 1859-1863," in *Not Just Pin Money: Selected Essays on the History of Women's Work in British Columbia,* ed. Barbara K. Latham and Roberta J. Pazdro (Victoria, BC: Camosun College, 1984), 111.
9 Peter Stearns, "Stages of Consumerism: Recent Work on the Issues of Periodization," *Journal of Modern History* 69 (March 1997): 106, 102; Bill Lancaster, *The Department*

Store: A Social History (London: Leicester University Press, 1995), 8; Michael B. Miller, *The Bon Marché: Bourgeois Culture and the Department Store, 1869-1920* (Princeton, NJ: Princeton University Press, 1981), 25, 31; "Ville de Paris: Population and Density from 1365," http://www.demographia.com/dm-par90.htm.

10 Susan Porter Benson, *Counter Cultures: Saleswomen, Managers, and Customers in American Department Stores, 1890-1940* (Urbana and Chicago: University of Illinois Press, 1988), 13; Miller, *The Bon Marché*, 30-31; Sidney Redner, "Population History of New York from 1790 to 1990," http://physics.bu.edu/~redner/projects/population/index.html.

11 Miller, *The Bon Marché*, 167-68, 29-31, 47, quote p. 40; Benson, *Counter Cultures*, 14-15.

12 H. Pasdermadjian, *The Department Store: Its Origins, Evolution and Economics* (New York: Arno Press, 1976 [1954]), 36-37; Geoffrey Crossick and Serge Jaumain, "The World of the Department Store: Distribution, Culture and Social Change," in *Cathedrals of Consumption: The European Department Store, 1850-1939*, ed. Geoffrey Crossick and Serge Jaumain (Aldershot, UK: Ashgate, 1999), 1-45; Miller, *The Bon Marché*, 36-37; Monod, *Store Wars*, 123.

13 Finkel and Conrad, *History of the Canadian Peoples*, 2:118.

14 Wallace Ward, "Morgan's on the March," *The Montréaler*, October 1951, 19.

15 Santink, *Timothy Eaton*, 70, 82.

16 Pasdermadjian, *The Department Store*, 7; Lancaster, *The Department Store*, 20, 23, 46.

17 Henry Klasson, *Eye on the Future: Business People in Calgary and the Bow Valley, 1870-1900* (Calgary: University of Calgary Press, 2002), 265.

18 Santink, *Timothy Eaton*, 111, 98, 110, 124-25, 166; Eileen O'Connor, "The Eaton's Mail-Order Catalogue, 1884-1976: An Archival Analysis," unpublished paper, 1996, Canadian Museum of Civilization, Library, Archives, and Documentation, History Records, 21-164, 15; Miller, *The Bon Marché*, 46-47. Harrods, Macy's, and Eaton's sales totals are provided in dollars by Santink in *Timothy Eaton*, page 266. She does not specify whether these dollars are Canadian or American. According to Denise Chong, however, the Canadian dollar was "fixed at parity with the American dollar until World War One": Denise Chong, *The Concubine's Children* (Toronto: Penguin Books, 1994), xiii.

19 "250 Water Street," *Canada's Historic Places/Lieux patrimoniaux du Canada*, http://www.historicplaces.ca/.

20 Statistics Canada, *Historical Statistics of Canada* (1983), Series A67-69, http://www.statcan.gc.ca/bsolc/olc-cel/olc-cel?catno=11-516-X&lang=eng; Finkel and Conrad, *History of the Canadian Peoples*, 2:118; John William Ferry, *A History of the Department Store* (New York: Macmillan, 1960), 328-29; David Spencer Limited, *Golden Jubilee: 1873-1923* (Victoria: David Spencer, 1923), 6; Jean Barman, *The West beyond the West: A History of British Columbia*, rev. ed. (Toronto: University of Toronto Press, 1999), 390; Catherine C. Cole, "Comparative Analysis of the Toronto and Winnipeg Editions of the Eaton's Mail-Order Catalogue," unpublished paper, Canadian Museum of Civilization, Library, Archives and Documentation, History Records, 1995, Box 1-164, p. 1; Henry Klassen, "T.C. Power & Bro.: The Rise of a Small Western Department Store, 1870-1902," *Business History Review* 66, 4 (Winter 1992), http://www.gale.cengage.com/AcademicOneFile/; "Anderson Department Store Fonds: Elgin County Archives," *Ontario History* 99, 2 (Autumn 2007): 248; Elizabeth Sifton, "Montréal's Fashion Mile: St. Catherine Street, 1890-1930," in *Fashion: A Canadian Perspective, 1890-1930*, ed. Alexandra Palmer (Toronto: University of Toronto Press, 2004), 205-6; Carla J. Wheaton, "'- as modern as some of the fine new departmental stores ... can

make it': A Social History of the Large Water Street Stores, St. John's, Newfoundland, 1892-1949" (PhD diss., Memorial University of Newfoundland, 2002), 64-68.

21 Klassen, *Eye on the Future,* 277-85; H.T. Lockyer, "The Rise of H.B.C. Vancouver Retail Establishment," *The Beaver* (December 1920): 20-21; Christopher Moore, *Adventurers: Hudson's Bay Company – The Epic Story* (Hong Kong: Quantum Book Group, 2000), 7; "Report on the Hudson's Bay Stores in Canada," Mr. Burbridge, 1912, HBCA, A. 102-2504.

22 Ferry, *History,* 311; R. Simpson Company, *The Story of Simpson's: 68 Years of Progress* (Toronto: Wood, Gudy, 1940), 2, in RG17/1Q/24, HBCHS; "Our Story," Training Department, *The Every-Tuesday-Morning Bulletin,* no. 134 (1932), in HBCHS, RG17/1S/1; Santink, *Timothy Eaton,* 159.

23 Cole, "Comparative Analysis," 2; Santink, *Timothy Eaton,* 130, 140, 143, 170, 180, 266; Miller, *The Bon Marché,* 46-47; James C. Worthy, *Shaping an American Institution: Robert E. Wood and Sears, Roebuck* (Urbana and Chicago: University of Illinois Press, 1984), 31; "Population of Great Britain and Ireland, 1871-1931," *GenDocs:* http://homepage. ntlworld.com/hitch/gendocs/pop.html#EW; "Population of France," *New York Times,* 11 September 1904, http://www.nytimes.com/ref/membercenter/nytarchive.html; Texas State Data Center and Office of the State Demographer, "Resident Population of States in the United States, 1900-2000," http://txsdc.utsa.edu/txdata/apport/hist_a.php.

24 Liverant, "Buying Happiness: English Canadian Intellectuals and the Development of Canadian Consumer Culture" (PhD diss., University of Alberta, 2008), 22; Monod, *Store Wars,* 25, 33.

25 Miller, *The Bon Marché;* Asa Briggs, *Friends of the People: The Centenary History of Lewis's* (London: B.T. Batsford, 1956), 21; Ralph Hower, *History of Macy's of New York, 1858-1919* (Cambridge: Harvard University Press, 1943), 120; Sifton, "Montréal's Fashion Mile," 205-6; Santink, *Timothy Eaton,* 92, 97.

26 Monod, *Store Wars,* 27-28.

27 Bettina Bradbury, *Working Families: Age, Gender, and Daily Survival in Industrializing Montreal* (Toronto: University of Toronto Press, 2007); Santink, *Timothy Eaton,* 92, 97; Untitled report, ca. 1960s, AO, TEP, Series 162, Box 18, File 674.

28 Monod, *Store Wars,* 105-7, 109, quote p. 104.

29 Bradbury, *Working Families;* Finkel and Conrad, *History of the Canadian Peoples,* 2:49.

30 Liverant, "Buying Happiness," 28-40.

31 Keith Walden, *Becoming Modern in Toronto: The Industrial Exhibition and the Shaping of a Late Victorian Culture* (Toronto: University of Toronto Press, 1997), 85-86, 125; Stearns, "Stages of Consumerism," 111-12.

32 Susan Porter Benson, "Living on the Margin: Working-Class Marriages and Family Survival Strategies in the United States, 1919-1941," in *The Sex of Things: Gender and Consumption in Historical Perspective,* ed. Victoria de Grazia and Ellen Furlough (Berkeley: University of California Press, 1996), 212-43; Henry Thomas Lockyer, Manager of HBC Vancouver, BC Royal Commission on Labour, 1912-14, BCA, GR-0684, Box 2, File 1; Kathy Peiss, *Cheap Amusements: Working Women and Leisure in Turn-of-the-Century New York* (Philadelphia: Temple University Press, 1986); Carolyn Strange, *Toronto's Girl Problem: The Perils and Pleasures of the City, 1880-1930* (Toronto: University of Toronto Press, 1995), 116-74.

33 Dirk Hoerder, *Creating Societies: Immigrant Lives in Canada* (Montréal and Kingston: McGill-Queen's University Press, 1999), 199-202.

34 O'Connor, "The Eaton's Mail-Order Catalogue," 15; William Leach, *Land of Desire: Merchants, Power, and the Rise of a New American Culture* (New York: Pantheon Books, 1993), 334; Santink, *Timothy Eaton,* 228-32, 266.

35 Moore, *Adventurers,* 7; "Report on the Hudson's Bay Stores in Canada," Mr. Burbridge, 1912, HBCA, A. 102-2504; "Sight-Seeing Calgary Store," *The Beaver* (March 1932): 420-21.

36 Statistics Canada, *Historical Statistics of Canada,* 1983, Series A2-14, "Population of Canada, by Province, Census Dates, 1851-1976," http://www.statcan.gc.ca/bsolc/olc-cel/olc-cel?catno=11-516-X&lang=eng; David Spencer, Ltd., *Golden Jubilee,* 29-30; R. Simpson Company, *The Story of Simpson's,* 2, in RG17/1Q/24, HBCHS.

37 Statistics Canada, *Historical Statistics of Canada,* 1983, Series A2-14; Newfoundland and Labrador, *Historical Statistics of Newfoundland and Labrador* (St. John's, NF: Queen's Printer, 1970), 6, http://www.stats.gov.nl.ca/Publications/Historical/PDF/Foreword.pdf; Wheaton, "– as modern," 188; Rannie Gillis, *Historic North Sydney: Images of Our Past* (Halifax, NS: Nimbus Publishing, 2005); L.D. McCann, "Metropolitanism and Branch Businesses in the Maritimes, 1881-1931," *The Acadiensis Reader,* vol. 2: *Atlantic Canada after Confederation,* ed. P.A. Buckner and David Frank (Fredericton: Acadiensis Press, 1985), 202-15.

38 Monod, *Store Wars,* 123.

39 Ferry, *A History of the Department Store,* 324; Sifton, "Montréal's Fashion Mile," 213, 216; Mary Catherine Matthews, "Working for Family, Nation, and God: Paternalism and the Dupuis Frères Department Store, Montréal, 1926-1952" (MA thesis, McGill University, 1997), 2-3; Statistics Canada, *Department Stores in Canada,* 13-14; Santink, *Timothy Eaton,* 266; Worthy, *Shaping an American Institution,* 31.

40 Monod, *Store Wars,* 111-12, 211-13; Dominion Bureau of Statistics, *Seventh Census of Canada, 1931,* vol. 10, *Merchandising and Service Establishments – Part I, Retail Merchandise Trade* (Ottawa: J.O. Patenaude, 1931), xix-xx, lxxxiii.

41 Leach, *Land of Desire,* 273-74; Monod, *Store Wars,* 124-27, 358; Statistics Canada, *Department Stores in Canada,* 16; Lancaster, *The Department Store,* 85-86; H.H. Stevens, *Report,* 201.

42 Monod, *Store Wars,* 122-25; Worthy, *Shaping an American Institution,* 83; Leach, *Land of Desire,* 275.

43 Worthy, *Shaping an American Institution,* 82, 86; Leach, *Land of Desire,* 280-81; Lancaster, *The Department Store,* 90; "Westward to the Sea," *Contacts,* 17 July 1945; Monod, "Bay Days," 15; McCann, "Metropolitanism and Branch Businesses," 202-15.

44 "Westward to the Sea," *Contacts,* 17 July 1945; Monod, "Bay Days," 15; McCann, "Metropolitanism and Branch Businesses," 202-15; Eileen Sufrin, *The Eaton Drive: The Campaign to Organize Canada's Largest Department Store, 1948-1952* (Toronto: Fitzhenry and Whiteside, 1982), 14.

45 Monod, *Store Wars,* 123; Stevens, *Report of the Royal Commission,* 202; Dominion Bureau of Statistics, *Seventh Census of Canada,* xxiv-xxv; Hower, *History of Macy's,* 399; Worthy, *Shaping an American Institution,* 103.

46 Statistics Canada, *Department Stores in Canada,* 16; Lancaster, *The Department Store,* 103-4; Stevens, *Report of the Royal Commission on Price Spreads,* 207.

47 Monod, *Store Wars,* 213.

48 R. Simpson Company, *Thumbnail Sketches* (Toronto: Robert Simpson, 1927), in RG17/1Q/24, HBCHS.

49 Monod, *Store Wars,* 215; Monod, "Bay Days," 12; Ferry, *The Department Store,* 301-2.

50 "Vancouver's Big Store Operations," *Vancouver Sun,* 6 June 1934, 11; Ferry, *A History of the Department Store,* 331; Sifton, "Montréal's Fashion Mile," 213, 216; Matthews, "Working for Family, Nation, and God," 2-3; "250 Water Street," *Canada's Historic Places/ Lieux patrimoniaux du Canada,* http://www.historicplaces.ca/visit-visite/com-ful _e.aspx?id=10088.

51 Statistics Canada, *Department Stores in Canada,* 17; Monod, *Store Wars,* 218-19.

52 "Woodward Profits Shown at Ottawa," *Vancouver Province,* 6 June 1934, 1; "Eaton's Raised Mark-Up to 44 Per Cent Last Year," *Vancouver Province,* 13 June 1934, 4; Monod, *Store Wars,* 218-19; Hower, *History of Macy's,* 381-82; Lancaster, *The Department Store,* 85-86.

53 Tebbel, *The Marshall Fields,* 147; Hower, *History of Macy's,* 405; Pasdermadjian, *The Department Store,* 52-54; Crossick and Jaumain, "The Department Store," 22; Lancaster, *The Department Store,* 103, 148; Worthy, *Shaping an American Institution,* 83.

Chapter 2: Creating Modern Canada

1 As quoted in "Eaton's Closures a Major Blow to Smaller Cities: An Icon on the Wane," *National Post,* 14 July 1999, C6.

2 Deirdre Kelly, "Just One Thing: Yanks Get the Point," *Globe and Mail,* 16 December 2000, 1.

3 Deborah Fulsang, "Beyond Blankets," *Globe and Mail,* 11 October 2003, L1.

4 Roland Marchand, *Advertising the American Dream: Making Way for Modernity, 1920-1940* (Berkeley: University of California Press, 1985), xx.

5 Miaso Batts, "Eaton's and Its Catalogues: An Expression of Canadian Social History," *Costume* 7 (1973): 68-69.

6 Archives of Ontario (AO), "The Archives of Ontario Remembers an Eaton's Christmas," http://www.archives.gov.on.ca/english/on-line-exhibits/eatons/index.aspx; Library and Archives Canada (LAC), "Canadian Mail Order Catalogues," http://www. collectionscanada.ca/mailorder/index-e.html; Canadian Museum of Civilization (hereafter CMC), "Before E-commerce: A History of Canadian Mail-Order Catalogues," http://www.civilization.ca/cmc/exhibitions/cpm/catalog/cat0000e.shtml.

7 William Leach, *Land of Desire: Merchants, Power, and the Rise of a New American Culture* (New York: Pantheon Books, 1993), 42; Mary Vipond, *The Mass Media in Canada,* 3rd ed. (Toronto: James Lorimer and Company, 2000), 18.

8 Russell Johnston, *Selling Themselves: The Emergence of Canadian Advertising* (Toronto: University of Toronto Press, 2001), 29.

9 Vipond, *The Mass Media in Canada,* 18-20. Readers wishing to learn more about the rise of the Canadian advertising industry – including the evolution of ad layouts, the production of advertisements, the size of newspapers' advertising accounts, and various types of advertising campaigns – should consult Johnston, *Selling Themselves,* which offers exceptionally detailed discussions of these processes.

10 Susan Strasser, *Satisfaction Guaranteed: The Making of the American Mass Market* (New York: Pantheon Books, 1989); Ralph Hower, *History of Macy's of New York, 1858-1919* (Cambridge, MA: Harvard University Press, 1943), 266.

11 Vipond, *The Mass Media in Canada,* 19.

12 Hower, *History of Macy's,* 269; Michael B. Miller, *The Bon Marché: Bourgeois Culture and the Department Store, 1869-1920* (Princeton, NJ: Princeton University Press, 1981), 173-75; Asa Briggs, *Friends of the People: The Centenary History of Lewis's* (London: B.T. Bats-

ford, 1956), 46; Eileen O'Connor, "The Eaton's Mail-Order Catalogue, 1884-1976: An Archival Analysis," 1996, CMC, Library, Archives, and Documentation, History Records, 21-164, 15.

13 Valerie J. Korinek, *Roughing It in the Suburbs: Reading Chatelaine Magazine in the Fifties and Sixties* (Toronto: University of Toronto Press, 2000), 126.

14 "The Eaton Policy," *Golden Jubilee*, 115; also "Typical Eaton Principles," Winnipeg Eaton's advertisement (Winnipeg: T. Eaton, 1919), AO, TEP, Series 162, File 682.

15 Monod, *Store Wars*, 5-64.

16 Norman Patterson, "Evolution of a Departmental Store," *Canadian Magazine*, September 1906, 438.

17 R. Simpson Company, *Thumbnail Sketches* (Toronto: Robert Simpson, 1927), 12-13, in RG17/1Q/24, Hudson's Bay Company Corporate Collection (hereafter HBCCC).

18 Patterson, "Evolution of a Departmental Store," 438; "Human Side of Eaton Factories," ca. 1924, AO, TEP, Series 162, File 682.

19 "Morgan Structure Forms a Memorial of Steady Growth," *Montréal Gazette*, 13 November 1923, HBCCC, MOR-A1.1, Historical Record Scrapbook, 1839-1936.

20 "H.B.C. Helped Settlers Remain on Land During 'Lean Years,'" *The Beaver* (February 1921): 20.

21 See, for example, *The Shopping Guide of the West* (Vancouver: Woodward Department Stores, 1914), HBCCC, 161.

22 "Eaton-Made Goods in Western Canada," Winnipeg Eaton's advertisement (Winnipeg: T. Eaton, ca. 1920s), AO, TEP, Series 162, File 682.

23 Patterson, "Evolution of a Departmental Store," 425.

24 R. Simpson Company, *Thumbnail Sketches*, RG17/1Q/24.

25 *Canada's Greatest Store* (Toronto: T. Eaton, 1905), AO, TEP, Series 162, File 1331.

26 Pamphlet distributed ca. 1908 (Toronto: T. Eaton, 1908), AO, TEP, Series 162, File 1331.

27 See, for example, "The Hudson's Bay Company: 'Adventurers of England' – A Great Feat of Development – Furs and Department Stores," HBC advertisement in *The Canadian Gazette and Export Trader,* 19 October 1933, 55.

28 Sir William Schooling, K.B.E., "Fur – And Further," *Manitoba Free Press*, 3 May 1920, clipping in HBCA, RG2/74/2.

29 "Canada's Most Magnificent Store," *The Empire*, 3 December 1894, 3.

30 *Canadian Shopper's Hand-Book and Repertoire of Fashion*, 1896-1897 Fall/Winter (Toronto: R. Simpson, 1896), HBCCC, RG17/1B/2.

31 "A Canadian Enterprise!" advertisement in *Massey-Harris Illustrated,* May-June 1898, HBCCC, RG17/1Q/6.

32 *Eaton's: Largest Institution of Its Kind under the British Flag* (Winnipeg: T. Eaton, ca. 1925), AO, TEP, Series 162, File 1537.

33 "Robert Simpson Company, Limited," *Good Neighbors: Studies in Corporate Citizenship* (Toronto: Financial Post, 1940), HBCCC, RG17/Q/17.

34 *Canada's Greatest Store.*

35 Edith MacDonald, *Golden Jubilee, 1869-1919* (Toronto and Winnipeg: T. Eaton, 1919), 231.

36 Ibid., 234-35.

37 "Victoria Day Celebration," *The Beaver* (July 1922): 32-33.

38 *Canadian Shoppers' Hand-Book and Repertoire of Fashion*, Spring and Summer 1892 (Toronto: R. Simpson, 1892), 172, HBCCC, RG17/1B/2.

39 "Eaton's Early Closing Movement," Winnipeg Eaton's advertisement (Winnipeg: T. Eaton, ca. 1920s), AO, TEP, Series 162, File 682.

40 H. Lee Wilson, "253 Years Old May 2nd," *The Beaver* (May 1923): 297.

41 Bill Lancaster, *The Department Store: A Social History* (London: Leicester University Press, 1995), 75.

42 Ibid., 80.

43 *Canadian Shopper's Hand-Book and Repertoire of Fashion,* Fall and Winter, 1896-97 (Toronto: Simpson's, 1896), 103, HBCCC, RG17/1B/2.

44 "Modern Store Building for John Murphy Co.," *The Gazette* (Montréal), 7 March 1929, 12-13.

45 Norman Patterson, "Evolution of a Departmental Store," *Canadian Magazine*, September 1906, 438.

46 From "The Great Mail Order House of the West – Catalogue No. 31," reproduced in *The Shopping Guide of the West: Woodward's Catalogue, 1898-1953,* ed. Vancouver Centennial Museum (Vancouver: J.J. Douglas, 1977), inside front cover.

47 *Eaton's of Canada* (Toronto: T. Eaton, 1956), 36, AO, TEP, Series 69, Box 8, File "[1947 to mid-60s]."

48 Pamphlet distributed ca. 1908 (Toronto: T. Eaton, 1908), AO, TEP, Series 162, File 1331.

49 Cynthia Wright, "'The Most Prominent Rendezvous of the Feminine Toronto': Eaton's College Street and the Organization of Shopping in Toronto, 1920-1950" (PhD diss., University of Toronto, 1992), 105.

50 Eaton's pamphlet distributed ca. 1908.

51 *The Evolution of a Store: A Sketch of 42 Years of Unexampled Growth* (Toronto: T. Eaton, 1911), AO, TEP, Series 162, Box 41, File 1333.

52 "The Four Corners and the Metropolis," Simpson's advertisement in *Massey-Harris Illustrated,* May-June 1898, 86, HBCCC, RG17/1Q/6.

53 *Canada's Greatest Store* (Toronto: T. Eaton, 1905), AO, TEP, Series 162, File 1331.

54 *About a Great Store* (Toronto: T. Eaton, 1908), unpaginated, AO, TEP, Series 162, File 1331.

55 *An Artist's Impressions upon a Visit to a Great Store,* unpaginated, AO, TEP, Series 162, File 1331.

56 Briggs, *Friends of the People,* 21.

57 "The Great Mail Order House," inside front cover. Emphasis in original.

58 *Canada's Greatest Store.*

59 University College London, Bentham Project, http://www.ucl.ac.uk/Bentham-Project/info/jb.htm.

60 "Typical Eaton Principles" (Toronto: T. Eaton, circa 1928), AO, TEP, Series 162, File 682.

61 Judith G. Coffin, "A 'Standard' of Living? European Perspectives on Class and Consumption in the Early Twentieth Century," *International Labor and Working-Class History* 55 (Spring 1999): 22.

62 Ibid., 6.

63 Eaton letter in *Free Press Prairie Farmer,* 26 September 1934, AO, TEP, Series 117, Box 1, File: Misc. Letters – Testimonials.

64 Mail Order Supervision to Mrs. H.W. Hunt, 11 December 1935, AO, TEP, Series 117, Box 1, File: Misc. Letters – Testimonials, 1935-38.

65 *Evolution of a Store,* last page.

66 John Kasson, *Rudeness and Civility: Manners in Nineteenth-Century Urban America* (New York: Hill and Wang, 1990), 34, 43.

67 Booklet produced by the T. Eaton Company, ca. 1910, unpaginated, AO, TEP, Series 162, File 1331.

68 *Canada and Toronto* (Toronto: Robert Simpson, 1927), HBCCC, box of brochures.

69 Jack Prest, "From Pioneer Trading Post to Great Department Store," *The Beaver* (March 1921): 2-4.

70 Jack Prest, "Indians and Edmonton Store," *The Beaver* (June 1925): 144; Jack Prest, "H.B.C. Still the Standby of the Indians," *The Beaver* (March 1923): 250.

71 Pamphlet produced by the T. Eaton Company, 1911, unpaginated, AO, TEP, Series 162, File 1333.

72 MacDonald, *Golden Jubilee, 1869-1919,* as quoted in John Brehl, "Eaton's: The Big Store Is Now 100 Years Old," *Toronto Star,* January 1963, in *A Century of Service to Canadian Shoppers* (Toronto: Toronto Star, 1969), unpaginated.

73 William Stephenson, *The Store That Timothy Built* (Toronto: McClelland and Stewart, 1969), 54.

74 "When Eaton's Opened in Winnipeg," Winnipeg Eaton's advertisement (Winnipeg: T. Eaton, ca. 1920s), AO, TEP, Series 162, File 682.

75 Augustus Bridle, "The Founder and His Successor," in MacDonald, *Golden Jubilee,* 107.

76 MacDonald, *Golden Jubilee,* 180.

77 Marchand, *Advertising the American Dream,* 192-93.

78 Prest, "H.B.C. Still the Standby," 250; Prest, "Indians and Edmonton Store," 144.

79 *The Pricemaker* (Calgary: Hudson's Bay Company, 1 September 1926), 2-3, HBCA, RG2-41-B/5.

80 "English as She Is Wrote," *The Beaver* (June 1921): 31.

81 "A Summer Trip to the Arctic," *The Beaver* (June 1925): 120-22.

82 "Happy 'Topsy,'" Simpson's 1933 Christmas Sale Catalogue (Toronto: R. Simpson, 1933), 67, HBCCC, RG17/1B/19.

83 Moncton Spring and Summer Catalogue, 1920 (Moncton: T. Eaton, 1920), 449.

84 "The Great Mail Order House," 87.

85 Eaton's 1896 Spring and Summer Catalogue (Toronto: T. Eaton, 1896), 184, LAC.

86 T.J. Jackson Lears, "From Salvation to Self-Realization: Advertising and the Therapeutic Roots of the Consumer Culture, 1880-1930," in *The Culture of Consumption: Critical Essays in American History, 1880-1980,* ed. Richard Wightman Fox and T.J. Jackson Lears (New York: Pantheon Books, 1983), 18.

87 Ibid., 19, 9; Marchand, *Advertising the American Dream,* 359.

88 John Levi Martin, "The Myth of the Consumption-Oriented Economy and the Rise of the Desiring Subject," *Theory and Society* 28, 3 (June 1999): 431.

89 *Canadian Shopper's Hand-Book and Repertoire of Fashion,* Fall-Winter 1896-87 (Toronto: R. Simpson, 1896), 123, in box of Simpson's catalogues, HBCCC.

90 HBC's 1904 Spring and Summer Catalogue (Winnipeg: Hudson's Bay Company, 1904), 49, in a box of HBC catalogues, HBCCC. See also Keith Walden, *Becoming Modern in Toronto: The Toronto Industrial Exhibition and the Shaping of a Late Victorian Culture* (Toronto: University of Toronto Press, 1997), 86; Carolyn Strange, *Toronto's Girl Problem: The Perils and Pleasures of the City, 1880-1930* (Toronto: University of Toronto Press, 1995), 19-30.

91 Simpson's 1922 Spring and Summer Catalogue (Toronto: R. Simpson, 1922), HBCCC, RG17/1B/12.

92 Walden, *Becoming Modern,* 85-86.

93 Kathy Peiss, *Hope in a Jar: The Making of America's Beauty Culture* (New York: Owl Books, 1999), esp. 166-202; see also Kathy Peiss, "Making Up, Making Over: Cosmetics, Consumer Culture, and Women's Identity," in *The Sex of Things: Gender and Consumption in Historical Perspective,* ed. Victoria de Grazia and Ellen Furlough (Berkeley and Los Angeles: University of California Press, 1996), 311-36.

94 *Introducing Christmas with a Week of Sales* (Montréal: Henry Morgan and Co., Limited, 1934), 9, box of Morgan's catalogues, HBCCC.

95 "A Beauty and Fashion Revue," advertisement, *Globe and Mail,* 18 November 1932, RG17/1P/13, HBCCC.

96 "How Five Girls Became Fast Friends," *Eaton's News Weekly,* 6 September 1924, 19, LAC.

97 *Canadian Shopper's Hand-Book,* 1896 (Toronto: R. Simpson, 1896), 29, box of Simpson's catalogues, HBCCC.

98 Simpson's Fall/Winter 1922-23 Catalogue (Toronto: R. Simpson, 1922), 50, box of Simpson's catalogues, HBCCC.

99 Simpson's Fall/Winter 1933-34 Catalogue (Toronto: R. Simpson, 1933), 56, box of Simpson's catalogues, HBCCC.

100 Vance Packard, *The Waste Makers* (New York: Van Rees Press, 1960).

101 "Unsurpassed in the British Empire: Voluntary Opinion English Journalist," *Sunday World,* 10 September 1907, AO, TEP, Series 162, File 660; Miss L.A. Jones to Sir John Eaton, 5 January 1919, AO, Series 162, Box 17, File 614.

102 Bessie McKillop to Management of the T. Eaton Co., AO, TEP, Series 162, Box 13, File 508; R.J. Charbonneau to Sirs, September 1937, AO, TEP, Series 162, Box 13, File 508.

103 Anonymous memo, summer 1937, AO, TEP, Series 117, Box 1.

104 G.A. Sims, "A Valuable Discovery," summer 1937, AO, TEP, Series 117, Box 1.

105 Patricia Phenix, *Eatonians: The Story of the Family Behind the Family* (Toronto: McClelland and Stewart, 2001), 138-39.

106 Miller, *The Bon Marché,* 183.

107 Dirk Hoerder, *Creating Societies: Immigrant Lives in Canada* (Montréal and Kingston: McGill-Queen's University Press, 1999), 200-1.

108 Hower, *History of Macy's,* 337.

109 Brehl, "Eaton's," unpaginated; Customer letter to Mr. John David Eaton, 4 November 1969, AO, TEP, Series 162, Box 13, File 508.

110 *Last Post* staff, "The Company," *Last Post,* February 1970, 14

111 T. Beauregard to the T. Eaton Co., 14 January 1976, AO, TEP, Series 162, Box 13, File 508; Cecelia Dickie to the T. Eaton Co., 4 February 1976, AO, TEP, Series 162, Box 13, File 508.

112 Fredelle Bruser Maynard, "Satisfaction Guaranteed: The 1928 Eaton's Catalogue," *Raisins and Almonds* (Toronto: Doubleday Canada, 1972), 39-51. Quotations are taken from pages 50-51.

113 Letter to the T. Eaton Co., 22 July 1983, AO, TEP, Series 162, Box 17, File 614.

114 Mildred J. Young, "Bachelor Ordered a Wife from EATON'S CATALOGUE," *Early Canadian Life,* April 1978, 21.

115 "Eaton's Closures a Major Blow to Smaller Cities: An Icon on the Wane," *National Post,* 14 July 1999, C6; Catherine Carstairs, "Roots Nationalism: Branding English Canada Cool in the 1980s and 1990s," *Histoire sociale/Social History* 77 (May 2006): 236-37.

116 Alison Isenberg, *Downtown America: A History of the Place and the People Who Made It* (Chicago: University of Chicago Press, 2004), 255-311; Phenix, *Eatonians,* 176. See also Cynthia Wright, "Rewriting the Modern: Reflections on Race, Nation, and the Death of a Department Store," *Histoire sociale/Social History* 33 (May 2000): 153-67.

117 Simone Weil Davis, *Living Up to the Ads: Gender Fictions of the 1920s* (Durham, NC: Duke University Press, 2000), 1.

Chapter 3: Fathers of Mass Merchandising

1 Letter to T. Eaton Co., 4 February 1976, Archives of Ontario (hereafter AO), T. Eaton Papers (hereafter TEP), Series 162, Box 13, File 508.

2 Michael Miller, *The Bon Marché: Bourgeois Culture and the Department Store, 1869-1920* (Princeton, NJ: Princeton University Press, 1981), 9; Roland Marchand, *Creating the Corporate Soul: The Rise of Public Relations and Corporate Imagery in American Big Business* (Berkeley and Los Angeles: University of California Press, 1998), 11; Gail Reekie, "'Humanising Industry': Paternalism, Welfarism, and Labour Control in Sydney's Big Stores, 1890-1930," *Labour History* 53 (November 1987): 1-19; Bill Lancaster, *The Department Store: A Social History* (London: Leicester University Press, 1995). See also Theresa McBride, "A Woman's World: Department Stores and the Evolution of Women's Employment, 1870-1920," *French Historical Studies* 10 (Autumn 1978): 664-83.

3 Marchand, *Creating the Corporate Soul*, 2.

4 John Tebbel, *The Marshall Fields: A Study in Wealth* (New York: E.P. Dutton, 1947), 70.

5 David Monod, *Store Wars: Shopkeepers and the Culture of Mass Marketing, 1890-1939* (Toronto: University of Toronto Press, 1996), 64. See also Gail Reekie, *Temptations: Sex, Selling and the Department Store* (Sydney: Allen and Unwin, 1993), 9; Carla Wheaton, "'– as modern as some of the fine new department stores – can make it': A Social History of the Large Water Street Stores, St. John's, Newfoundland, 1892-1949" (PhD diss., Memorial University, 2001), 330.

6 Wallace Ward, "Morgan's on the March," *The Montréaler,* October 1951, C1; Monod, *Store Wars*, 60, 64; "Rules and Regulations," 1854, Morgan's "Search File," Hudson's Bay Company Archives (hereafter HBCA).

7 Joy L. Santink, *Timothy Eaton and the Rise of His Department Store* (Toronto: University of Toronto Press, 1990), 11-12, quote p. 183; John C. Porter, *The Men Who Put the Show on the Road* (Toronto: Clarke, Irwin, 1952), unpaginated; R. Simpson Co., *The Simpsons Century* (Toronto: Toronto Star, 1971), unpaginated; William Stephenson, *The Store That Timothy Built* (Toronto: McClelland and Stewart, 1969), 30; Augustus Bridle, "The Founder and His Successor," in Edith MacDonald, *Golden Jubilee, 1869-1919* (Toronto and Winnipeg: T. Eaton, 1919), 80, 89.

8 R. Simpson Co., *Simpson's* (Toronto: R. Simpson, 1949), 5.

9 James Emmerson, "A Famous Canadian Store Strides into Its 100th Year," in R. Simpson Co., *The Simpsons Century* (Toronto: Toronto Star, 1972), unpaginated.

10 As quoted in Porter, *The Men Who Put the Show on the Road,* unpaginated.

11 Marchand, *Creating the Corporate Soul*, 11.

12 David Spencer, Ltd., *Golden Jubilee, 1873-1923* (Victoria: Spencer's, 1923), 2-7, 10-11.

13 Marchand, *Creating the Corporate Soul*, 27.

14 Bridle, "The Founder and His Successor," 69, 75.

15 Lancaster, *The Department Store,* 144.

16 Bridle, "The Founder and His Successor," 100, 108.

17 "Timothy Eaton Opens in Winnipeg," *The Winnipeg Daily Tribune,* 17 July 1905, 11.

18 Andrea Tone, *The Business of Benevolence: Industrial Paternalism in Progressive America* (Ithaca and London: Cornell University Press, 1997), 11; Reekie, "'Humanising Industry,'" 6; Susan Porter Benson, *Counter Cultures: Saleswomen, Managers, and Customers in American Department Stores, 1890-1940* (Urbana and Chicago: University of Illinois

Press, 1988), 42; William Leach, *Land of Desire: Merchants, Power, and the Rise of a New American Culture* (New York: Pantheon Books, 1993), 121.

19 MacDonald, *Golden Jubilee,* 176, 222; *Store Topics,* June 1927, 20; "Simpson Employes [sic] Guests at Barrymede," *Mail and Empire,* ca. July 1925, Hudson's Bay Company Corporate Collection (hereafter HBCCC), RG17/1E/74.

20 "Gratifying to Staff of Hudson's Bay Co.," unreferenced clipping, 1920, HBCA, RG2/74/2.

21 Benson, *Counter Cultures,* 139. See also Joan Sangster, *Earning Respect: The Lives of Working Women in Small-Town Ontario, 1920-1960* (Toronto: University of Toronto Press, 1995), 194.

22 Marchand, *Creating the Corporate Soul,* 12-13; Leach, *Land of Desire,* 116-17.

23 Susan Forbes, "The Influence of the Social Reform Movement and T. Eaton Company's Business Practices on the Leisure of Eaton's Female Employees during the Early Twentieth Century" (PhD diss., University of Western Ontario, 1998), 47-49; Mary Catherine Matthews, "Working for Family, Nation, and God: Paternalism and the Dupuis Frères Department Store, Montréal, 1926-1952" (MA thesis, McGill University, 1997), 65; *Simpson's Essay Contest* (Toronto: R. Simpson, 1929), HBCCC, RG17/1P/50; HBCA, RG2/74/3; "Special Features in a Big Store," undated advertisement, ca. 1920s (Winnipeg: T. Eaton, undated), AO, TEP, Series 162, File 682.

24 Correspondence regarding Jubilee promotions, 1927, HBCCC, RG17/1P/6; MacDonald, *Golden Jubilee,* 38.

25 Leach, *Land of Desire,* 134.

26 "Great Dry Goods Exhibition," 1891, AO, TEP, Series 162, Box 17, File 636; "Special Features in a Big Store," undated advertisement, ca. 1920s (Winnipeg: T. Eaton, undated), AO, TEP, Series 162, File 682.

27 Cynthia Wright, "'The Most Prominent Rendezvous of the Feminine Toronto': Eaton's College Street and the Organization of Shopping in Toronto, 1920-1950" (PhD diss., University of Toronto, 1992); Lorraine O'Donnell, "Visualizing the History of Women at Eaton's, 1869 to 1976" (PhD diss., McGill University, 2002), 308; Erika Diane Rappaport, *Shopping for Pleasure: Women in the Making of London's West End* (Princeton, NJ: Princeton University Press, 2000), 79-107, quote p. 100.

28 *Eaton's Fall and Winter Dry Goods Catalogue, 1887-1888* (Toronto: T. Eaton Company, 1887), 4; "The Four Corners and the Metropolis," *Massey-Harris Illustrated,* May-June 1898, 88.

29 "The Four Corners and the Metropolis," 88; "Simpson's Introduces the Grill for Men," unreferenced clipping, 1933, HBCCC, RG 17/1T/19; *About a Great Store* (Toronto and Winnipeg: T. Eaton Company, 1908), unpaginated; *The Little Helper* (Toronto: T. Eaton Company, 1908), AO, TEP, Series 162, Box 48, File 1548; "Electric Cooking Demonstration," brochure, 1932, HBCCC, RG17/1P/77.

30 "The Four Corners and the Metropolis," 88.

31 Untitled clipping about the opening of Morgan's new store, 1891, HBCCC, MOR-A1.1, Morgan's Scrapbooks.

32 *Eaton's Fall and Winter Dry Goods Catalogue, 1887-1888* (Toronto: T. Eaton Company, 1887), unpaginated. Also see "Simpson's for Silks," ca. 1903, back of Simpson's restaurant bill of fare (Toronto: R. Simpson, ca. 1903), HBCCC, RG17/1Q/3.

33 *The Shopping Guide of the West,* Spring and Summer 1929 (Vancouver: Woodward's, 1929), cover.

34 MacDonald, *Golden Jubilee, 1873-1923,* 16.

35 McBride, "'A Woman's World,'" 679; Leach, *Land of Desire,* 118; Reekie, "'Humanising Industry,'" 1-19; Marchand, *Creating the Corporate Soul,* 154; Joan Sangster, "The Softball Solution: Female Workers, Male Managers and the Operation of Paternalism at Westclox, 1923-60," *Labour/Le Travail* 32 (Fall 1993): 167-99; Hugh Grant, "Solving the Labour Problem at Imperial Oil: Welfare Capitalism in the Canadian Petroleum Industry, 1919-29," *Labour/Le Travail* 41 (Spring 1998): 69-95; Tone, *The Business of Benevolence,* 7-8, 11.

36 Ian Murray, "Employees – Welfare," 23 December 1965, AO, TEP, Series 162, Box 31, File 990; "Quarter-Century of Meritorious Service!" *Contacts,* June 1935, 10, AO, TEP, Series 141; Simpson's, *The History of Employee Benefits at Simpson's* (June 1952), unpaginated, HBCCC, RG17/1Q/3; "Welfare," *Bay Window,* March 1938, HBCA; MacDonald, *Golden Jubilee,* 232; Assistant Secretary, Board of Directors, to Mr. R.W. Eaton, 14 May 1920, AO, TEP, Series 162, Box 31, File 990; "Beaver Club Notes," *The Beaver* (September 1931): 306; *Eaton's and You* (Toronto 1940), 17-25, AO, TEP, Series 171, Box 1; Morgan's Historical Record Scrapbook, 1839-1936, untitled clipping, 1931, A.1 Morgan's Records, HBCCC.

37 *Contacts,* 17 July 1939, AO, TEP, Series 141; Forbes, "The Influence," 117, 167; William Stephenson, *The Store That Timothy Built* (Toronto: McClelland and Stewart, 1969), 78-80; MacDonald, *Golden Jubilee,* 226-28; "New Life for Calgary HBAAA," *The Beaver* (May 1921): 38; "Employees' Association Formed," *The Beaver* (February 1922): 34; "New Tennis and Quoits Courts," *The Beaver* (October 1920): 21.

38 Summary of Eleanor Thompson's interview with participant, 25 March 1995, 1, Canadian Museum of Civilization (hereafter CMC), History Records, Eaton's Mail-Order Catalogue, Eaton's Employees, Oral History Project, Box: I-164; Sangster, "The Softball Solution," 183; "Junior Executive Club," *The Beaver* (March 1930): 382; "HBC Business Club," *The Beaver* (September 1931): 307; "Beaver Club Notes," *The Beaver* (September 1931): 306; "Welfare," *Bay Window,* March 1938, HBCA; Forbes, "The Influence," 118-19; MacDonald, *Golden Jubilee,* 228.

39 Susan Forbes, "Gendering Corporate Welfare Practices: Female Sports and Recreation at Eaton's during the Depression," *Rethinking History* 5 (2001): 68.

40 Tone, *The Business of Benevolence,* 142; Carolyn Strange, *Toronto's Girl Problem: The Perils and Pleasures of the City, 1880-1930* (Toronto: University of Toronto Press, 1996), 208-11; Eaton's Girls' Club brochure, 1932, "Notices to Employees," AO, TEP, Series 171, 1.

41 McBride, "A Woman's World," 671.

42 MacDonald, *Golden Jubilee,* 176, 224; *Sherbourne House Club,* ca. 1920s, HBCCC; "Fudger House Rules," no date, HBCA, Simpson's Search File; Strange, *Toronto's Girl Problem,* 178; Joy Parr, *The Gender of Breadwinners: Women, Men, and Change in Two Industrial Towns, 1880-1950* (Toronto: University of Toronto Press, 1990), 36; Sangster, "Softball Solution," 186.

43 Letter to T. Eaton Co., 3 March 1919, in AO, TEP, Series 117, Box 1.

44 Letter to Sir, 17 September 1934, and Letter to Management of the T. Eaton Co., 27 June 1937, both in AO, TEP, Series 117, Box 1.

45 Matthews, "Working for Family, Nation, and God," 62.

46 Sangster, "Softball Solution," 180.

47 Matthews, "Working for Family, Nation, and God," 62; Phenix, *Eatonians,* 2.

48 J. Brooks, "Report on Staff Organization and Training," February 1925, HBCA, RG2/54/9; MacDonald, *Golden Jubilee,* 123; *A Little Chat about Selling* (Toronto: T. Eaton, 1931), 5-11, AO, TEP, Series 162, Box 24, File 816.

49 As quoted in Wright, "'The Most Prominent,'" 199.

50 Reekie, *Temptations,* 56.

51 Joy Parr, *Domestic Goods: The Material, the Moral, and the Economic in the Postwar Years* (Toronto: University of Toronto Press, 1999), 204.

52 Matthews, "Working for Family, Nation, and God," 75; Sandra Aylward, "Experiencing Patriarchy: Women, Work and Trade Unionism at Eaton's" (PhD diss., McMaster University, 1991), 97; "Supervisors, Group Managers, Heads of Departments and Assistants," June 1929, AO, TEP, Series 162, File 764; Flora McCrea Eaton, *Memory's Wall: The Autobiography of Flora McCrea Eaton* (Toronto: Clarke, Irwin, 1956), 151.

53 "To H.B.C. Girls," *The Beaver* (November 1920): 11; Summary of Eleanor Thompson's interview with participant, 20 March 1995, CMC, History Records, Eaton's Mail Order Catalogue, Box I-164; AO, TEP, F 1176, Series C, Box 3 (name withheld to protect privacy).

54 Emily Cowley to the T. Eaton Co. Limited, no date, AO, TEP, Series 162, File 669; Phenix, *Eatonians,* 128; "This Actually Happened," *Flash,* 16 September 1935, 3; AO, TEP, Series 141.

55 Santink, *Timothy Eaton,* 188; Lillian M. Poulter, ca. 1958, AO, TEP, Series 162, File 901.

56 Strange, *Toronto's Girl Problem,* 193; Phenix, *Eatonians,* 127.

57 Edward Meek to Messrs Donald, Mason, White and Foulds, 3 November 1919, AO, TEP, Series 35, Box 1, File 22 (emphasis in original); Josephine Rist to Lady Eaton, 7 May 1919, TEP, Series 35, Box 1, File 22.

58 Santink, *Timothy Eaton,* 199; Mercedes Steedman, *Angels of the Workplace: Women and the Construction of Gender Relations in the Canadian Clothing Industry, 1890-1940* (Toronto: Oxford University Press, 1997), 83; Phenix, *Eatonians,* 37; Andrew Neufeld, *Union Store: The History of the Retail Clerks Union in British Columbia, 1899-1999* (Vancouver: United Food and Commercial Workers Union Local 1518, 1999), 14, 28-29, 33-34.

59 Mr. M. Levy to Jack Eaton, 12 June 1912, AO, TEP, Series 35, Box 5, File 131; Eaton, *Memory's Wall,* 150-51; "Press Continually Finds News in HBC," *The Bay Window,* June 1934, 2.

60 Paul Yee, *Saltwater City: An Illustrated History of the Chinese in Vancouver* (Vancouver: Douglas and McIntyre, 2006), 87.

61 "Alberta Indians," *The Beaver* (January 1922): 5; "How H.B.C. Acquired Its Farm Lands," *The Beaver* (November 1923): 50.

62 Poem in *The Bayonet,* July 1935.

63 "Nigger Humour," *The Beaver* (March 1926): 4.

64 *The Eaton News,* as quoted in Wright, "'The Most Prominent Rendezvous,'" 195.

65 "Eaton Customers," *Flash,* April 1940, AO, TEP, Series 117, Box 1, File – Toronto Testimonials, 1930s-40s.

Chapter 4: Crafting the Consumer Workforce

1 Arlie Russell Hochschild, *The Managed Heart: Commercialization of Human Feeling* (Berkeley: University of California Press, 2003 [1983]), 187-89; Pei-Chia Lan, "Working in a Neon Cage: Bodily Labor of Cosmetics Saleswomen in Taiwan," 29 *Feminist Studies* 29 (Spring 2003): 39, 32; Joan Sangster, "The Softball Solution: Female Workers, Male Managers and the Operation of Paternalism at Westclox, 1923-60," *Labour/Le Travail* 32 (Fall 1993): 193.

2 John Maynard Keynes, *The General Theory of Employment, Interest, and Money* (London and Basingstoke: Macmillan, 1936), 89.

3 Stephen Meyer III, *The Five Dollar Day: Labor Management and Social Control in the Ford Motor Company, 1908-1921* (Albany: State University of New York Press, 1981), 106-8, 119, 200.

4 August Bridle, "The Founder and His Successor," in Edith MacDonald, *Golden Jubilee, 1869-1919* (Toronto: T. Eaton, 1919), 82; *Flash,* 2 December 1935, 2; *Flash,* 5 July 1937, 3; H.M. Tucker to Miss C. Rowe, 27 August 1926, Archives of Ontario (hereafter AO), T. Eaton Papers (hereafter TEP), Series 162, Box 31, File 990; "Shower of China," *The Beaver* (August-September 1921): 32; "Mrs. L. McDermid to Edmonton," *The Beaver* (March 1923): 251; "Saskatoon Store News," *The Beaver* (September 1923): 459; "General News," *The Beaver* (September 1925): 43; "Staff Supplement," *The Beaver* (September 1929): 272-73; "Hoover Company," *The Beaver* (September 1928): 84; MacDonald, *Golden Jubilee,* 232-34; "The Top Ten Privileges," *Bayonet,* May 1940, Hudson's Bay Company Archives (hereafter HBCA); *Bay Builder,* April 1937, HBCA; quote is from MacDonald, *Golden Jubilee,* 233.

5 "Miss Morris Honored," *The Beaver* (February 1922): 34. There is an extended sociological literature on gift giving. Interested readers should start with David Cheal, *The Gift Economy* (New York: Routledge, 1988).

6 Herbert H. Bishop, Superintendent of David Spencer, Ltd., to BC Commission on Labour, 1912 to 1914, British Columbia Archives (hereafter BCA), GR-0684, Box 2, File 2; "Employees' Shopping," *The Beaver* (January 1923): 177; *The History of Employee Benefits at Simpson's* (Toronto: Simpson's, 1952), HBCCC, RG17/1Q/3; "Discounts," HBCA, RG2/10/Base-Notes, File 59; *Employees' Book of Information* (Toronto 1933), pp. 23-25, AO, TEP, Series 162, Box 23, File 792.

7 "Who's Your Hatter?" AO, TEP, Series 171, Box 1; *The Every-Tuesday-Morning Bulletin,* no. 163 (ca. 1937), 1, Hudson's Bay Company Corporate Archives (hereafter HBC-CC), RG17/1S/1.

8 Mary Catherine Matthews, "Working for Family, Nation, and God: Paternalism and the Dupuis Frères Department Store, Montreal, 1926-1952" (MA thesis, McGill University, 1997); "What Are Your Wants?" *The Beaver* (October 1921): 14.

9 *Store Topics,* April 1927, 4.

10 "The Gingham Girl," *Contacts,* April 1934, 3.

11 Michael Miller, *The Bon Marché: Bourgeois Culture and the Department Store, 1869-1920* (Princeton, NJ: Princeton University Press, 1981), 221.

12 "Eaton Choral Society Theatre Night," *Eaton News Weekly,* ca. 1920s, Library and Archives Canada (hereafter LAC); "Choir Concert Pleases Many," *The Bay Builder,* May 1935, 4.

13 "Here and There with Eatonians," *Flash,* 9 December 1935, 3.

14 Ian McKay, "'By Wisdom, Wile or War': The Provincial Workmen's Association and the Struggle for Working-Class Independence in Nova Scotia, 1879-97," *Labour/Le Travail* 18 (Fall 1986): 13-62, esp. 18; "Eaton's Proclaims Saturday Holiday," Winnipeg newspaper advertisement, late 1920s, AO, TEP, Series 162, File 682.

15 MacDonald, *Golden Jubilee,* 235; "H.B.C. Vernon Accountant Winning Fame as an Author," *The Beaver* (December 1920): 51.

16 Andrea Tone, *The Business of Benevolence: Industrial Paternalism in Progressive America* (Ithaca and London: Cornell University Press, 1997), 126, 58.

17 Mariana Valverde, *The Age of Light, Soap, and Water: Moral Reform in English Canada, 1885-1925* (Toronto: University of Toronto Press, 1991), 104, 119; Paul Voisey, *Vulcan: The Making of a Prairie Community* (Toronto: University of Toronto Press, 1988), 28, 30, 32.

18 *Report of the Ontario Commission on Unemployment* (Toronto: A.T. Wilgress, 1916), 176.
19 F.H. Richmond, "Report on Stores etc.," 1925, 39, HBCCC.
20 Patricia Phenix, *Eatonians: The Story of the Family behind the Family* (Toronto: McClelland and Stewart, 2002), 41.
21 Cynthia Wright, "'The Most Prominent Rendezvous of the Feminine Toronto':
    Eaton's College Street and the Organization of Shopping in Toronto, 1920-1950"
    (PhD diss., University of Toronto, 1992), 208.
22 Ibid., 209-10.
23 "Keep Employees Well," *The Beaver* (March 1926): 76.
24 *Our Mail Order System* (Toronto: T. Eaton, 1905), AO, TEP, Series 162, Box 48, File 1535.
25 *Canada and Toronto* (Toronto: R. Simpson, 1931), unpaginated, HBCCC, box of Simpson's brochures; *About a Great Store* (Toronto and Winnipeg: T. Eaton, 1908), unpaginated, AO, TEP, Series 162, File 1331; Wayne Roberts, "The Last Artisans: Toronto
    Printers, 1896-1914," in *Essays in Canadian Working-Class History,* ed. Gregory S. Kealey
    and Peter Warrian (Toronto: McClelland and Stewart, 1976), 138; *Our Mail Order
    System; Evolution of a Store* (Toronto: T. Eaton, 1911), AO, TEP, Series 162, Box 41, File
    1333.
26 MacDonald, *Golden Jubilee,* 232; "1914-1919," *The Beaver* (December 1925): 32-33;
    Jonathan Vance, *Death So Noble: Memory, Meaning, and the First World War* (Vancouver:
    UBC Press, 1997), 135.
27 "May Festival of Eaton Girls' Club," *Eaton News Weekly,* 11 June 1927, 19.
28 "Beauty Contest," *The Beaver* (February 1922): 25; see also "Social Notes," *The Beaver*
    (February 1923): 201; "Queen of the May," *The Beaver* (May 1923): 313; "Models of
    Fashion," *The Beaver* (October 1921): 25.
29 "Windswept, Streamlined, and Going Places!" *Contacts,* April 1934, 2; "The Store Sets
    High Mark in Style Exhibit," *The Beaver* (October 1921): 24; see also Donica Belisle,
    "Exploring Postwar Consumption: The Campaign to Unionize Eaton's in Toronto,
    1948-1952," *Canadian Historical Review* 86, 4 (December 2005): 662-64.
30 "Complaint Column," *The Little Helper,* 11 April 1908, 8, AO, TEP, Series 162, Box 48,
    File 1548; "Misdemeanors," 15 March 1900, AO, TEP, Series 162, File 651.
31 "Store Warns Employees about Male Customers," *Winnipeg Free Press,* 7 January 1972,
    AO, TEP, Series 162, Box 18, File 656; "Uniformity and Neatness in Dress," *The Beaver*
    (March 1921): 41; *Employees' Book of Information* (Toronto: T. Eaton, 1933), 8, AO, TEP,
    Series 162, Box 23, File 792; "Customers Don't Like," *The Beaver* (September 1928): 75;
    "What Is the Essence of Good Salesmanship?" *Contacts,* October 1935, 3; see also Susan
    Porter Benson, *Counter Cultures: Saleswomen, Managers, and Customers in American De-
    partment Stores, 1890-1940* (Urbana and Chicago: University of Illinois Press, 1986),
    128-36; Susan Forbes, "The Influence of the Social Reform Movement and T. Eaton
    Company's Business Practices on the Leisure of Eaton's Female Employees during the
    Early Twentieth Century" (PhD diss., University of Western Ontario, 1998), 144.
32 "Let's Make-Up," *Contacts,* April 1934, 13; "C.E.A. Savage, "Physical Exercise and Store
    Life," *The Beaver* (June 1931): 241; *Every-Tuesday Morning Bulletin,* 24 August 1937,
    HBCCC; MacDonald, *Golden Jubilee,* 123; Marie-Emmanelle Chessel, "Training Sales
    Personnel in France between the Wars," in *Cathedrals of Consumption: The European
    Department Store, 1850-1939,* ed. Geoffrey Crossick and Serge Jaumain (Aldershot, UK:
    Ashgate, 1999), 286-92; J. Brooks, "Report on Staff Organization and Training," February 1925, HBCA, RG2/54/9.
33 *Employees' Book of Information* (Toronto 1933), 17, AO, TEP, Series 162, Box 23, File
    792; "All Fingers," *Contacts,* March 1933, 8.

34 "Tested Selling Sentences," *Contacts,* September 1933, 4-5; "What Are You Selling?" *Contacts,* June 1933, 15. See also Benson, *Counter Cultures,* 156.

35 *A Little Chat about Selling* (Toronto: T. Eaton, 1931), 5, AO, TEP, Series 162, Box 24, File 816. In the 1950s, such reification reached a new level when Eaton's – again following US developments – added two more stages to their three-step model: determining customers' needs and suggesting additional items (*5 Star Salesmanship at EATON'S* [Toronto: T. Eaton, 1958], AO, TEP, Series 162, Box 24, File 816).

36 Georg Lukács, "Reification and the Consciousness of the Proletariat," in *History and Class Consciousness: Studies in Marxist Dialectics,* trans. Rodney Livingstone (London: Basingstoke, 1968), 83; Hochschild, *The Managed Heart,* 187-89.

Chapter 5: Shopping, Pleasure, and Power

1 Elizabeth Kowaleski-Wallace, *Consuming Subjects: Women, Shopping, and Business in the Eighteenth Century* (New York: Columbia University Press, 1997), 4, 5.

2 Isabel Ecclestone Mackay, *The House of Windows* (London, New York, and Toronto: Cassell, 1912), 125.

3 Joy Parr, *Domestic Goods: The Material, the Moral, and the Economic in the Postwar Years* (Toronto: University of Toronto Press, 1999), 7.

4 William Leach, "Transformations in a Culture of Consumption: Women and Department Stores, 1890-1925," *Journal of American History* 71 (September 1984): 321. See also Stuart Ewen, *Captains of Consciousness: Advertising and the Social Roots of the Consumer Culture* (New York: McGraw Hill, 1976), and Betty Friedan, *The Feminine Mystique* (New York: Norton, 2001 [1963]).

5 As quoted in Victoria de Grazia, "Changing Consumption Regimes," in *The Sex of Things: Gender and Consumption in Historical Perspective,* ed. Victoria de Grazia with Ellen Furlough (Berkeley, Los Angeles, and London: University of California Press, 1996), 14.

6 Ibid., 17-19.

7 Erika Diane Rappaport, *Shopping for Pleasure: Women in the Making of London's West End* (Princeton, NJ: Princeton University Press, 2000), 10.

8 Elaine Abelson, *When Ladies Go A-Thieving: Middle-Class Shoplifters in the Victorian Department Store* (New York and Oxford: Oxford University Press, 1989), 9-16; Susan Porter Benson, *Counter Cultures: Saleswomen, Managers, and Customers in American Department Stores, 1890-1940* (Urbana and Chicago: University of Illinois Press, 1988), 18; Karen Halttunen, "From Parlor to Living Room: Domestic Space, Interior Decoration, and the Culture of Personality," in *Consuming Visions: Accumulation and the Display of Goods in America, 1880-1920,* ed. Simon J. Bronner (New York: Norton, 1989), 157-90; Parr, *Domestic Goods,* 10, 169, 187.

9 Benson, *Counter Cultures,* 78. See also Parr, *Domestic Goods.*

10 Cynthia Wright, "'The Most Prominent Rendezvous of the Feminine Toronto': Eaton's College Street and the Organization of Shopping in Toronto, 1920-1950" (PhD diss., University of Toronto, 1992), 42.

11 Ibid., 195-204.

12 H.H. Stevens, *Report of the Royal Commission on Price Spreads* (Ottawa: J.O. Patenaude, 1937), 207.

13 Ishbel Maria Marjoribanks Gordon, 16 April 1896, *The Canadian Journal of Lady Aberdeen,* ed. John T. Saywell (Toronto: Champlain Society, 1960), 517; Tremblay is quoted in Wright, "'The Most Prominent Rendezvous,'" 204.

14 Interior Decorating Bureau to Mr. G. Hanna, College Street Service Bureau, 24 October 1958, AO, TEP, Series 69, Box 17; Archives of Ontario (hereafter AO), T. Eaton Papers (hereafter TEP), Series 69, Box 16, and Hudson's Bay Company Archives (hereafter HBCA), A.102/552; Mrs. Jean McDermott, "A Happy Mother," to Christmas Memories, 20 November 1977, AO, TEP, Series 162, Box 17, File 615; Gladys McGregor to Mr. David Eaton, 2 February 1976, AO, TEP, Series 162, Box 13, File 508.

15 William Stephenson, *The Store That Timothy Built* (Toronto: McClelland and Stewart, 1969), 25; David Monod, *Store Wars: Shopkeepers and the Culture of Mass Marketing, 1890-1939* (Toronto: University of Toronto Press, 1996), 118; Dorothy Keene, "Eaton's ... The Dollar Skirt, and the 'Glorious 17th,'" 1968, AO, TEP, Series 162, Box 17, File 652; AO, TEP, Series 162, Box 18, File 162; Katrina Srigley, "Clothing Stories: Consumption, Identity, and Desire in Depression-Era Toronto," *Journal of Women's History* 19, 1 (Spring 2007), 93; Mildred E. Smith to Mr. John D. Eaton, 25 June 1969, AO, TEP, Series 162, Box 17, File 614.

16 Monod, *Store Wars,* 119; Mrs. G.V. Greene to Mr. Stephenson, 1968, AO, TEP, Series 162, Box 17, File 614; Helen Scott to Sir, 22 May 1975, AO, TEP, Series 162, Box 17, File 614.

17 "Thousands Patronized Big Salvage Sale," *Vancouver Province,* 24 November 1908, 7; Mark Chisholm to Mr. John D. Eaton, 27 December 1963, AO, TEP, Series 162, Box 17, File 614; Wright, "'The Most Prominent Rendezvous,'" 204-5; Katrina Srigley, "'You Always Saved Your Best Dress for Sundays': Working Girls, Clothing, and Consumption in a Depression-Era City," paper presented to the "Labouring Feminism: Feminism and Working-Class History" conference, University of Toronto, September 2005; Kathleen Strange, "Rural Manitoba in a Downtown Store," *Contacts,* July 1943, 22-23, AO, TEP, Series 162, File 665-Over-Size S54.

18 "Thousands Patronized Big Salvage Sale," *Vancouver Province,* 24 November 1908, 7; "A Customer for More Than Half Century," *Moncton Transcript,* 6 February 1935, AO, TEP, Series 117, Box 1; Chas. Stephenson, P.M. to T. Eaton Co., 6 August 1934, AO, TEP, Series 117, Box 1; Fred Paine to Hudson's Bay Company, 6 October 1953, HBCA, A.102/552; B.L. Williams to the Governor and Merchant, 17 January 1948, HBCA, A.102/552.

19 "Timothy Eaton Opens in Winnipeg," *Winnipeg Daily Tribune,* 17 July 1905, 11.

20 "Christmas Shopping," *Gateway,* 8 December 1927, 1.

21 Stuart Somerville, Ottawa, ON, to The T. Eaton Co., 2 November 1942, AO, TEP, Series 117, Box 1; Doris Ashdown to General Manager, 30 May 1950, HBCA, A.102/552.

22 Cynthia Comacchio, *The Infinite Bonds of Family: Domesticity in Canada, 1850-1940* (Toronto: University of Toronto Press, 1999), 15-47.

23 Bettina Bradbury, *Working Families: Age, Gender, and Daily Survival in Industrializing Montreal* (Toronto: McClelland and Stewart, 1993), 152-81; Alice Prentice et al., *Canadian Women: A History* (Toronto: Harcourt Brace, 1996), 126-28.

24 Dana Frank, *Purchasing Power: Consumer Organizing, Gender, and the Seattle Labor Movement, 1919-1929* (Cambridge: Cambridge University Press, 1999), 126; Bessie McKillop to Management of the T. Eaton Co., 27 June 1937, AO, TEP, Series 117, Box 1; Mrs. F.E. Horwood to the T. Eaton Co., 17 April 1941, AO, TEP, Series 117, Box 1.

25 E.L.H. to the T. Eaton Co., 19 October 1932, AO, TEP, Series 117, Box 1; Vera McIntosh to Sirs, 23 August 1935, AO, TEP, Series 117, Box 1.

26 Letter to Manager, 1 March 1939; Mrs. William Simpson to Mr. Frederick Eaton, President, 3 November 1982, both in AO, TEP, Series 117, Box 1; Letter to the T. Eaton Co., 17 November 1947; Letter to the T. Eaton Co., 20 April 1938; Letter to the

T. Eaton Co., 25 August 1938; Letter to T. Eaton, 20 August 1934, all in AO, TEP, Series 117, Box 1; Parr, *Domestic Goods,* 256.

27 Mrs. Thom T. Nixon to T. Eaton Company, 25 August 1934, AO, TEP, Series 117, Box 1; Mrs. E.R. Reinhardt to Eaton's, 19 November 1969, AO, TEP, Series 162, Box 13, File 508; Mrs. William Lees to T. Eaton Co., AO, TEP, Series 162, Box 13, File 508.

28 "Investigation among 197 Households," *The Beaver* (December 1920): 45; (Mrs. C.L.) Alice H. Rogers to the T. Eaton Co., 2 December 1940, AO, TEP, Series 117, Box 1; Mrs. Georgina Leonard to Manager, Eatons of Canada, 17 January 1976, AO, TEP, Series 162, Box 13, File 508.

29 Mrs. Georgina Leonard to Manager; Bill and Laura Chase, "Recalling the Years 1935-1941," as quoted in Robert D. Watt, "Introduction," *The Shopping Guide of the West: Woodward's Catalogues, 1898-1953,* ed. Vancouver Centennial Museum (Vancouver: J.J. Douglas, 1977), xii-xiii; Letter to Mr. Bill Stephenson, 16 August 1968, AO, TEP, Series 162, Box 17, File 615.

30 Mrs. Georgina Leonard to Manager; Bill and Laura Chase, "Recalling the Years 1935-1941," xii-xiii; Letter to Mr. Bill Stephenson, 16 August 1968, AO, TEP, Series 162, Box 17, File 615; Janet A. Betts, as quoted in Robert D. Watt, "Introduction," *The Shopping Guide of the West,* xii.

31 Mrs. Charles Roach, Grand Falls, NB, to T. Eaton Co., February 1958, AO, TEP, Series 162, Box 13, File 508; Mrs. E.R. Reinhardt to Eaton's Archives Dept., 20 November 1969, AO, TEP, Series 162, Box 18, File 674; Anna Foidart, as summarized by Jean Bruce and Eleanor Thompson, "Eaton's Mail-Order Catalogue Oral History Project," Canadian Museum of Civilization (hereafter CMC), Library, Archives, and Documentation, History Records, Box: I-164.

32 Mrs. Daisy Waddell, Nanaimo, BC, to Sir, 15 January 1976, AO, TEP, Series 162, Box 13, File 508; Mrs. E.R. Reinhardt to Eaton's; Joy Parr, "Household Choices as Politics and Pleasure in 1950s Canada," *International Labor and Working-Class History* 55 (Spring 1999): 112-28.

33 "Big Stores Were Formally Opened," *Vancouver Province,* 24 November 1903, 3; Craig Heron, *Booze: A Distilled History* (Toronto: Between the Lines, 2003), 105-21.

34 Letter to Charlie, undated, author's name illegible, AO, TEP, Series 162, Box 17, File 614; "W.C.T.U.," *Wetaskiwin Times,* 11 June 1931, 7.

35 Bruce and Thompson, "Eaton's Mail-Order Catalogue Oral History Project"; John Brehl, "Eaton's: The Big Store Is Now 100 Years Old," in *A Century of Service to Canadian Shoppers* (Toronto: The Toronto Star, 1969), unpaginated; Nellie McClung, *The Second Chance* (Toronto: William Briggs, 1910), 13.

36 Irene Stewart to the President, 24 January 1976, AO, TEP, Series 162, Box 13, File 508; Mrs. Thelma Hayes, as summarized by Bruce and Thompson, "Eaton's Mail-Order Catalogue Oral History Project."

37 Karen Dubinsky, *Rape and Heterosexual Conflict in Ontario, 1880-1929* (Chicago: University of Chicago Press, 1993).

38 Penny Tinkler and Cheryl Krasnick Warsh, "Feminine Modernity In Interwar Britain and North America: Corsets, Cars, and Cigarettes," *Journal of Women's History* 20, 3 (Fall 2008): 113-43; Robert J.C. Stead, *Grain* (Toronto: McClelland and Stewart, 1969 [1926]), 74; Jean Louis Perron, as summarized by Bruce and Thompson, "Eaton's Mail-Order Catalogue Oral History Project."

39 Letter to Eaton's Archives Dept., 20 November 1969, AO, TEP, Series 162, Box 18, File 674; Jean Louis Perron, as summarized by Bruce and Thompson, "Eaton's Mail-Order Catalogue Oral History Project."

40 "Over 10,000 Dresses Sold by Simpson's Yesterday," *The Globe,* 9 January 1932, clipping at Hudson's Bay Company Corporate Collection (hereafter HBCCC), RG17/1T/20.
41 Denyse Baillargeon, *Making Do: Women, Family and Home in Montreal during the Great Depression,* trans. Yvonne Klein (Waterloo, ON: Wilfrid Laurier Press, 1999).
42 "The Shoppers' Philosophy," in "Around the Fireside," *Grain Growers' Guide,* 21 June 1911, 21.
43 "University Fashion Tea," *The Beaver* (December 1930): 134. This paragraph draws from detailed readings of interwar employee magazines and newspaper clippings. Complete lists of organizations selling tickets to Eaton's fashion shows during the late 1940s and 1950s are in AO, TEP, Series 151, Box 2, File 58.
44 "Fashion Review, Blue Bonnets," unreferenced clipping, Autumn 1932; "Fashion Is Winner at Blue Bonnets," *Montreal Daily Star,* 7 September 1933, HBCCC, MOR-A1.1, Morgan's Scrapbooks. For a detailed look at the Montreal Junior League, see Elise Chenier, "Class, Gender, and the Social Standard: The Montreal Junior League, 1912-1939," *Canadian Historical Review* 90, 4 (December 2009): 671-710.
45 Mrs. Thelma Hayes, as summarized by Bruce and Thompson, "Eaton's Mail-Order Catalogue Oral History Project"; Anna Foidart, as summarized by Bruce and Thompson, "Eaton's Mail-Order Catalogue Oral History Project."
46 Diaries of Beatrice Brigden, October 1904, 1912, 1914, Archives of Manitoba, PS816, Files 1, 6, 7.
47 Untitled report, ca. 1960s, AO, TEP, Series 162, Box 18, File 674.
48 Letter to Sir, 17 September 1934, AO, TEP, Series 117, Box 1; Mrs. F. Grieve to the T. Eaton Co., August 1934, AO, TEP, Series 117, Box 1.
49 Mrs. Georgina Leonard to Manager; Mrs. W.P. Lister to Manager, Mail Order, 4 October 1939, AO, TEP, Series 117, Box 1.
50 Rosalind Williams, *Dream Worlds: Mass Consumption in Late Nineteenth-Century France* (Berkeley and Los Angeles: University of California Press, 1982), 65-66.
51 Female customer (name withheld to protect privacy), "Christmas Memories," 1977, AO, TEP, Series 162, Box 17, File 615; Audrey W. Steele to Eaton's, 1977, AO, TEP, Series 162, Box 17, File 615; Margaret Howe, Toronto, "Eaton's at Christmas," 1977, AO, TEP, Series 162, Box 17, File 615.
52 "First Stage of Inquest," *Star,* 20 November 1906, AO, TEP, Series 162, File 665, OOS54.
53 Insurance Claims," HBCA, RG 2, Series 17, File C/1; Miss F. Goodman, Toronto, ON, to General Manager, 29 March 1944, AO, TEP, Series 69, Box 16.
54 "Returns," ca. 1910s, RG17/1T/20; "Complaint Column," *The Little Helper,* 11 April 1908, 8, AO, TEP, Series 162, Box 48, File 1548.
55 AO, TEP, Series 69, Boxes 16 and 17; AO, TEP, Series 162, Box 17, File 614; HBCA, A.102/552; HBCA, RG2/8/771-774.
56 Miss L. Garrett to General Manager, 1953, AO, TEP, Series 69, Box 16; Theresa G. Falkner to Mr. George Leyland, Customers' Deposit Account Department, 14 October 1947, AO, TEP, Series 69, Box 16; Mrs. Margaret Moslen, London, ON, to Sir, 5 September 1945, AO, TEP, Series 69, Box 16.
57 G.W. Barber, Memo, 8 September 1948; Mrs. A.S. Davies, Toronto, 6 December 1945; Joan Rumney to Personnel Department, 11 March 1946; Mrs. J. Lorna South to Mr. Mercer, 17 August 1950; all in AO, TEP, Series 69, Box 16.
58 "Complaint Column," *The Little Helper,* 11 April 1908, 8, AO, TEP, Series 162, Box 48, File 1548; Gladys A. Munroe, M.D., to Mr. John David Eaton, 8 October 1946, AO, TEP, Series 69, Box 16.

59 Doris Ashdown, Vancouver, BC, to General Manager, 30 May 1950, HBCA, A.102/552; Srigley, "Clothing Stories," 94; M. Hill to Sirs, 5 February 1958, AO, TEP, Series 69, Box 16.

60 Mrs. E. Straiton to Superintendent, 29 March 1957, AO, TEP, Series 69, Box 36.

61 Chief Constable to Messrs T. Eaton and Company, 7 December 1897, AO, TEP, Series 35, Box 1, File 24A; Joy L. Santink, *Timothy Eaton and the Rise of His Department Store* (Toronto: University of Toronto Press, 1990), 193; "Mrs. Baar Was Allowed To Go," *News,* 14 September 1912, AO, TEP, Series 162, OOS54, File 665. See also Elaine Abelson, *When Ladies Go A-Thieving: Middle-Class Shoplifters in the Victorian Department Store* (Oxford and New York: Oxford University Press, 1989), 6.

62 Wright, "'The Most Prominent Rendezvous,'" 204.

63 Harriet Bateman to T. Eaton Co., 21 August 1934, AO, TEP, Series 117, Box 1; Mrs. H. Blandy to T. Eaton Co., September 1934, AO, TEP, Series 117, Box 1; Laurene Gardiner to T. Eaton Company, 14 March 1940, AO, TEP, Series 117, Box 1; Bill and Laura Chase, "Recalling the Years 1935-1941," xii-xiii.

64 Gladys McGregor, Toronto, to Mr. David Eaton, 2 February 1976, AO, TEP, Series 162, Box 13, File 508; Elizabeth Bilash, as summarized by Bruce and Thompson, "Eaton's Mail-Order Catalogue Oral History Project."

65 Mary Quayle Innis, "Holiday," *Canadian Forum* (January 1932): 140-42.

66 Innis, "Holiday."

67 Gabrielle Roy, *Enchantment and Sorrow: The Autobiography of Gabrielle Roy,* trans. Patricia Claxton (Toronto: Lesser and Orphen Henrys Publishers, 1987), 3-7.

68 Ibid., 3-7.

69 Booklet produced by the T. Eaton Company, ca. 1910, unpaginated, AO, TEP, Series 162, File 1331.

70 Wright, "'The Most Prominent Rendezvous,'" 207.

71 "Nigger Humour," *The Beaver* (March 1926): 4; "Wise or Otherwise," *Store Topics,* April 1927, 20; Johnny Young, poem in *The Bayonet,* July 1935; untitled joke, *Store Topics,* Christmas 1925, 13; untitled joke, *Store Topics,* Christmas 1925, 13; "English as She Is Wrote," *The Beaver* (June 1921): 31.

Chapter 6: Working at the Heart of Consumption

1 Susan Porter Benson, *Counter Cultures: Saleswomen, Managers, and Customers in American Department Stores, 1890-1940* (Urbana and Chicago: University of Illinois Press, 1988), 181.

2 *Historical Statistics of Canada,* 2nd ed. (Ottawa: Statistics Canada, 1999), D86-106.

3 Graham S. Lowe, "Women, Work, and the Office: The Feminization of Clerical Occupations in Canada, 1901-1931," in *Rethinking Canada: The Promise of Women's History,* 3rd ed., ed. Veronica Strong-Boag and Anita Clair Fellman (Toronto: Oxford University Press, 1997), 265, 255; Veronica Strong-Boag, *The New Day Recalled: Lives of Girls and Women in English Canada, 1919-1939* (Toronto: Copp Clark Pitman, 1993), 59.

4 "Mention of Women Employees in the Early Days," ca. 1960s, Archives of Ontario (hereafter AO), T. Eaton Papers (hereafter TEP), Series 162, Box 18, File 680; Edith MacDonald, *Golden Jubilee, 1869-1919* (Toronto: The T. Eaton Co., 1919), 57-68; Joy L. Santink, *Timothy Eaton and the Rise of His Department Store* (Toronto: University of Toronto Press, 1991), 83, 114, 191; Patricia Phenix, *Eatonians: The Story of the Family behind the Family* (Toronto: McClelland and Stewart, 2002), 170; Wayne Roberts, *Honest Womanhood: Feminism, Femininity and Class Consciousness among Toronto Working Women, 1893 to 1914* (Toronto: New Hogtown Press, 1976), 26.

5 Marie Gérin-Lajoie, "Le syndicalisme féminin," *Québécoises du 20e siècle,* ed. Michèle Jean (Montréal: Éditions du jour, 1974 [1921]), 110-11; Winnipeg University Women's Club, *The Work of Women and Girls in the Department Stores of Winnipeg,* 1914, 8, University of Manitoba Libraries; *Report of the Ontario Commission on Unemployment* (Toronto: A.T. Wilgress, 1916), 59.

6 Ministry of Trade and Commerce, *Seventh Census of Canada, 1931,* vol. 10, *Merchandising and Service Establishments* (Ottawa: J.O. Patenaude, 1934), xxvi, 36; Summary of Eleanor Thompson's interview with participant, 25 March 1995, 1, Canadian Museum of Civilization (hereafter CMC), History Records, Eaton's Mail-Order Catalogue, Eaton's Employees, Oral History Project, Box: I-164; Elizabeth Brown to "Bob," 10 September 1930 and 28 November 1932, AO, F 1176, Series C, Box 2; Marie Lavigne and Jennifer Stoddart, "Ouvriéres et travailleuses montréalaises, 1900-1940," in *Travailleuses et féministes: Les femmes dans la société québecoise,* ed. Marie Lavigne and Yolande Pinard (Montréal: Boréal Express, 1983), 106; "Count of Toronto Staff," 1939, *Statistics Notebook,* AO, TEP, Series 181, Box 1.

7 Winnipeg University Women's Club, *The Work of Women and Girls,* 16-17; Enid Price, *Industrial Occupations of Women* (Montréal: Canadian Reconstruction Association, 1919), 59.

8 Marjorie MacMurchy, *The Canadian Girl at Work: A Book of Vocational Guidance* (Toronto: A.T. Wilgress, 1919), 15-16, 13; Miss Lola Belle Campbell, ca. 1958, Life Story Recording Project, AO, TEP, Series 162, File 901; "50 Years Here," *Flash,* 27 October 1947, 2, AO, TEP, Series 141.

9 Santink, *Timothy Eaton,* 82; Charles Luther Burton, *A Sense of Urgency: Memoirs of a Canadian Merchant* (Toronto: Clark, 1952), 185; Winnipeg University Women's Club, *The Work of Women and Girls,* 13; "Miss Louise Black," *Flash,* ca. July 1947, 12, AO, TEP, Series 141.

10 For example, *The Bay Builder,* November 1936. Lorraine O'Donnell offers detailed explorations of buyers' experiences in "Visualizing the History of Women at Eaton's, 1869 to 1976" (PhD diss., McGill University, 2002).

11 *Store Merchandise Departments,* 1940, 1-15, AO, TEP, Series 59, Box 2, File 15; Phenix, *Eatonians,* 82-86.

12 Adelaide Hoodless, "Trades and Industries," in *Women of Canada: Their Life and Work* (National Council of Women of Canada, 1900), 95; *Report of the Ontario Commission on Unemployment,* 59; J.E. Wilton to BC Commission on Labour, 1912 to 1914, British Columbia Archives (hereafter BCA), GR-0684, Box 2, File 1; Summary of Eleanor Thompson's interview with participant, 22 March 1995, 1, CMC, History Records, Eaton's Mail-Order Catalogue, Eaton's Employees, Oral History Project, Box I-164; Summary of Eleanor Thompson's interview with participant, 25 March 1995, 13, CMC, History Records, Eaton's Mail-Order Catalogue, Eaton's Employees, Oral History Project, Box I-164; Summary of Eleanor Thompson's interview with participant, 25 March 1995, 1, CMC, History Records, Eaton's Mail-Order Catalogue, Eaton's Employees, Oral History Project, Box I-164.

13 Mrs. William Forbes MacDonald, Vancouver Local Council of Women, to British Columbia Commission on Labour, 1912-14, BCA, GR-0684, Box 2, File 1; Strong-Boag, *The New Day Recalled,* 42; Denyse Baillargeon, *Making Do: Women, Family, and Home in Montreal during the Great Depression,* trans. Yvonne Klein (Waterloo, ON: Wilfrid Laurier University Press, 1999), 34; Suzanne Morton, *Ideal Surroundings: Domestic Life in a Working-Class Suburb in the 1920s* (Toronto: University of Toronto Press, 1995), 140; Santink, *Timothy Eaton,* 112; Winnipeg University Women's Club, *The Work of*

Women and Girls, 14; Henry Thomas Lockyer, Manager HBC Vancouver Store, to the BC Commission on Labour, 1912 to 1914, BCA, GR-0684, Box 2, File 2; "Three Celebrate 35 Years with Eaton's," *Flash,* 31 January 1949, 11.

14 Annie Hyder, ca. 1958, Life Story Recording Project, AO, TEP, Series 162, File 901; "Welcome to the Quarter Century Club," *Flash,* 9 January 1950, 5; Elizabeth Brown's letters to "Bob," AO, F 1176, Series C, Box 3.

15 Linda Kealey, *Enlisting Women for the Cause: Women, Labour, and the Left in Canada, 1890-1920* (Toronto: University of Toronto Press, 1998), 16-17; Strong-Boag, *The New Day Recalled,* 41; *Report of the Ontario Commission on Unemployment,* 178-79; Winnipeg University Women's Club, *The Work of Women and Girls,* 19; Summary of Eleanor Thompson's interview with participant, 20 March 1995, CMC, History Records, Eaton's Mail-Order Catalogue, Eaton's Employees, Oral History Project, Box: I-164.

16 David Spencer, Ltd., *Golden Jubilee, 1873-1923* (Victoria, BC: David Spencer, 1923), 20; Miss Margaret O'Meara, ca. 1958, Life Story Recording Project, AO, TEP, Series 162, File 901; *Contacts,* October 1933, 7.

17 "Lethbridge," *The Beaver* (June 1920): 35; "Honor Roll Call," *The Bay Builder,* 2 May 1940, 9; "Eatonians Abroad," *Flash,* 9 July 1935, 1, AO, TEP, Series 141; I.R. Lewis, "Mem. re Women's Employment Situation," 19 November 1930, AO, TEP, Series 9, Box 6, File: Factory Matters; Jean Thomson Scott, *The Conditions of Female Labour in Ontario* (Toronto: Warwick and Sons, 1892), 25; "Count of Toronto Staff," 1939, *Statistics Notebook,* AO, TEP, Series 181, Box 1.

18 Annie Hyder, ca. 1958, Life Story Recording Project, AO, TEP, Series 162, File 901; "Welcome to the Quarter Century Club," *Flash,* 6 March 1950, 6; "Welcome to the Quarter Century Club," *Flash,* 20 February 1950, 6; Summary of Eleanor Thompson's interview with participant, 20 March 1995, 1, CMC, History Records, Eaton's Mail-Order Catalogue, Eaton's Employees, Oral History Project, Box I-164; Robyn Margaret Dowling, "Shopping and the Construction of Femininity in the Woodward's Department Store, Vancouver, 1945 to 1960" (MA thesis, University of British Columbia, 1991), 90.

19 Dirk Hoerder, *Creating Societies: Immigrant Lives in Canada* (Montréal and Kingston: McGill-Queen's University Press, 1999), 202; Santink, *Timothy Eaton,* 192-93; A. Ross McCormack, "Networks among British Immigrants and Accommodation to Canadian Society: Winnipeg, 1900-1914," *Histoire sociale/Social History* 17 (November 1984): 372-73; "Congratulations to Four on 35 Years' Service," *Flash,* 14 March 1949, 12; "Congratulations to Four on 35th Anniversaries," *Flash,* ca. July 1947, 12, TEP, Series 141; "35th Anniversary Honours for Thirteen," *Flash,* 25 May 1948, 6; "Welcome to the Quarter Century Club," *Flash,* 6 March 1950, 6; "More Eatonians Reach 35 Year Mark," *Flash,* 4 July 1949, 4; "Four Celebrate Thirty-Five Years at Eaton's," *Flash,* 25 April 1949, 4; "Ten Celebrate 35th Anniversaries," *Flash,* 21 June 1948, 12.

20 Mary Catherine Matthews, "Working for Family, Nation, and God: Paternalism and the Dupuis Frères Department Store, 1926-1952" (MA thesis, McGill University, 1997).

21 *Chinook Winds,* April-May 1937, cover.

22 Alison Prentice et al., *Canadian Women: A History* (Toronto: Harcourt Brace Jovanovich, 1988), 426; Anne Klein and Wayne Roberts, "Besieged Innocence: The 'Problem' and Problems of Working Women – Toronto, 1896-1914," in *Women at Work: Ontario, 1850-1930,* ed. Janice Acton et al. (Toronto: Women's Press Publications), 225-27; Scott, *The Conditions of Female Labour,* 19; Veronica Strong-Boag, "The Girl of the New Day: Canadian Working Women in the 1920's," in *The Consolidation of Capitalism, 1896-1929,* ed.

Gregory Kealey (Toronto: McClelland and Stewart, 1983), 176; Baillargeon, *Making Do*, 37.

23 D.W. Poupard to the BC Commission on Labour, 1912 to 1914, BCA, GR-0684, Box 3, File 2; T.H. Howard to Mr. I.R. Lewis, 7 October 1938, AO, TEP, Series 162, Box 31, File 990; Untitled clipping, ca. 1931, HBCCC, MOR-A1.1; "Employer Shares His Pleasures with Employees," *Daily Telegraph*, 1 August 1913, HBCCC, MOR-A1.1.

24 Mrs. Emily Cowley to T. Eaton Co. Limited, no date, TEP, Series 162, File 669; Carolyn Strange, *Toronto's Girl Problem: The Perils and Pleasures of the City, 1880-1930* (Toronto: University of Toronto Press, 1995), 9-11.

25 Prentice et al., *Canadian Women*, 128. For this paragraph, see Joan Sangster, "The Softball Solution: Female Workers, Male Managers, and the Operation of Paternalism at Westclox, 1923-60," *Labour/Le Travail* 32 (Fall 1993): 188; Phenix, *Eatonians*, 45. See also Morton, *Ideal Surroundings*, 146.

26 Sangster, "The Softball Solution," 188; "Store Warns Employees about Male Customers," *Winnipeg Free Press*, 7 January 1972, AO, TEP, Series 162, Box 18, File 656; MacDonald, *Golden Jubilee*, 274; "Courtesy," *The Beaver* (December 1924): 14; Rev. Blevin Atkinson, "Ambition," *The Beaver* (September 1925): 180-81; "Efficiency," *The Beaver* (April 1922): 38; "Wholesome Minds," *The Beaver* (July 1921): 30; "Eaton's Early Closing Movement," Winnipeg newspaper advertisement, ca. 1926, in AO, TEP, Series 162, File 682.

27 Scott, *The Conditions of Female Labour*, 19; "The T. Eaton Company," 1963, AO, TEP, Series 162, File 669; also Phenix, *Eatonians*, 128; *Rules and Regulations and General Information* (Winnipeg: T. Eaton, ca. 1920), 2, AO, TEP, Series 162, Box 23, File 799.

28 "General News," *The Beaver* (December 1925): 43.

29 Morton, *Ideal Surroundings*, 147; Matthews, "Working for Family, Nation and God," 78.

30 W.C. Woodward, Secretary of Woodward's Departmental Store, to BC Commission on Labour, 1912 to 1914, BCA, GR-0684, Box 2, File 2; Phenix, *Eatonians*, 127-28; *The Bay Window*, December 1934; "An Early Simpsons Rule," *The Simpsons Century* (Toronto Star Limited, 1970), unpaginated, HBCCC, RG17/1Q/34; "Store Warns Employees about Male Customers," *Winnipeg Free Press*, 7 January 1972, AO, TEP, Series 162, Box 18, File 656; *Bayonet*, Summer 1936; "Congratulations to Four on 35 Years' Service," *Flash*, 14 March 1949, 12.

31 Phenix, *Eatonians*, 2; Lillian M. Poulter, ca. 1958, Life Story Recording Project, AO, TEP, Series 162, File 901; Santink, *Timothy Eaton*, 183; "Articles," 1958, AO, TEP, Series 162, Box 1, File 901; Miss E.M. Giroux, ca. 1958, Life Story Recording Project, AO, TEP, Series 162, File 901.

32 Santink, *Timothy Eaton*, 197; Summary of Eleanor Thompson's interview with participant, 25 March 1995, 1, CMC, History Records, Eaton's Mail-Order Catalogue, Box I-164; "More about Eaton Operatic Society," *Flash*, 30 December 1935, 3, AO, TEP, Series 141; "The Visiting Pickle-Packers," *Contacts*, June 1933, 10, AO, TEP, Series 141; "Hilda Booth Stars with Bay Girls Net Squad," *The Bay Window*, November 1934, 4, HBCA.

33 E.M. Knox, *Girl of the New Day* (Toronto: McClelland and Stewart, 1919), 101-2.

34 "Praise for the City Order," *Flash*, 30 December 1935, 2.

35 Interview with former employee, "Re Telephone Order," 1940, HBCCC, RG17/1P/15.

36 "Welcome to the Quarter Century Club," *Flash*, 17 April 1950, 11.

37 Miss Margaret O'Meara, Life Story Recording Project, ca. 1958, TEP, Series 162, Box 1, File 901.

38 Letter to the Manager [Vancouver], 21 April 1939, *The Bay Builder,* October 1940, 8.

39 "Six Superior Sales Clerks," *The Bayonet,* June 1938, 1.

40 "35th Anniversary Honours for Thirteen," *Flash,* 25 May 1948, 6.

41 MacMurchy, *The Canadian Girl at Work,* 9.

42 "Welcome to the Quarter Century Club," *Flash,* 17 April 1950, 11.

43 Miss Emily May Caine, ca. 1958, Life Story Recording Project, AO, TEP, Series 162, File 901.

44 "The Status of the Wage-Earner in Retail Trade," 13, ca. 1934, Library and Archives Canada (hereafter LAC), RG 33, Vol. 53.

45 Winnipeg University Women's Club, *The Work of Women and Girls,* 15-16; Local Council of Women of Victoria Representative to the BC Commission on Labour, 1912 to 1914, BCA, GR-0684, Box 3, File 2; Vancouver Local Council of Women, "Report of Committee on Employments for Women," submitted to the BC Commission on Labour, 1912 to 1914, BCA, GR-0684, Box 4, File 15.

46 Santink, *Timothy Eaton,* 189, 202; Scott, *The Conditions of Female Labour,* 22; Herbert H. Bishop, Superintendent of David Spencer, Ltd., to BC Commission on Labour, 1912 to 1914, BCA, GR-0684, Box 2, File 2; Winnipeg University Women's Club, *The Work of Women and Girls,* 14; "Departmental Stores," *Saturday Night,* 27 March 1897, 3; W.C. Woodward, Secretary of Woodward's Departmental Store, to BC Commission on Labour, 1912 to 1914, BCA, GR-0684, Box 2, File 2.

47 Local Council of Women of Victoria to the BC Commission on Labour, 1912 to 1914, BCA, GR-0684, Box 3, File 2; W.C. Woodward, Secretary of Woodward's Departmental Store, to BC Commission on Labour, 1912 to 1914, BCA, GR-0684, Box 2, File 2; Henry Thomas Lockyer, Manager HBC Vancouver Store, to the BC Commission on Labour, 1912 to 1914, BCA, GR-0684, Box 2, File 2; Herbert H. Bishop, Superintendent of David Spencer, Ltd., to BC Commission on Labour, 1912 to 1914, BCA, GR-0684, Box 2, File 2; Daisy Gibson to John Cairns, 3 January 1938, Saskatchewan Archives Board (hereafter SAB), LA, I.117, Department of Labour; John Cairns to T.M. Molloy, Esq., 3 January 1939, SAB, LA, I.117, Department of Labour; H. Williams to Thos. M. Molloy, 20 April 1935, SAB, LA, I.117, Department of Labour; Anonymous to Minimum Wage Board, no date, SAB, LA, I.117, Department of Labour; R.R. Kreitzwieser, Saskatoon Young Man's Liberal Association, to Mr. Johnstone, Commissioner of Labour, 17 October 1939, SAB, LA, I.117, Department of Labour.

48 Miss C. Fullerton to Russell Harvey, no date, LAC, MG 31 B 31, Vol. 1.

49 Margaret Hoskins to the Board of Directors, 23 March 1931, AO, TEP, Series 162, Box 31, File 990; Isabel Ross to Irving W. Ford, 28 March 1945, AO, TEP, Series 162, Box 31, File 990.

50 Micheline Dumont et al., *Québec Women: A History,* trans. Roger Gannon and Rosalind Gill (Toronto: Women's Press, 1987), 217; J.E. Wilton to BC Commission on Labour, 1912 to 1914, BCA, GR-0684, Box 2, File 1; R.R. Kreitzwieser, Saskatoon Young Man's Liberal Association, to Mr. Johnstone, Commissioner of Labour, 17 October 1939, SAB, LA, I.117, Department of Labour; Mrs. D.C. Grainger to the Minister of Labour, April 1934, SAB, LA, I.117, Department of Labour; Minimum Wage Inspector to Mrs. D.C. Grainger, 5 May 1934, SAB, LA, I.117, Department of Labour.

51 Santink, *Timothy Eaton,* 196; Mrs. William Forbes MacDonald to BC Commission on Labour, 1912 to 1914, BCA, GR-0684, Box 2, File 1; "A Lament," *Bay Chuckwagon,* September 1939, HBCA.

52 Winnipeg University Women's Club, *The Work of Women and Girls,* 18; Ralph B. Peck, "Your Attitude Toward Your Customer," *Contacts,* May 1932, 6, AO, TEP, Series 141.

53 "Customer's Complaint," *The Bayonet,* April 1934, HBCA. For this paragraph, see also Winnipeg University Women's Club, *The Work of Women and Girls,* 18; Peck, "Your Attitude Toward Your Customer," *Contacts.*

54 "Contents of Some Letters between T. Eaton Co. and City Hall," AO, TEP, Series 162, Box 18, File 667; Winnipeg University Women's Club, *The Work of Women and Girls,* 18; Miss E.M. Giroux, ca. 1958, AO, TEP, Series 162, File 901; Mrs. Janet Kemp, Vancouver Local Council of Women, to the BC Commission on Labour, 1912 to 1914, BCA, GR-0684, Box 2, File 1; Winnipeg University Women's Club, *The Work of Women and Girls,* 6; Mme Arthur Gibeault, "Les employées de magasins," *La Bonne Parole,* May 1927, 13; Lillian M. Poulter, ca. 1958, AO, TEP, Series 162, File 901.

55 Santink, *Timothy Eaton,* 202.

56 "Does Shirley Temple Know?" in Barry Broadfoot, ed., *Ten Lost Years, 1929-1939: Memories of Canadians Who Survived the Depression* (Toronto: Doubleday, 1973), 265.

57 "A Bevy of Beauties to Smooth Customer's Ups and Downs," *The Bayonet,* June 1938, 1.

58 "Hudson's Bay Field Day," *The Beaver* (June 1923): 356; "Swimming Awards Presented," *Contacts,* November 1932, 10; see also Helen Smith and Pamela Wakewich, "'Beauty and the Helldivers': Representing Women's Work and Identities in a Warplant Newspaper," *Labour/Le Travail* 44 (Fall 1999): 77-107.

59 "A Trip Through Fruitland," *Store Topics,* June 1927, 11.

60 "Misdemeanors," 15 March 1900, AO, TEP, Series 162, File 651; "Rules and Regulations for the Guidance of Employees," July 1912, HBCA, Search Files: Morgan and Company; Benson, *Counter Cultures,* 245; *Employees' Book of Information* (Toronto: T. Eaton, 1933), 18, AO, TEP, Series 162, Box 23, File 792; "Customers Don't Like," *The Beaver* (September 1928): 75; "Lapses," *Contacts,* April 1935, 18.

61 Santink, *Timothy Eaton,* 191-92.

62 Benson, *Counter Cultures,* 231.

63 *Rules and Regulations and General Information* (Winnipeg: T. Eaton, ca. 1920), 9, AO, TEP, Series 162, Box 23, File 799; *Employees' Book of Information;* "Rules and Regulations for the Guidance of Employees," July 1912, HBCA, Search Files: Morgan and Company; "Twenty Sins of Salesmanship and Their Opposite Virtues," *Contacts,* June 1933, 3.

64 Peck, "Your Attitude Toward Your Customer," 6; Isabel Ecclestone Mackay, *The House of Windows* (London, New York, and Toronto: Cassell, 1912) 75; Lindsey McMaster, "The Urban Working Girl in Turn-of-the-Century Canadian Fiction," *Essays on Canadian Writing* 77 (Fall 2002): 10.

65 *Employees' Book of Information,* 8, AO, TEP, Series 162, Box 23, File 792; *Rules and Regulations and General Information;* "An Ode to Our Flappers," *The Beaver* (February 1921): 31.

66 Susan L. Forbes, "Gendering Corporate Welfare Practices: Female Sports and Recreation at Eaton's during the Depression," *Rethinking History* 5 (2001): 63, 68-69.

67 As quoted in Matthews, "Working for Family, Nation, and God," 75.

68 Elvina Ralph to F.M. Molloy, Secretary Minimum Wage Board, 1 August 1923, SAB, Department of Labour, LA, I.117; Andrew Neufeld, *Union Store: The History of the Retail Clerks Union in British Columbia, 1899-1999* (Vancouver: United Food and Commercial Workers Union Local 1518, 1999), 32.

69 Santink, *Timothy Eaton,* 199; "One of Them" to the Honourable H. Stevens, 23 May 1931, LAC, RG 33, Volume 5.

70 "Employers Free to Choose Hands," *Mail,* 29 December 1906, AO, TEP, Series 162, File 665, OOS54; John Cairns to H.S. Johnstone, Esq, 8 July 1939 and "The Hudson

Bay Beauty Salon," no date, both in SAB, LA, I.117, Department of Labour; R.R. Kreitzwieser, Saskatoon Young Man's Liberal Association, to Mr. Johnstone, Commissioner of Labor, 17 October 1939, SAB, LA, I.117, Department of Labour.

71 Fair Play to the Minimum Wage Board, 12 December 1927, SAB, LA, I.117, Department of Labour; J.M. McMillan, Trades and Labour Council, Vancouver, to BC Commission on Labour, 1912 to 1914, BCA, GR-0684, Box 1, File 1; Neufeld, *Union Store*, 32.

72 Santink, *Timothy Eaton*, 199.

73 As quoted in Neufeld, *Union Store*, 14.

74 As quoted in Mercedes Steedman, *Angels of the Workplace: Women and the Construction of Gender Relations in the Canadian Clothing Industry, 1890-1940* (Toronto: Oxford University Press, 1997), 83.

75 Phenix, *Eatonians*, 37.

76 Neufeld, *Union Store*, 33-34.

77 Report on Wages, 22 November 1934, AO, TEP, Series 9, Box 5, File F8 Matter – Eaton's Reports.

78 Neufeld, *Union Store*, 28-29, 34.

79 "Tie-Up in Winnipeg is Now Complete," *New York Times*, 21 May 1919, *New York Times Archives*, http://www.nytimes.com.

80 "All Winnipeg under Rule of Strikers," *Chicago Daily Tribune*, 21 May 1919, and *Chicago Tribune Archives*, http://pqasb.pqarchiver.com/chicagotribune.

81 "Sorters and Trimmers," *Winnipeg Telegram Strike Edition*, 29 May 1919, 23; "Wanted At Once," *Winnipeg Telegram Strike Edition*, 4 June 1919, 11; "Wanted," *Winnipeg Telegram Strike Edition*, 10 June 1919, 11; "Wanted," *Winnipeg Telegram Strike Edition*, 11 June 1919, 11; "Wanted," *Winnipeg Telegram Strike Edition*, 12 June 1919, 11; "Wanted," *Winnipeg Telegram Strike Edition*, 13 June 1919, 13; "Wanted," *Winnipeg Telegram Strike Edition*, 17 June 1919, 12; "Wanted," *Winnipeg Telegram Strike Edition*, 18 June 1919, 13; Wanted," *Winnipeg Telegram Strike Edition*, 27 June 1919, 14.

82 "Committee of 1,000 Organize Opposition Solders' Parade," *Western Labor News*, 5 June 1915, 4; "Great War Veterans Endorse Strike," *Western Labor News*, 5 June 1919, 4; J.E. Robinson to Mr. H. McGee, 8 July 1919, AO, TEP, Series 7, Box 1.

83 Elvina Ralph to F.M. Molloy, Secretary Minimum Wage Board, 1 August 1923, SAB, LA, I.117, Department of Labour; Gary Cross and Peter Shergold, "'We Think We Are of the Oppressed: Gender, White Collar Work, and the Grievances of Late Nineteenth-Century Women," *Labour History* 28 (Winter 1987): 32; Neufeld, *Union Store*, 26.

84 Benson, *Counter Cultures*, 269; Neufeld, *Union Store*, 38-39.

85 Benson, *Counter Cultures*, 269.

86 J.E. Robinson to Mr. H. McGee, 8 July 1919, AO, TEP, Series 7, Box 1; "Retail Clerks Doing Fine," *Western Labor News*, 27 May 1919, 2; Harry McGee, 27 June 1919, AO, TEP, Series 162, Box 30, File 981.

87 MG 31 B 31, Volume 1, File 5, LAC; Kealey, *Enlisting Women for the Cause*, 165.

88 In that these forms of resistance were informal and ongoing, they resemble those undertaken by the peasants examined by James C. Scott in *Weapons of the Weak: Everyday Forms of Peasant Resistance* (New Haven, CT: Yale University Press, 1985).

Chapter 7: Criticizing the Big Stores

1 "Riot Act Read to 2,000 Vancouver Relief Strikers," *The Globe*, 24 April 1935, 1-2.

2 Michael Miller, *The Bon Marché: Bourgeois Culture and the Department Store, 1869-1920* (Princeton, NJ: Princeton University Press, 1981), 190-212; Lisa Tiersten, "Marianne

in the Department Store: Gender and the Politics of Consumption in Turn-of-the-Century Paris," in *Cathedrals of Consumption: The European Department Store, 1850-1939*, ed. Geoffrey Crossick and Serge Jaumain (Aldershot, UK: Ashgate, 1999), 116-34; Geoffrey Crossick and Serge Jaumain, "The World of the Department Store: Distribution, Culture and Social Change," in *Cathedrals of Consumption*, 1-45; Susan Porter Benson, *Counter Cultures: Saleswomen, Managers, and Customers in American Department Stores, 1890-1940* (Urbana and Chicago: University of Illinois Press, 1988), 134-36; Elaine Abelson, *When Ladies Go A-Thieving: Middle-Class Shoplifters in the Victorian Department Store* (New York and Oxford: Oxford University Press, 1989).

3 Andreas Huyssen, "Mass Culture as Woman: Modernism's Other," *After the Great Divide: Modernism, Mass Culture, Postmodernism* (Bloomington: Indiana University Press, 1986), 44-64; Carolyn Strange, *Toronto's Girl Problem: The Perils and Pleasures of the City, 1880-1930* (Toronto: University of Toronto Press, 1995).

4 David Monod, *Store Wars: Shopkeepers and the Culture of Mass Marketing, 1890-1930* (Toronto: University of Toronto Press, 1996); Strange, *Toronto's Girl Problem;* Ruth Frager, "Class, Ethnicity, and Gender in the Eaton Strikes of 1912 and 1934," in *Gender Conflicts: New Essays in Women's History*, ed. Franca Iacovetta and Mariana Valverde (Toronto: University of Toronto Press), 189-228; Cynthia Wright, "'Feminine Trifles of Vast Importance: Writing Gender into the History of Consumption," *Gender Conflicts*, 229-60; Andrew Neufeld, *Union Store: The History of the Retail Clerks Union in British Columbia, 1899-1999* (Vancouver: United Food and Commercial Workers Union Local 1518, 1999); Ian MacPherson, *Each for All: A History of the Co-operative Movement in English Canada, 1900-1945* (Ottawa: Macmillan of Canada, 1979).

5 Joy L. Santink, *Timothy Eaton and the Rise of His Department Store* (Toronto: University of Toronto Press, 1991), 205.

6 Monod, *Store Wars*, 231.

7 Mack, "The Barnums of Business," *Saturday Night*, 8 May 1897, 3; "'Loss Leaders' to Be Fought," *Victoria Daily Times*, 23 November 1937, 14.

8 Mack, "The Barnums of Business," *Saturday Night*, 15 May 1897, 8. The earliest articles in this series are titled "Departmental Stores."

9 Mack, "The Barnums of Business," *Saturday Night*, 15 May 1897, 8. For more on P.T. Barnum, see "P.T. Barnum," *Wikipedia*, http://en.wikipedia.org/wiki/P._T._Barnum.

10 Mack, "Departmental Stores," *Saturday Night*, 3 April 1897, 8; Mack, "The Barnums of Business," *Saturday Night*, 8 May 1897, 3; Mack, "The Barnums of Business," *Saturday Night*, 17 April 1897, 8; Mack, "The Barnums of Business," *Saturday Night*, 5 June 1897, 6; Mack, "Departmental Stores," *Saturday Night*, 3 April 1897, 8; Mack, "The Barnums of Business," *Saturday Night*, 15 May 1897, 8; Mack, "The Barnums of Business," *Saturday Night*, 24 April 1897, 8.

11 Ernest E. Leigh, "Departmental Stores," included in Mack, "The Barnums of Business," *Saturday Night*, 27 March 1897, 3.

12 "Ketchem, Skinem and Cookem's Mammoth Department Store," *Saturday Night*, 27 February 1897, 8.

13 Mack, "The Barnums of Business," *Saturday Night*, 12 June 1897, 6; Mack, "Departmental Stores," *Saturday Night*, 27 March 1897, 3.

14 As quoted in Santink, *Timothy Eaton*, 206-7.

15 Mack, "Departmental Stores," *Saturday Night*, 13 March 1897, 8.

16 As quoted in Eileen Sufrin, *The Eaton Drive: The Campaign to Organize Canada's Largest Department Store, 1948-1952* (Toronto: Fitzhenry and Whiteside, 1982), 19.

17 Alice Chown, *The Stairway* (Toronto: University of Toronto Press, 1988 [1921]), 120.
18 William Stephenson, *The Store That Timothy Built* (Toronto: McClelland and Stewart, 1969), 98.
19 "Big Stores' Bid for Trade Cuts Wages of 10,000," *The Globe,* 8 June 1934, 1.
20 Mack, "The Barnums of Business," *Saturday Night,* 22 May 1897, 8; Santink, *Timothy Eaton,* 219; "Isaac B. Johnston Again on the Warpath," article in a Toronto newspaper, ca. 1904, AO, TEP, Series 162, OOS54, File 664.
21 As quoted in Santink, *Timothy Eaton,* 221.
22 Mack, "Departmental Stores," *Saturday Night,* 20 March 1897, 3.
23 As summarized by Jean Bruce and Eleanor Thompson, "Eaton's Mail-Order Catalogue Oral History Project," CMC, Library, Archives, and Documentation, History Records, Box: I-164.
24 Stephenson, *The Store,* 48.
25 "$1,000,000 for Stores in Clothing Orders," *The Leader-Post,* 17 September 1937, 1.
26 Mack, "The Barnums of Business," *Saturday Night,* 8 May 1897, 3; "Next Week in Parkdale," article in a Toronto newspaper, ca. 1904, in AO, TEP, Series 162, OOS54, File 664; Stephenson, *The Store,* 66; Untitled article in a Toronto newspaper, 18 February 1910, in AO, TEP, Series 162, OOS54, File 664.
27 H.H. Stevens, *Report of the Royal Commission on Price Spreads* (Ottawa: J.O. Patenaude, 1937), 1.
28 Monod, *Store Wars,* 311.
29 A.J. Logan, Chairman, Independent Retail Merchants of Yorkton, to W.L. McQuarrie, 2 March 1934, RG 33, Volume 57, File: Exhibit 51.
30 C.P. Moore, of C.P. Moore Limited, Heavy and Shelf Hardware, Sydney, NS, to Honorable W.W. Kennedy, M.P., 14 March 1935, LAC, RG 33, Volume 4, File: Chain and Department Stores General.
31 J.E. McCurdy, McCurdy and Company, Sydney, NS, to Mr. W.W. Kennedy, Chairman: Royal Commission, 1 April 1935, LAC, RG 33, Volume 4, File: Chain and Department Stores General.
32 J.M. Ferguson to Mr. W.L. McQuarrie, 2 March 1934, LAC, RG 33, Volume 57, Exhibit 50.
33 E.F. Chesney, Hardware and Harness, Wolseley, SK, to the Retail Merchants Association of Saskatoon and W.L. McQuarry, 27 February 1934, LAC, RG 33, Volume 57, Exhibit 50.
34 J.W. Harris to W.L. McQuarrie, 8 March 1934, LAC, RG 33, Volume 57, Exhibit 50.
35 Monod, *Store Wars,* 305, 316.
36 Roy Rosenzweig, *Eight Hours for What We Will: Workers and Leisure in an Industrial City, 1870-1920* (Cambridge: Cambridge University Press, 1983).
37 Neufeld, *Union Store,* 10.
38 Marten Estey, "Early Closing: Employer-Organized Origin of the Retail Labor Movement," *Labor History* 13 (Fall 1972): 560-70.
39 Alan Metcalfe, "The Evolution of Organized Physical Recreation in Montréal, 1840-1895," *Histoire sociale/Social History* 21 (May 1978): 148.
40 Santink, *Timothy Eaton,* 198.
41 Edith MacDonald, *Golden Jubilee: 1869-1919* (Toronto: T. Eaton, 1919), 125-34; "Eaton's Eight Hour Day," *The Financial Post,* 11 January 1919, 10.
42 Neufeld, *Union Store,* 10.
43 Ibid., 26.

44 D.W. Poupard, Secretary of the Retail Employees' Association of British Columbia, to BC Royal Commission on Labour, 1912-14, BCA, GR-0684, Box 3, File 2.

45 Ibid.

46 Neufeld, *Union Store,* 34.

47 Phenix, *Eatonians,* 37.

48 Wayne Roberts, "The Last Artisans: Toronto Printers, 1896-1914," in *Essays in Canadian Working-Class History,* ed. Gregory S. Kealey and Peter Warrian (Toronto: McClelland and Stewart, 1976), 125-42.

49 Both the 1912 strike and the 1934 lockout are examined in Frager, "Class, Ethnicity, and Gender."

50 Roberts, "The Last Artisans," 138.

51 Phenix, *Eatonians,* 37.

52 Frager, "Class, Ethnicity, and Gender," 205.

53 Ibid., 201.

54 As quoted in Roberts, "The Last Artisans," 138.

55 As quoted in Frager, "Class, Ethnicity, and Gender," 202-3.

56 As quoted in John Brehl, "Eaton's: The Big Store Is Now 100 Years Old," *A Century of Service to Canadian Shoppers* (Toronto: Toronto Star, 1969), unpaginated.

57 Chown, *The Stairway,* 121.

58 As quoted in Frager, "Class, Ethnicity, and Gender," 202-3.

59 "Mephistoph, Eat'em and Co.," *Saturday Night,* 10 April 1897, 3.

60 As quoted in Sufrin, *The Eaton Drive,* 19; Chown, *The Stairway,* 117-18.

61 Stevens, *Report of the Royal Commission on Price Spreads,* 1.

62 "The Rubicon," *Western Labor News,* 31 May 1919, 3.

63 "Weston Women Wreck Stores' Delivery Rigs – Threaten to Murder Drivers and Special Policemen Sent as Guards," *Winnipeg Evening Tribune,* 6 June 1919, 2; Linda Kealey, *Enlisting Women for the Cause: Women, Labour, and the Left in Canada, 1890-1920* (Toronto: University of Toronto Press, 1998), 226-27. It should be noted that not all saleswomen were strikebreakers. As Chapter 5 shows, some walked off the job and were afterwards dismissed.

64 Chown, *The Stairway,* 117.

65 William Filtness, "Report of Department Store Labour," 16 January 1913, presented to BC Royal Commission on Labour, 1912-14, BCA, GR-0684, Box 1, File 10.

66 "The Status of the Wage-Earner in Retail Trade," 13, ca. 1934, LAC, RG 33, Vol. 53, Report.

67 Mack, "The Barnums of Business," *Saturday Night,* 22 May 1897, 8.

68 "Notes on Eaton's Early Days," authored by a former manager and sent to Eaton's Archives, no date, 2, AO, TEP, Series 162, File 669.

69 "A Mass Meeting," Poster, in AO, TEP, Series 162, OOS54, File 664.

70 Frager, "Class, Ethnicity, and Gender," 216.

71 Dana Frank, "Where Are the Workers in Consumer-Worker Alliances? Class Dynamics and the History of Consumer-Labor Campaigns," *Politics and Society* 31 (September 2003): 366.

72 Ibid., 367.

73 Notes on Eaton's early days, authored by a former manager and sent to Eaton's Archives, 2, AO, TEP, Series 162, File 669.

74 As quoted in Frager, "Class, Ethnicity, and Gender," 195.

75 As quoted in Ian MacPherson, *Each for All: A History of the Co-operative Movement in English Canada, 1900-1945* (Ottawa: Macmillan, 1979), 118.

76 *Regina Manifesto,* 1933, available at LAC.

77 "Co-operative System Only Answer to Anarchy of Competition," *Canadian Co-operator,* November 1931, 13, LAC.

78 H.H., "Cooperative Societies," "Mail Bag," *Grain Growers' Guide,* 27 January 1915, 9; "Co-operative Stores," *Grain Growers' Guide,* 27 January 1915, 9, 20; J.W. Ward, "Co-operation for Western Farmers," *Grain Growers' Guide,* 27 January 1915, 10, 55.

79 MacPherson, *Each for All,* 56-57.

80 Ibid., 56, quote p. 38. See also Scott MacAuley, "The Smokestack Leaned toward Capitalism," *Journal of Canadian Studies* 37, 1 (Spring 2002): 44.

81 Chown, *The Stairway,* 118.

82 MacPherson, *Each for All,* 65.

83 Rusty Neal, as quoted in MacAuley, "The Smokestack Leaned toward Capitalism," 63.

84 MacPherson, *Each for All,* 141.

85 Santink, *Timothy Eaton,* 216; "The Destroyer," ca. 1907, article in a Toronto newspaper, ca. 1904, in AO, TEP, Series 162, OOS54, File 664; Frager, "Class, Ethnicity, and Gender," 192.

86 Frager, "Class, Ethnicity, and Gender," 208; "The Company," *Last Post,* February 1970, 14; Sufrin, *The Eaton Drive,* 30.

87 Strange, *Toronto's Girl Problem;* Mariana Valverde, *The Age of Light, Soap, and Water: Moral Reform in English Canada, 1885-1925* (Toronto: University of Toronto Press, 1991); Rebecca Coulter, "The Working Young of Edmonton, 1921-1931," in *Childhood and Family in Canadian History,* ed. Joy Parr (Toronto: McClelland and Stewart, 1982), 144; and Anne Klein and Wayne Roberts, "Besieged Innocence: The 'Problem' and Problems of Working Women – Toronto, 1896-1914," in *Women at Work: Ontario, 1850-1930,* ed. Janice Acton, Penny Goldsmith, and Bonny Shepard (Toronto: Women's Press, 1974), 212.

88 Charlotte Fuhrer, as quoted in Constance Backhouse, *Petticoats and Prejudice: Women and Law in Nineteenth-Century Canada* (Toronto: Women's Press, 1991), 261, 263.

89 Jean Thompson Scott, *The Conditions of Female Labour in Ontario* (Toronto: Warwick and Sons, 1892), 92; Kealey, *Enlisting Women for the Cause,* 35-36; Phenix, *Eatonians,* 34; Mme Arthur Gibeault, "Les employées de magasins," *La Bonne Parole,* May 1927, 13-14.

90 "Fight Satan with Fire," *The Evening Star,* 15 April 1897, 2; Member of the Victoria LCW, to BC Royal Commission on Labour, 1912-14, BCA, GR-0684, Box 4, File 18.

91 Strange, *Toronto's Girl Problem,* 89; Frager, "Class, Ethnicity, and Gender," 202-3.

92 Toronto Council of Women, *Nothing New under the Sun* (Ottawa: National Library of Canada, 1978), 30; Veronica Strong-Boag, *Parliament of Women: The National Council of Women of Canada, 1893-1929* (Ottawa: National Museum of Man, 1976), 199; Kealey, *Enlisting Women,* 26, 32, 34-36; Margaret E. MacCallum, "Keeping Women in Their Place: The Minimum Wage in Canada, 1910-1925," *Labour/Le Travail* 17 (Spring 1986), 31; "Store Girls of Québec Given Raise," *Star Weekly,* 2 July 1934, AO, TEP, Series 37, Box 13, File: Minimum Wage – Québec Corresp. Etc.

93 J.E. Wilton to BC Royal Commission on Labour, 1912-14, BCA, GR-0684, Box 2, File 1.

94 Josephine Perfect Harshaw, *When Women Work Together: A History of the Young Women's Christian Association in Canada* (Toronto: YWCA, 1966), 15-16; Marie Gérin-Lajoie, "Le

syndicalisme féminin," in *Québécoises du 20e siècle,* ed. Michèle Jean (Montréal: Éditions du jour, 1974), 107-10.

95 H. Belton to Mr. C.L. Burton, "Re: Sherbourne House Club Foundation," 15 June ca. 1951, HBCCC; Stephenson, *The Store,* 74.

96 Toronto Council of Women, *Nothing New under the Sun,* 43; Frank, "Where Are the Workers ...?" 368.

97 Mrs. Mitchell, Executive, Local Council of Women of Victoria, to BC Royal Commission on Labour, 1912-14, BCA, GR-0684, Box 3, File 3.

98 "Disloyal to Toronto," article in a Toronto newspaper, ca. 1907, in AO, TEP, Series 162, OOS54, File 664; Margaret Hobbs, "Equality and Difference: Feminism and the Defence of Women Workers during the Great Depression," *Labour/Le Travail* 32 (Fall 1993): 201-23; Marie Lavigne and Jennifer Stoddart, "Ouvriéres et travailleuses montréalaises, 1900-1940," *Travailleuses et féministes: Les femmes dans la société québecoise,* ed. Marie Lavigne and Yolande Pinard (Montréal: Boréal Express, 1983), 106.

99 Frager, "Class, Ethnicity, and Gender," 198-99, 213.

100 Chown, *The Stairway,* 120.

101 Lindsey McMaster, "The Urban Working Girl in Turn-of-the-Century Canadian Fiction," *Essays on Canadian Writing* 77 (Fall 2002): 10.

102 Isabel Ecclestone Mackay, *The House of Windows* (London, New York, and Toronto: Cassell, 1912), 18-19, 43.

103 Ibid., 2, 37-38, 144-45, 119.

104 Monod, *Store Wars,* 236; A.J. Logan, Chairman, Independent Retail Merchants of Yorkton, to W.L. McQuarrie, 2 March 1934, RG 33, Volume 57, File: Exhibit 51.

105 Santink, *Timothy Eaton,* 212-13; "Where Great Danger Lies," article in a Toronto newspaper, ca. 1907, in AO, TEP, Series 162, OOS54, File 664.

106 Monod, *Store Wars,* 234.

107 As quoted in Cynthia Wright, "'Feminine Trifles of Vast Importance': Writing Gender into the History of Consumption," in *Gender Conflicts: New Essays in Women's History,* ed. Franca Iacovetta and Mariana Valverde (Toronto: University of Toronto Press, 1992), 240-41.

108 Ibid.

109 As quoted in Stephenson, *The Store,* 66.

110 Robert J. Moorehead, "Mrs. Grundy against God Almighty," *Fighting the Devil's Triple Demons* (Brantford, ON: Bradley-Garretson, 1911), 115-25.

111 William Leach, "Transformations in a Culture of Consumption: Women and Department Stores, 1890-1925," *Journal of American History* 71 (September 1984): 336.

112 N.A. Baillieul, Dealer in Groceries and Confectionery, Port Hawkesbury, NS, to Mr. W.W. Kennedy, 12 March 1935, RG 33, Volume 4, File: Chain and Department Stores General.

113 "Ordering by Mail," *Red and White* (St. Dunstan's University student newspaper), June 1910, 32-36.

114 "Conservation of Local Currency," *Evening Chronicle,* Port Arthur, 10 September 1910, AO, TEP, Series 162, OOS54, File 665.

115 John Deyell to the T. Eaton Co., Winnipeg, 1 September 1934, TEP, Series 162, Box 13, File 508; James Day to T. Eaton Co., 27 August 1934, AO, TEP, Series 162, Box 13, File 508.

116 "False Lights They Are," article in a Toronto newspaper, ca. 1907, AO, TEP, Series 162, OOS54, File 664.

117 Henry Thomas Lockyer, Manager of HBC Vancouver, BC Royal Commission on Labour, 1912-14, BCA, GR-0684, Box 2, File 1.

Epilogue: Canadian Institutions?

1 R. Stevens, Raincity, and MercuryBlue, "HBC Sold to New U.S. Owner," Comments, CBC News: http://www.cbc.ca/money/story/2008/07/16/hudsonbaynrdc.html#social comments.
2 Dave Miles and Claire Beatty, "HBC Sold to New U.S. Owner."
3 Olivia P and Josephus HAP, as quoted in "HBC Sold to New U.S. Owner."
4 Catherine Carstairs, "Roots Nationalism: Branding English Canada Cool in the 1980s and 1990s," *Histoire sociale/Social History* 77 (May 2006): 235-55.
5 Ibid., 250, 247.
6 Ibid., 254.

Bibliography

Archival References

Archives of Manitoba (AM)
Beatrice Brigden Collection
Hudson's Bay Company Catalogues

Archives of Ontario (AO)
Joshua Brown Family Papers
T. Eaton Company Papers (TEP), including:
  Chinook Winds
  Contacts
  Flash
T. Eaton Company Photographs

British Columbia Archives (BCA)
Papers of the British Columbia Royal Commission on Labour, 1912-14

Canadian Museum of Civilization (CMC)
Mail Order Historical Records

City of Vancouver Archives
Spencer's *Store Topics,* in the City Time Capsule Collection

City of Victoria Archives
Spencer Papers

Hudson's Bay Company Archives (HBCA) and Library
A12 Files
A102 Files
Record Group 2
Monod, David. "Bay Days: The Managerial Revolution and the Hudson's Bay Company Stores Department," PP 1986-10, 1990.

Hudson's Bay Company Corporate Collection (HBCCC)
Hudson's Bay Company Records
Morgan's Records
Simpson's Records
Woodward's Records

Library and Archives Canada (LAC)
Eaton's Catalogues
Eaton News Weekly
The Beaver
Papers of the Royal Commission on Price Spreads, 1934-38

McGill University Archives (MUA)
Morgan's Records

Saskatchewan Archives Board (SAB)
Department of Labour Files

Serials (Excluding Department Store Publications)
Dry Goods Review
Evening Star
Financial Post
Gateway
Grain Growers' Guide
La Bonne Parole
Maclean's
Montrealer
Montreal Gazette
Red and White
Regina Leader-Post
Saturday Night
Toronto Globe
Toronto Mail and Empire
Vancouver Sun
Vancouver Province
Victoria Daily Times
Victoria Times Colonist
Western Labor News
Winnipeg Telegram
Winnipeg Tribune
Woman's Century

Other References

"250 Water Street." *Canada's Historic Places/Lieux patrimoniaux du Canada.* http://www. historicplaces.ca/.

Abelson, Elaine S. *When Ladies Go A-Thieving: Middle-Class Shoplifters in the Victorian Department Store.* New York and Oxford: Oxford University Press, 1989.

Adilman, Tamara. "A Preliminary Sketch of Chinese Women and Work in British Columbia, 1858-1950." In *Not Just Pin Money: Selected Essays on the History of Women's Work in British Columbia,* ed. Barbara K. Latham and Roberta J. Pazdro, 53-78. Victoria, BC: Camosun College, 1984.

Adorno, Theodor, and Max Horkheimer. "The Culture Industry: Enlightenment as Mass Deception." In *Dialectic of Enlightenment,* trans. John Cumming, 120-67. New York: Continuum Publishing Group, 1976.

Agnew, Jean-Christophe. "Coming Up for Air: Consumer Culture in Historical Perspective." In *Consumer Society in American History: A Reader,* ed. Lawrence B. Glickman, 373-98. Ithaca and London: Cornell University Press, 1999.

Anderson, Carol, and Katharine Mallinson. *Lunch with Lady Eaton: Inside the Dining Rooms of a Nation.* Toronto: ECW Press, 2004.

"Anderson Department Store Fonds: Elgin County Archives." *Ontario History* 99, 2 (Autumn 2007): 247-49.

Atwood, Margaret. "Introduction to *Roughing It in the Bush.*" *Moving Targets: Writing with Intent, 1982-2004,* 34-42. Toronto: Anansi, 2004.

Auslander, Leora. "The Gendering of Consumer Practices in Nineteenth-Century France." In *The Sex of Things: Gender and Consumption in Historical Perspective,* ed. Victoria de Grazia and Ellen Furlough, 79-112. Berkeley: University of California Press, 1996.

Ayer, Shirley. *A Great Church in Action: A History of Timothy Eaton Memorial Church, Toronto, Canada, 1909-1977.* Whitby, ON: Plum Hollow Books, 1978.

Aylward, Sandra. "Experiencing Patriarchy: Women, Work, and Trade Unionism at Eaton's." PhD diss., McMaster University, 1991.

Backhouse, Constance. *Petticoats and Prejudice: Women and Law in Nineteenth-Century Canada.* Toronto: Women's Press, 1991.

Baillargeon, Denyse. *Making Do: Women, Family and Home in Montreal during the Great Depression.* Trans. Yvonne Klein. Waterloo, ON: Wilfrid Laurier University Press, 1999.

Baldwin, Betsey. "Canadian Nationalism and Eaton's Catalogues," 1999. Canadian Museum of Civilization, Library, Archives and Documentation, History Records, Box 1-164.

–. "The Displacement of Hat-Making as a Professional Art at Eaton's," 1999. Canadian Museum of Civilization, Library, Archives and Documentation, History Records, Box 1-164.

Bannerman, Josie, Kathy Chopik, and Ann Zurbrigg. "Cheap at Half the Price: The History of the Fight for Equal Pay in BC." In *Not Just Pin Money: Selected Essays on the History of Women's Work in British Columbia,* ed. Barbara K. Latham and Roberta J. Pazdro, 297-313. Victoria, BC: Camosun College, 1984.

Bates, Christina. "Shop and Factory: The Ontario Millinery Trade in Transition, 1870-1930." In *Fashion: A Canadian Perspective,* ed. Alexandra Palmer, 113-38. Toronto: University of Toronto Press, 2004.

Batts, Miaso. "Eaton's and Its Catalogues: An Expression of Canadian Social History." *Costume* 7 (1973): 68-69.

Belisle, Donica. "Consuming Producers: Retail Workers and Commodity Culture at Eaton's in Mid-Twentieth-Century Toronto." MA thesis, Queen's University, 2001.

–. "Exploring Postwar Consumption: The Campaign to Unionize Eaton's in Toronto, 1948-1952." *Canadian Historical Review* 86, 4 (December 2005): 641-72.

–. "A Labour Force for the Consumer Century: Commodification at Canada's Largest Department Stores, 1890 to 1940." *Labour/Le Travail* 58 (Fall 2006): 107-44.

–. "Negotiating Paternalism: Women and Canada's Largest Department Stores, 1890 to 1960." *Journal of Women's History* 19, 1 (Spring 2007): 58-81.

–. "Toward a Canadian Consumer History." *Labour/Le Travail* 52 (Fall 2003): 181-206.

Benson, Susan Porter. *Counter Cultures: Saleswomen, Managers, and Customers in American Department Stores, 1890-1940.* Urbana and Chicago: University of Illinois Press, 1988.

–. "Gender, Generation, and Consumption in the United States: Working-Class Families in the Interwar Period." In *Getting and Spending: European and American Consumer Societies in the Twentieth Century,* ed. Susan Strasser, Charles McGovern, and Matthias Judt, 223-40. Cambridge: Cambridge University Press, 1998.

–. "Living on the Margin: Working-Class Marriages and Family Survival Strategies in the United States, 1919-1941." In *The Sex of Things: Gender and Consumption in Historical Perspective,* ed. Victoria de Grazia and Ellen Furlough, 212-43. Berkeley: University of California Press, 1996.

Berger, Carl. *The Sense of Power: Studies in the Ideas of Canadian Imperialism, 1867-1914.* Toronto: University of Toronto Press, 1970.

"Big Stores Wage Western War." *Trade and Commerce in Western Canada,* March 1955, 4-7.

Binder, Sarah. "Shoppers Bid a Sad Farewell as Eaton's Doors Close." *National Post,* 22 October 1999, C5.

Blanke, David. *Sowing the American Dream: How Consumer Culture Took Root in the Rural Mid-West.* Athens: Ohio University Press, 2000.

Bliss, Michael. *A Living Profit: Studies in the Social History of Canadian Business, 1883-1911.* Toronto: McClelland and Stewart, 1972.

Bluestone, Barry. *The Retail Revolution: Market Transformation, Investment, and Labor in the Modern Department Store.* Boston: Auburn House Publishing, 1981.

Bosnitch, Katherine. "A Little on the Wild Side: Eaton's Prestige Fashion Advertising Published in the *Montreal Gazette,* 1952-1972." MA thesis, Concordia University, 2000.

Bosworth, Fred. "Simpson's vs. Eaton's: The Battle of the Big Stores." In *Canada in the Fifties: From the Archives of* Maclean's, 58-69. Toronto: Maclean Hunter Publishing, 1999.

Bourdieu, Pierre. *Distinction: A Social Critique of the Judgement of Taste.* Trans. R. Robert Nice. Cambridge, MA: Harvard University Press, 1984.

Bradbury, Bettina. *Working Families: Age, Gender, and Daily Survival in Industrializing Montreal.* Toronto: University of Toronto Press, 2007.

Brandes, Stuart. *American Welfare Capitalism, 1880-1940.* Chicago and London: University of Chicago Press, 1970.

Breckman, Warren. "Disciplining Consumption: The Debate about Luxury in Wilhelmine Germany, 1890-1914." *Journal of Social History* 24, 3 (Spring 1991): 485-505.

Brehl, John. "Eaton's: The Big Store Is Now 100 Years Old." In *A Century of Service to Canadian Shoppers,* 1-3. Toronto: Toronto Star Limited, 1969.

Briggs, Asa. *Friends of the People: The Centenary History of Lewis's.* London: B.T. Batsford, 1956.

Broadfoot, Barry, ed. "Does Shirley Temple Know?" *Ten Lost Years, 1929-1939: Memories of Canadians Who Survived the Depression.* Toronto: Doubleday, 1973.

–, ed. *The Pioneer Years, 1895-1914: Memories of the Settlers Who Opened the West.* Toronto and New York: Doubleday, 1976.

Buck-Morss, Susan. *The Dialectics of Seeing: Walter Benjamin and the Arcades Project.* Cambridge, MA: MIT Press, 1989.

Burke, Timothy. *Lifebuoy Men, Lux Women: Commodification, Consumption, and Cleanliness in Modern Zimbabwe.* Durham and London: Duke University Press, 1996.

Burley, Edith I. *Servants of the Honourable Company: Work, Discipline, and Conflict in the Hudson's Bay Company, 1770-1879.* Toronto: Oxford University Press, 1997.

Burton, Charles Luther. *A Sense of Urgency: Memoirs of a Canadian Merchant.* Toronto: Clark, 1952.

Burton, G. Allan. *A Store of Memories.* Toronto: McClelland and Stewart, 1986.

Byl, John. "The Margaret Eaton School, 1901-1942: Women's Education in Elocution, Drama, and Physical Education." PhD diss., State University of New York at Buffalo, 1992.

Callwood, June. "She's Organizing Eaton's." *Maclean's,* 1 October 1950, 20, 48-50.

Carrier, Roch. *The Hockey Sweater and Other Stories.* Trans. Sheila Fischman. Toronto: House of Anansi Press, 1979.

Carstairs, Catherine. "Roots Nationalism: Branding English Canada Cool in the 1980s and 1990s." *Histoire sociale/Social History* 77 (May 2006): 235-55.

Cheal, David. *The Gift Economy.* New York: Routledge, 1988.

Chessel, Marie-Emmanuelle. "Training Sales Personnel in France between the Wars." In *Cathedrals of Consumption: The European Department Store, 1850-1939,* ed. Geoffrey Crossick and Serge Jaumain, 286-92. Aldershot: Ashgate, 1999.

Chong, Denise. *The Concubine's Children.* Toronto: Penguin Books, 1994.

Chown, Alice. *The Stairway.* Toronto: University of Toronto Press, 1988 [1921].

Clarke, John. "'Mine Eyes Dazzle': Cultures of Consumption." In *New Times and Old Enemies: Essays on Cultural Studies and America,* 73-112. London: HarperCollins Academic, 1991.

Cobble, Dorothy Sue. "Organizing the Postindustrial Workforce: Lessons from the History of Waitress Unionism." *Industrial and Labor Relations Review* 44 (April 1991): 419-36.

Coffin, Judith G. "A 'Standard' of Living? European Perspectives on Class and Consumption in the Early Twentieth Century." *International Labor and Working-Class History* 55 (Spring 1999): 6-26.

Cohen, Lizabeth. *A Consumer's Republic: The Politics of Mass Consumption in Postwar America.* New York: Alfred A. Knopf, 2003.

–. "Embellishing a Life of Labor: An Interpretation of the Material Culture of American Working-Class Homes, 1885-1915." In *Material Cultural Studies in America,* ed. Thomas J. Schlereth, 289-305. Nashville: American Association for State and Local History, 1982.

–. "Encountering Mass Culture at the Grassroots: The Experience of Chicago Workers in the 1920s." *American Quarterly* 41 (March 1989): 6-33.

–. "Escaping Steigerwald's 'Plastic Cages': Consumers as Subjects and Objects in Modern Capitalism." *Journal of American History* 93, 2 (September 2006): 409-13.

–. *Making a New Deal: Industrial Workers in Chicago, 1919-1939.* Cambridge: Cambridge University Press, 1990.

–. "The Mass in Mass Consumption." *Reviews in American History* 18 (1990): 549-55.

–. "The New Deal State and the Making of Citizen Consumers." In *Getting and Spending: European and American Consumer Societies in the Twentieth Century,* ed. Susan Strasser, Charles McGovern, and Matthias Judt, 111-25. Washington, DC: Cambridge University Press, 1998.

Coish, Calvin. "The Eaton's Catalogue: A Newfoundland Tradition." *Distant Shores: Pages from Newfoundland's Past,* 138-44. Grand Falls-Windsor: Lifestyle Books, 1994.

Cole, Catherine C. "Comparative Analysis of the Toronto and Winnipeg Editions of the Eaton's Mail-Order Catalogue." 1995. Canadian Museum of Civilization, Library, Archives and Documentation, History Records, Box 1-164.

Collins, Jackie L. *Threads: Gender, Labor, and Power in the Global Apparel Industry.* Chicago: University of Chicago Press, 2003.

Comacchio, Cynthia. *The Infinite Bonds of Family: Domesticity in Canada, 1850-1940.* Toronto: University of Toronto Press, 1999.

Comeau, Michelle. "Les grands magasins de la Rue Sainte-Catherine à Montréal: Des lieux de modernisation, d'homogénéisation et de différenciation des modes de consommation." *Material History Review* 41 (Spring 1995): 58-68.

Conor, Liz. "The Flapper's Ontological Ambivalence: Prosthetic Visualities, the Feminine and Modernity." *Dealing with Difference: Essays in Gender, Culture and History,* ed. Patricia Grimshaw and Diane Kirkby, 178-97. Melbourne: Department of History, University of Melbourne, 1997.

Conrad, Margaret, and Alvin Finkel, with Cornelius Jaenen. *History of the Canadian Peoples: Beginnings to 1867.* 2 vols. 2nd ed. Toronto: Copp Clark, 1998.

Coulter, Rebecca. "The Working Young of Edmonton, 1921-1931." In *Childhood and Family in Canadian History,* ed. Joy Parr, 143-59. Toronto: McClelland and Stewart, 1982.

Cross, Gary. *An All-Consuming Century: Why Commercialism Won in Modern America.* New York: Columbia University Press, 2000.

–. *Time and Money: The Making of Consumer Culture.* New York and London: Routledge, 1993.

Cross, Gary, and Peter Shergold. "'We Think We Are of the Oppressed': Gender, White Collar Work, and the Grievances of Late Nineteenth-Century Women." *Labor History* 28 (Winter 1987): 23-53.

Crossick, Geoffrey, and Serge Jaumain. "The World of the Department Store: Distribution, Culture and Social Change." In *Cathedrals of Consumption: The European Department Store, 1850-1939,* ed. Geoffrey Crossick and Serge Jaumain, 1-45. Aldershot: Ashgate, 1999.

David Spencer, Ltd. *Golden Jubilee, 1873-1923.* Victoria, BC: David Spencer, 1923.

Davis, Simone Weil. *Living Up to the Ads: Gender Fictions of the 1920s.* Durham, NC: Duke University Press, 2000.

de Grazia, Victoria. "Changing Consumption Regimes." In *The Sex of Things: Gender and Consumption in Historical Perspective,* ed. Victoria de Grazia with Ellen Furlough, 11-24. Berkeley, Los Angeles, and London: University of California Press, 1996.

–. "Introduction." In *The Sex of Things: Gender and Consumption in Historical Perspective,* ed. Victoria de Grazia and Ellen Furlough, 1-10. Berkeley: University of California Press, 1996.

–. *Irresistible Empire: America's Advance through 20th-Century Europe.* Cambridge, MA: Harvard University Press, 2005.

de Grazia, Victoria, and Lizabeth Cohen. "Introduction" to "Class and Consumption." Special issue, *International Labor and Working-Class History* 55 (Spring 1999): 1-5.

Denison, Murrell. *This Is Simpson's.* Toronto: Simpson's, 1958.

Dennis, Thelma. "Eaton's Catalogue: Furnishings for Rural Alberta, 1886-1930." *Alberta History* 27 (1989): 21-31.

Dominion Bureau of Statistics. *Seventh Census of Canada, 1931.* Vol. 10, *Merchandising and Service Establishments: Part I, Retail Merchandise Trade.* Ottawa: J.O. Patenaude, 1931.

Dowling, Robyn Margaret. "Shopping and the Construction of Femininity in the Woodward's Department Store, Vancouver, 1945 to 1960." MA thesis, University of British Columbia, 1991.

Dry Goods and Stylewear Review. "Mail Order Decline: Departmental Losses Feature Eaton and Simpson Evidence." *Dry Goods and Stylewear Review* (June 1934): 5-12.

Dubinsky, Karen. *Rape and Heterosexual Conflict in Ontario, 1880-1929.* Chicago: University of Chicago Press, 1993.

–. *The Second Greatest Disappointment: Honeymooning and Tourism at Niagara Falls.* Toronto: Between the Lines, 1999.

Dupuis-Leman, Josette. *Dupuis-Frères: Le Magasin du Peuple.* Montréal: Stanké, 2001.

Eaton, Flora McCrea. *Memory's Wall: The Autobiography of Flora McCrea Eaton.* Toronto: Clarke, Irwin, 1956.

Elvins, Sarah. *Sales and Celebrations: Retailing and Regional Identity in Western New York State, 1920-1940.* Athens: Ohio University Press, 2004.

Emmerson, James. "A Famous Canadian Store Strides into Its 100th Year." In *The Simpson's Century,* unpaginated. Toronto: Toronto Star, 1972.

Enstad, Nan. *Ladies of Labor, Girls of Adventure: Working Women, Popular Culture, and Labor Politics at the Turn of the Twentieth Century.* New York: Columbia University Press, 1999.

Estey, Marten. "Early Closing: Employer-Organized Origin of the Retail Labor Movement." *Labor History* 13 (1972): 560-70.

Ewen, Stuart. *Captains of Consciousness: Advertising and the Social Roots of the Consumer Culture.* New York: McGraw Hill, 1976.

Fahrni, Magda. "Counting the Costs of Living: Gender, Citizenship, and a Politics of Prices in 1940s Montreal." *Canadian Historical Review* 83, 4 (December 2002): 483-504.

Feldster, Ruth. *Motherhood in Black and White: Race and Sex in American Liberalism, 1930-1965.* Ithaca and London: Cornell University Press, 2000.

Ferry, John William. *A History of the Department Store.* New York: Macmillan, 1960.

Finn, Margot. "Sex and the City: Metropolitan Modernities in English History." *Victorian Studies* 44, 1 (Autumn 2001): 25-32.

Finnegan, Margaret. *Selling Suffrage: Consumer Culture and Votes for Women.* Columbia: Columbia University Press, 1999.

Forbes, Susan L. "Gendering Corporate Welfare Practices: Female Sports and Recreation at Eaton's during the Depression." *Rethinking History* 5 (2001): 59-74.

–. "The Influence of the Social Reform Movement and T. Eaton Company's Business Practices on the Leisure of Eaton's Female Employees during the Early Twentieth Century." PhD diss., University of Western Ontario, 1998.

Frager, Ruth. "Class, Ethnicity, and Gender in the Eaton Strikes of 1912 and 1934." In *Gender Conflicts: New Essays in Women's History,* ed. Franca Iacovetta and Mariana Valverde, 189-228. Toronto: University of Toronto Press, 1992.

–. *Sweatshop Strife: Class, Ethnicity and Gender in the Jewish Labour Movement of Toronto, 1900-1939.* Toronto: University of Toronto Press, 1992.

Frager, Ruth, and Carmela Patrias. *Discounted Labour: Women Workers in Canada, 1870-1939.* Toronto: University of Toronto Press, 2005.

Frank, Dana. *Purchasing Power: Consumer Organizing, Gender, and the Seattle Labor Movement, 1919-1929.* Cambridge: Cambridge University Press, 1994.

–. "Where Are the Workers in Consumer-Worker Alliances? Class Dynamics and the History of Consumer-Labor Campaigns." *Politics and Society* 31 (September 2003): 363-79.

Freiman, Lawrence. *Don't Fall Off the Rocking Horse: An Autobiography.* Toronto: McClelland and Stewart, 1978.

Friedan, Betty. *The Feminine Mystique.* New York: Norton, 2001 [1963].

Geller, Peter. "Creating Corporate Images of the Fur Trade: The Hudson's Bay Company and Public Relations in the 1930s." In *The Fur Trade Revisited: Selected Papers of the Sixth*

North American Fur Trade Conference, Mackinac Island, Michigan, 1991, ed. Jennifer Brown, William John Eccles, and Donald P. Heldman, 409-26. Michigan: Mackinac State Historical Parks, 1991.

Gereffi, Gary, and Miguel Korzeniewicz, eds. *Commodity Chains and Global Capitalism.* Westport, CT: Praeger, 1994.

Gérin-Lajoie, Marie. "Le syndicalisme féminin." In *Québécoises du 20e siècle,* ed. Michèle Jean, 103-16. Montréal: Éditions du jour, 1974 [1921].

Giles, Judy. *The Parlour and the Suburb: Domestic Identities, Class, Femininity and Modernity.* Oxford and New York: Berg, 2004.

Gillis, Rannie. *Historic North Sydney: Images of Our Past.* Halifax: Nimbus Publishing, 2005.

Glazebrook, G.T. De, Katharine B. Brett, Judith MacErvel, and Leslie Smart. *A Shopper's View of Canada's Past: Pages from Eaton's Catalogues, 1886-1930.* Toronto: University of Toronto Press, 1969.

Glazer, Nona Y. *Women's Paid and Unpaid Labor: The Work Transfer in Health Care and Retailing.* Philadelphia: Temple University Press, 1993.

Glickman, Lawrence B. *A Living Wage: American Workers and the Making of Consumer Society.* Ithaca and London: Cornell University Press, 1997.

–. "Workers of the World, Consume: Ira Steward and the Origins of Labor Consumerism." *International Labor and Working-Class History* 52 (Fall 1997): 72-86.

Gordon, Ishbel Maria Marjoribanks. *The Canadian Journal of Lady Aberdeen.* Edited by John T. Saywell. Toronto: Champlain Society, 1960.

Gorham, Deborah. "Flora MacDonald Denison: Canadian Feminist." In *A Not Unreasonable Claim: Women and Social Reform in Canada, 1880s-1920s,* ed. Linda Kealey, 47-70. Toronto: Women's Press, 1979.

Grant, Hugh. "Solving the Labour Problem at Imperial Oil: Welfare Capitalism in the Canadian Petroleum Industry, 1919-29." *Labour/Le Travail* 41 (Spring 1998): 69-95.

Green, Nancy L. *Ready-to-Wear, Ready-to-Work: A Century of Industry and Immigrants in Paris and New York.* Durham, NC: Duke University Press, 1997.

Gresko, Jacqueline. "'Roughing It in the Bush' in British Columbia: Mary Moody's Pioneer Life in New Westminster, 1859-1863." In *Not Just Pin Money: Selected Essays on the History of Women's Work in British Columbia,* ed. Barbara K. Latham and Roberta J. Pazdro, 38-51. Victoria, BC: Camosun College, 1984.

Griffiths, N.E.S. *The Splendid Vision: Centennial History of the National Council of Women of Canada, 1893-1993.* Ottawa: Carleton University Press, 1993.

Guard, Julie. "Women Worth Watching: Radical Housewives in Cold War Canada." In *Whose National Security? Canadian State Surveillance and the Creation of Enemies,* ed. Gary Kinsman, Dieter K. Buse, and Mercedes Steedman, 73-88. Toronto: Between the Lines, 2000.

Haight, Susan. "Machines in Suburban Gardens: The 1936 T. Eaton Company Architectural Competition for House Designs." *Material History Review* 44 (Fall 1996): 23-43.

Halttunen, Karen. "From Parlor to Living Room: Domestic Space, Interior Decoration, and the Culture of Personality." *Consuming Visions: Accumulation and the Display of Goods in America, 1880-1920,* ed. Simon J. Bronner, 157-90. New York: Norton, 1989.

Hannis, Prudence. "Survey of the Eaton's Catalogue: 1881-1976 – Household Appliances," 1996. Canadian Museum of Civilization, Library, Archives and Documentation, History Records, Box 1-164.

Hardy, Stephen. "'Adopted by All the Leading Clubs'": Sporting Goods and the Shaping of Leisure, 1800-1900." In *For Fun and Profit: The Transformation of Leisure into Consumption*, ed. Richard Butsch, 71-104. Philadelphia: Temple University Press, 1990.

Harker, Douglas E. *The City and the Store*. Vancouver: Woodwards Stores, 1958.

–. *The Woodwards: A Family Story of Ventures and Traditions*. Vancouver: Mitchell Press, 1976.

Harshaw, Josephine Perfect. *When Women Work Together: A History of the Young Women's Christian Association in Canada*. Toronto: YWCA, 1966.

Hart, E.J. *The Selling of Canada: The CPR and the Beginnings of Canadian Tourism*. Banff: Altitude Publishing, 1983.

Harvey, David. *The Condition of Postmodernity: An Enquiry into the Origins of Cultural Change*. Cambridge: Basil Blackwell, 1989.

Haug, Wolfgang Fritz. *Critique of Commodity Aesthetics: Appearance, Sexuality, and Advertising in Capitalist Society*. Trans. Robert Bock. London: Polity Press, 1971.

Hennessy, Rosemary. *Profit and Pleasure: Sexual Identities in Late Capitalism*. New York: Routledge, 2000.

Henry Morgan and Company Limited. *80 Years of Merchandising*. Montréal: Henry Morgan, 1927.

Heron, Craig. *Booze: A Distilled History*. Toronto: Between the Lines, 2003.

Hilton, Marjorie. "Retailing the Revolution: The State Department Store (GUM) and Soviet Society in the 1920s." *Journal of Social History* 37, 4 (Summer 2004): 939-64.

Historical Statistics of Canada, 2nd ed. Ottawa: Statistics Canada, 1999.

Hochschild, Arlie Russell. *The Managed Heart: Commercialization of Human Feeling*. Berkeley: University of California Press, 2003 [1983].

Hoerder, Dick. *Creating Societies: Immigrant Lives in Canada*. Montréal and Kingston: McGill-Queen's University Press, 1999.

Hoodless, Adelaide. "Trades and Industries." In *Women of Canada: Their Life and Work*, compiled by the National Council of Women of Canada, 91-95. National Council of Women of Canada, 1900.

Horodyski, Mary. "'That was quite a strike alright ...': Women and the Winnipeg General Strike of 1919." *Fireweed* 26 (4 April 1988) from *Gender Watch* (ProQuest Information and Learning Company online database).

Hosgood, Christopher P. "'Doing the Shops' at Christmas: Women, Men and the Department Store in England, c. 1880-1914." *Cathedrals of Consumption: The European Department Store, 1850-1939*, ed. Geoffrey Crossick and Serge Jaumain, 97-115. Aldershot: Ashgate, 1999.

–. "'Mercantile Monasteries': Shops, Shop Assistants, and Shop Life in Late-Victorian Britain." *Journal of British Studies* 38 (July 1999): 322-52.

Howard, Vicki. "'The Biggest Small-Town Store in America': Independent Retailers and the Rise of Consumer Culture." *Enterprise and Society* 9, 3 (2008): 457-86.

Howell, Alison. "Retail Unionization: An Historical Approach to the Suzy Shier Case." Honours Thesis, Trent University, 2000.

Howell, Colin D. *Blood, Sweat, and Cheers: Sport and the Making of Modern Canada*. Toronto: University of Toronto Press, 2001.

Hower, Ralph. *History of Macy's of New York, 1858-1919*. Cambridge, MA: Harvard University Press, 1943.

Huyssen, Andreas. "Mass Culture as Woman: Modernism's Other." *After the Great Divide: Modernism, Mass Culture, Postmodernism*, 44-64. Bloomington: Indiana University Press, 1986.

Iacovetta, Franca. "Postmodern Ethnography, Historical Materialism, and Decentring the (Male) Authorial Voice: A Feminist Conversation." *Histoire sociale/Social History* 32 (November 1999): 275-93.

–. "Recipes for Democracy? Gender, Family, and Making Female Citizens in Cold War Canada." *Canadian Woman Studies* 20 (Summer 2000): 12-21.

Iacovetta, Franca, and Valerie Korinek. "Jello Salads, One-Stop Shopping, and Maria the Homemaker: The Gender Politics of Food." In *Sisters or Strangers? Immigrant Women, Minority Women, and the Racialized Other in Canadian History,* ed. Marlene Epp, Franca Iacovetta, and Frances Swyripa, 190-232. Toronto: University of Toronto Press, 2004.

Innis, Mary Quayle. "Holiday." *Canadian Forum* (January 1932): 141-42.

Isenberg, Alison. *Downtown America: A History of the Place and the People Who Made It.* Chicago: University of Chicago Press, 2004.

Jackman, Mary R. *The Velvet Glove: Paternalism and Conflict in Gender, Class, and Race Relations.* Berkeley: University of California Press, 1994.

Jacoby, Sanford M. *Modern Manors: Welfare Capitalism since the New Deal.* Princeton, NJ: Princeton University Press, 1997.

James, Kathleen. "From Messel to Mendelsohn: German Department Store Architecture in Defence of Urban and Economic Change." In *Cathedrals of Consumption: The European Department Store, 1850-1939,* ed. Geoffrey Crossick and Serge Jaumain, 252-78. Aldershot, UK: Ashgate, 1999.

Jameson, Fredric. "Reification and Utopia in Mass Culture." In *The Jameson Reader,* ed. Michael Hardt and Kathi Weeks, 123-48. New York: Blackwell, 2000.

Johnston, Russell. *Selling Themselves: The Emergence of Canadian Advertising.* Toronto: University of Toronto Press, 2001.

Johnstone Walker Limited. *The Story of JW: 75 Years in Edmonton, 1886-1961.* Edmonton: Johnstone Walker, 1961.

Jones, Jennifer. "*Coquettes* and *Grisettes:* Women Buying and Selling in Ancien Régime Paris." In *The Sex of Things: Gender and Consumption in Historical Perspective,* ed. Victoria de Grazia and Ellen Furlough, 25-53. Berkeley: University of California Press, 1996.

Joyce, Patrick. *Work, Society and Politics: The Culture of the Factory in Later Victorian England.* London: Harvester Press, 1980.

Kasson, John. *Rudeness and Civility: Manners in Nineteenth-Century Urban America.* New York: Hill and Wang, 1990.

Kealey, Linda. *Enlisting Women for the Cause: Women, Labour, and the Left in Canada, 1890-1920.* Toronto: University of Toronto Press, 1998.

Keynes, John Maynard. *The General Theory of Employment, Interest, and Money.* London and Basingstoke: Macmillan, 1936.

Kidd, Alan J., and David Nicholls, eds. *Gender, Civic Culture, and Consumerism: Middle-Class Identity in Britain, 1800-1940.* Manchester and New York: Manchester University Press, 1999.

Klasson, Henry. *Eye on the Future: Business People in Calgary and the Bow Valley, 1870-1900.* Calgary: University of Calgary Press, 2002.

–. "T.C. Power & Bro.: The Rise of a Small Western Department Store, 1870-1902." *Business History Review* 66, 4 (Winter 1992). http://www.gale.cengage.com/Academic OneFile/.

Klein, Anne, and Wayne Roberts. "Besieged Innocence: The 'Problem' and Problems of Working Women – Toronto, 1896-1914." In *Women at Work: Ontario, 1850-1930,* ed. Janice Acton, Penny Goldsmith, and Bonnie Shepard, 211-60. Toronto: Women's Press Publications, 1974.

Klein, Naomi. *No Logo: Taking Aim at the Brand Bullies.* Toronto: Vintage Canada, 2000.

Knox, E.M. *The Girl of the New Day.* Toronto: McClelland and Stewart, 1919.

Korinek, Valerie J. *Roughing It in the Suburbs: Reading* Chatelaine *Magazine in the Fifties and Sixties.* Toronto: University of Toronto Press, 2000.

Kowaleski-Wallace, Elizabeth. *Consuming Subjects: Women, Shopping, and Business in the Eighteenth Century.* New York: Columbia University Press, 1997.

Lan, Pei-Chia. "Working in a Neon Cage: Bodily Labor of Cosmetics Saleswomen in Taiwan." *Feminist Studies* 29 (Spring 2003): 21-45.

Lancaster, Bill. *The Department Store: A Social History.* London: Leicester University Press, 1995.

Last Post. "The Company." *Last Post,* February 1970, 10-22.

Lavigne, Marie, Yolande Pinard, and Jennifer Stoddart. "The Féderation Nationale Saint-Jean-Baptiste and the Women's Movement in Quebec." In *A Not Unreasonable Claim: Women and Social Reform in Canada, 1880s-1920s,* ed. Linda Kealey, 71-87. Toronto: Women's Press, 1979.

Lavigne, Marie, and Jennifer Stoddart. "Ouvrières et travailleuses montréalaises, 1900-1940." In *Travailleuses et féministes: Les femmes dans la société québécoise,* ed. Marie Lavigne and Yolande Pinard, 98-113. Montréal: Boréal Express, 1983.

Leach, William. *Land of Desire: Merchants, Power, and the Rise of a New American Culture.* New York: Pantheon Books, 1993.

–. "Transformations in a Culture of Consumption: Women and Department Stores, 1890-1925." *The Journal of American History* 71 (September 1984): 319-42.

Lears, Jackson. *Fables of Abundance: A Cultural History of Advertising in America.* New York: Basic Books, 1994.

–. "From Salvation to Self-Realization: Advertising and the Therapeutic Roots of the Consumer Culture, 1880-1930." In *The Culture of Consumption: Critical Essays in American History, 1880-1980,* ed. Richard Wightman Fox and T.J. Jackson Lears, 1-38. New York: Pantheon Books, 1983.

–. *No Place of Grace: Antimodernism and the Transformation of American Culture, 1880-1920.* New York: Pantheon Books, 1981.

Lévesque, Andrée. *Making and Breaking the Rules: Women in Quebec, 1919-1939.* Trans. Yvonne M. Klein. Toronto: McClelland and Stewart, 1994.

Licht, Walter. "Fringe Benefits: A Review Essay of the American Workplace." *International Labor and Working-Class History* 53 (Spring 1998): 164-78.

Lindstrom, Richard. "'It would break my heart to see you behind a counter!': Business and Reform at L.S. Ayres & Company in the Early Twentieth Century." *Indiana Magazine of History* 93, 4 (December 1997): 345-76.

Liverant, Bettina. "Buying Happiness: English Canadian Intellectuals and the Development of Canadian Consumer Culture." PhD diss., University of Alberta, 2008.

Loeb, Lori Anne. *Consuming Angels: Advertising and Victorian Women.* New York and Oxford: Oxford University Press, 1994.

Lowe, Graham S. "Women, Work, and the Office: The Feminization of Clerical Occupations in Canada, 1901-1931." In *Rethinking Canada: The Promise of Women's History,* 3rd ed., ed. Veronica Strong-Boag and Anita Clair Fellman, 253-70. Toronto: Oxford University Press, 1997.

Lukács, Georg. "Reification and the Consciousness of the Proletariat." In *History and Class Consciousness: Studies in Marxist Dialectics,* trans. Rodney Livingstone, 83-222. London: Basingstoke, 1968.

MacAuley, Scott. "The Smokestack Leaned Toward Capitalism." *Journal of Canadian Studies* 37, 1 (Spring 2002): 43-67.

MacCallum, Margaret E. "Keeping Women in Their Place: The Minimum Wage in Canada, 1910-1925." *Labour/Le Travail* 17 (Spring 1986): 29-56.

MacDonald, Edith [The Scribe]. *Golden Jubilee, 1869-1919.* Toronto and Winnipeg: T. Eaton Company, 1919.

Mackay, Isabel Ecclestone. *The House of Windows.* London, New York, and Toronto: Cassell, 1912.

MacMurchy, Marjorie. *The Canadian Girl at Work: A Book of Vocational Guidance.* Toronto: A.T. Wilgress, 1919.

MacPherson, Ian. *Each for All: A History of the Co-operative Movement in English Canada, 1900-1945.* Ottawa: MacMillan of Canada, 1979.

MacPherson, Mary-Etta. *Shopkeepers to a Nation: The Eatons.* Toronto: McClelland and Stewart, 1963.

Mallory, Enid. *Over the Counter: The Country Store in Canada.* Toronto: Fitzhenry and Whiteside, 1985.

Manitoba Culture, Heritage, and Tourism, "T. Eaton Company Store, Winnipeg: Synopsis of Significance." Winnipeg: Government of Manitoba, 2001.

Marchand, Roland. *Advertising the American Dream: Making Way for Modernity, 1920-1940.* Berkeley and Los Angeles: University of California Press, 1985.

–. *Creating the Corporate Soul: The Rise of Public Relations and Corporate Imagery in American Big Business.* Berkeley and Los Angeles: University of California Press, 1998.

Martin, John Levi. "The Myth of the Consumption-Oriented Economy and the Rise of the Desiring Subject." *Theory and Society* 28, 3 (June 1999): 425-53.

Martin, Michèle. *Hello Central: Gender, Technology, and Culture in the Formation of Telephone Systems.* Montréal and Kingston: McGill-Queen's University Press, 1991.

Matthews, Mary Catherine. "Working for Family, Nation, and God: Paternalism and the Dupuis Fréres Department Store, 1926-1952." MA thesis, McGill University, 1997.

Maynard, Fredelle Bruser. "Satisfaction Guaranteed: The 1928 Eaton's Catalogue." *Raisins and Almonds,* 39-51. Toronto: Doubleday Canada, 1972.

McBride, Theresa. "A Woman's World: Department Stores and the Evolution of Women's Employment, 1870-1920." *French Historical Studies* 10 (Autumn 1978): 664-83.

McCann, L.D. "Metropolitanism and Branch Businesses in the Maritimes, 1881-1931." In *The Acadiensis Reader,* Vol. 2, *Atlantic Canada after Confederation,* ed. P.A. Buckner and David Frank, 202-15. Fredericton: Acadiensis Press, 1985.

McClintock, Anne. *Imperial Leather: Race, Gender, and Sexuality in the Colonial Contest.* New York: Routledge, 1995.

McClung, Nellie. *The Second Chance.* Toronto: William Briggs, 1910.

McCormack, A. Ross. "Networks among British Immigrants and Accommodation to Canadian Society: Winnipeg, 1900-1914." *Histoire sociale/Social History* 17 (November 1984): 357-74.

McGovern, Charles. "Consumption and Citizenship in the United States, 1900-1940." In *Getting and Spending: European and American Consumer Societies in the Twentieth Century,* ed. Susan Strasser, Charles McGovern, and Matthias Judt, 37-58. Washington: Cambridge University Press, 1998.

McKay, Ian. "'By Wisdom, Wile or War': The Provincial Workmen's Association and the Struggle for Working-Class Independence in Nova Scotia, 1879-97." *Labour/Le Travail* 18 (Fall 1986): 13-62.

McMaster, Lindsey. "The Urban Working Girl in Turn-of-the-Century Canadian Fiction." *Essays on Canadian Writing* 77 (Fall 2002): 1-25.

McQueen, Rod. *The Eatons: The Rise and Fall of Canada's Royal Family.* Rev. ed. Toronto: Stoddart, 1999.

Mehaffy, Marilyn. "Advertising Race/Racing Advertising: The Feminine Consumer (Nation), 1876-1900." *Signs: Journal of Women in Culture and Society* 23, 1 (1997): 131-74.

Metcalfe, Alan. "The Evolution of Organized Physical Recreation in Montreal, 1840-1895." *Histoire sociale/Social History* 21 (May 1978): 144-66.

Meyer, Stephen, III. *The Five Dollar Day: Labor Management and Social Control in the Ford Motor Company, 1908-1921.* Albany: State University of New York Press, 1981.

Miller, Michael B. *The Bon Marché: Bourgeois Culture and the Department Store, 1869-1920.* Princeton, NJ: Princeton University Press, 1981.

Ministry of Trade and Commerce, *Seventh Census of Canada, 1931.* Vol. 10, *Merchandising and Service Establishments.* Ottawa: J.O. Patenaude, 1934.

Monod, David. *Store Wars: Shopkeepers and the Culture of Mass Marketing, 1890-1939.* Toronto: University of Toronto Press, 1996.

Moore, Christopher. *Adventurers: Hudson's Bay Company – The Epic Story.* Hong Kong: Quantum Book Group, 2000.

Moorehead, Robert J. *Fighting the Devil's Triple Demons.* Brantford, ON: Bradley-Garretson, 1911.

Morgan, David. *The Morgans of Montreal.* Toronto: David Morgan, 1992.

Mort, Frank. *Cultures of Consumption: Masculinities and Social Space in Late Twentieth-Century Britain.* London and New York: Routledge, 1996.

–. "The Politics of Consumption." In *New Times: The Changing Face of Politics in the 1990s,* ed. Stuart Hall and Martin Jacques, 160-72. London: Lawrence and Wishart, 1989.

Morton, Suzanne. *At Odds: Gambling and Canadians, 1919-1969.* Toronto: University of Toronto Press, 2003.

–. *Ideal Surroundings: Domestic Life in a Working-Class Suburb in the 1920s.* Toronto: University of Toronto Press, 1995.

–. "The June Bride as the Working-Class Bride: Getting Married in a Halifax Working-Class Neighbourhood in the 1920s." In *Canadian Family History: Selected Readings,* ed. Bettina Bradbury, 360-79. Toronto: Copp Clark Pitman, 1992.

Nasmith, George. *Timothy Eaton.* Toronto: McClelland and Stewart, 1923.

Nava, Mica. "Consumerism Reconsidered: Buying and Power." *Cultural Studies* 5, 2 (May 1991): 157-73.

–. "Framing Advertising: Cultural Analysis and the Incrimination of Visual Texts." In *Buy This Book: Studies in Advertising and Consumption,* 35-50. New York: Routledge, 1997.

Neufeld, Andrew. *Union Store: The History of the Retail Clerks Union in British Columbia, 1899-1999.* Vancouver: United Food and Commercial Workers Union, Local 1518, 1999.

Newfoundland and Labrador. *Historical Statistics of Newfoundland and Labrador.* St. John's, NF: Queen's Printer, 1970. www.stats.gov.nl.ca/Publications/Historical/PDF/Foreword.pdf.

Newman, Peter C. *Empire of the Bay: An Illustrated History of the Hudson's Bay Company*. Ed. John Geiger. Toronto: Viking Studio/Madison Press, 1989.

–. *Merchant Princes: Company of Adventurers*. Vol. 3. Toronto: Viking, 1991.

Noel, Jan. "Defrocking Dad: Masculinity and Dress in Montreal, 1700-1867." In *Fashion: A Canadian Perspective*, ed. Alexandra Palmer, 68-89. Toronto: University of Toronto Press, 2004.

O'Connor, Eileen. "Constructing Medical Social Authority on Dress in Victorian Canada." *Canadian Bulletin of Medical History* 25, 2 (2005): 335-50.

–. "The Eaton's Mail-Order Catalogue, 1884-1976: An Archival Analysis," 1996. Canadian Museum of Civilization, Library, Archives and Documentation, History Records, Box 1-164.

O'Donnell, Lorraine. "Visualizing the History of Women at Eaton's, 1869 to 1976." PhD diss., McGill University, 2002.

–. "Le voyage virtuel: Les consommatrices, le monde de l'étranger et Eaton à Montréal, 1880-1980." *Revue d'histoire de l'Amérique française* 59 (Spring 2005): 535-68.

Owram, Douglas. "Canadian Domesticity in the Postwar Era." In *The Veterans Charter and Post-World War II Canada*, ed. Peter Neary and J.L. Granatstein, 205-23. Montréal and Kingston: McGill-Queen's University Press, 1998.

Palmer, Bryan D. *Working-Class Experience: Rethinking the History of Canadian Labour, 1800-1991*. 2nd ed. Toronto: McClelland and Stewart, 1992.

Parr, Joy. *Domestic Goods: The Material, the Moral, and the Economic in the Postwar Years*. Toronto: University of Toronto Press, 1999.

–. *The Gender of Breadwinners: Women, Men, and Change in Two Industrial Towns, 1880-1950*. Toronto: University of Toronto Press, 1990.

–. "Household Choices as Politics and Pleasure in 1950s Canada." *International Labor and Working-Class History* 55 (Spring 1999): 112-28.

–. "Reinventing Consumption." *The Beaver* 80, 1 (2000): 66-73.

Pasdermadjian, H. *The Department Store: Its Origins, Evolution and Economics*. New York: Arno Press, 1976 [1954].

Patterson, Norman. "Evolution of a Departmental Store." *Canadian Magazine*, September 1906, 425-38.

Peiss, Kathy. *Cheap Amusements: Working Women and Leisure in Turn-of-the-Century New York*. Philadelphia: Temple University Press, 1986.

–. *Hope in a Jar: The Making of America's Beauty Culture*. New York: Owl Books, 1999.

–. "Making Up, Making Over: Cosmetics, Consumer Culture, and Women's Identity." In *The Sex of Things: Gender and Consumption in Historical Perspective*, ed. Victoria de Grazia and Ellen Furlough, 311-36. Berkeley: University of California Press, 1996.

Penfold, Steve. *The Donut: A Canadian History*. Toronto: University of Toronto Press, 2008.

Perkins, Elizabeth. "The Consumer Frontier: Household Consumption in Early Kentucky." *Journal of American History* 78, 2 (September 1991): 486-510.

Perry, Adele. *On the Edge of Empire: Gender, Race, and the Making of British Columbia, 1849-1871*. Toronto: University of Toronto Press, 2001.

Phenix, Patricia. *Eatonians: The Story of the Family behind the Family*. Toronto: McClelland and Stewart, 2002.

"Population of Great Britain and Ireland, 1871-1931." *GenDocs*. http://homepage.ntlworld.com/hitch/gendocs/pop.html#EW.

"Population of France." *New York Times*, 11 September 1904. http://www.nytimes.com/ref/membercenter/nytarchive.html.

Porter, John C. *The Men Who Put the Show on the Road.* Toronto: Clarke, Irwin, 1952.

Porter, McKenzie. "'Bargain' is a Naughty Word at Morgan's." *MacLean's,* 15 June 1953, 24-25, 64-67, 71.

Porter, Roy. "Pre-Modernism and the Art of Shopping." *Critical Inquiry* 34, 4 (Winter 1992): 3-14.

Pragnell, Bradley. "Organizing Department Store Workers: The Case of the RWDSU at Eaton's, 1983-1987." Kingston: Industrial Relations Centre, Queen's University, 1989.

Prentice, Alison, Paula Bourne, Gail Cuthbert Brandt, Beth Light, Wendy Mitchinson, and Naomi Black. *Canadian Women: A History.* Toronto: Harcourt Brace Jovanovich, 1988.

Price, Enid. *Industrial Occupations of Women.* Montréal: Canadian Reconstruction Association, 1919.

R. Simpson Company. *Simpson's.* Toronto: Simpson's, 1949.

–. *The Simpsons Century.* Toronto: Toronto Star, 1972.

–. *The Story of Simpson's: 68 Years of Progress.* Toronto: Wood, Gundy, 1940.

–. *This Is Simpson's.* Simpson's, 1947.

–. *Thumbnail Sketches.* Toronto: Simpsons, 1927.

Rappaport, Erika D. "Acts of Consumption: Musical Comedy and the Desire of Exchange." In *Cathedrals of Consumption: The European Department Store, 1850-1939,* ed. Geoffrey Crossick and Serge Jaumain, 189-207. Aldershot, UK: Ashgate, 1999.

–. *Shopping for Pleasure: Women in the Making of London's West End.* Princeton, NJ: Princeton University Press, 2000.

Redner, Sidney. "Population History of New York from 1790 to 1990." http://physics. bu.edu/~redner/projects/population/index.html.

Reekie, Gail. "'Humanising Industry': Paternalism, Welfarism, and Labour Control in Sydney's Big Stores, 1890-1930." *Labour History* 53 (November 1987): 1-19.

–. "Impulsive Women, Predictable Men: Psychological Constructions of Sexual Difference in Sales Literature to 1930." *Australian Historical Studies* 24 (1991): 359-77.

–. *Temptations: Sex, Selling, and the Department Store.* Sydney: Urban and Unwin, 1993.

Reiter, Esther. *Making Fast Food: From the Frying Pan into the Fryer.* Montréal and Kingston: McGill-Queen's University Press, 1996.

Report of the Ontario Commission on Unemployment. Toronto: A.T. Wilgress, 1916.

Roberts, Evan. "'Don't Sell Things, Sell Effects': Overseas Influences in New Zealand Department Stores, 1909-1956." *Business History Review* 77, 2 (Summer 2003): 265-89.

–. "Gender in Store: Salespeople's Working Hours and Union Organisation in New Zealand and the United States, 1930-60." *Labour History* 83 (November 2002): http://www.historycooperative.org/journals/lab/83/roberts.html.

Roberts, Wayne. *Honest Womanhood: Feminism, Femininity and Class Consciousness among Toronto Working Women, 1893 to 1914.* Toronto: New Hogtown Press, 1976.

–. "The Last Artisans: Toronto Printers, 1896-1914." In *Essays in Canadian Working-Class History,* ed. Gregory S. Kealey and Peter Warrian, 125-42. Toronto: McClelland and Stewart, 1976.

–. "'Rocking the Cradle for the World': The New Woman and Maternal Feminism, Toronto, 1877-1914." In *A Not Unreasonable Claim: Women and Social Reform in Canada, 1880s-1920s,* ed. Linda Kealey, 15-46. Toronto: Women's Press, 1979.

Robinson, Daniel J. *The Measure of Democracy: Polling, Market Research, and Public Life, 1930-1945.* Toronto: University of Toronto Press, 1999.

Rosenzweig, Roy. *Eight Hours For What We Will: Workers and Leisure in an Industrial City, 1870-1920.* Cambridge: Cambridge University Press, 1983.

Ross, Judy Tomlinson. "Eaton's Beauty Dolls." In *Dolls of Canada: A Reference Guide,* ed. Evelyn Robson Stahlendorf, 57-85. Ottawa: Booklore Publishers, 1986.

Roy, Gabrielle. *Enchantment and Sorrow: The Autobiography of Gabrielle Roy.* Translated by Patricia Claxton. Toronto: Lesser and Orpen Dennys Publishers, 1987.

Rudy, Jarrett. *The Freedom to Smoke: Tobacco Consumption and Identity.* Montréal and Kingston: McGill-Queen's University Press, 2005.

Rutherford, Paul. *Endless Propaganda: The Advertising of Public Goods.* Toronto: University of Toronto Press, 2000.

Sager, Eric W. "The Transformation of the Canadian Domestic Servant, 1871-1931." *Social Science History* 31, 4 (Winter 2007): 509-37.

Sangster, Joan. "Consuming Issues: Women on the Left, Political Protest, and the Organization of Homemakers, 1920-1960." In *Framing Our Past: Canadian Women's History in the Twentieth Century,* ed. Sharon Anne Cook, Lorna McLean, and Kate O'Rourke, 240-47. Montréal and Kingston: McGill-Queen's University Press, 2001.

–. *Dreams of Equality: Women on the Canadian Left, 1920-1950.* Toronto: McClelland and Stewart, 1989.

–. *Earning Respect: The Lives of Working Women in Small-Town Ontario, 1920-1960.* Toronto: University of Toronto Press, 1995.

–. "Making a Fur Coat: Women, the Labouring Body, and Working-Class History." *International Review of Social History* 52 (2007): 241-70.

–. "The Softball Solution: Female Workers, Male Managers, and the Operation of Paternalism at Westclox, 1923-60." *Labour/Le Travail* 32 (Fall 1993): 164-99.

–. *Transforming Labour: Women and Work in Post-War Canada.* Toronto: University of Toronto Press, 2010.

Santink, Joy L. *Timothy Eaton and the Rise of His Department Store.* Toronto: University of Toronto Press, 1990.

Schmidt, Leigh Eric. "The Commercialization of the Calendar: American Holidays and the Culture of Consumption, 1870-1930." *Journal of American History* 78, 3 (December 1991): 887-916.

Scott, James. *Weapons of the Weak: Everyday Forms of Peasant Resistance.* New Haven, CT: Yale University Press, 1985.

Scott, Jean Thomson. *The Conditions of Female Labour in Ontario.* Toronto: Warwick and Sons, 1892.

Scranton, Philip, ed. *Beauty and Business: Commerce, Gender, and Culture in Modern America.* New York and London: Routledge, 2001.

Shannon, Brent. "ReFashioning Men: Fashion, Masculinity, and the Cultivation of the Male Consumer in Britain, 1860-1914." *Victorian Studies* 46, 4 (Summer 2004): 597-630.

Sifton, Elizabeth. "Montreal's Fashion Mile: St. Catherine Street, 1890-1930." In *Fashion: A Canadian Perspective, 1890-1930,* ed. Alexandra Palmer, 203-66. Toronto: University of Toronto Press, 2004.

Simmers, Otto C. "Consumer Opinion of Retail Store Clerks." London, ON: University of Western Ontario, 1933.

Simpson's-Sears. *Simpson's-Sears: The First Twenty-Five Years.* Toronto: Simpson's-Sears, 1978.

Smith, Helen, and Pamela Wakewich. "'Beauty and the Helldivers': Representing Women's Work and Identities in a Warplant Newspaper." *Labour/Le Travail* 44 (1999): 77-107.

Spiekermann, Uwe. "Theft and Thieves in German Department Stores, 1895-1930: A Discourse on Morality, Crime and Gender." In *Cathedrals of Consumption: The European*

Department Store, 1850-1939, ed. Geoffrey Crossick and Serge Jaumain, 135-59. Aldershot, UK: Ashgate, 1999.

Srigley, Katrina. "Clothing Stories: Consumption, Identity, and Desire in Depression-Era Toronto." *Journal of Women's History* 19, 1 (Spring 2007): 82-104.

–. "'In case you hadn't noticed!': Race, Ethnicity, and Women's Wage-Earning in a Depression-Era City." *Labour/Le Travail* 55 (2005): 69-105.

–. "'You Always Saved Your Best Dress for Sundays': Working Girls, Clothing, and Consumption in a Depression-Era City." Paper presented at the "Labouring Feminism: Feminism and Working-Class History" conference, University of Toronto, September 2005.

Statistics Canada. *Department Stores in Canada/Les grands magasins au Canada, 1923-1976.* Ottawa: Statistics Canada, 1979.

–. *Historical Statistics of Canada,* 1983. http://www.statcan.gc.ca/.

Stead, Robert J.C. *Grain.* Toronto: McClelland and Stewart, 1969 [1926].

Stearns, Peter N. *Consumerism in World History: The Global Transformation of Desire.* 2nd ed. London and New York: Routledge, 2006.

–. "Stages of Consumerism: Recent Work on the Issues of Periodization." *Journal of Modern History* 69 (March 1997): 102-17.

Steedman, Mercedes. *Angels of the Workplace: Women and the Construction of Gender Relations in the Canadian Clothing Industry, 1890-1940.* Toronto: McClelland and Stewart, 1997.

Steigerwald, David. "All Hail the Republic of Choice: Consumer History as Contemporary Thought." *Journal of American History* 93 (September 2006): 385-403.

Stephenson, William. *The Store That Timothy Built.* Toronto: McClelland and Stewart, 1969.

Stevens, H.H. *Report of the Royal Commission on Price Spreads.* Ottawa: J.O. Patenaude, 1937.

Strange, Carolyn. *Toronto's Girl Problem: The Perils and Pleasures of the City, 1880-1930.* Toronto: University of Toronto Press, 1995.

Strasser, Susan. "Making Consumption Conspicuous: Transgressive Topics Go Mainstream." *Technology and Culture* 43 (October 2002): 755-70.

–. *Satisfaction Guaranteed: The Making of the American Mass Market.* New York: Pantheon Books, 1989.

Strasser, Susan, Charles McGovern, and Matthias Judt, eds. *Getting and Spending: European and American Consumer Societies in the Twentieth Century.* Cambridge: Cambridge University Press, 1998.

Strong-Boag, Veronica. "The Girl of the New Day: Canadian Working Women in the 1920's." In *The Consolidation of Capitalism, 1896-1929,* ed. Gregory Kealey, 169-210. Toronto: McClelland and Stewart, 1983.

–. *The New Day Recalled: Lives of Girls and Women in English Canada, 1919-1939.* Toronto: Copp Clark Pitman, 1988.

–. *The Parliament of Women: The National Council of Women of Canada, 1893-1929.* Ottawa: National Museum of Man, 1976.

Sufrin, Eileen. *The Eaton Drive: The Campaign to Organize Canada's Largest Department Store, 1948-1952.* Toronto: Fitzhenry and Whiteside, 1982.

Sussman, Charlotte. *Consuming Anxieties: Consumer Protest, Gender, and British Slavery, 1713-1833.* Palo Alto, CA: Stanford University Press, 2000.

Swiencicki, Mark A. "Consuming Brotherhood: Men's Culture, Style and Recreation as Consumer Culture, 1880-1930." In *Consumer Society in American History: A Reader,* ed. Lawrence B. Glickman, 207-40. Ithaca and London: Cornell University Press, 1999.

T. Eaton Company. *Eaton's of Canada: The Story of the Largest Retail Organization in the British Empire, Including a Digest of Information about the Canadian Market.* Toronto: T. Eaton Company, 1956.

–. "The Greatest Departmental Store in the British Empire." *Toronto: An Illustrated Tour through Its Highways and Byways.* Toronto: Canadian Gravure Company Limited, ca. 1931.

–. *The Story of a Store.* Toronto: T. Eaton, 1952.

Tamari, Tomoko. "Rise of the Department Store and the Aestheticization of Everyday Life in Early 20th-Century Japan." *International Journal of Japanese Sociology* 15 (2006): 99-118.

Tebbel, John. *The Marshall Fields: A Study in Wealth.* New York: E.P. Dutton, 1947.

Texas State Data Center and Office of the State Demographer. "Resident Population of States in the United States, 1900-2000." http://txsdc.utsa.edu/txdata/apport/hist_a.php.

Thompson, Eleanor. "Eaton's Mail Order Catalogue, Oral History Project," 1995. Canadian Museum of Civilization, Library, Archives and Documentation, History Records, Box 1-164.

Tiersten, Lisa. "Marianne in the Department Store: Gender and the Politics of Consumption in Turn-of-the-Century Paris." In *Cathedrals of Consumption: The European Department Store, 1850-1939,* ed. Geoffrey Crossick and Serge Jaumain, 116-34. Aldershot, UK: Ashgate, 1999.

–. *Marianne in the Market: Envisioning Consumer Society in Fin-de-Siècle France.* Berkeley and Los Angeles: University of California Press, 2001.

Tinkler, Penny, and Cheryl Krasnick Warsh. "Feminine Modernity in Interwar Britain and North America: Corsets, Cars, and Cigarettes." *Journal of Women's History* 20, 3 (Fall 2008): 113-43.

Tippet, Maria. *Making Culture: English-Canadian Institutions and the Arts before the Massey Commission.* Toronto: University of Toronto Press, 1990.

Tone, Andrea. *The Business of Benevolence: Industrial Paternalism in Progressive America.* Ithaca and London: Cornell University Press, 1997.

Toronto Council of Women. *Nothing New under the Sun.* Ottawa: National Library of Canada, 1978.

Toronto Star. A Century of Service to Canadian Shoppers. Toronto: Toronto Star, 1969.

–. "Timothy Eaton: He Started It All." *Eaton's: A Century of Service to Canadian Shoppers,* 4-8. Toronto: Toronto Star, 1969.

Trentmann, Frank. "Beyond Consumerism: New Historical Perspectives on Consumption." *Journal of Contemporary History* 39, 3 (July 2004): 373-401.

Valverde, Mariana. *The Age of Light, Soap, and Water: Moral Reform in English Canada, 1885-1925.* Toronto: University of Toronto Press, 1991.

Vance, Jonathan. *Death So Noble: Memory, Meaning, and the First World War.* Vancouver: UBC Press, 1997.

Veblen, Thorstein. *Theory of the Leisure Class: An Economic Study of Institutions.* New York: New American Library, 1912 [1899].

Vickery, Amanda. "His and Hers: Gender, Consumption and Household Accounting in Eighteenth-Century England." *Past and Present* (2006), Supplement 1, 12-38.

Vipond, Mary. *The Mass Media in Canada.* 3rd ed. Toronto: James Lorimer and Company, 2000.

Voisey, Paul. *Vulcan: The Making of a Prairie Community.* Toronto: University of Toronto Press, 1988.

Wachtel, Paul L. *The Poverty of Affluence: A Psychological Portrait of the American Way of Life.* New York: Free Press, 1983.

Walden, Keith. *Becoming Modern in Toronto: The Toronto Industrial Exhibition and the Shaping of a Late Victorian Culture.* Toronto: University of Toronto Press, 1997.

–. "Speaking Modern: Language, Culture, and Hegemony in Grocery Window Displays, 1887-1920." *Canadian Historical Review* 70 (September 1989): 285-310.

Walkowitz, Judith. *City of Dreadful Delight: Narratives of Sexual Danger in Late-Victorian London.* Chicago: University of Chicago Press, 1992.

Walsh, Claire. "The Newness of the Department Store: A View from the Eighteenth Century." In *Cathedrals of Consumption: The European Department Store, 1850-1939,* ed. Geoffrey Crossick and Serge Jaumain, 46-71. Aldershot, UK: Ashgate, 1999.

Ward, Wallace. "Morgan's on the March." *The Montrealer,* October 1951, 18-23.

Watt, Robert D. "Introduction." In *The Shopping Guide of the West: Woodward's Catalogues, 1898-1953,* ed. Vancouver Centennial Museum, v-xxviii. Vancouver: J.J. Douglas, 1977.

Weiers, Margaret. "Modern Apartments Preferred to This." *Toronto Star,* 3 October 1963.

Wetherell, Donald G. "Making New Identities: Alberta Small Towns Confront the City, 1900-1950." *Journal of Canadian Studies* 39, 1 (Winter 2005): 175-97.

Wheaton, Carla. "'– as modern as some of the fine new department stores – can make it': A Social History of the Large Water Street Stores, St. John's, Newfoundland, 1892-1949." PhD diss., Memorial University, 2001.

Williams, Rosalind H. *Dream Worlds: Mass Consumption in Late Nineteenth-Century France.* Berkeley: University of California Press, 1982.

Willis, Ellen. "'Consumerism' and Women." In *Voices from Women's Liberation,* ed. Leslie B. Tanner, 307-13. New York: New American Library, 1971.

Willis, John. "Cette manche au syndicat – La grève chez Dupuis Frères en 1952." *Labour/Le Travail* 57 (Spring 2006): 43-92.

–. "The Mail Order Catalogue: An Achievement in Mass Distribution and Labour." In *Les territoires de l'entreprise/The Territories of Business,* ed. Claude Bellavance and Pierre Lanthier, 174-99. Sainte-Foy, PQ: Les Presses de l'Université Laval, 2004.

Worthy, James C. *Shaping an American Institution: Robert E. Wood and Sears, Roebuck.* Urbana and Chicago: University of Illinois Press, 1984.

Wright, Cynthia. "'Feminine Trifles of Vast Importance: Writing Gender into the History of Consumption." In *Gender Conflicts: New Essays in Women's History,* ed. Franca Iacovetta and Mariana Valverde, 229-60. Toronto: University of Toronto Press, 1992.

–. "'The Most Prominent Rendezvous of the Feminine Toronto': Eaton's College Street and the Organization of Shopping in Toronto, 1920-1950." PhD diss., University of Toronto, 1992.

–. "Rewriting the Modern: Reflections on Race, Nation, and the Death of a Department Store." *Histoire sociale/Social History* 33 (May 2000): 153-67.

Yee, Paul. *Saltwater City: An Illustrated History of the Chinese in Vancouver.* Vancouver: Douglas and McIntyre, 2006.

Young, Louise. "Marketing the Modern: Department Stores, Consumer Culture, and the New Middle Class in Interwar Japan." *International Labor and Working-Class History* 55 (Spring 1999): 52-70.

Young, Mildred J. "Bachelor Ordered a Wife from EATON'S CATALOGUE." *Early Canadian Life* (April 1978): 21.

Index

Note: "(i)" after a page number indicates an illustration; HBC stands for Hudson's Bay Company

department stores, 84; on Royal Commission on Price Spreads, 203, 206
Montgomery, Lucy Maud, 202, 228
Montgomery Ward's, 21, 38-39
Montréal, QC, 16, 20, 22, 35. *See also* Morgan's
Moodie, Susannah, 17
Moody, Mary, 17
Moore, C.P., 204
Moorehead, Robert J., 228-29
Morgan, Henry, 20, 87
Morgan's (1860s and 1870s), 20, 21, 71-72
Morgan's (1880s and 1890s): carriage trade the target consumer group, 27, 130; Colonial House Department Store, 22, 23(i); market share compared with Eaton's, 25; premier department store in Québec, 4, 20, 22, 23(i)
Morgan's advertising, 47, 50
Morgan's employees, 181
Morgan's paternalism: benefits for employees, 99; fatherly or courtly toward female customers, 95; paternal regard for female employees' reputations, 168; philanthropy, 86; provision of lavatories for female customers, 94; sense of security and belonging in employees, 98-99; tributes to founder, 83-84
Morton, Suzanne, 6
Moslen, Margaret, 149
Munroe, Gladys, 150
Murdock, Annie, 161
Murphy's (Montréal, QC), 22, 30, 40
Mysteries of Montreal (Fuhrer), 220

National Consumers' League (US), 224
National Council of Women of Canada (NCWC), 219
national identity and department stores: advertising promoted ties to Britain, 54-57, 118, 166; branded nationalism, 79, 237-38; conflation of consumerism with nationalism, 238, 240; construction of nation as white, English, consumerist, Protestant, middle-class, and status-seeking, 7, 10, 46, 78, 79-81, 133-34, 238; department stores as symbols of national identity, 234-35; Eaton's

self-portrayal as symbol of national identity, 78-79, 155, 234-35; English Canadians' yearning for common identity, 236; link between mass retail and Canadian identity, 75-76, 76-79, 235-36, 237-38; patriotic advertising, 4, 54-57, 118-19, 234-35, 236; perceptions of Eaton's role in building modern Canada, 75-76, 76-78, 235; stores as capitalist solutions to lack of common heritage, 79
National Tattler, 221, 222(i)
Neal, Rusty, 217
Neufeld, David, 190
New Brunswick population (1901 to 1921), 33-34
Newfoundland population (1901 to 1921), 34
newspapers and department stores, 46-48, 200, 218. *See also The Globe*
Nine Hours Labour League, 206
Noel, Jan, 16-17
Northwest Company, 15
Nova Scotia, 33-34

Ogilvy's (Ottawa, ON), 35
O'Meara, Margaret, 165, 172-73
One Big Union (OBU), 207-8
Ottawa, ON, 20, 35

Packard, Vance, 74
Paine, Fred, 133
Paris and *magasins de nouveautés* (1840s), 17-18
Parkin, George, 29
Parr, Joy, 5, 6, 100, 136
Parsons, Florence, 162
paternalism of department stores: consequences of, 98-107; counteracting negative publicity, 84-85; customers' beliefs in honesty of store, 98; familialism (familial corporate identity), 88-92, 107; male breadwinner/female homemaker model, 102, 107; masculine authority over female customers and staff, 7-8, 10, 86-87; modern business practices' merger with paternalism, 85-86; mythologizing of founders, 82-83, 83(i), 84, 88-89, 90(i), 107; origins in pre-industrial merchants, 84, 87-88; philanthropy, 86, 92-93, 98;